CSET
114-115

Social Science
Teacher Certification Exam

By: Sharon Wynne, M.S.
Southern Connecticut State University

"And, while there's no reason yet to panic, I think it's only prudent that we make preparations to panic."

XAMonline, INC.
Boston

XAMonline, Inc.
21 Orient Ave.
Melrose, MA 02176
Toll Free 1-800-509-4128
Email: info@xamonline.com
Web www.xamonline.com
Fax: 1-781-662-9268

Library of Congress Cataloging-in-Publication Data

Wynne, Sharon A.
    Social Science 114, 115: Teacher Certification / Sharon A. Wynne. -2nd ed.
    ISBN 978-1-58197-340-2
    1. Social Science 114, 115   2. Study Guides.   3. CSET
    4. Teachers' Certification & Licensure.   5. Careers

Disclaimer:
The opinions expressed in this publication are the sole works of XAMonline and were created independently from the National Education Association, Educational Testing Service, or any State Department of Education, National Evaluation Systems or other testing affiliates.

Between the time of publication and printing, state specific standards as well as testing formats and website information may change that is not included in part or in whole within this product. Sample test questions are developed by XAMonline and reflect similar content as on real tests; however, they are not former tests. XAMonline assembles content that aligns with state standards but makes no claims nor guarantees teacher candidates a passing score. Numerical scores are determined by testing companies such as NES or ETS and then are compared with individual state standards. A passing score varies from state to state.

Printed in the United States of America   œ-1

CSET: Social Science 114, 115
ISBN: 978-1-58197-340-2

TEACHER CERTFICATION STUDY GUIDE

TABLE OF CONTENTS

DOMAIN 1:   **WORLD HISTORY**

COMPETENCY 1.1   ANCIENT CIVILIZATIONS..1

Skill 1.1a   Describe the early physical and cultural development of humankind from the Paleolithic era to the agricultural revolution, explaining how the methods of archaeology and anthropology contribute to the understanding of prehistory..1

Skill 1.1b   Describe and analyze the impact of human interaction with the physical environment on the development of the ancient cultures of the Fertile Crescent, Persia, Egypt, Kush, Greece, India, China, Rome, and pre-Columbian America 3

Skill 1.1c   Describe and analyze the ancient cultures of Mesopotamia, Persia, Egypt, Kush, Greece, India, China, Rome, and pre-Columbian America, and describe and analyze their intellectual, ethical, scientific, artistic accomplishments and values. 4

Skill 1.1d   Describe and analyze the foundations of western political and philosophical thought in ancient Greek, Roman, and Judeo-Christian traditions...9

Skill 1.1e   Describe and analyze the foundations of Asian political and philosophical thought found in ancient Chinese and Indian traditions. 10

Skill 1.1f   Describe and analyze the importance and patterns of expansion and contraction of empires, religions, and trade that influenced various regional cultures through the decline of the Roman Empire 12

COMPETENCY 1.2   MEDIEVAL AND EARLY MODERN TIMES 15

Skill 1.2a   Analyze the impact of geography, including both human and physical features, on the development of medieval and early-modern Asian, African, Middle Eastern, pre-Columbian American, and European civilizations. 15

Skill 1.2b   Trace the decline of the Western Roman Empire and the development of the Byzantine Empire, and analyze the emergence of these two distinct European civilizations and their views on religion, culture, society, and politics. 17

SOCIAL SCIENCE   i

Skill 1.2c   Describe the role and expansion of Christianity in medieval and early modern Europe and the Middle East. 18

Skill 1.2d   Identify the basic tenets of Islam, and describe Islamic society and culture between the beginning of the 7th century and the end of the 18th century.. 19

Skill 1.2e   Analyze the religious and secular contributions of Islam to European, African and Asian civilizations and the impact of medieval Muslim civilization on Asia, Africa, and Europe between the 7th century and the 18th century. 24

Skill 1.2f   Analyze and compare and contrast the development of feudalism as a social, political, and economic system in Europe and Japan 26

Skill 1.2g   Compare and contrast the geographic, political, economic, religious, and social structures of pre-Columbian American civilizations in North and South America between A.D. 500 and the end of the 18th century. 28

Skill 1.2h   Analyze the geographic, political, economic, religious, and social structures of Asia and Africa between A.D. 500 and the end of the 18th century.. 30

Skill 1.2i   Analyze the art, literature, music, science, and technology of the Renaissance and their diffusion and impact throughout Europe. ..32

Skill 1.2j   Analyze the political and religious transformations caused by the Reformation and their impact on Europe. 34

Skill 1.2k   Analyze the historical developments of the Scientific Revolution and the ideas of the Enlightenment and their effects on social, religious, political, economic, and cultural institutions................................. 35

COMPENTENCY 1.3   MODERN WORLD HISTORY 38

Skill 1.3a   Describe and evaluate the significance of the "Age of Exploration," and the main ideas of the Enlightenment and their influences on social, political, religious, and economic thought and practice. 38

Skill 1.3b   Compare and contrast the American Revolution and the French Revolution and their enduring worldwide effects on political expectations for self-government and individual liberty. 40

Skill 1.3c   Describe and analyze the emergence of nationalism in the 18th and 19th centuries and its impact on Western, African, and Asian societies. 41

Skill 1.3d   Analyze the causes and effects of the Industrial Revolution, including its impact on science, technology, and society. 42

Skill 1.3e   Describe the emergence and origins of new theories regarding politics, economics, literature, and the arts in the 18th, 19th, and 20th centuries. 43

Skill 1.3f   Analyze the economic, political, social, and geographic factors contributing to the emergence of 19th-century imperialism, and evaluate its impact on Africa, Southeast Asia, China, India, Latin America, and the Philippines. 45

Skill 1.3g   Compare and contrast the social, political, and economic factors that influenced the Russian Revolutions of 1905 and 1917. 46

Skill 1.3h   Analyze the origins and course of World War I and its effects on Europe and the rest of the world, including its impact on science, technology, the arts, politics, society, economics, and geography 48

Skill 1.3i   Analyze the conflict between fascist and Marxist/communist ideologies, and the rise, goals, and policies of dictatorships and totalitarian governments between the two World Wars. 50

Skill 1.3j   Analyze the origins, course, and consequences of World War II, including the human cost of the war, the resulting redrawing of boundaries, and the movement of peoples in Europe, Asia, Africa, and the Middle East. 56

Skill 1.3k   Analyze the international developments of the post-World War II era, including decolonization, nationalism, nation-building, the development of international organizations, and global migration 60

Skill 1.3l   Analyze the Cold War from its origins in the post-World War II 1940s to the dissolution of the Soviet Union in 1991, including its impact on social, cultural, political, economic, technological, and geographic developments in the world. 62

Skill 1.3m   Analyze the emergence of a global economy and its impact on the environment, epidemiology, and demographics, and the development and impact of the information, technology, and communications revolutions. 64

Skill 1.3n   Describe the causes and effects of genocide in the 20th century, including, but not limited to, the Armenian genocide, the Holocaust, and post-World War II "ethnic cleansing." 66

Skill 1.3o   Explain and evaluate the strategic importance of the Middle East and the volatile political relations within the region. 69

DOMAIN 2:   **U.S. HISTORY**

COMPETENCY 2.1   PRE-REVOLUTIONARY ERA AND THE WAR FOR INDEPENDENCE 72

Skill 2.1a   Describe the major American Indian cultural groups and their contributions to early American society. 72

Skill 2.1b   Explain and analyze the struggle for the control of North America among European powers and the emergence of the 13 colonies under English rule 74

Skill 2.1c   Analyze the effects of English, French, Dutch, and Spanish colonial rule on social, economic, and governmental structures in North America, and the relationships of these colonies with American Indian societies. 79

Skill 2.1d   Describe the institutionalization of African slavery in the Western Hemisphere and analyze its consequences in sub-Saharan Africa 81

Skill 2.1e   Analyze the causes for the War for Independence, the conduct of the war the war, and its impact on Americans. 82

COMPETENCY 2.2   THE DEVELOPMENT OF THE CONSTITUTION AND THE EARLY REPUBLIC 89

Skill 2.2a   Describe and evaluate the impact of the Enlightenment and the unique colonial experiences on the writing of the Declaration of Independence, Articles of Confederation, the Federalist Papers, the Constitution, and the Bill of Rights. 89

Skill 2.2b   Examine the issues regarding ratification of the Constitution, and compare and contrast the positions of the Federalists and Anti-Federalists. 94

COMPETENCY 2.3   THE EMERGENCE OF A NEW NATION.....................95

Skill 2.3a   Describe the differing visions of the early political parties and explain the reasons for the respective successes and failures of those parties. 95

Skill 2.3b   Compare the significant political and socioeconomic ideas and issues during the Jeffersonian and Jacksonian periods and contrast how they were implemented in policy and practice. 98

Skill 2.3c   Describe American foreign policy prior to the Civil War.................99

Skill 2.3d   Identify and describe the political, social, religious, economic, and geographic factors that led to the formation of distinct regional and sectional identities and cultures..101

Skill 2.3e   Describe the purpose, challenges, and economic incentives associated with settlements of the West, including the concept of Manifest Destiny. 103

Skill 2.3f   Map and analyze the expansion of U.S. borders and the settlement of the West, and describe how geographic features influenced this expansion. 105

Skill 2.3g   Analyze the evolution of American Indian policy up to the Civil War 106

Skill 2.3h   Describe and analyze the impact of slavery on American society, government, and economy, and the contributions of enslaved Africans to America, and trace the attempts to abolish slavery in the first half of the 19th century. 107

Skill 2.3i   Describe and compare and contrast early 19th-Century social and reform movements and their impact on antebellum American society. 112

COMPETENCY 2.4   CIVIL WAR AND RECONSTRUCTION 116

Skill 2.4a   Interpret the debates over the doctrines of nullification and state secession. 116

Skill 2.4b   Compare and contrast the strengths and weaknesses of the Union and Confederacy. 117

Skill 2.4c   Describe the major military and political turning points of the war 118

Skill 2.4d   Describe and analyze the physical, social, political, and economic impact of the war on combatants, civilians, communities, states, and the nation...119

Skill 2.4e   Compare and contrast plans for Reconstruction with its actual implementation. 121

Skill 2.4f   Explain and assess the development and adoption of segregation laws, the influence of social mores on the passage and implementation of these laws, and the rise of white supremacist organizations. 123

Skill 2.4g   Analyze the relationship of the 13th, 14th, and 15th Amendments to Reconstruction, and compare and contrast their initial and later interpretations...125

COMPETENCY 2.5   THE GILDED AGE...128

Skill 2.5a   Describe and analyze the role of entrepreneurs and industrialists and their impact on the United States economy. 128

Skill 2.5b   Describe and analyze the effects of industrialization on the American economy and society, including increased immigration, changing working conditions, and the growth of early labor organizations. 130

Skill 2.5c   Explain and analyze the causes for, and the impact of, Populism and Progressivism. 131

Skill 2.5d   Explain the development of federal Indian policy – including the environmental consequences of forced migration into marginal regions – and its consequences for American Indians. 133

Skill 2.5e   Analyze the impact of industrialism and urbanization on the physical and social environments of the United States................134

COMPETENCY 2.6   THE U.S. AS A WORLD POWER...............................136

Skill 2.6a   Evaluate the debate about American imperialistic policies before, during and following the Spanish-American War........................136

Skill 2.6b   Analyze the political, economic, and geographic significance of the Panama Canal, the "Open Door" policy with China, Theodore Roosevelt's "Big Stick" Diplomacy, William Howard Taft's "Dollar" Diplomacy, and Woodrow Wilson's Moral Diplomacy.................137

Skill 2.6c   Evaluate the political, economic, social, and geographic consequences of World War I in terms of American foreign policy and the war's impact on the American home front......................139

COMPETENCY 2.7   THE 1920s 142

Skill 2.7a   Analyze domestic events that resulted in, or contributed to, the Red Scare, Marcus Garvey's Back to Africa movement, the Ku Klux Klan, the American Civil Liberties Union, the National Association for the Advancement of Colored People, and the Anti-Defamation League. 142

Skill 2.7b   Analyze the significance of the passage of the 18th and 19th Amendments as they related to the changing political and economic roles of women in society. 145

Skill 2.7c   Assess changes in American immigration policy in the 1920s.....146

Skill 2.7d   Describe new trends in literature, music, and art, including the Harlem Renaissance and the Jazz Age.....................................147

Skill 2.7e   Assess the impact of radio, mass production techniques, and the growth of cities on American society. 148

COMPETENCY 2.8   THE GREAT DEPRESSION AND THE NEW DEAL ..150

Skill 2.8a   Analyze the differing explanations for the 1939 stock market crash, Herbert Hoover's and Congress' responses to the crisis, and the implementation of Franklin Delano Roosevelt's New Deal policies 150

Skill 2.8b   Describe and assess the human toll of the of the Great Depression, including the impact of natural disasters and agricultural practices on the migration from rural Southern and Eastern regions to urban and Western areas. 155

Skill 2.8c   Analyze the effects of, and controversies arising from, New Deal policies, including the social and physical consequences of regional programs 157

Skill 2.8d   Trace and evaluate the gains and losses of organized labor in the in the 1930s. 157

COMPETENCY 2.9   WORLD WAR II 160

Skill 2.9a   Explain the origins of American involvement in World War II, including reactions to events in Europe, Africa, and Asia. 160

Skill 2.9b   Analyze American foreign policy before and during World War II 161

Skill 2.9c   Evaluate and analyze significant events, issues, and experiences during World War II and the experiences and contributions of American fighting forces, including the role of minorities. 162

Skill 2.9d   Assess American foreign policy in the aftermath of World War II, using geographic, political, and economic perspectives. 167

COMPETENCY 2.10   POST-WORLD WAR II AMERICA 170

Skill 2.10a   Describe and evaluate the significance of changes in international migration patterns and their impact on society and the economy 170

Skill 2.10b   Describe the increased role of the federal government in response to World War II and the Cold War and assess the impact of this increased role on regional economic structures, society, and the political system. 171

Skill 2.10c   Describe the effects of technological developments on society, politics, and the economy since 1945. 172

Skill 2.10d   Analyze the major domestic policies of presidential administrations from Harry S Truman to the present. 174

COMPETENCY 2.11   POST-WORLD WAR II U.S. FOREIGN POLICY 177

Skill 2.11a   Trace the origins of the Cold War. 177

Skill 2.11b   Analyze the roles of the Truman Doctrine, the Marshall Plan, and military alliances, including the North American Treaty Organization (NATO), the South East Asian Treaty Organization (SEATO), and the Warsaw Pact. 177

Skill 2.11c   Trace the origins and consequences of the Korean War. 178

Skill 2.11d   Explain and analyze the relationship between domestic and foreign policy during the Cold War. 179

Skill 2.11e   Analyze the foreign policies of post-World War II presidential administrations and their effect on the Cold War. 180

Skill 2.11f   Trace the causes, controversies, and consequences of the Vietnam War, its effects on American combatants and civilians, and its continued impact on American society. 183

COMPETENCY 2.12   CIVIL RIGHTS MOVEMENT 186

Skill 2.12a   Examine and analyze the key people, events, policies, and court cases in the field of civil rights from varying perspectives. 186

Skill 2.12b   Describe the civil rights movements of African Americans and other minority groups and their impacts on government, society, and the economy. 190

Skill 2.12c   Analyze the development of the women's rights movement and its connections to other social and political movements. 191

DOMAIN 3:   CALIFORNIA HISTORY

COMPETENCY 3.1   PRE-COLUMBIAN PERIOD THROUGH THE END OF MEXICAN RULE 193

Skill 3.1a   Describe the geography, economic life, and culture of California's American Indian peoples as well as their relationship with the environment. 193

Skill 3.1b   Define and assess the impact of Spanish exploration and colonization, including the establishment of the mission system, ranchos, and pueblos, and their influences on the development of the agricultural economy of early California 196

Skill 3.1c   Describe the causes of the Mexican-American War and assess its impact on California. 197

COMPETENCY 3.2   FROM THE GOLD RUSH TO THE PRESENT 200

Skill 3.2a   Describe the discovery of gold and assess its consequences on the cultures, societies, politics, and economies of California, including its impact on California Indians and Californios 200

Skill 3.2b   Describe the international migration to California in the 19th century, the social, economic, and political responses to this migration, and the contributions of immigrants to the development of California 201

Skill 3.2c   Analyze key principles in California's constitutional and political development and compare and contrast the California and U.S. Constitutions...205

Skill 3.2d   Describe 20th century migration to California from the rest of the U.S. and the world, and analyze its impact on the cultural, economic, social, and political evolution of the state 208

Skill 3.2e   Identify major environmental issues in California history and their economic, social, and political implications. 211

DOMAIN 4:   PRINCIPLES OF AMERICAN DEMOCRACY

COMPETENCY 4.1   PRINCIPLES OF AMERICAN DEMOCRACY 213

Skill 4.1a   Analyze the influence of ancient Classical and Enlightenment political thinkers and the pre-Revolutionary colonial and indigenous peoples' experience on the development of the American government, and consider the historical contexts in which democratic theories emerged. 213

Skill 4.1b   Explain and analyze the principles of the Declaration of Independence and how the U.S. Constitution reflects a balance between classical republican and classical liberal thinking..........213

Skill 4.1c   Evaluate the Founding Fathers' contribution to the establishment of a constitutional system as articulated in the Federalist Papers, constitutional debates, and the U.S. Constitution. 214

Skill 4.1d   Describe the significance of the Bill of Rights and the 14th Amendment as limits on government in the American constitutional process as compared to English Common Law. 216

Skill 4.1e   Describe the nature and importance of law in U.S. political theory, including the democratic procedures of law making, the rule of adherence to the law, and the role of civil disobedience. 218

Skill 4.1f   Analyze the significance and evolving meaning of the principles of American democracy. 219

Skill 4.1g   Describe the meaning and importance of each of the rights guaranteed in the Bill of Rights and analyze the reciprocal nature of citizenship..221

Skill 4.1h   Explain the basis and practice of acquiring American citizenship 222

COMPETENCY 4.2   FUNDAMENTAL VALUES AND PRINCIPLES OF CIVIL SOCIETY..225

Skill 4.2a   Explain and analyze the historical role of religion, religious diversity, and religious discrimination and conflict in American life.............225

Skill 4.2b   Analyze citizen participation in governmental decision-making in a large modern society and the challenges Americans faced historically to their political participation......................................227

Skill 4.2c   Analyze the evolving practices of citizen collaboration and deliberation, and special interest influence in American democratic decision-making. 229

Skill 4.2d   Compare and contrast the role of the individual in democratic and authoritarian societies..230

Skill 4.2e   Explain how civil society provides opportunities for individuals to promote private or public interests...231

COMPETENCY 4.3   THE THREE BRANCHES OF GOVERNMENT 234

Skill 4.3a   Analyze Articles I, II, and III as they relate to the legislative, executive, and judicial branches of government.........................234

Skill 4.3b   Analyze how and why the existing roles and practices of the three branches of government have evolved. 236

Skill 4.3c   Describe and analyze the issues that arise as a result of the checks and balances system..236

Skill 4.3d   Explain the process by which the Constitution is amended. 236

COMPETENCY 4.4   LANDMARK U.S. SUPREME COURT CASES 239

Skill 4.4a   Analyze the changing interpretations of the Bill of Rights and later constitutional amendments. 239

Skill 4.4b   Evaluate the effects of the Court's interpretations of the
               Constitution. Give examples. 239

Skill 4.4c   Describe and analyze the controversies that have resulted over the
               changing interpretations of civil rights. 241

COMPETENCY 4.5   ISSUES REGARDING CAMPAIGNS FOR NATIONAL, STATE, AND LOCAL ELECTIVE OFFICES.............. 244

Skill 4.5a   Analyze the origin, development, and role of political parties. 244

Skill 4.5b   Describe the means that citizens use to participate in the political
               process. 244

Skill 4.5c   Explain the function and evolution of the College of Electors and
               analyze its role in contemporary American politics. 245

Skill 4.5d   Describe and evaluate issues of state redistricting and the political
               nature of reapportionment. 248

COMPETENCY 4.6   POWERS AND PROCEDURES OF THE NATIONAL, STATE, LOCAL AND TRIBAL GOVERNMENTS 249

Skill 4.6a   Identify the various ways in which federal, state, local, and tribal
               governments are organized. 249

Skill 4.6b   Analyze the issues that arise out of the divisions of jurisdiction
               among federal, state, local, and tribal governments at each level of
               government; consider their impacts on those different levels of
               government. 250

Skill 4.6c   Analyze the sources of power and influence in democratic politics,
               such as access to and use of the mass media, money, economic
               interests, and the ability to mobilize groups. 251

COMPETENCY 4.7   THE MEDIA IN AMERICAN POLITICAL LIFE 254

Skill 4.7a   Describe the significance of a free press, including the role of the
               broadcast, print, and electronic media in American society and
               government. 254

Skill 4.7b   Analyze the interaction between public officials and the media to
               communicate and influence public opinion. 256

COMPETENCY 4.8   POLITICAL SYSTEMS **258**

Skill 4.8a   Explain and analyze different political systems and the philosophies that underlie them, including the parliamentary system. 258

Skill 4.8b   Analyze problems of new democracies in the 19th and 20th centuries and their internal struggles. 259

COMPETENCY 4.9   TENSIONS WITHIN OUR CONSTITUTIONAL DEMOCRACY **262**

Skill 4.9a   Analyze the constitutional interpretations of the First Amendment's statement about the separation of church and state...................262

Skill 4.9b   Debate the adequacy of the solution of majority rule and the role of minority rights in a majority-rules system. 264

DOMAIN 5:   PRINCIPLES OF ECONOMICS

COMPETENCY 5.1   ECONOMIC TERMS AND CONCEPTS AND ECONOMIC REASONING **266**

Skill 5.1a   Describe the causal relationship between scarcity and choices, and explain opportunity cost and marginal benefit and marginal cost 266

Skill 5.1b   Identify the difference between monetary and non-monetary incentives and how changes in incentives cause changes in behavior..267

Skill 5.1c   Debate the role of private property as an incentive in conserving and improving scarce resources, including renewable and nonrenewable natural resources. 268

Skill 5.1d   Describe and analyze the debate concerning the role of a market economy versus a planned economy in establishing and preserving political and personal liberty. 269

COMPETENCY 5.2   ELEMENTS OF AMERICA'S MARKET ECONOMY IN A GLOBAL SETTING **271**

Skill 5.2a   Describe and analyze the relationship of the concepts of incentives and substitutes to the law of supply and demand. 271

Skill 5.2b   Describe the effects of changes in supply and/or demand on the relative scarcity, price, and quantity of particular products. 272

Skill 5.2c   Explain and analyze the roles of property rights, competition, and profit in a market economy. 273

Skill 5.2d   Explain and analyze how prices reflect the relative scarcity of goods and services and perform the function of allocation in a market economy. 274

Skill 5.2e   Explain the process by which competition among buyers and sellers determines a market price. 276

Skill 5.2f   Describe the effect of price controls on buyers and sellers 277

Skill 5.2g   Analyze how domestic and international competition in a market economy affects the quality, quantity, and price of goods and services produced. 278

Skill 5.2h   Explain the role of profit as the incentive to entrepreneurs in a market economy... 279

Skill 5.2i   Describe the functions of the financial markets. 280

COMPETENCY 5.3   THE RELATIONSHIP BETWEEN POLITICS AND ECONOMICS 282

Skill 5.3a   Analyze the effects of federal, state, and local policies on the distribution of resources and economic decision-making. 282

Skill 5.3b   Describe the economic and social effects of government fiscal policies. 283

Skill 5.3c   Describe the aims and tools of monetary policy and its economic and social effects. 284

Skill 5.3d   Assess the tradeoff between efficiency and equality in modern mixed economies, using social policies as examples. 285

Skill 5.3e   Apply the principles of economic decision-making to a current or historical social problem in America. 286

COMPETENCY 5.4   ELEMENTS OF THE U.S. LABOR MARKET IN A GLOBAL SETTING..288

Skill 5.4a   Describe the circumstances surrounding the establishment of principal American labor unions, procedures that unions use to gain benefits for their members, and the effects of unionization, the minimum wage, and unemployment insurance. 288

Skill 5.4b   Analyze the current U.S. economy and the global labor market 289

Skill 5.4c   Analyze wage differences between jobs and professions, using the laws of supply and demand and the concept of productivity........290

Skill 5.4d   Analyze the effects of international mobility of capital, labor, and trade on the U.S. economy...291

COMPETENCY 5.5   AGGREGATE ECONOMIC BEHAVIOR OF THE AMERICAN ECONOMY..293

Skill 5.5a   Describe how measures of economic output are adjusted using indexes. 293

Skill 5.5b   Define, calculate, and analyze the significance of the changes in rates of unemployment, inflation, and real Gross Domestic Product 294

Skill 5.5c   Distinguish between short- and long-term interest rates and explain their relative significance. 295

COMPETENCY 5.6   INTERNATIONAL TRADE AND THE AMERICAN ECONOMY..297

Skill 5.6a   Use the concept of comparative advantage to identify the costs of and gains from international trade. 297

Skill 5.6b   Define, calculate, and analyze the significance of the changes in rates of unemployment, inflation, and real GDP 298

Skill 5.6c   Distinguish between short- and long-term interest rates and explain their relative significance. 299

Skill 5.6d   Describe how international currency exchange rates are determined and their significance 300

DOMAIN 6:   PRINCIPLES OF GEOGRAPHY

COMPETENCY 6.1   TOOLS AND PERSPECTIVES OF GEOGRAPHIC STUDY 302

Skill 6.1a   Describe the criteria for defining regions and identify why places and regions are important..302

Skill 6.1b   Explain the nature of map projections and use maps, as well as other geographic representations and technologies to acquire, process, and report information from a spatial perspective 307

COMPETENCY 6.2   GEOGRAPHIC DIVERSITY OF NATURAL LANDSCAPES AND HUMAN SOCIETIES.................311

Skill 6.2a   Analyze how unique ecologic settings are encouraged by various combinations of natural and social phenomena, including bio-geographic relationships with climate, soil, and terrain................311

Skill 6.2b   Analyze the patterns and networks of economic interdependence across the earth's surface during the agricultural, industrial, and post-industrial revolutions, including the production and processing of raw materials, marketing, consumption, transportation, and other measures of economic development...313

Skill 6.2c   Describe the processes, patterns, and functions of human settlements from subsistence agriculture to industrial metropolis 316

Skill 6.2d   Analyze the forces of cooperation and conflict among peoples and societies that influence the division and control of the earth's surface..317

COMPETENCY 6.3   CULTURE AND THE PHYSICAL ENVIRONMENT....318

Skill 6.3a   Describe and analyze ways in which human societies and settlement patterns develop in response to the physical environment, and explain the social, political, economic, and physical processes that have resulted in today's urban and rural landscapes. 318

Skill 6.3b   Recognize the interrelationship of environmental and social policy 320

BIBLIOGRAPHY 321

SAMPLE TEST 323

ANSWER KEY 349

RIGOR TABLE 350

RATIONALES WITH SAMPLE QUESTIONS 351

Study and Testing Tips

In the preface, emphasis was placed upon the idea of focusing on the right material, in other words, *what* to study in order to prepare for the subject assessments. But equally important is *how* you study.

learning (lurn'ing) n. 1. the acquiring of knowledge of or skill in (a subject, trade, art, etc.) by study; experience, etc. 2. to come to know (of or about) 3. acquired knowledge or skill. *(Definition courtesy of Webster's New World Dictionary of the American Language, 1987)*

What we call "learning" is actually a very complicated process built around multi-faceted layers of sensory input and reinforcement.

When you were a child, learning largely consisted of trial and error experimentation, (i.e. don't touch that, it's *hot*! Or this tastes *good*!). But as we grow older and the neurotransmitters within our brain develop, learning takes on deeper, subtler levels. As adults the neural pathways are fully in place, allowing us to make abstract connections, synthesizing all of our previous experiences (which is essentially what knowledge is), into tremendously complicated, cohesive thoughts.

However, you can increase your chances of truly mastering the information by taking some simple, but effective steps.

Study Tips:

1. <u>Some foods aid the learning process.</u> Foods such as milk, nuts, seeds, rice, and oats help your study efforts by releasing natural memory enhancers called CCKs (*cholecystokinin*) composed of *tryptophan*, *choline*, and *phenylalanine*. All of these chemicals enhance the neurotransmitters associated with memory. Before studying, try a light, protein-rich meal of eggs, turkey, and fish. All of these foods release the memory enhancing chemicals. The better the c connections, the more you comprehend.

Likewise, before you take a test, stick to a light snack of energy boosting and relaxing foods. A glass of milk, a piece of fruit, or some peanuts all release various memory-boosting chemicals and help you to relax and focus on the subject at hand.

2. Learn to take great notes. A by-product of our modern culture is that we have grown accustomed to getting our information in short doses (i.e. TV news sound bites or USA Today style newspaper articles.)

Consequently, we've subconsciously trained ourselves to assimilate information better in neat little packages. If your notes are scrawled all over the paper, it fragments the flow of the information. Strive for clarity. Newspapers use a standard format to achieve clarity. Your notes can be much clearer through use of proper formatting. A very effective format is called the **Cornell Method:**

> Take a sheet of loose-leaf lined notebook paper and draw a line all the way down the paper about 1-2" from the left-hand edge.

> Draw another line across the width of the paper about 1-2" up from the bottom. Repeat this process on the reverse side of the page.

Look at the highly effective result. You have ample room for notes, a left hand margin for special emphasis items or inserting supplementary data from the textbook, a large area at the bottom for a brief summary, and a little rectangular space for just about anything you want.

3. Dissect the material. Too often we focus on the details and don't gather an understanding of the concept. However, if you simply memorize only dates, places, or names, you may well miss the whole point of the subject.

A key way to understand things is to put them in your own words. If you are working from a textbook, automatically summarize each paragraph in your mind. If you are outlining text, don't simply copy the author's words, **rephrase** them in your own words. You remember your own thoughts and words much better than someone else's, and subconsciously tend to associate the important details to the core concepts.

4. Turn every heading and caption into a question. Pull apart written material paragraph by paragraph and don't forget the captions under the illustrations.

Example: If the heading is "Stream Erosion," flip it around to read: "Why do streams erode?" Then answer the questions.

If you train your mind to think in a series of questions and answers, not only will you learn more, but it also helps to lessen the test anxiety because you are used to answering questions.

5. <u>Read, Read, Read.</u> Even if you only have 10 minutes, put your notes or a book in your hand. Your mind is similar to a computer; you have to input data in order to have it processed. *By reading, you are storing data for future retrieval.* The more times you read something, the more you reinforce the storage of data. Even if you don't fully understand something on the first pass, *your mind stores much of the material for later recall.*

6. <u>Create the right study atmosphere</u>. Our bodies respond to an inner clock called biorhythms. Burning the midnight oil works well for some people, but not everyone. If possible, set aside a particular place to study that is free of distractions. Shut off the television, cell phone, pager and exile your friends and family during your study period.

If you really are bothered by silence, try background music. Not rock, not hip-hop, not country, but classical. Light classical music at a low volume has been shown to aid in concentration. Don't pick anything with lyrics; you end up singing along. Try just about anything by Mozart, generally light and airy, it subconsciously evokes pleasant emotions and helps relax you.

7. <u>Limit the use of highlighters.</u> At best, it's difficult to read a page full of yellow, pink, blue, and green streaks.Try staring at a neon sign for a while and you'll soon see my point; the horde of colors obscure the message. A quick note, a brief dash of color, an underline, and an arrow pointing to a particular passage is much clearer than a horde of highlighted words.

8. <u>Budget your study time</u>. Although you shouldn't ignore any of the material, *allocate your available study time in the same ratio that topics may appear on the test.*

Testing Tips:

1. Don't outsmart yourself. Don't read anything into the question. Don't make an assumption that the test writer is looking for something else than what is asked. Stick to the question as written and don't read extra things into it.

2. Read the question and all the choices *twice* before answering the question. You may miss something by not carefully reading, and then re-reading both the question and the answers.

If you really don't have a clue as to the right answer, leave it blank on the first time through. Go on to the other questions as they may provide a clue as to how to answer the skipped questions.If later on, you still can't answer the skipped ones . . . ***Guess.*** The only penalty for guessing is that you *might* get it wrong. Only one thing is certain; if you don't put anything down, you will get it wrong!

3. Turn the question into a statement. Look at the way the questions are worded. The syntax of the question usually provides a clue. Does it seem more familiar as a statement rather than as a question? Does it sound strange?

By turning a question into a statement, you may be able to spot if an answer sounds right, and it may also trigger memories of material you have read.

4. Look for hidden clues. It's actually very difficult to compose multiple-foil (choice) questions without giving away part of the answer in the options presented. In most multiple-choice questions you can often readily eliminate one or two of the potential answers. This leaves you with only two real possibilities and automatically your odds go to fifty-fifty for very little work.

5. Trust your instincts. For every fact that you have read, you subconsciously retain something of that knowledge. On questions that you aren't really certain about, go with your basic instincts. **Your first impression on how to answer a question is usually correct.**

6. Mark your answers directly on the test booklet. Don't bother trying to fill in the optical scan sheet on the first pass through the test.

Just be very careful not to miss-mark your answers when you eventually transcribe them to the scan sheet.

7. Watch the clock! You have a set amount of time to answer the questions. Don't get bogged down trying to answer a single question at the expense of 10 questions you can more readily answer.

Are these tips foolproof? *No.* The Educational Testing Service (ETS) test writers are well versed in the "art" of writing assessments, and very seldom present "flawed" (read very easy to dissect) questions.

However, by applying these tips, you can generally improve your odds of making the right choices.

COMPETENCY 1.1   ANCIENT CIVILIZATIONS

Skill 1.1a   **Describe what is known of the early physical and cultural development of humankind from the Paleolithic era to theagricultural revolution, explaining how the methods of archaeology and anthropology contribute to the understanding of prehistory.**

ANTHROPOLOGY is the scientific study of human culture and humanity, the relationship between man and his culture. Anthropologists study different groups, how they relate to other cultures, and patterns of behavior, similarities and differences. Their research is two fold: **cross-cultural** and **comparative**. The major method of study is referred to as **participant observation**. The anthropologist studies and learns about the people being studied by living among them and participating with them in their daily lives. Other methods may be used but this is the most characteristic method used.

ARCHAEOLOGY is the scientific study of past human cultures by studying the remains they left behind--objects such as pottery, bones, buildings, tools, and artwork. Archaeologists locate and examine any evidence to help explain the way people lived in past times. They use special equipment and techniques to gather the evidence and make special effort to keep detailed records of their findings because a lot of their research results in destruction of the remains being studied.

The first step is to locate an archaeological site using various methods. Next, surveying the site takes place starting with a detailed description of the site with notes, maps, photographs, and collecting artifacts from the surface. Excavating follows either by digging for buried objects or by diving and working in submersible decompression chambers, when underwater. They record and preserve the evidence for eventual classification, dating, and evaluating their find.

Sources of knowledge about early humans:

- Fossils derived from burial pits
- Occasional bones found in rock deposits
- Archaeological excavations of tools, pottery, well paintings
- Study of living primitives

Although written records go back about 4,500 years, scientists have pieced together evidence that documents the existence of humans (or "man-apes) as much as 600,000 years ago. The first manlike creatures arose in many parts of the world about one million years ago. By slow stages, these creatures developed into types of men who discovered fire and tools. These creatures had human-sized brains and inbred to produce **Cro-Magnon** type creatures (25,000 years ago), from which **homo sapiens** descended.

These primitive humans demonstrated wide behavior patterns and great adaptability. Little is known in the way of details, including when language began to develop. They are believed to have lived in small communities that developed on the basis of the need to hunt. Cave paintings reveal a belief that magic pictures of animals could conjure up real ones. Some figurines seem to indicate belief in fertility gods and goddesses. Belief in some form of afterlife is indicated by burial formalities.

Fire and weapons were in use quite early. Archaeological evidence points to the use of hatchets, awls, needles and cutting tools in the Old Stone Age, or **Paleolithic** (one million years ago). Artifacts of the New Stone Age, or **Neolitihic**, (6,000-8,000 BCE) include indications of polished tools, domesticated animals, the wheel, and some agriculture. Pottery and textiles have been found dating to the end of the New Stone Age. The discovery of metals in the **Bronze Age** (3,000 BCE) is concurrent with the establishment of what are believed to be the first civilizations. The Iron Age, followed quickly on the heels of the Bronze Age.

By 4,000 BCE, humans lived in villages, engaged in animal husbandry, grew grains, sailed in boats, and practiced religions. Civilizations arose earliest in the fertile river valleys of the Nile, Mesopotamia, the Indus, and the Hwang Ho Valleys.

Prerequisites of civilization:

- Use of metals rather than stone for tools and weapons
- A system of writing
- A calendar
- A territorial state organized on the basis of residence in the geographic region

Skill 1.1b   **Describe and analyze the impact of human interaction with the physical environment on the development of the ancient cultures of the Fertile Crescent.**

The earliest known civilizations developed in the **Tigris-Euphrates Valley** of Mesopotamia (modern Iraq) and the **Nile Valley** of Egypt between 4000 BCE and 3000 BCE. Because these civilizations arose in river valleys, they are known as **fluvial civilizations**. Geography and the physical environment played a critical role in the rise and the survival of both of these civilizations.

First, the rivers provided a source of water that would sustain life, including animal life. The hunters of the society had ample access to a variety of animals, initially for hunting to provide food, as well as hides, bones, antlers, etc. from which clothing, tools and art could be made. Second, the proximity to water provided a natural attraction to animals which could be herded and husbanded to provide a stable supply of food and animal products. Third, the rivers of these regions overflowed their banks each year, leaving behind a deposit of very rich soil. As these early people began to experiment with growing crops rather than gathering food, the soil was fertile and water was readily available to produce sizeable harvests. In time, the people developed systems of irrigation that channeled water to the crops without significant human effort on a continuing basis.

The **Fertile Crescent** was bounded on the West by the Mediterranean Sea, on the South by the Arabian Desert, on the north by the Taurus Mountains, and on the east by the Zagros Mountains.

The designation "Fertile Crescent" was applied by the famous historian and Egyptologist James Breasted to the part of the Near East that extended from the Persian Gulf to the Sinai Peninsula. It included Mesopotamia, Syria and Palestine. This region was marked by almost constant invasions and migrations. These invaders and migrants seemed to have destroyed the culture and civilization that existed. Upon taking a longer view, however, it becomes apparent that they actually absorbed and supplemented the civilization that existed before their arrival. This is one of the reasons the civilization developed so quickly and created so such an advanced culture.

Skill 1.1c   **Describe and analyze the religious, social, economic, and political structures of the ancient cultures of Mesopotamia,Persia, Egypt, Kush, Greece, India, China, Rome, and pre-Columbian America, and describe and analyze their intellectual, ethical, scientific, and artistic accomplishments and values.**

Ancient civilizations were those cultures that developed to a greater degree and were considered advanced. There are a number of ancient civilizations worth examining, each with its own major accomplishments.

The ancient civilization of the **Sumerians** invented the wheel, developed irrigation through use of canals, dikes, and devices for raising water, devised the system of cuneiform writing, learned to divide time, and built large boats for trade. The **Babylonians** devised the famous **Code of Hammurabi**, the first written code of laws, which would later form the basis for our modern laws. **Egypt** made numerous significant contributions including construction of the great pyramids, development of hieroglyphic writing, preservation of bodies after death, making paper from papyrus, the invention of the method of counting in groups of 1-10 (the decimal system), completion of a solar calendar; and laying the foundation for science and astronomy.

The civilizations of the Sumerians, Amorites, Hittites, Assyrians, Chaldeans, and Persians controlled various areas of the land we call Mesopotamia. The culture of **Mesopotamia** was definitely autocratic in nature. The various civilizations that criss-crossed the Fertile Crescent were very much top-heavy, with a single ruler at the head of the government and, in many cases, also the head of the religion. The people followed his strict instructions or faced the consequences, which were usually dire and often life-threatening.

For example, each Sumerian city-state (and there were a few) had its own god, with the city-state's leader doubling as the high priest of worship of that local god. Subsequent cultures had a handful of gods as well, although they had more of a national worship structure, with high priests centered in the capital city as advisers to the tyrant. With few exceptions, tyrants and military leaders controlled the vast majority of aspects of society, including trade, religions, and the laws.

Trade was vastly important to these civilizations since they had access to some but not all of the things that they needed to survive. Some trading agreements led to occupation, as was the case with the Sumerians, who didn't bother to build walls to protect their wealth of knowledge. Egypt and the Phoenician cities were powerful and regular trading partners of the various Mesopotamian cultures.

Legacies handed down to us from these people include:
- The first use of writing, the wheel, and banking (Sumeria);
- The first written set of laws (Code of Hammurabi);
- The first epic story (*Gilgamesh*);
- The first library dedicated to preserving knowledge (instituted by the Assyrian leader Ashurbanipal);
- The Hanging Gardens of Babylon (built by the Chaldean Nebuchadnezzar)

The earliest historical record of **Kush** is in Egyptian sources. They describe a region upstream from the first cataract of the Nile as "wretched." This civilization was characterized by a settled way of life in fortified mud-brick villages. They subsisted on hunting and fishing, herding cattle, and gathering grain. Skeletal remains suggest that the people were a blend of Negroid and Mediterranean peoples. This civilization appears to be the second-oldest in Africa (after Egypt). Either the people were Egyptian or heavily influenced by Egyptians at a very early period in the development of the society. They appear to have spoken Nilo-Saharan languages. The area in which they lived is called Nubia. The capital city was Kerma, a major trading center between the northern and southern parts of Africa.

During the period of Egypt's **Old Kingdom** (ca. 2700-2180 BCE), this civilization was essentially a diffused version of Egyptian culture and religion. When Egypt came under the domination of the Hyksos, Kush reached its greatest power and cultural energy (1700-1500 BCE). When the Hyksos were eventually expelled from Egypt, the New Kingdom brought Kush back under Egyptian colonial control. The collapse of the **New Kingdom** in Egypt (ca. 1000 BCE), provided the second opportunity for Kush to develop independently of Egyptian control and to conquer all of the Nubian region. The capital was then moved to Napata.

For the most part, the Kushites apparently considered themselves Egyptian and inheritors of the pharoanic tradition. Their society was organized on the Egyptian model, adopting Egyptian royal titles, etc. Even their art and architecture was based on Egyptian models. But their pyramids were smaller and steeper. In what has been called "**a magnificent irony of history**" the Kushites conquered Egypt in the eighth century, creating the twenty-fifth dynasty. The dynasty ended in the seventh century when Egypt was defeated by the Assyrians.

In government, the king ruled through a law of custom that was interpreted by priests. The king was elected from the royal family. Descent was determined through the mother's line (as in Egypt). But in an unparalleled innovation, the Kushites were ruled by a series of **female monarchs**. The Kushite religion was polytheistic, including all of the primary Egyptian gods. There were, however, regional gods which were the principal gods in their regions. Derived from other African cultures, there was also a lion warrior god. This civilization was vital through the last half of the first millennium BC, but it suffered about 300 years of gradual decline until it was eventually conquered by the Nuba people.

The **Phoenicians** were sea traders well known for their manufacturing skills in glass and metals and the development of their famous purple dye. They became so very proficient in the skill of navigation that they were able to sail by the stars at night. Further, they devised an alphabet using symbols to represent single sounds, which was an improved extension of the Egyptian principle and writing system. The ancient **Assyrians** were warlike and aggressive due to a highly organized military and used horse drawn chariots.

The **Hebrews**, also known as the ancient Israelites instituted "monotheism," which is the worship of one God, Yahweh, and combined the 66 books of the Hebrew and Christian Greek scriptures into the Bible we have today. The ancient **Persians** developed an alphabet; contributed the religions and philosophies of **Zoroastrianism**, **Mithraism**, and **Gnosticism**; and allowed conquered peoples to retain their own customs, laws, and religions.

The **Minoans** had a system of writing using symbols to represent syllables in words. They built palaces with multiple levels containing many rooms, water and sewage systems with flush toilets, bathtubs, hot and cold running water, and bright paintings on the walls. The **Mycenaeans** changed the Minoan writing system to aid their own language and used symbols to represent syllables.

The classical civilization of **Greece** was based on the foundations already laid by such ancient groups as the Egyptians, Phoenicians, Minoans, and Mycenaeans. The modern **Olympic Games** are a revival of an ancient Greek tradition and many of the events are recreations of original contests. Greek mythology, centered around a pantheon of gods and the mortals they interact with, has been the source of inspiration for literature into the present day. Among the more important contributions of Greece were the Greek alphabet derived from the Phoenician letters which formed the basis for the Roman alphabet and our present-day alphabet. Extensive trading and colonization resulted in the spread of the Greek civilization.

Other important areas that the Greeks are credited with influencing include drama, epic and lyric poetry, fables, myths centered on the many gods and goddesses, science, astronomy, medicine, mathematics, philosophy, art, architecture, and recording historical events. The works of the Greek epic poet **Homer** are considered the earliest in western literature, and are still read and taught today. The tradition of the theater was born in Greece, with the plays of **Aristophanes** and others. In the field of mathematics, **Pythagoras** and **Euclid** laid the foundation of geometry and Archimedes calculated the value of pi. **Herodotus** and **Thucydides** were the first to apply research and interpretation to written history. In the arts, Greek sensibilities were held as perfect forms to which others might strive. In sculpture, the Greeks achieved an idealistic aesthetic that had not been perfected before that time.

The conquests of **Alexander the Great** spread Greek ideas to the areas he conquered and brought to the Greek world many ideas from Asia. Above all, the value of ideas, wisdom, curiosity, and the desire to learn as much about the world as possible was a major objective of the conquests.

The ancient civilization of **Rome** lasted approximately 1,000 years including the periods of Republic and Empire, although its lasting influence on Europe and its history was for a much longer period. There was a very sharp contrast between the curious, imaginative, inquisitive Greeks and the practical, simple, down-to-earth, no-nonsense Romans, who spread and preserved the ideas of ancient Greece and other culture groups. The contributions and accomplishments of the Romans are numerous but their greatest included language, engineering, building, law, government, roads, trade, and the "**Pax Romana.**" Pax Romana was the long period of peace enabling free travel and trade, spreading people, cultures, goods, and ideas all over a vast area of the known world.

A most interesting and significant characteristic of the Greek, Hellenic, and Roman civilizations was "**secularism**" where emphasis shifted away from religion to the state. Men were not absorbed in or dominated by religion as had been the case in Egypt and the nations located in Mesopotamia. Religion and its leaders did not dominate the state and its authority was greatly diminished.

In **India**, Hinduism was a continuing influence along with the rise of Buddhism. Industry and commerce developed along with extensive trading with the Near East. Indian goods found their way to western ports through trade with the ancient Mediterranean civilizations, including Rome. The resulting cultural exchange was good for both sides of the equation. Outstanding advances in the fields of science and medicine were made along with being the first to be active in navigation and maritime enterprises during this time. The caste system was developed, the principle of zero in mathematics was discovered, and the major religion of Hinduism was begun.

China is considered by some historians to be the oldest, uninterrupted civilization in the world and was in existence around the same time as the ancient civilizations founded in Egypt, Mesopotamia, and the Indus Valley. The Chinese studied nature and weather; stressed the importance of education, family, and a strong central government; followed the religions of Buddhism, Confucianism, and Taoism; and invented such things as gunpowder, paper, printing, and the magnetic compass.

China began building the **Great Wall**, practiced crop rotation and terrace farming, increased the importance of the silk industry, and developed caravan routes across Central Asia for extensive trade. Also, they increased proficiency in rice cultivation and developed a written language based on drawings or pictographs (there is no alphabet symbolizing sounds, as each word or character had a form different from all others). Chinese people became very proficient at producing beautiful artworks and exporting them, along with silk, to the rest of the world along the **Silk Road**. China was also the birthplace of many of the world's most familiar inventions, including paper, printing, paper money, and gunpowder.

The civilization in **Japan** appeared during this time having borrowed much of their culture from China. It was the last of the classical civilizations to develop. Although they used, accepted, and copied Chinese art, law, architecture, dress, and writing, the Japanese refined these into their own unique way of life, including incorporating the religion of Buddhism into their culture.

The civilizations in **Africa** south of the Sahara were developing the refining and use of iron, especially for farm implements and later for weapons. Trading was overland using camels and at important seaports. The Arab influence was extremely important, as was their later contact with Indians, Christian Nubians, and Persians. In fact, their trading activities were probably the most important factor in the spread of and assimilation of different ideas and stimulation of cultural growth.

The people who lived in the Americas before Columbus arrived had a thriving, connected society. The civilizations in North America tended to spread out more and were in occasional conflict but maintained their sovereignty for the most part. The South American civilizations, however, tended to migrate into empires, with the strongest city or tribe assuming control of the lives and resources of the rest of the nearby peoples.

Native Americans in North America had a spiritual and personal relationship with the various Spirits of Nature and a keen appreciation of the ways of woodworking and metalworking. Various tribes dotted the landscape of what is now the United States. They struggled against one another for control of resources such as food and water but had no concept of ownership of land, since they believed that they were living on the land with the permission of the Spirits. The North Americans mastered the art of growing many crops and, to their credit, were willing to share that knowledge with the various Europeans who eventually showed up. Artwork made of hides, beads, and jewels was popular at this time.

The most well-known empires of South America were the Aztec, Inca, and Maya. Each of these empires had a central capital in which lived the emperor, who controlled all aspects of the lives of his subjects. The empires traded with other peoples; and if the relations soured, the results were usually absorption of the trading partners into the empire. These empires, especially the **Aztecs**, had access to large numbers of metals and jewels, and they created weapons and artwork that continues to impress historians today. The **Inca Empire** stretched across a vast period of territory down the western coast of South America and was connected by a series of roads. A series of messengers ran along these roads, carrying news and instructions from the capital, Cusco. The Incas, however, did not have the wheel. The **Mayas** are most well-known for their famous pyramids and calendars, as well as their language, which still stumps archaeologists.

Skill 1.1d   **Describe and analyze the foundations of western political and philosophical thought in ancient Greek, Roman, and Judeo-Christian traditions.**

Ancient Greece is often called the "**Cradle of Western Civilization**" because of the enormous influence it had not only on the time in which it flourished, but on western culture ever since. Early Greek institutions have survived for thousands of years, and have influenced the entire world.

The **Athenian form of democracy**, with each citizen having an equal vote in his own government, is a philosophy upon which all modern democracies are based. In the United States, the Greek tradition of democracy was honored in the choice of **Greek architectural** styles for the nation's government buildings. In philosophy, **Aristotle** developed an approach to learning that emphasized observation and thought, and **Socrates** and **Plato** contemplated the nature of being and the origins and ideals of government and political relations.

Greece was responsible for the rise of independent, strong city-states. Note the complete contrast between independent, freedom-loving Athens with its practice of pure democracy i.e. direct, personal, active participation in government by qualified citizens and the rigid, totalitarian, militaristic Sparta.

The Greek civilization served as an inspiration to the **Roman Republic**, which followed in its tradition of democracy, and was directly influenced by its achievements in art and science. Later, during the Renaissance, European scholars and artists would rediscover ancient Greece's love for dedicated inquiry and artistic expression, leading to a surge in scientific discoveries and advancements in the arts.

The ancient **Israelites** and **Christians** created a powerful legacy of political and philosophical traditions, much of which survives to this day. In law and religion, especially, we can draw a more or less straight line from then to now.

Israel was not the first ancient civilization to have a series of laws for its people to follow. However, thanks to the staggering popularity of the **Ten Commandments**, we think of the Israelites in this way. This simple set of laws, some of which are not laws at all but societal instructions, maintains to this day a central role in societies the world over. Such commandments as the ones that prohibit stealing and killing were revolutionary in their day because they applied to everyone, not just the disadvantaged. In many ancient cultures, the rich and powerful were above the law because they could buy their way out of trouble and because it wasn't always clear what the laws were. Echoing the Code of Hammurabi and preceding Rome's Twelve Tables, the Ten Commandments provided a written record of laws, so all knew what was prohibited.

The civilization of Israel is also known as the first to assume a worship of just one god, or **monotheism**. The Christian communities built on this tradition, and both faiths exist and are expanding today, especially in western countries. Rather than a series of gods, each of which was in charge of a different aspect of nature or society, the ancient Israelites and Christians believed in just one god, called Yahweh or God, depending on which religion you look at. This divine being was, these peoples believed, the "one, true god," lord over all. This worship of just one god had more of a personal nature to it, and the result was that the believers thought themselves able to talk (or, more properly, pray) directly to their god, whereas the peoples of Mesopotamia and Egypt thought the gods distant and unapproachable.

Modern western societies owe a tremendous debt to both the legal and religious aspects of these ancient societies.

(See also Skill 1.1c)

Skill 1.1e   Describe and analyze the foundations of Asian political and philosophical thought found in ancient Chinese and Indian traditions.

Large elements of ancient times resonate today in both India and China, most prominently in the areas of philosophy and politics. **India** in ancient times had the shining light of Mohenjo-Daro, which was a planned community that had wide, straight streets and modern plumbing, among other comforts that we would consider "modern" innovations. The city-state, made so famous by the ancient Greeks, could be found in India as well, in the period after the Aryan invasion. The idea of a united India, which exists now, was realized very early on in the country's history, although the vast majority of rulers have been strong-handed and strong-willed emperors and kings.

Hinduism was begun by the people known as Aryans around 1500 BCE and spread into India. The Aryans blended their culture with the culture of the Dravidians, natives they conquered. Today it has many sects, promotes worship of hundreds of gods and goddesses and belief in reincarnation. Though forbidden today by law, a prominent feature of Hinduism in the past was a rigid adherence to and practice of the infamous caste system.

Buddhism developed in India from the teachings of Prince Gautama and spread to most of Asia. Its beliefs opposed the worship of numerous deities, the Hindu caste system and the supernatural. Worshippers must be free of attachment to all things worldly and devote themselves to finding release from life's suffering.

One tremendous bit of legacy that we can trace to the Aryans is the **caste** system, which permeates nearly all aspects of Indian society today. The prohibitions might be less severe these days, but the castes are still there. The great twin religions of Hinduism and Buddhism had their genesis in India; both are still very much alive today, emphasizing their doctrines of rebirth, enlightenment, nirvana, and more. The Hindu doctrine of reincarnation especially went hand-in-hand with the caste system, making it nearly impossible for the disadvantaged to ever improve their fortunes.

Ancient **China** was a land in constant turmoil. Tribes warred with one another almost from the first, with the **Great Wall of China** being a consolidation of walls built to keep out invaders. The Great Wall was built at the direction of China's emperor, and the idea of an emperor or very strong "government of one" was the rule of law until the twentieth century.

Two of the world's most important religions originated in China: Taoism and Confucianism. Confucius, especially, is one of the most famous figures in world history; his ethics teachings continue to form the basis of thought for many Chinese people.

Confucianism is a Chinese religion based on the teachings of the Chinese philosopher Confucius. There is no clergy, no organization, and no belief in a deity or in life after death. It emphasizes political and moral ideas with respect for authority and ancestors. Rulers were expected to govern according to high moral standards.

Taoism is a native Chinese religion with worship of more deities than almost any other religion. It teaches all followers to make the effort to achieve the two goals of happiness and immortality. Practices and ceremonies include meditation, prayer, magic, reciting scriptures, special diets, breath control, beliefs in witchcraft, fortune telling, astrology, and communicating with the spirits of the dead.

Shinto is the native religion of Japan developed from native folk beliefs worshipping spirits and demons in animals, trees, and mountains. According to its mythology, deities created Japan and its people, which resulted in worshipping the emperor as a god. Shinto was strongly influenced by Buddhism and Confucianism but never had strong doctrines on salvation or life after death.

Skill 1.1f   **Describe and analyze the importance and patterns of expansion and contraction of empires, religions, and trade that influenced various regional cultures through the decline of the Roman Empire.**

The first empire in history was probably in Mesopotamia, and it was probably the Akkadians, led by Sargon, conqueror of Sumeria. Sargon didn't last long as an emperor, however. He was succeeded as the master of Mesopotamia by a host of famous names, including the Amorite leader Hammurabi, he of the famous Code. Another of the famous leaders of the Middle Eastern peoples was Nebuchadnezzar, leader of the Chaldeans. We know this name better for two famous episodes in world history: the building of the Hanging Gardens of Babylon and the Babylonian Captivity, the capture of and transport of the ancient Israelites. Other rulers of the Fertile Crescent include the warrior-tribes the Hittites and the Assyrians, both powerful and successful in their day. But the Middle East empire-building phase didn't really build until Darius the Great came onto the scene.

Darius was the man who built a collection of cities and satraps into the Persian Empire, one of the largest the world had ever seen. It stretched from Egypt, which it conquered eventually, to the boundaries of India. Millions of people owed their lives and their allegiances to Darius and to his successors. The head of the Persian Empire was the most powerful man in the world. He was also the head of the various religions that dotted his large empire, with various locations believing in local gods and spirits representing aspects of Nature. This was not a new idea, since it had been done in Mesopotamian empires before and especially well in Egypt.

It should be mentioned here that Egypt had an empire of its own, of sorts. The Egyptian civilization encompassed many cities up and down the Nile River in northeastern and east-central Africa, and the production capacity and religious fervor of these Egyptians was incredibly high. The **pharaohs** who were in command of all aspects of the lives of the Egyptian people were also heads of the various religions. Even though each Egyptian god had its own temple and each temple had its own priests, the pharaoh was the liaison between the people and their gods. Egyptian goods flowed from ports and trade centers to locations all over the Mediterranean area and into central Asia. Egypt also was a captivating takeover goal for many neighbors; the only ones to succeed were a Persian, a Macedonian, and a Roman.

As big as the Empire was, the Persians always wanted more. They grew covetous of the growing Greek civilization, which was looking to expand in all directions, especially to the east, to areas claimed by the Persians. A series of disagreements escalated into a series of battles and then a full-blown war, which the Greeks refer to as the Persian Wars. This struggle had some of the most famous battles in the world, including Marathon, in which the Greeks won despite being vastly outnumbered; Thermopylae, in which a valiant group of Spartans held off thousands of Persian warriors for several days; Salamis, a naval battle that the Greeks won despite being outgunned and outnumbered; and Plataea, in which the Greeks sealed the deal by finally outnumbering the Persians. These victories convinced the Persians not to attempt another invasion of Greece, but it didn't mean the end of the Empire. **(See Skill 1.1c).**

That end came at the hands of **Alexander the Great**, a Macedonian general who conquered both Greece and Persia, eventually adding Egypt, Phoenician cities, and part of India, creating an empire that was staggering in its geography and impact. This empire more than any other resulted in cultural exchange. This was known as **Hellenization**, and it brought the Greek enlightened way of life to the peoples of the East while also bringing the exotic goods and customs of the East to Greece. Until this time, the peoples of East and West exchanged goods and customs in small ways but were overall suspicious of their enemies. Alexander changed all that, bringing both sides together under one banner and beginning an exchange of ideas, beliefs, and goods that would capture the imagination of rulers for years after his untimely death.

Rome was the next and most successful of the ancient empires, building itself from one town that borrowed from its Etruscan neighbors into a worldwide empire stretching from the wilds of Scotland to the shores of the Middle East. Building on the principles of Hellenization, Rome imported and exported goods and customs galore, melding the production capabilities and the belief systems of all it conquered into a heterogeneous yet distinctly Roman civilization. Like no other empire before it, Rome conquered and absorbed what it got. Trade, religion, science, political structure—all these things were incorporated into the Roman Empire, with all of the benefits that assimilation brought being passed on to the Empire's citizens. **(See Skill 1.1d)**

The official end of the **Roman Empire** came when Germanic tribes took over and controlled most of Europe. The five major tribes were the Visigoths, Ostrogoths, Vandals, Saxons, and the Franks. In later years, the Franks successfully stopped the invasion of southern Europe by Muslims by defeating them under the leadership of Charles Martel at the Battle of Tours in 732 AD. Thirty-six years later in 768 AD, the grandson of Charles Martel became King of the Franks and is known throughout history as **Charlemagne**. Charlemagne was a man of war but was unique in his respect for and encouragement of learning. He made great efforts to rule fairly and ensure just treatment for his people.

The East had its share of empires as well, especially in China. From an early age, China had emperors who were in charge of vast territories and vast numbers of people. The Chinese, especially, were good at exporting their goods and customs, especially along the famous Silk Road. Exotic spices flowed along this road to the Middle East and to Rome. The Chinese empire steadily expanded, rivaling even Rome in breadth and accomplishments by the time of the famous Han Dynasty. When Rome fell, China lived on.

COMPETENCY 1.2   MEDIEVAL AND EARLY MODERN TIMES

Skill 1.2a   Analyze the impact of geography, including both human and physical features, on the development of medieval and early-modern Asian, African, Middle Eastern, pre-Columbian American, and European civilizations.

As civilizations progressed through the Middle Ages and on into early modern times, the ways in which people communicated, explored, fought, and traded expanded. Methods of transportation were being updated all the time, with land-based vehicles growing ever larger and ships increasing in size and purpose as well. Ways to build, as in cities and towns, were increasing technologically as well. At the same time that an emphasis was being put on connecting to the outside world, people were increasingly looking inward, both in their pursuit of "the next life," as most religions would style it, and in their desire to protect what they had earned. The same groups of people that worked together to build ships to sail the high seas also worked together to build tall castles to watch over their houses and towns. Advances in technology extended to warfare as well, with powerful new weapons like gunpowder making old ways of fighting obsolete. It was a turbulent time throughout the world.

Mountains and rivers still formed formidable boundaries for countries and civilizations, of course. The ways that men killed other men had advanced, but the ways in which men crossed rivers and mountains hadn't kept pace. Mountains still had to be marched over, and rivers still had to be ferried or rafted across. If the defender was at the top of the mountain or on the other side of the river, it didn't matter how many advanced weapons the attackers had; the defender still had the edge.

This was true in the high mountains of Asia and South America. It was true in the delta-dotted plains of India and Central Asia. It was even true in Europe, which boasted more than its fair share of high mountains (Alps and Pyrenees) and wide rivers (like the Rhine and the Rhone). This was the case everywhere around the world, except, of course, in the sands of sub-Saharan Africa, where struggles took the form of wars of attrition, the victors being those who weathered the sandstorms and lack of water the best. The Middle East, with its preponderance of flat lands interrupted by only a few hills, rivers, and isolated mountains, saw more than its fair share of combat, as was the case in the earliest days and as continues to be the case even today.

As in the earliest days of civilization, people lived near waterways because they depended on those waterways for trade. The larger the boats, the more they could carry; this certainly increased the efficiency of trade. Foods and spices that previously were nonexistent in the markets of Europe because they would spoil before they ever reached their destination were increasingly for sale, since travel times had dramatically decreased because of improvements in travel technology.

Following the stunningly successful example of the Roman Empire, more and more people built serviceable roads, making land-based trade less of a desperate adventure and more a viable alternative to water trading. Especially in the deserts of northern Africa and the jungles of South America, people depended on rivers and lakes for their very survival, both for drinking water and for sustenance for the ever-increasing number and variety of crops that they grew.

Especially in Europe during this period, the **castle** was a dominant feature on the landscape of many a town, village, or country. Castles housed kings, soldiers, retinues, and plain old peasants. They also served as watchtowers, guardhouses, and barracks. If you wanted to take over a country, you had better take over the castles, so your enemy couldn't stockpile soldiers and resources and make a counterstrike when you least expected it. Some conquerors made a habit of targeting castles, taking them over, and then razing them, in order to eliminate the enemy's ability to fight back. Other conquerors felt compelled to build castles every few miles, as guard towers or, more likely, as symbols of the newfound authority.

In a way, the castle was the new "high ground." In battles of old, the army that held the high ground held the advantage because its opponents would have to tire themselves out running uphill just to engage, while the high ground holders could pepper them with rocks, arrows, and other airborne weapons. Walled cities were certainly popular as defensible positions throughout history, but they weren't as easy to create as castles were and they couldn't be as easily defended. By building castles, the people of these periods changed their landscape in their favor, in effect creating a huge advantage where none had been before.

This was perhaps the way that the landscapes of the world changed the most—the way that people changed it. Where broad plains had been before, towns and villages, castles and fortifications, ports and trade centers dotted the landscape. Despite such episodes as the devastating **Black Plague** and a seemingly endless series of wars, the populations of the world continued to expand, with people always seeking to expand their living spaces. More people meant not only more living space but also more demand for basic and exotic goods. As civilization spread outward from its beginnings in the Fertile Crescent, ancient Africa, and along the rivers Indus and Yangtze, the needs and signatures of mankind spread out with it.

Skill 1.2b   **Trace the decline of the Western Roman Empire and the development of the Byzantine Empire, and analyze the emergence of these two distinct European civilizations and their views on religion, culture, society, and politics.**

The decline of the Western Roman Empire was due to a variety of factors, including the increasing sprawl of the Empire; the resilience of the Germanic and other "barbarian" foes; and the spread of dissatisfaction of the Empire's residents themselves with the administration of the vast social, economic, and political network. At the same time, the splitting of the empire in the early fourth century had, intentionally or not, tipped the balance in favor of the Eastern Empire, which was closer to Asia, farther away from Germany, and easier to defend.

The early religion of the Empire was one of many gods, representing the various parts of Nature and the skies. As Rome conquered various peoples with varied religions, the Empire assimilated the religions of those peoples as well. By the time that the Eastern Empire was created, the Empire as a whole was a melting pot of beliefs and faiths. Christianity, however, had come to the fore, especially when Constantine made it the state religion in 312. The Eastern Empire basically started out this way, whereas the Western Empire ended as such. The main difference in the east, however, was that the emperor was head of the church, not the other way around.

The Eastern Empire became The **Byzantine Empire**, which was closer to the Middle East and so better inherited the traditions of Mesopotamia and Persia. This was in stark contrast to the Western Empire, which inherited the traditions of Greece and Carthage. Byzantium was known for its exquisite artwork including the famous church **Hagia Sophia**. Perhaps the most wide-ranging success of the Byzantine Empire was in the area of trade. Uniquely situated at the gateway to both West and East, Byzantium could control trade going in both directions. Indeed, the Eastern Empire was much more centralized and rigid in its enforcement of its policies than the feudal West.

The **Byzantine** and **Saracenic** (or Islamic) civilizations were both dominated by religion. The major contributions of the Saracens were in the areas of science and philosophy including accomplishments in astronomy, mathematics, physics, chemistry, medicine, literature, art, trade and manufacturing, agriculture, and a marked influence on the Renaissance Period of history. The Byzantines (Christians) made important contributions in art and the preservation of Greek and Roman achievements including architecture - especially in eastern Europe and Russia, the Code of Justinian, and Roman law.

Skill 1.2c   Describe the role and expansion of Christianity in medieval and early modern Europe and the Middle East.

The rise of Christianity in early modern Europe was due as much to the iron hand of feudalism as it was to the Church itself. **Feudalism**, more than any other element, helped the Church get its grip on Europe. Like the caste system in India, feudalism kept people in strict control according to their social class. If you were a peasant, you had been born that way and you had an excellent chance of staying that way for your entire life. The rich and powerful were also the highest class in society, and the friends of the rich and powerful were the clergy.

The Church, through its warnings of death and damnation without salvation, had rigid control of the belief systems of most of the people throughout Europe. In this way, the Church was able to assume more than just traditionally religious roles in people's lives. Clergy were respected and trusted members of society, and people consulted them on secular matters as well as religious ones.

In a way that governments never could, Christianity unified Europe. Especially with the Pope at the head of the religion, the peoples of Europe could correctly be called Christendom because they all had the same beliefs, the same worries, and the same tasks to perform in order to achieve the salvation that they so desperately sought. The Church was only too happy to capitalize on this power, which increased throughout the Middle Ages until it met a stalwart from Germany named Martin Luther.

Also at this time, a desire to travel to the Holy Land, to Palestine and what is now Israel, grew significantly. The Church encouraged this, and pilgrimage routes sprang up. The purpose of the **Crusades** was to rid Jerusalem of Muslim control and these series of violent, bloody conflicts did affect trade and stimulated later explorations seeking the new, exotic products such as silks and spices. The Crusaders came into contact with other religions and cultures and learned and spread many new ideas.

Also coming into importance at this time was the era of knighthood and its code of chivalry as well as the tremendous influence of the Church (Roman Catholic). During the period of the Renaissance, the Church was the only place where people could be educated. The Bible and other books were hand-copied by monks in the monasteries. Cathedrals were built and were decorated with art depicting religious subjects.

Skill 1.2d   **Identify the basic tenets of Islam, and describe Islamic society and culture between the beginning of the 7th century and the end of the 18th century.**

A few years after the death of the Emperor Justinian, **Mohammed** was born (570 CE) in a small Arabian town near the Red Sea. Before this time, Arabians played only an occasional role in history. Arabia was a vast desert of rock and sand, except the coastal areas on the Red Sea. It was populated by nomadic wanderers called **Bedouin**, who lived in scattered tribes near oases where they watered their herds. Tribal leaders engaged in frequent war with one another. The family or tribe was the social and political unit, under the authority of the head of the family, within which there was cruelty, infanticide, and suppression of women.

Their religion was a crude and superstitious paganism and idolatry. Although there was regular contact with Christians and Jews through trading interactions, the idea of monotheism was foreign. What vague unity there was within the religion was based upon common veneration of certain sanctuaries. The most important of these was a small square temple called **the Kaaba** (cube), located in the town of **Mecca**. Arabs came from all parts of the country in annual pilgrimages to Mecca during the sacred months when warfare was prohibited. For this reason, Mecca was considered the center of Arab religion.

In about 610 a prophet named **Mohammed** came to some prominence. He called his new religion **Islam** (submission [to the will of God]) and his followers were called **Moslems** – those who had surrendered themselves. His first converts were members of his family and his friends. As the new faith began to grow, it remained a secret society. But when they began to make their faith public, they met with opposition and persecution from the pagan Arabians who feared the new religion and the possible loss of the profitable trade with the pilgrims who came to the Kaaba every year.

Islam slowly gained ground, and the persecutions became more severe around Mecca. In 622, Mohammed and his close followers fled the city and found refuge in **Medina** to the North. His flight is called the **Hegira**. This event marks the beginning of the Moslem calendar. Mohammed took advantage of the ongoing feuds between Jews and Arabs in the city and became the rulers of Medina, making it the capital of a rapidly growing state.

In the years that followed, Islam changed significantly. It became a fighting religion and Mohammed became a political leader. The group survived by raiding caravans on the road to Mecca and plundering nearby Jewish tribes. This was a victorious religion that promised plunder and profit in this world and the blessings of paradise after death. It attracted many converts from the Bedouin tribes. By 630, Mohammed was strong enough to conquer Mecca and make it the religious center of Islam, toward which all Moslems turned to pray, and the *Kaaba* the most sacred **Mosque** or temple. Medina remained the political capital.

By taking over the pilgrimage, the sacred city and the sanctuary from paganism, Mohammed made it easier for converts to join the religion. By the time of his death in 632, most of the people of Arabia had become at least nominal adherents of Islam.

Mohammed left behind a collection of divine revelations (**surahs**) he believed were delivered by the angel Gabriel. These were collected and published in a book called the **Koran** (reading), which has since been the holy scripture of Islam. The revelations were never dated or kept in any kind of chronological order. After the prophet's death they were organized by length (in diminishing order). The *Koran* contains Mohammed's teachings on moral and theological questions, his legislation on political matters, and his comments on current events.

Islam has five basic principles, known as the **Pillars of Islam**:

1. The oneness and omnipotence of God – **Allah**.
    - Mohammed is the prophet of Allah to whom all truth has been revealed by God.
    - To each of the previous prophets (Adam, Noah, Abraham, Moses and Jesus) a part of the truth was revealed.
2. One should **pray five times a day** at prescribed intervals, facing Mecca,
3. **Charity** – for the welfare of the community.
4. **Fasting** from sunrise to sunset every day during the holy month of Ramadan to cleanse the spirit.
5. **Pilgrimage to Mecca** should be made if possible and if no one suffers thereby.

The moral principles of Islam are:

- The practice of the virtues of charity, humility and patience,
- Enemies are to be forgiven,
- Avarice, lying and malice are condemned, and
- Drinking (alcohol), eating pork, and gambling are prohibited.

Mohammed believed that on the Day of Judgment all souls would be judged. The infidel would be condemned to a hell (**gehennem**) of perpetual fire; the good/faithful would go to Paradise, a beautiful place of cool waters, sensual delights, and ease. He emphasized a strong sense of predestination. The **Koran** elevated the level of women. A man could marry as many as four wives if he loved them equally. Divorce was easy, but the wife had to be given a dowry.

Mohammed drew freely upon Christianity, Judaism, and Arab paganism. His knowledge of the first two was limited to what he learned through casual conversation. The resulting doctrine was a mixture of ideas that is original when taken as a whole. It appealed to both the simple Arab of the prophet's day and to the faith of more civilized people.

Mohammed died without either a political or a religious succession plan. His cousin, Ali, who had married Mohammed's daughter Fatima, believed his kinship and his heroism as a warrior gave him a natural claim to leadership. But Moslems in Medina thought one of their own should succeed Mohammed. **Abu Bakr** was finally chosen. He took the title of **Caliph**. The title was retained throughout the duration of the Moslem Empire.

These Moslem Arabians immediately launched an amazing series of conquests which, in time, extended the empire from the Indus River Valley to Spain. It has often been said that these conquests were motivated by religious fanaticism and the determination to force Islam upon the infidel. In fact, however, the motives were economic and political.

During the period of expansion there was a brief civil war that occurred because Ali was proclaimed Caliph at Medina. He was opposed by an aristocratic family of Mecca called the **Umayyad**. Ali was assassinated in 661, and the Umayyads emerged supreme, handing the caliphate down in their family for nearly a century. Because their strongest support was in Syria, they moved the capital from Medina to Damascus.

There were significant changes during the century of Umayyad rule. First, there was little effort to convert conquered people. Infidels were taxed, the faithful were not. But taxation encouraged conversion. **Conversion** brought not only freedom from taxation, but a role in politics and other privileges reserved for the faithful. By the end of the seventh century, great numbers of conquered people had adopted Islam. Second, the Arabs, though still the ruling class, had become scattered and they were mingling with the other peoples and races of the empire. Last, Islam, rather than Arab nationalism, was becoming the important factor in Moslem patriotism.

The Umayyads had always represented Arabian rather than broader Moslem interests. More devout Moslems, especially in Persia, were unhappy with their rule. They turned to the **Abbasid** family for leadership. This family was descended from Abbas, the uncle of Mohammed. They relied on their relation to the prophet's family to attract the loyalty of devout Moslems of all races. The Abbasid dynasty began with the overthrow of the Umayyad family in 750, although an Umayyad emir continued to rule in Spain. This group then became separated from the rest of the empire. Persia then replaced Syria as the center of the empire, and the capital was moved from Damascus to Baghdad.

The Arab aristocracy was succeeded by a mixed official aristocracy drawn from all of the Moslem races. The caliphs modeled themselves after the Persian kings. Moslem civilization became a composite of Arabs, Persians and Greeks who were united by the teachings of Islam and the Arabic language. The Abbasid dynasty ushered in a period of great prosperity and absolute power that lasted for about 75 years. It was during the reign of Haroun al Rashid (786-809) that the caliphate reached its greatest power. Baghdad was one of the richest cities in the world, center of an empire that reached from central Asia to the Atlantic. But the empire was too large and its people too diverse to be held together by a single individual for very long. Shortly after Haroun's reign, the caliph began to lose power and the empire began to disintegrate. This continued through the tenth century.

The Umayyad emir in Spain took the title Caliph of Cordova; in Egypt a descendant of Mohammed's daughter (Fatima) founded the caliphate of Cairo, which later came to include Syria. From 945-1055 the caliphs of Baghdad were completely dominated by a Persian dynasty of emirs, until they were conquered by the Seljuk Turks, who had come down from central Asia and adopted Islam with fanatical zeal. The Turkish emirs and sultans ruled for 200 years, reviving the political strength of the empire for a time and recovering Syria. It was the Turkish emirs who dealt with the crusaders. Finally, in the middle of the thirteenth century they were overcome by a fresh invasion from Asia – the Mongol hordes. The Abbasid caliphate disappeared.

Despite these political divisions, the Moslem world maintained strong economic, religious and cultural unity throughout this period. Mohammed had taught that all Moslems are brothers, equal in the sight of God. Conversion to Islam erased the differences between peoples of different ethnic origin.

The converts to Islam, who brought their cultural traditions, probably contributed more to this emerging synthetic civilization than the Arabs. This blending of cultures, facilitated by a common language, a common religion, and a strong economy, created learning, literature, science, technology and art that surpassed anything found in the Western Christian world during the Early Middle Ages. Interestingly, the most brilliant period of Moslem culture was from the eighth century through the eleventh, coinciding with the West's darkest cultural period.

Reading and writing in Arabic, the study of the Koran, arithmetic and other elementary subjects were taught to children in schools attached to the mosques. In larger and wealthier cities, the mosques offered more advanced education in literature, logic, philosophy, law, algebra, astronomy, medicine, science, theology and the tradition of Islam. Books were produced for the large reading public. The wealthy collected private libraries, and public libraries arose in large cities.

The most popular subjects were theology and the law. But the more important field of study was philosophy. The works of the Greek and Hellenistic philosophers were translated into Arabic and interpreted with commentaries. These were later passed on to the Western Christian societies and schools in the twelfth and thirteenth centuries. The basis of Moslem philosophy was Aristotelian and Neo-platonic ideas, which were essentially transmitted without creative modification.

The Moslems were also interested in natural science. They translated the works on Galen and Hippocrates into Arabic and added the results of their own experience in medicine. Avicenna was regarded in Western Europe as one of the great masters of medicine. They also adopted the work of the Greeks in the other sciences and modified and supplemented them with their own discoveries. Much of their work in chemistry was focused on alchemy (the attempt to transmute base metals into gold). The **Muslim** culture outdistanced the Western world in the field of medicine, primarily because the people weren't constrained by the sort of superstitious fervor that had so embraced the West at this time. The Muslim doctor **Al-Razi** was one of the most well-known physicians in the world and was the author of a medical encyclopedia and a handbook for smallpox and measles.

Adopting the heritage of Greek mathematics, the Moslems also borrowed a system of numerals from India. This laid the foundation for modern arithmetic, geometry, trigonometry and algebra.

Moslem art and architecture tended to be mostly uniform in style, allowing for some regional modification. They borrowed from Byzantine, Persian and other sources. The floor plan of the mosques was generally based on Mohammed's house at Medina. The notable unique elements were the tall **minarets** from which the faithful were called to prayer. Interior decoration was the style now called **arabesque**. Mohammed had banned paintings or other images of living creatures. These continued to be absent from mosques, although they occasionally appeared in book illustration and secular contexts. But their skilled craftsmen produced the finest art in jewelry, ceramics, carpets, and carved ivory.

The Moslems also produced sophisticated literature in both prose and poetry. The flexibility of the Arabic language was very well adapted to poetry. Little, however, of their poetry or prose was carried down by Western culture. The best-known works of this period are the short stories known as the **Arabian Nights** and the poems of **Omar Khayyam**.

Skill 1.2e **Analyze the religious and secular contributions of Islam to European, African and Asian civilizations and the impact of medieval Muslim civilization on Asia, Africa, and Europe between the beginning of the 7th century and the end of the 18th century.**

The Islamic contributions to Europe, Africa, and Asia are many and varied, in the areas of religion, economics, and culture. The area that benefited most was Africa.

The Muslim religion began in the Middle East, in the Arabian Peninsula, with the **Hegira** of Muhammad to Medina and then his triumphant return to Mecca. The religion's message of equality for all (at least, all men) was a powerful draw for the poor residents of Arabia and northern Africa, who were starving and had little hope of a better life. So was the idea of immortality, which you could achieve by following the precepts of Islam and otherwise live a good life. In less than 100 years, Islam had spread across the whole of northern Africa and into Spain.

These areas of northern African are mainly desert, even to this day. In the seventh and eighth centuries, the sands were a bit different and maybe a bit less. But they were still prevalent. One major contribution that the Muslim culture made to these areas was to perfect methods of **irrigation** that brought water and, as a result, food at levels that hadn't been available to these people before. The existing canals of the Middle East were extended as well, bringing much-needed resources to people living in the arid areas of the Arabian Peninsula. These advancements were especially welcome because, despite the harsh conditions, populations in these areas were growing all the time.

The breadth of territory in the lands controlled by the Muslim peoples at this time encompassed a correspondingly large variety of crops, including wheat, fruits, sugar, olives, wines, cotton, and flax. The trade routes and trade centers that had developed made distribution of these crops easier than it might have been otherwise, and the goods were distributed not only within the Muslim lands but elsewhere, to Europe and to Asia. The main vehicles of distribution of all of these goods were boats; Arabian horses; and camels, the "**ships of the desert**." In the same way that Asian and European goods influenced the business and society in Muslim trade centers and towns, goods and practices from the Muslim world made themselves known in other parts of the world.

In the trade centers of the Muslim world and of Europe, merchants made a name for themselves with their shrewd business practices. They were some of the first businessmen to take checks and give receipts. We can trace the terms *bazaar*, *tariff*, and *caravan* to them as well. Not surprisingly, many merchants in the Muslim world had rather large incomes. Like their European counterparts, these merchants lived in large homes with servants and other benefits that that income allowed. As in Russia and in Europe, many Muslim merchant estates had serfs or slaves. Even though the Muslim doctrine of equality before Allah was in full force, the practice of slavery was allowed under the same sort of logic that allowed men to disallow women basic rights. (It should be noted here that women enjoyed extended rights in very few places in the world at this time. Their treatment at the hands of their men in the Muslim world was more harsh on average than in Europe, however.)

In science, especially, the Muslim world often outshone the European world at this time. One of the main Muslim contributions to mathematics was the introduction of the number **zero**. It seems difficult to comprehend using our modern way of thinking that the number zero did not always exist; yet neither the Greeks nor the early Romans had the idea to assign a number to the mathematical equivalent of nothing. Much moreso than Europeans in the early years, Muslim explorers made their way to the Far East, both over land and on the high seas, bringing back with them not only goods but also knowledge. Muslim explorers also had versions of the compass and the astrolabe long before their European counterparts did.

Muslim doctors were diagnosing diseases, prescribing cures, and even performing advanced surgeries in modernized hospitals, things that European countries certainly could not boast of. The Muslim doctor Al-Razi was one of the most well-known physicians in the world and was the author of a medical encyclopedia and a handbook for smallpox and measles.

Most of the civilizations of Asia at this time were too far to be influenced by Muslim armies. Europe was a different story. Lured by the promise of greener pastures and greater opportunity, Muslim armies repeatedly marched north in an effort to spread their religion and influence into Europe. Spain was about as far as they got, thanks to a concerted European effort that resulted in a smashing victory at Tours in 732.

Muslim armies, however, controlled Palestine and Jerusalem, considered by most of Christendom, as Europe was known in those days, as the **Holy Land**. In a series of campaigns and battles that have been collectively called the **Crusades**, European armies sailed and marched to the Holy Land in an attempt to return it to European hands, in which it rested as recently as the sixth and seventh centuries, in the waning days of the Roman Empire. Muslim military leaders, especially the gallant **Saladin**, were able to unite their armies in a way that European leaders never did. The battles of the Crusades, especially the epic struggles for control of Jerusalem, involved new weapons and new tactics.

Skill 1.2f   **Analyze and compare and contrast the development of feudalism as a social, political, and economic system in Europe and Japan.**

During the Middle Ages, the system of **feudalism** became a dominant feature of the economic and social system in Europe. Feudalism began as a way to ensure that a king or nobleman could raise an army when needed. In exchange for the promise of loyalty and military service, **lords** would grant a section of land, called a **fief** to a **vassal**, as those who took this oath of loyalty were called. The vassal was then entitled to work the land and benefit from its proceeds or to grant it in turn as a fief to another. At the bottom of this ladder were **peasants** or **serfs** who actually worked the land. At the top was the king to whom all lands might legally belong. The king could ensure loyalty among his advisors by giving them use of large sections of land which they in turn could grant as fiefs.

It was a system of loyalty and protection. The strong protected the weak that returned the service with farm labor, military service, and loyalty. Improved tools and farming methods made life more bearable although most never left the manor or traveled from their village during their lifetime. The lord or noble, in return for the serfs' loyalty, offered them his protection. In practical effect, the serf was considered property owned by his lord with little or no rights at all. The lord's sole obligation to the serfs was to protect them so they could continue to work for him (in most cases, though not all lords were men). This system would last for many centuries. In Russia it would last until the 1860s.

Manorialism, which also arose during the Middle Ages is similar to feudalism in structure, but consisted of self-contained manors that were often owned outright by a nobleman. Some manors were granted conditionally to their lords, and some were linked to the military service and oaths of loyalty found in feudalism, meaning that the two terms overlap somewhat. Manors usually consisted of a large house for the lord and his family, surrounded by fields and a small village that supported the activities of the manor. The lord of the manor was expected to provide certain services for the villagers and laborers associated with the manor including the support of a church.

Also coming into importance at this time was the era of **knighthood** and its code of **chivalry** as well as the tremendous influence of the Roman Catholic Church . Until the period of the Renaissance, the Church was the only place where people could be educated. The **Bible** and other books were hand-copied by monks in the monasteries. Cathedrals were built and were decorated with art depicting religious subjects.

Land is a finite resource, and as the population grew in the middle centuries of the Middle Ages, the manorial/feudal system became less and less effective as a system of economic organization. The end of the feudal manorial system was sealed by the outbreak and spread of the infamous **Black Death**, which killed over one-third of the total population of Europe. Those who survived and were skilled in any job or occupation were in demand and many serfs or peasants found freedom and, for that time, a decidedly improved standard of living.

With the increase in trade and travel, cities sprang up and began to grow. Craft workers in the cities developed their skills to a high degree, eventually organizing **guilds** to protect the quality of the work and to regulate the buying and selling of their products. City government developed and flourished, centered around strong town councils. Active in city government and the town councils were the wealthy businessmen who made up the rising middle class. Strong nation-states became powerful and people developed a renewed interest in life and learning.

Feudalism developed in Japan later than it did in Europe and lasted longer as well. Japan dodged one huge historical bullet when a huge Mongol invasion was driven away by the famed **kamikaze**, or "divine wind," in the twelfth century. Japan was thus free to continue to develop itself as it saw fit and to refrain from interacting with the West, especially. This isolation, and thus the feudal system, lasted until the nineteenth century.

From its beginnings, Japan had morphed into an imperial form of government, with the divine emperor being able to do no wrong and, therefore, serving for life. **Kyoto**, the capital, became one of the largest and most powerful cities in the world. Slowly, though, as in Europe, the rich and powerful landowners, the nobles, grew powerful. Eventually, they had more power than the emperor. This required a great attitude change in the minds of the Japanese people, but change their attitudes they did.

The nobles were lords of great lands and were called **Daimyos**. They were of the highest social class and had working for them people of lower social classes, including the lowly peasants, who had few privileges other than being allowed to work for the great men that the Daimyos told everyone they were. The Daimyos had warriors serving them known as **samurai**, who were answerable only to the Daimyo. The samurai code of honor was an exemplification of the overall Japanese belief that every man was a soldier and a gentleman.

The main economic difference between imperial and feudal Japan was that the money that continued to flow into the country from trade with China, Korea, and other Asian countries and from good, old-fashioned plundering on the high seas made its way no longer into the emperor's coffers but rather the pockets of the Daimyos.

Skill 1.2g   Compare and contrast the geographic, political, economic, religious, and social structures of pre-Columbian American civilizations in North and South America between A.D. 500 and the end of the 18th century.

The North American and South American Native Americans could not have been more different, yet in some ways they were the same as well. Differences in geography, economic focus, and the preponderance of visitors from overseas produced differing patterns of occupation, survival, and success.

In North America, the landscape was much more hospitable to settlement and exploration. The North American continent, especially in what is now the United States, had a few mountain ranges and a handful of wide rivers but nothing near the dense jungles and staggeringly high mountains that South America did. The area that is now Canada was cold but otherwise conducive to settlement. As a result, the Native Americans in the northern areas of the Americas were more spread out and their cultures more diverse than their South American counterparts.

One of the best known of the North American tribes were the **Pueblo**, who lived in what is now the American Southwest.. The Pueblos chose their own chiefs. This was perhaps one of the oldest representative governments in the world. Known also for their organized government were the **Iroquoi**, who lived in the American Northeast. The famous **Five Nations** of the Iroquois made treaties among themselves and shared leadership of their peoples.

For the North Americans, life was all about finding and growing food. The people were great farmers and hunters. They grew such famous crops as **maize**, or corn, and potatoes and squash and pumpkins and beans; and they hunted all manner of animals for food, including deer, bears, and buffalo. Despite the preponderance of crop-growing areas, many Native Americans, however, did not domesticate animals except for dogs. They might have killed pigs and chickens for food, but they certainly made it easy on themselves by growing them in pens right outside their houses.

The Native Americans who lived in the wilds of Canada and in the Pacific Northwest lived off the land as well and, in this case, the nearby water. Fishing was a big business in these places. The people used fish to eat and for trade, exchanging the much-needed food for supplies from neighboring tribes.

Religion was a personal affair for nearly all of these tribes, with beliefs in higher powers extending to Spirits in the sky and elsewhere in Nature. Native Americans had none of the one-god-only mentality that developed in Europe and the Middle East, nor did they have the wars associated with the conflict that those monotheistic religions had with one another.

Those people who lived in North America had large concentrations of people and houses, but they didn't have the kind of large civilization centers like cities elsewhere in the world. The communities did not have any formal government. Each individual was responsible for governing himself or herself, particularly with regard to the rights of other members of the community. The chiefs generally carried out the will of the tribe. Each tribe was a discrete unit with its own lands. Boundaries of tribal territories were determined by treaties with neighbors. There was an organized confederation among certain tribes, often called a nation.

Though not greatly differing from each other in degree of civilization, the native peoples north of Mexico varied widely in customs, housing, dress, and religion. Among the native peoples of North America there were at least 200 languages and 1500 dialects. Each of the hundreds of tribes was somewhat influenced by its neighbors. Communication between tribes that spoke different languages was conducted primarily through a very elaborate system of sign language.

Those people who lived in North America had large concentrations of people and houses, but they didn't have the kind of large civilization centers like the cities of elsewhere in the world. These people didn't have an exact system of writing, either. These were two technological advances that were found in many other places in the world, including, to varying degrees, South America. There we know the most about the empires of the Aztec, Inca, and Maya. People lived in South America before the advent of these empires, of course. One of the earliest people of record were the **Olmecs**, who left behind little to prove their existence except a series of huge carved figures.

The **Aztecs** dominated Mexico and Central America. They weren't the only people living in these areas, just the most powerful ones. The Aztecs had many enemies, some of whom were only too happy to help Hernan Cortes precipitate the downfall of the Aztec society. The Aztecs had access to large numbers of metals and jewels, and they used these metals to make weapons and these jewels to trade for items they didn't already possess. Actually, the Aztecs didn't do a whole lot of trading; rather, they conquered neighboring tribes and demanded tribute from them; this is the source of so much of the Aztec riches. They also believed in a handful of gods and believed that these gods demanded human sacrifice in order to continue to smile on the Aztecs. The center of Aztec society was the great city of **Tenochtitlan**, which was built on an island so as to be easier to defend and boasted a population of 300,000 at the time of the arrival of the conquistadors. Tenochtitlan was known for its canals and its pyramids, none of which survive today.

The **Inca** Empire stretched across a vast period of territory down the western coast of South America and was connected by a series of roads. A series of messengers ran along these roads, carrying news and instructions from the capital, Cusco, another large city along the lines of but not as spectacular as Tenochtitlan. The Incas are known for inventing the *quipu*, a string-based device that provided them with a method of keeping records. The Inca Empire, like the Aztec Empire, was very much a centralized state, with all income going to the state coffers and all trade going through the emperor as well. The Incas worshiped the dead, their ancestors, and nature and often took part in what we could consider strange rituals.

The most advanced Native American civilization were the **Maya**, who lived primarily in Central America. They were the only Native American civilization to develop writing, which consisted of a series of symbols that has still not been deciphered. The Mayas also built huge pyramids and other stone figures and sculptures, mostly of the gods they worshiped. The Mayas are most famous, however, for their **calendars** and for their mathematics. The Mayan calendars were the most accurate on the planet until the sixteenth century. The Mayas also invented the idea of zero, which might sound like a small thing except that no other culture had thought of such a thing. Maya worship resembled the practices of the Aztec and Inca, although human sacrifices were rare. The Mayas also traded heavily with their neighbors.

Skill 1.2h   Analyze the geographic, political, economic, religious, and social structures of Asia and Africa between A.D. 500 and the end of the 18th century.

Between the fourth and ninth centuries, Asia was a story of religions and empires, of kings and wars, and of increasing and decreasing contact with the West.

India began this period recovering from the invasion of Alexander the Great. One strong man who met the great Alexander was **Chandragupta Maurya**, who began one of his country's most successful dynasties. Chandragupta conquered most of what we now call India. His grandson, **Asoka**, was more of a peaceful ruler but powerful nonetheless. He was also a great believer in the practices and power of Buddhism, sending missionaries throughout Asia to preach the ways of the Buddha. Succeeding the Mauryas were the Guptas, who ruled India for a longer period of time and brought prosperity and international recognition to their people.

The **Guptas** were great believers in science and mathematics, especially their uses in production of goods. They invented the decimal system and had a concept of zero, two things that put them ahead of the rest of the world on the mathematics timeline. They were the first to make cotton and calico, and their medical practices were much more advanced than those in Europe and elsewhere in Asia at the time. These inventions and innovations created high demand for Indian goods throughout Asia and Europe.

The idea of a united India continued after the Gupta Dynasty ended. It was especially favorable to the invading Muslims, who took over in the eleventh century, ruling the country for hundreds of years through a series of sultanates. The most famous Muslim leader of India was **Tamerlane**, who founded the Mogul Dynasty and began a series of conquests that expanded the borders of India. Tamerlane's grandson **Akbar** is considered the greatest Mogul. He believed in freedom of religion and is perhaps most well-known for the series of buildings that he had built, including mosques, palaces, forts and tombs, some of which are still standing today. During the years that Muslims ruled India, Hinduism continued to be respected, although it was a minority religion; Buddhism, however, died out almost entirely from the country that begot its founder.

The imposing mountains to the north of India served as a deterrent to Chinese expansion. India was more vulnerable to invaders who came from the west or by sea from the south. The Indian people were also vulnerable to the powerful monsoons, which came driving up from the south a few times every year, bringing howling winds and devastation in their wake.

The story of **China** during this time is one of dynasties controlling various parts of what is now China and Tibet. The **Tang Dynasty** was one of the most long-lasting and the most proficient, inventing the idea of civil service and the practice of block printing. Next was the Sung Dynasty, which produced some of the world's greatest paintings and porcelain pottery but failed to unify China in a meaningful way. This would prove instrumental in the takeover of China by the Mongols, led by Genghis Khan and his most famous grandson, Kublai.

Genghis Khan was known as a conqueror, and Kublai was known as a uniter. They both extended the borders of their empire, however; and at its height, the Mongol Empire was the largest the world has ever seen, encompassing all of China, Russia, Persia, and central Asia. Following the Mongols were the Ming and Manchu Dynasties, both of which focused on isolation. As a result, China at the end of the eighteenth century knew very little of the outside world, and vice versa. **Ming** artists created beautiful porcelain pottery, but not much of it saw its way into the outside world until much later. The **Manchus** were known for their focus on farming and road-building, two practices that were instituted in greater numbers in order to try to keep up with expanding population. Confucianism, Taoism, and ancestor worship—the staples of Chinese society for hundreds of years—continued to flourish during all this time.

The other major power in Asia was **Japan**, which developed independently and tried to keep itself that way for hundreds of years. Early Japanese society focused on the emperor and the farm, in that order. Japan was often influenced early on by China, from which it borrowed many things, including religion (Buddhism), a system of writing, calendar, and even fashion. The Sea of Japan protected Japan from more than Chinese invasion, including the famous Mongol one that was blown back by the "divine wind." The power of the emperor declined as it was usurped by the era of the Daimyo and his loyal soldiers, the **samurai**. Japan flourished economically and culturally during many of these years, although the policy of isolation the country developed kept the rest of the world from knowing such things. Buddhism and local religions were joined by Christianity in the sixteenth century, but it wasn't until the mid-nineteenth century that Japan rejoined the world community.

African civilizations during these centuries were few and far between. Most of northern coastal Africa had been conquered by Moslem armies. The preponderance of deserts and other inhospitable lands restricted African settlements to a few select areas. The city of Zimbabwe became a trading center in south-central Africa in the fifth century but didn't last long. More successful was **Ghana**, a Muslim-influenced kingdom that arose in the ninth century and lasted for nearly 300 years. Ghanaians had large farming areas and also raised cattle and elephants. They traded with people from Europe and the Middle East. Eventually overrunning Ghana was Mali, whose trade center **Timbuktu** survived its own empire's demise and blossomed into one of the world's caravan destinations. Iron, tin, and leather came out of Mali with a vengeance. The succeeding civilization of the Songhai had relative success in maintaining the success of their predecessors. Religion in all of these places was definitely Muslim, and even after extended contact with other cultures technological advancements were few and far between.

Skill 1.2i   Analyze the art, literature, music, science, and technology of the Renaissance and their diffusion and impact throughout Europe.

The word "**Renaissance**" literally means "rebirth", and signaled the rekindling of interest in the glory of ancient classical Greek and Roman civilizations. It was the period in human history marking the start of many ideas and innovations leading to our modern age. A combination of a renewed fascination with the classical world and new infusion of money into the hands of those so fascinated brought on the Renaissance. In the areas of art, literature, music, and science, the world changed for the better.

The Renaissance began in Italy with many of its ideas starting in Florence, controlled by the infamous **Medici** family. Education, especially for some of the merchants, required reading, writing, math, the study of law, and the writings of classical Greek and Roman writers.

Most famous are the Renaissance artists, The more important artists were Giotto and his development of perspective in paintings; **Leonardo da Vinci** who was not only an artist but also a scientist and inventor; **Michelangelo** who was a sculptor, painter, and architect; and others including Raphael, Donatello, Titian, and Tintoretto. All of these men pioneered a new method of painting and sculpture— that of portraying real events and real people as they really looked, not as the artists imagined them to be. One need look no further than Michelangelo's *David* to illustrate this.

Literature was a focus as well during the Renaissance. **Humanists**, a group which included **Petrarch, Boccaccio, Erasmus**, and **Sir Thomas More**, advanced the idea of being interested in life here on earth and the opportunities it can bring, rather than constantly focusing on heaven and its rewards. The monumental works of **Shakespeare, Dante,** and **Cervantes** found their origins in these ideas as well as the ones that drove the painters and sculptors. All of these works, of course, owe much of their existence to the invention of the printing press, which occurred during the Renaissance.

The Renaissance changed music as well. No longer just a religious experience, music could be fun and composed for its own sake, to be enjoyed in fuller and more humanistic ways than in the Middle Ages. Musicians worked for themselves, rather than for the churches, as before, and so could command good money for their work, increasing their prestige.

Science advanced considerably during the Renaissance, especially in the area of physics and astronomy. **Copernicus, Kepler,** and **Galileo** led a Scientific Revolution in proving that the earth was round and certainly not perfect, an earth-shattering revelation to those who clung to medieval ideals of a geocentric, church-centered existence.

All of these things encouraged people to see the world in a new way, more real, more realized, and more realistic than ever before. Other contributions of the Italian Renaissance period were in:

Political philosophy - the writings of **Machiavelli**

Literature - the writings of **Petrarch** and **Boccaccio**

Medicine - the work of Brussels-born **Andrea Vesalius** earned him the title of "father of anatomy" and had a profound influence on the Spaniard **Michael** Servetus and the Englishman **William Harvey**

In Germany, Gutenberg's invention of the **printing press** with movable type facilitated the rapid spread of Renaissance ideas, writings and innovations, thus ensuring the enlightenment of most of Western Europe. Contributions were also made by Durer and Holbein in art and by Paracelsus in science and medicine.

The effects of the Renaissance in the Low Countries can be seen in the literature and philosophy of **Erasmus** and the art of **van Eyck** and **Breughel the Elder**. **Rabelais** and **de Montaigne** in France also contributed to literature and philosophy. In Spain, the art of **El Greco** and **de Morales** flourished, as did the writings of **Cervantes** and **De Vega**. In England, Sir Thomas More and **Sir Francis Bacon** wrote and taught philosophy and were inspired by **Vesalius**. **William Harvey** made important contributions in medicine. The greatest talent was found in literature and drama and given to mankind by **Chaucer, Spenser, Marlowe, Jonson**, and the incomparable Shakespeare.

The Renaissance ushered in a time of curiosity, learning, and incredible energy sparking the desire for trade to procure these new, exotic products and to find better, faster, cheaper trade routes to get to them. The work of geographers, astronomers and mapmakers made important contributions and many studied and applied the work of such men as Hipparchus of Greece, Ptolemy of Egypt, Tycho Brahe of Denmark, and Fra Mauro of Italy.

Skill 1.2j   Analyze the political and religious transformations caused bythe Reformation and their impact on Europe.

The **Reformation** period consisted of two phases: the **Protestant Revolution** and the **Catholic Reformation**. The Protestant Revolution came about because of religious, political, and economic reasons. The religious reasons stemmed from abuses in the Catholic Church including fraudulent clergy with their scandalous immoral lifestyles; the sale of religious offices, indulgences, and dispensations; different theologies within the Church; and frauds involving sacred relics.

The political reasons for the **Protestant Revolution** involved the increase in the power of rulers who were considered "absolute monarchs", who desired all power and control, especially over the Church. The growth of "nationalism" or patriotic pride in one's own country was another contributing factor.

Economic reasons included the greed of ruling monarchs to possess and control all lands and wealth of the Church, the deep animosity against the burdensome papal taxation, the rise of the affluent middle class and its clash with medieval Church ideals, and the increase of an active system of "intense" capitalism.

The Protestant Revolution began in Germany with the revolt of **Martin Luther** against Church abuses. It spread to Switzerland where it was led by **Calvin**. It began in England with the efforts of King Henry VIII to have his marriage to Catherine of Aragon annulled so he could wed another and have a male heir. The results were the increasing support given not only by the people but also by nobles and some rulers, and of course, the attempts of the Church to stop it.

The **Catholic Reformation** was undertaken by the Church to "clean up its act" and to slow or stop the Protestant Revolution. The major efforts to this end were supplied by the Council of Trent and the Jesuits. Six major results of the Reformation included:

- Religious freedom,
- Religious tolerance,
- More opportunities for education,
- Power and control of rulers limited,
- Increase in religious wars, and
- An increase in fanaticism and persecution.

Skill 1.2k   Analyze the historical developments of the Scientific Revolution and the ideas of the Enlightenment and their effects on social, religious, political, economic, and cultural institutions.

The Scientific Revolution and the Enlightenment were two of the most important movements in the history of civilization, resulting in a new sense of self-examination and a wider view of the world than ever before.

The **Scientific Revolution** was, above all, a shift in focus from **belief to evidence**. Scientists and philosophers wanted to see the proof, not just believe what other people told them. It was an exciting time, if you were a forward-looking thinker.

A Polish astronomer, **Nicolaus Copernicus**, began the Scientific Revolution. He crystallized a lifetime of observations into a book that was published about the time of his death; in this book, Copernicus argued that the Sun, not the Earth, was the center of a solar system and that other planets revolved around the Sun, not the Earth. This flew in the face of established (read: Church-mandated) doctrine. The Church still wielded tremendous power at this time, including the power to banish people or sentence them to prison or even death.

The Danish astronomer **Tycho Brahe** was the first to catalog his observations of the night sky, of which he made thousands. Building on Brahe's data, German scientist **Johannes Kepler** instituted his theory of planetary movement, embodied in his famous Laws of Planetary Movement. Using Brahe's data, Kepler also confirmed Copernicus's observations and argument that the Earth revolved around the Sun.

The most famous defender of this idea was **Galileo Galilei**, an Italian scientist who conducted many famous experiments in the pursuit of science. He is most well-known, however, for his defense of the **heliocentric** (sun-centered) idea. He wrote a book comparing the two theories, but most readers could tell easily that he favored the new one. He was convinced of this mainly because of what he had seen with his own eyes. He had used the relatively new invention of the telescope to see four moons of Jupiter. They certainly did not revolve around the Earth, so why should everything else? His ideas were not at all favored with the Church, which continued to assert its authority in this and many other matters. The Church was still powerful enough at this time, especially in Italy, to order Galileo to be placed under house arrest.

Galileo died under house arrest, but his ideas didn't die with him. Picking up the baton was an English scientist named **Isaac Newton**, who became perhaps the most famous scientist of all. He is known as the discoverer of gravity and a pioneering voice in the study of optics (light), calculus, and physics.

More than any other scientist, Newton argued for (and proved) the idea of a mechanistic view of the world: You can see how the world works and prove how the world works through observation; if you can see these things with your own eyes, they must be so. Up to this time, people believed what other people told them; this is how the Church was able to keep control of people's lives for so long. Newton, following in the footsteps of Copernicus and Galileo, changed all that.

This naturally led to the **Enlightenment**, a period of intense self-study that focused on ethics and logic. More so than at any time before, scientists and philosophers questioned cherished truths, widely held beliefs, and their own sanity in an attempt to discover why the world worked—from within. "I think, therefore I am" ("Cogito ergo sum" in Latin) was one of the famous sayings of that or any day. It was uttered by **Rene Descartes**, a French scientist-philosopher whose dedication to logic and the rigid rules of observation were a blueprint for the thinkers who came after him.

One of the giants of the era was England's **David Hume**. A pioneer of the doctrine of empiricism, or believing things only when you've seen the proof for yourself, Hume was also a prime believer in the value of skepticism; in other words, he was naturally suspicious of things that other people told him to be true and constantly set out to discover the truth for himself. These two related ideas influenced a great many thinkers after Hume, and his writings (of which there are many) continue to inspire philosophers to this day.

The Enlightenment thinker who might be the most famous is **Immanuel Kant** of Germany. He was both a philosopher and a scientist, and he took a definite scientific view of the world. He wrote the movement's most famous essay, "Answering the Question: What Is Enlightenment?" and he answered his famous question with the motto "Dare to Know." For Kant, the human being was a rational being capable of hugely creative thought and intense self-evaluation. He encouraged all to examine themselves and the world around them. He believed that the source of morality lay not in the nature of the grace of God but in the human soul itself. He believed that man believed in God for practical, not religious or mystical, reasons.

Also prevalent during the Enlightenment was the idea of the "**social contract**," the belief that government existed because people wanted it to, that the people had an agreement with the government that they would submit to it as long as it protected them and didn't encroach on their basic human rights. This idea was first made famous by the Frenchman Jean-Jacques Rousseau but was also adopted by England's John Locke and America's Thomas Jefferson.

John Locke was one of the most influential political writers of the seventeenth century who put great emphasis on human rights and put forth the belief that when governments violate those rights people should rebel. He wrote the book "Two Treatises of Government" in 1690, which had tremendous influence on political thought in the American colonies and helped shaped the U.S. Constitution and Declaration of Independence.

COMPENTENCY 1.3   MODERN WORLD HISTORY.

Skill 1.3a   Describe and evaluate the significance of the "Age of Exploration," and the main ideas of the Enlightenment and their influences on social, political, religious, and economic thoughtand practice.

The **Age of Exploration** actually had its beginnings centuries before exploration actually took place. The rise and spread of Islam in the seventh century and its subsequent control over the holy city of Jerusalem led to the European so-called holy wars, the Crusades, to free Jerusalem and the Holy Land from this control. Even though the Crusades were not a success, those who survived and returned to their homes and countries in Western Europe brought back with them new products such as silks, spices, perfumes, new and different foods. Luxuries that were unheard of gave new meaning to colorless, drab, dull lives.

New ideas, new inventions, and new methods also went to Western Europe with the returning Crusaders and from these new influences was the intellectual stimulation which led to the period known as the Renaissance. The revival of interest in classical Greek art, architecture, literature, science, astronomy, medicine and increased trade between Europe and Asia and the invention of the printing press helped to push the spread of knowledge and start exploring.

For many centuries, various mapmakers made many maps and charts, which in turn stimulated curiosity and the seeking of more knowledge. At the same time, the Chinese were using the magnetic compass in their ships. Pacific Islanders were going from island to island, covering thousands of miles in open canoes navigating by sun and stars. Arab traders were sailing all over the Indian Ocean in their **dhows**.

The trade routes between Europe and Asia were slow, difficult, dangerous, and very expensive. Between sea voyages on the Indian Ocean and Mediterranean Sea and the camel caravans in central Asia and the Arabian Desert, the trade was still controlled by the Italian merchants in **Genoa** and **Venice**. It would take months and even years for the exotic luxuries of Asia to reach the markets of Western Europe. A faster, cheaper way had to be found. A way had to be found which would bypass traditional routes and end the control of the Italian merchants.

Prince Henry of Portugal (also called the Navigator) encouraged, supported, and financed the Portuguese seamen who led in the search for an all-water route to Asia. A shipyard was built along with a school teaching navigation. New types of sailing ships were built which would carry the seamen safely through the ocean waters. Experiments were conducted in newer maps, newer navigational methods, and newer instruments. These included the **astrolabe** and the **compass**, enabling sailors to determine direction as well as latitude and longitude for exact location.

Although Prince Henry died in 1460, the Portuguese kept on, sailing along and exploring Africa's west coastline. In 1488, **Bartholomew Diaz** and his men sailed around Africa's southern tip and headed toward Asia. Diaz wanted to push on but turned back because his men were discouraged and weary from the long months at sea, extremely fearful of the unknown, and just refusing to travel any further.

However, the Portuguese were finally successful ten years later in 1498 when **Vasco da Gama** and his men, continuing the route of Diaz, rounded Africa's Cape of Good Hope, sailing across the Indian Ocean, reaching India's port of Calicut (Calcutta). Although, six years earlier, Columbus had reached the New World and an entire hemisphere, da Gama had proved Asia could be reached from Europe by sea.

Christopher Columbus, sailing for Spain, is credited with the discovery of America although he never set foot on its soil. **Magellan** is credited with the first circumnavigation of the earth. Other Spanish explorers made their marks in parts of what are now the United States, Mexico, and South America.

The importance of the Age of Exploration was not only the discovery and colonization of the New World, but also a new hemisphere as a refuge from poverty, persecution, and a place to start a new and better life. It led to the development of better maps and charts and new, more accurate navigational instruments. It led to an increased knowledge, great wealth, and new and different foods and items not previously known in Europe. It was also proof that Asia could be reached by sea and that the earth was round. Ships and sailors would not sail off the edge of a flat earth and disappear forever into nothingness.

With the increase in trade and travel, cities germinated and began to grow. Craft workers in the cities developed their skills to a high degree, eventually organizing guilds to protect the quality of the work and regulate the buying and selling of their products. City government developed and flourished centered on strong town councils. Active in city government and the town councils were the wealthy businessmen who made up the growing middle class.

In addition, there were a number of individuals and events during the time of exploration and discoveries. The **Vivaldo brothers** and **Marco Polo** wrote of their travels and experiences, which signaled the early beginnings. From the Crusades, the survivors made their way home to different places in Europe bringing with them fascinating, new information about exotic lands, people, customs, and desired foods and goods such as spices and silks.

For France, claims to various parts of North America were the result of the efforts of such men as **Champlain, Cartier, LaSalle, Father Marquette** and **Joliet.** Dutch claims were based on the work of one **Henry Hudson. John Cabot** gave England its stake in North America along with **John Hawkins, Sir Francis Drake,** and the half-brothers **Sir Walter Raleigh and Sir Humphrey Gilbert.**

Actually the first Europeans in the New World were Norsemen led by **Eric the Red** and later, his son Leif the Lucky. However, before any of these, the ancestors of today's Native Americans and Latin American Indians crossed the Bering Strait from Asia to Alaska, eventually settling in all parts of the Americas.

Skill 1.3b   Compare and contrast the American Revolution and the French Revolution and their enduring worldwide effects on political expectations for self-government and individual liberty.

The American Revolution and the French Revolution were similar yet different, liberating their people from unwanted government interference and installing a different kind of government. They were both fought for the liberty of the common people, and they both were built on writings and ideas that embraced such an outcome; yet that is where the similarities end. Both Revolutions proved that people could expect more from their government and that such rights as self-determination were worth fighting - and - dying for.

The **American Revolution** resulted in the successful efforts of the English colonists in America to win their freedom from Great Britain. After more than one hundred years of mostly self-government, the colonists resented the increased British meddling and control, they declared their freedom, won the Revolutionary War with aid from France, and formed a new independent nation.

The **French Revolution** was the revolt of the middle and lower classes against the gross political and economic excesses of the rulers and the supporting nobility. It ended with the establishment of the first in a series of French Republics. Conditions leading to revolt included extreme taxation, inflation, lack of food, and the total disregard for the impossible, degrading, and unacceptable condition of the people on the part of the rulers, nobility, and the Church.

Several important differences need to be emphasized:

- The British colonists were striking back against unwanted taxation and other sorts of "government interference." The French people were starving and, in many cases, destitute and were striking back against an autocratic regime that cared more for high fashion and courtly love than bread and circuses.
- The American Revolution involved a years-long campaign, of often bloody battles, skirmishes, and stalemates. The French Revolution was bloody to a degree but mainly an overthrow of society and its outdated traditions
- The American Revolution resulted in a representative government, which marketed itself as a beacon of democracy for the rest of the world. The French Revolution resulted in a consulship, a generalship, and then an emperor—probably not what the perpetrators of the Revolution had in mind when they first struck back at the king and queen.

Still, both Revolutions are looked back on as turning points in history, as times when the governed stood up to the governors and said, "Enough."

Skill 1.3c   Describe and analyze the emergence of nationalism in the 18th and 19th centuries and its impact on Western, African, and Asian societies.

During the eighteenth and especially the nineteenth centuries, **nationalism** emerged as a powerful force in Europe and elsewhere in the world. Strictly speaking, nationalism was a belief in one's own nation and people. More so than in previous centuries, the people of the European nations began to think in terms of a nation of people who had similar beliefs, concerns, and needs. This was partly a reaction to a growing discontent with the autocratic governments of the day and also just a general realization that there was more to life than the individual. People could feel a part of something like their nation, making themselves more than just an insignificant soul struggling to survive.

Nationalism precipitated several changes in government, most notably in France; it also brought large groups of people together, as with the unifications of Germany and Italy. What it didn't do, however, is provide sufficient outlets for this sudden rise in national fervor. Especially in the 1700s and 1800s, European powers and peoples began looking to Africa and Asia in order to find colonies: rich sources of goods, trade, and cheap labor. Africa, especially, suffered at the hands of European imperialists, bent on expanding their reach outside the borders of Europe. Asia, too, suffered colonial expansion, most notably in India and Southeast Asia.

This colonial expansion would come back to haunt the European imperialists in a very big way, as colonial skirmishes spilled over into alliance that dragged the European powers into World War I. Some of these colonial battles were still being fought as late as the start of World War II as well.

Skill 1.3d   **Analyze the causes and effects of the Industrial Revolution, including its impact on science, technology, and society.**

The **Industrial Revolution**, which began in Great Britain in the 18th century and spread elsewhere, was the development of power-driven machinery (fueled by coal and steam) leading to the accelerated growth of industry with large factories replacing homes and small workshops as work centers. The lives of people changed drastically and a largely agricultural society changed to an industrial one. In Western Europe, the period of empire and colonialism began. The industrialized nations seized and claimed parts of Africa and Asia in an effort to control and provide the raw materials needed to feed the industries and machines in the "mother country". Later developments included power based on electricity and internal combustion, replacing coal and steam.

In general, the Industrial revolution is seen a process of change from an agrarian, handicraft economy to one dominated by industry and machine manufacture Technological changes included the use of iron and steel, new energy sources, the invention of new machines that increased production (including the steam engine and the spinning jenny), the development of the factory system, and important developments in transportation and communication (including the railroad and the telegraph).

The Industrial Revolution was largely confined to Britain from 1760 to 1830 and then spread to Belgium and France. Other nations lagged behind, but, once Germany, the U.S., and Japan achieved industrial power, they outstripped Britain's initial successes. Eastern European countries lagged into the 20th century, and not until the mid-20th century did the Industrial Revolution spread to such countries as China and India.

Symbolic of the industrial revolution was the use of **coal** as a source of energy. The conversion of coal to coke made cheaper iron ore smelting possible and simultaneously produced town gas, used from the early 19th century for lighting. Coal-fuelled boilers provided steam-power for mines drainage, factory machinery, and locomotives, making speed and repetitive activities less arduous and greatly augmenting output. Particularly associated with such changes were cotton textiles, made cheaply in large quantities.

Social changes occurred simultaneously. Many new jobs were created between the later 18th and the mid-19th century from the ever widening applications of technical innovations such as in gas-making, in the chemical industry, in canal and railway transport, and in textiles. New methods of industrial production also required many people to move to urban locations. In England, for example, some existing towns such as Manchester expanded very rapidly, whilst new towns emerged. Rapid urban growth posed many unforeseen problems of overcrowded houses, inadequate sanitation, and law and order.

Industrialization effected changes in economic, political, and social organization. These included a wider distribution of wealth and increased international trade; political changes resulting from the shift in economic power; sweeping social changes that included the rise of **working-class movements**, the development of managerial hierarchies to oversee the division of labour, and the emergence of new patterns of authority; and struggles against externalities such as industrial pollution and urban crowding.

Skill 1.3e **Describe the emergence and origins of new theories regarding politics, economics, literature, and the arts in the 18th, 19th, and 20th centuries.**

The overriding theme of life during the eighteenth through the twentieth centuries was progress. Technological advancements brought great and terrible things in all aspects of life. New theories in economics brought great changes in the way the world does business. New theories in government brought about new nations, uprisings, and wars galore. New theories in art changed the landscape of painting forever.

The driving forces in politics in the eighteenth century were **nationalism** and **liberalism**. The latter was a belief in the power of the people to approve of their government and, if they didn't, to form a new one; the former was a belief in a commonality of customs, practices, and outlooks by all peoples of a certain country or ethnicity. The eighteenth century ended with the American and French Revolutions, which overthrew monarchies in favor of representative governments. These two driving forces dominated the political landscape of the nineteenth and twentieth centuries as well, with nearly the entire map of Europe being rewritten in a wake of nationalist fervor. Some monarchies survived, but they were fewer and farther between.

Another impetus that drove many political actions in these two centuries was the desire for **colonization**. European powers carved up Africa in the search of greater resources and influence over their neighbors. Asia, too, fell under the yoke of European occupation, as did Central and South America. The United States and Russia (later the Soviet Union) got involved as well, in an ongoing struggle that culminated in the Cold War. Differences in political ideology, along with entangling alliances based on countering of competing influences and a sheer desire to possess more territory and resources to accommodate growing populations, led to nearly every major war during these 200 years.

One of the major political movements in the twentieth century was **communism**. Invented by a German philosopher, it found sway most famously in the Soviet Union but also in China and North Korea and Vietnam, where it survives to this day. Communism was, at its heart, an economic theory, with the famous doctrine of "class struggle" controlling every aspect of life, including what kind of government a people should live under.

Communist states controlled nearly every aspect of society, including religion and economics. The government owned factories and ports, machines and ships; this means that the income from goods produced therein went into the state-controlled coffers. This kind of economic theory was in stark contrast to the famous **laissez faire** attitude that occupied much of the Western nations during the 1700s, 1800s, and 1900s.

An American president, Calvin Coolidge, famously said, "The business of America is business"; yet in the U.S. and elsewhere, businesses were relatively free to pursue their own interests, make their innovations, and keep their own money, as long as they didn't break national or international laws along the way.

The **Industrial Revolution** of the eighteenth and nineteenth centuries had brought great progress in efficiency, but it also created sometimes horrendous working conditions. During these years, workers gathered together in increasing numbers and demanded better work environments, better benefits, and better pay. With varying degrees, they got what they wanted, although it took a lot longer than they wanted it to.

Things changed in the worlds of literature and art as well. The main development in the nineteenth century was **Romanticism**, an emphasis on emotion and the imagination that was a direct reaction to the logic and reason so stressed in the preceding Enlightenment. Famous Romantic authors included **John Keats, William Wordsworth, Victor Hugo,** and Johann Wolfgang von **Goethe.** The horrors of the Industrial Revolution gave rise to the very famous realists **Charles Dickens, Fyodor Dosteovsky, Leo Tolstoy,** and **Mark Twain**, who described life as they saw it, for better or for worse - usually worse.

The most famous movement of the 1800s, however, was **Impressionism**. The idea was to present an impression of a moment in time, one of life's fleeting moments memorialized on canvas. A list of famous impressionists is a who's who of the most famous painters in the world: **Monet, Degas, van Gogh, Manet, Cezanne, Renoi**r, and the list goes on. More than any other time in the history of the arts, Impressionism produced famous faces and famous canvases.

Echoing Dickens's dislike of an industrialized world, twentieth century authors stressed individual action and responsibility. The giants of the 1900s include **James Joyce, T.S. Eliot, John Steinbeck, Ernest Hemingway, William Faulkner,** and **George Orwell**, all of whom to varying degrees expressed distrust at the power of machines and weapons and most of modern society.

Can one man change the world? Many people think so if that man is **Pablo Picasso**. The young Spanish painter brought about a monumental revolution in his art in the early twentieth century with the advent of **Cubism**, which exaggerated perspective and people and things in a way never before seen. Art hasn't been the same since. A Russian painter, Vasili Kandinski, created what is believed to be the first completely abstract painting. Realism, impressionism, and the empiricist ideas of the past 400 years were dead: Abstraction ruled the day.

Following Cubism were a variety of art movements emphasizing different things: Surrealism, aiming to depict the subconscious mind on canvas; Dadaism, exploring formlessness; and pop art, which simultaneously mocked and celebrated popular culture. The most famous pop artist was, of course, **Andy Warhol**.

Skill 1.3f **Analyze the economic, political, social, and geographic factors contributing to the emergence of 19th-century imperialism, and evaluate its impact on Africa, Southeast Asia, China, India, Latin America, and the Philippines.**

In Europe, Italy and Germany each were totally united into one nation from many smaller states. There were revolutions in Austria and Hungary, the Franco-Prussian War, the dividing of Africa among the strong European nations, interference and intervention of Western nations in Asia, and the breakup of Turkish dominance in the Balkans. In Africa, France, Great Britain, Italy, Portugal, Spain, Germany, and Belgium controlled the entire continent except **Liberia** and **Ethiopia**. In Asia and the Pacific Islands, only **China, Japan**, and present-day **Thailand (Siam)** kept their independence. The others were controlled by the strong European nations.

An additional reason for **European imperialism** was the harsh, urgent demand for the raw materials needed to fuel and feed the great Industrial Revolution. These resources were not available in the huge quantity so desperately needed which necessitated (and rationalized) the partitioning of the continent of Africa and parts of Asia. In turn, these colonial areas would purchase the finished manufactured goods. Europe in the nineteenth century was a crowded place. Populations were growing but resources were not. The peoples of many European countries were also agitating for rights as never before. To address these concerns, European powers began to look elsewhere for relief.

One of the main places for European imperialist expansion was Africa. **Britain, France, Germany,** and **Belgium** took over countries in Africa and claimed them as their own. The resources (including people) were then shipped back to the mainland and claimed as colonial gains. The Europeans made a big deal about "civilizing the savages," reasoning that their technological superiority gave them the right to rule and "educate" the peoples of Africa.

Southeast Asia was another area of European expansion at this time, mainly by France. So, too, was India, colonized by Great Britain. These two nations combined with Spain to occupy countries in Latin America. Spain also seized the rich lands of the Philippines.

As a result of all this activity, a whole new flood of goods, people, and ideas began to come back to Europe and a whole group of people began to travel to these colonies, to oversee the colonization and to "help bring the people up" to the European level. European leaders could also assert their authority in these colonies as they could not back home.

In the United States, **territorial expansion** occurred in the expansion westward under the banner of **"Manifest Destiny."** In addition, the U.S. was involved in the War with Mexico, the Spanish-American War, and support of the Latin American colonies of Spain in their revolt for independence. In Latin America, the Spanish colonies were successful in their fight for independence and self-government.

The time from 1830 to 1914 is characterized by the extraordinary growth and spread of patriotic pride in a nation along with intense, widespread imperialism. Loyalty to one's nation included national pride; extension and maintenance of sovereign political boundaries; unification of smaller states with common language, history, and culture into a more powerful nation; or smaller national groups who, as part of a larger multi-cultural empire, wished to separate into smaller, political, cultural nations.

Skill 1.3g   Compare and contrast the social, political, and economicfactors that influenced the Russian Revolutions of 1905 and 1917.

Until the early years of the twentieth century Russia was ruled by a succession of **Czars**. The Czars ruled as autocrats or, sometimes, despots. Society was essentially feudalistic and was structured in three levels. The top level was held by the Czar. The second level was composed of the rich nobles who held government positions and owned vast tracts of land. The third level of the society was composed of the remaining people who lived in poverty as peasants or serfs. There were several unsuccessful attempts to revolt during the nineteenth century, caused largely by discontent among these three levels, especially the peasant, but they were quickly suppressed. The two revolutions of the early 20th Century, in 1905 and 1917, however, were quite different.

Discontent with the social structure, with the living conditions of the peasants, and with working conditions despite industrialization were among the causes of the **1905 Revolution**. This general discontent was aggravated by the **Russo-Japanese War** (1904-1905) with inflation, rising prices, etc. Peasants who had been able to eke out a living began to starve. Many of the fighting troops were killed in battles Russia lost to Japan because of poor leadership, lack of training, and inferior weaponry. Czar Nicholas II refused to end the war despite setbacks, and in January 1905 Port Arthur fell.

A trade union leader, Father Gapon, organized a protest to demand an end to the war, industrial reform, more civil liberties, and a constituent assembly. Over 150,000 peasants joined a demonstration outside the Czar's **Winter Palace**. Before the demonstrators even spoke, the palace guard opened fire on the crowd. This destroyed the people's trust in the Czar. Illegal trade unions and political parties formed and organized strikes to gain power.

The strikes eventually brought the Russian economy to a halt. This led Czar Nicholas II to sign the **October Manifesto** which created a constitutional monarchy, extended some civil rights, and gave the parliament limited legislative power. In a very short period of time, the Czar disbanded the parliament and violated the promised civil liberties.

The violation of the October Manifesto would help foment the **1917 Revolution**. There were other factors as well. Defeats on the battlefields during WWI caused discontent, loss of life, and a popular desire to withdraw from the war. The war had also caused another surge in prices and scarcity of many items. Most of the peasants could not afford to buy bread. In addition, the Czar's behavior triggered more unrest. The Czar continued to appoint unqualified people to government posts and handle the situation with general incompetence. The Czar also listened to his wife's (Alexandra) advice. She was strongly influenced by **Rasputin**. This caused increased discontent among all level of the social structure.

Workers in Petrograd went on strike in 1917 over the need for food. The Czar again ordered troops to suppress the strike. This time, however, the troops sided with the workers. The revolution then took a unique direction. The parliament created a provisional government to rule the country. The military and the workers also created their own governments called **soviets** (popularly elected local councils). The parliament was composed of nobles who soon lost control of the country when they failed to comply with the wishes of the populace. The result was chaos.

The most significant differences between the 1905 and 1917 revolutions were the formation of political parties and their use of propaganda and the support of the military and some of the nobles in 1917. The political leaders who had previously been driven into exile returned. **Lenin, Stalin** and **Trotsky** won the support of the peasants with the promise of "Peace, Land, and Bread". The parliament, on the other hand, continued the country's involvement in the war. Lenin and the **Bolshevik Party** gained the support of the **Red Guard** and together overthrew the provisional government. In short order they had complete control of Russia and established a new communist state.

World War I: 1914 to 1918

Emotions ran high in early 20th Century Europe, and minor disputes magnified into major ones and sometimes quickly led to threats of war. Especially sensitive to these conditions was the area of the states on the Balkan Peninsula. Along with the imperialistic colonization for industrial raw materials, military build-up (especially by Germany), and diplomatic and military alliances, the conditions for one tiny spark to set off the explosion were in place. In July 1914, a Serbian national assassinated **Archduke Ferdinand**, the Austrian heir to the throne, and his wife as they visited Sarajevo. War began a few weeks later. There were a few attempts to keep war from starting, but these efforts were futile. Eventually nearly 30 nations were involved, and the war didn't end until 1918.

One of the major causes of the war was the tremendous surge of **nationalism** during the 1800s and early 1900s. People of the same nationality or ethnic group sharing a common history, language or culture began uniting or demanding the right of unification, especially in the empires of Eastern Europe, such as Russian Ottoman and Austrian-Hungarian Empires. Getting stronger and more intense were the beliefs of these peoples in loyalty to common political, social, and economic goals considered to be before any loyalty to the controlling nation or empire. Other causes were the increasing strength of military capabilities, massive colonization for raw materials needed for industrialization and manufacturing, and military and diplomatic alliances.

World War I saw the introduction of such warfare as use of tanks, airplanes, machine guns, submarines, poison gas, and flame throwers. Fighting on the Western front was characterized by a series of **trenches** that were used throughout the war until 1918. The atrocities of war took everyone by surprise, and led to much of the animosity that marked the terms of the end of the war. It would lead to ban on certain weapons, particularly poison gas, and leave the nations of Europe unwilling to go to war again.

When Germany agreed in 1918 to an armistice, it assumed that the peace settlement would be drawn up on the basis of US President Woodrow Wilson's Fourteen Points, which it considered equitable and made no attempt at recriminations. Instead, at the Paris Peace Conference Germany was subjected to harsh reparations, being asked to pay the other countries for damages during the war. Heavy restrictions were placed on Germany as well, taking away arms and territories, losses that weighed heavily on the German psyche. The European powers even went so far as the force Germany to assume responsibility for causing the war.

In America, President Wilson lost in his efforts to get the U.S. Senate to approve the peace treaty. The Senate at the time was a reflection of American public opinion and its rejection of the treaty was a rejection of Wilson. The approval of the treaty would have made the U.S. a member of the League of Nations but Americans had just come off a bloody war to ensure that democracy would exist throughout the world. Americans just did not want to accept any responsibility that resulted from its new position of power and were afraid that membership in the League of Nations would embroil the U.S. in future disputes in Europe.

There were 28 nations involved in the war, not including colonies and territories. It began July 28, 1914 and ended November 11, 1918 with the signing of the Treaty of Versailles. Economically, the war cost a total of $337 billion; increased inflation and huge war debts; and caused a loss of markets, goods, jobs, and factories. Politically, old empires collapsed; many monarchies disappeared; smaller countries gained temporary independence; Communists seized power in Russia; and, in some cases, nationalism increased. Socially, total populations decreased because of war casualties and low birth rates. There were millions of displaced persons and villages and farms were destroyed. Cities grew while women made significant gains in the work force and the ballot box. There was less social distinction and classes. Attitudes completely changed and old beliefs and values were questioned. The peace settlement established the **League of Nations** to ensure peace, but it failed to do so.

Pre-war empires lost tremendous amounts of territories as well as the wealth of natural resources in them. New, independent nations were formed and some predominately ethnic areas came under control of nations of different cultural backgrounds. Some national boundary changes overlapped and created tensions and hard feelings as well as political and economic confusion. The wishes and desires of every national or cultural group could not possibly be realized and satisfied, resulting in disappointments for both; those who were victorious and those who were defeated. Germany received harsher terms than expected from the treaty which weakened its post-war government and, along with the world-wide depression of the 1930s, set the stage for the rise of Adolf Hitler and his Nationalist Socialist Party and World War II.

Skill 1.3i   Analyze the conflict between fascist and Marxist/communist ideologies, and the rise, goals, and policies of dictatorships and totalitarian governments between the two World Wars.

Socialism is a fairly recent political phenomenon though its roots can be traced pretty far back in time in many respects. At the core, both socialism and communism are fundamentally economic philosophies that advocate public rather than private ownership, especially over means of production, yet even here, there are many distinctions.

Karl Marx concentrated his attention on the industrial worker and on state domination over the means of production. In practice, this Marxian dogma has largely been followed the most in those countries that profess to be Communist. In conjunction with massive programs for the development of heavy industry, this emphasis on production regardless of the wants or comforts of the individual in the given society. Socialism by contrast, usually occurring where industry has already been developed, has concerned itself more with the welfare of the individual and the fair distribution of whatever wealth is available.

Communism has a rigid theology, and a bible (**Das Capital**) that sees Communism emerging as a result of almost cosmic laws. Modern socialism is much closer to the ground. It too sees change in human society and hopes for improvement, but there is no unchanging millennium at the end of the road. Communism is sure that it will achieve the perfect state and in this certainty it is willing to use any and all means, however ruthless, to bring it about.

Socialism on the other hand, confident only that the human condition is always changing, makes no easy approximation between ends and means and so cannot justify brutalities. This distinction in philosophy, of course, makes for an immense conflict in methods. Communism, believing that revolution is inevitable, works toward it by emphasizing class antagonisms. Socialism, while seeking change, insists on the use of democratic procedures within the existing social order of a given society. In it, the upper classes and capitalists are not to be violently overthrown but instead to be won over by logical persuasion. It is interesting to note that in every perfect, idealized community or society that people have dreamed about throughout history, where human beings are pictured living in a special harmony that transcends their natural instincts, there has been a touch of socialism.

This tendency was especially found in the **Utopian-Socialists** of the early nineteenth century, whose basic aim was the repudiation of the private-property system with its economic inefficiency and social injustice. Their criticisms rather than any actual achievements would linger after them. Like Marx, they envisioned industrial capitalism as becoming more and more inhumane and oppressive. They could not imagine the mass of workers prospering in such a system.

Yet the workers soon developed their own powerful organizations and institutions. They began to bend the economic system to their own benefit. Thus a split did occur. First, between those who after the growing success of the labor movement rejected the earlier utopian ideas as being impractical. Second, between those who saw in this newfound political awareness of the working class the key to organizing a realistic ability of revolution, who saw this as inevitable based on their previous observations and study of history.

Having reached a point where it has managed to jeopardize its very own survival, the inevitable revolution of those opposed to the present capitalist system had to occur. History has proven this so, and history is always right and irrefutable. These believers in the absolute correctness of this doctrine gathered around Marx in what he called **Scientific Socialism**, in contempt of all other kinds which he considered not to be scientific, and therefore, useless as a realistic political philosophy.

The next split would occur between those who believed in the absolute inevitability of the coming revolution (the Revolutionary Socialists or as they came to be known, the **Communists**), and those who while accepting the basic idea that the current capitalist system could not last, saw in the growing political awareness of the working class the beginnings of an ability to effect peaceful and gradual change in the social order. They believed this is better in the long run for everyone concerned as opposed to a cataclysmic, apocalyptic uprising (the **Democratic-Socialists**).

Major strides for the Democratic-Socialists were made before the First World War. A war that the Socialists, by philosophy pacifists, initially resisted, giving only reluctant support only once the struggle had begun. During the conflict, public sentiment against pacifism tended generally to weaken the movement, but with peace, reaction set in. The cause of world socialism leaped forward, often overcompensating by adhering to revolutionary communism which in the Revolution of 1917 had taken hold of in Russia. The between wars period saw the sudden spurt of socialism, whether their leanings were democratic or not, all socialists were bound together for a time in their resistance to fascism.

The decade following World War II saw tremendous growth in socialism. Economic planning and the nationalization of industry was undertaken in many countries and to this day have not been repudiated, though a subsequent return to self-confidence in the private business community and among voters, in general, has frequently weakened the socialist majority or reduced it to the status of an opposition party.

This political balance leaves most industrialized countries with a mixed socialist-capitalist economy. So long as there is no major world-wide depression, this situation may remain relatively stable. The consequences of World War II, particularly the independence of former European colonies, has opened vast new areas for the attempted development of socialist forms. Most have tried to aspire to the democratic type but very few have succeeded except where democratic traditions were strong.

Socialism though concentrating on economic relationships, has always considered itself a complete approach to human society. In effect, a new belief system and thus a world rather than a national movement. In this respect as well, it owes much to Great Britain for it was in London in 1864 that the first **Socialist International** was organized by Karl Marx. This radical leftist organization died off after limping along for twelve years, by which time its headquarters had moved to New York.

After the passage of about another twelve years, the **Second Socialist International** met in Paris to celebrate the anniversary of the fall of the Bastille in the French Revolution. By this time, serious factions were developing. There were the Anarchists, who wanted to tear down everything, Communists who wanted to tear down the established order and build another in its place, and the Democratic-Socialists majority who favored peaceful political action.

Struggling for internal peace and cohesion right up to the First World War, socialism would remain largely ineffectual at this critical international time. Peace brought them all together again in Bern, Switzerland, but by this time the Soviet Union had been created and the Russian Communists refused to attend the meeting on the grounds that the Second Socialist International opposed the type of dictatorship it saw as necessary in order to achieve revolutions. Thus the **Communist International** was created in direct opposition to the Socialist International. While the socialists went on to advocate the "triumph of democracy, firmly rooted in the principles of liberty". The main objective of this new Socialist International was to maintain the peace, an ironic and very elusive goal in the period between the two world wars.

The Nazi attack on Poland in September, 1939, completely shattered the organization. In 1946, however a new Socialist Information and Liaison Office was set up to reestablish old contacts, and in 1951 the Communist International was revived with a conference in Frankfurt, Germany. At which time, it adopted a document entitled "Aims and Tasks of Democratic Socialism". A summary of these objectives gives a good picture of modern Democratic-Socialism as it exists on paper in its ideal form.

The first principle is nationalized ownership of the major means of production and distribution. Usually public ownership is deemed appropriate for the strategically important services: public utilities, banking and resource industries such as coal, iron, lumber and oil. Farming has never been considered well adapted to public administration and has usually been excluded from nationalization. From this takeover of the free enterprise system, socialists expect a more perfect freedom to evolve, offering equal opportunity for all, minimizing class conflict, access to better products for less cost, and security from physical want or need.

At the international level, socialism seeks a world of free peoples living together in peace and harmony for the mutual benefit of all. That freedom, at least from colonial rule, has largely been won. Peace throughout the world, however, is still as far off in most respects as it has ever been. According to the socialist doctrine, putting an end to capitalism will do much to reduce the likelihood of war. Armies and business are seen to need each other in a marriage of the weapons-mentality and devotion to private profit through the economic exploitation of weaker countries.

While communism and socialism arose in reaction to the excesses of nineteenth century capitalism, all three have matured in the past 100 years. Capitalism has mellowed, while a sibling rivalry may continue to exist between communism and socialism. Officially, communism clings to the idea of revolution and the seizing of capitalist property by the state without compensation. Socialism accepts gradualism, feeling that a revolution, particularly in an industrial society would be ruinous. In fact, socialists and in some situations even communists, have come to realize that not all economic institutions function better in public hands. Private responsibility frequently offers benefits that go to the public good. This is particularly true in the agricultural sector, where personal ownership and cultivation of land have always been deeply ingrained.

All socialism denies certain freedoms, sometimes hidden in what it considers favorable terms. It deprives the minority of special economic privileges for the benefit of majority. The more left-wing, communistic socialism may deny the democratic process entirely. Traditionally defined, democracy holds to the idea that the people, exercising their majority opinion at the polls, will arrive at the common good by electing representative individuals to govern them. Communists would interpret this to mean the tyranny of an uneducated majority obliged to decide between a politically selected group of would-be leaders. There is no question that the democratic process has its limitations, but for want of a better method, contemporary socialism accepts democracy as a major principle.

The expressed goals of modern socialism are commendable, but goals of course are easy to state, especially when there is no real opportunity to carry them out in actual fact. The gulf between theory and practice is often insurmountable. The situation thus remains whether given the chance socialism can bring about a better world than now exists. Nowhere today does socialism exist in a pure and unchallenged form, but in many nations it has made impressive gains.

Fascism was the last important historical economic system to arise. It has been called a reaction against the last two ideologies discussed. It can, at times, cooperate with a Monarchy if it has to. In general, Fascism is the effort to create, by dictatorial means, a viable national society in which competing interests were to be adjusted to each other by being entirely subordinated to the service of the state.

Generally spealking, Fascism has several characeterisitcs in all of it's various manifestations. First, an origin at a time of serious economic disruption and of rapid and bewildering social change. Second, a philosophy that rejects democratic and humanitarian ideals and glorifies the **absolute sovereignty of the state**, the unity and destiny of the people, and their unquestioning loyalty and obedience to the dictator. Third, there is an **aggressive nationalism** which calls for the mobilization and regimentation of every aspect of national life and makes open use of violence and intimidation. Fourth is the **simulation of mass popular support,** accomplished by outlawing all but a single political party and by using suppression, censorship, and propaganda. Fifth and final is a program of vigorous action including economic reconstruction, industrialization, pursuit of economic self-sufficiency, territorial expansion and war which is dramatized as bold, adventurous, and promising a glorious future.

Fascist movements often had Socialist origins. For example, in Italy, where fascism first arose in place of socialism, **Benito Mussolini**, sought to impose what he called "**corporativism.**" A fascist "corporate" state would, in theory, run the economy for the benefit of the whole country like a corporation. It would be centrally controlled and managed by an elite who would see that its benefits would go to everyone.

Fascism has always declared itself the uncompromising enemy of communism, with which, however, fascist actions have much in common. In fact, many of the methods of organization and propaganda used by fascists were taken from the experience of the early Russian communists, along with the belief in a single strong political party, secret police, etc. The propertied interests and the upper classes, fearful of revolution, often gave their support to fascism on the basis of promises by the fascist leaders to maintain the status quo and safeguard property. Thus in effect accomplishing a revolution from above with their help as opposed from below against them. However, fascism did consider itself a revolutionary movement of a different type.

Once established, a fascist regime ruthlessly crushes communist and socialist parties as well as all democratic opposition. It regiments the propertied interests to its national goals and wins the potentially revolutionary masses to fascist programs by substituting a rabid nationalism for class conflict. Thus fascism may be regarded as an extreme defensive expedient adopted by a nation faced with the sometimes illusionary threat of communist subversion or revolution. Under fascism, capital is regulated as much as labor and fascist contempt for legal or constitutional guarantees effectively destroyed whatever security the capitalistic system had enjoyed under pre-fascist governments.

In addition, fascist or similar regimes are at times anti-Communist. This is evidenced by the Soviet-German **Molotov-Ribbentrop Treaty of 1939**. During the period of alliance created by the treaty, Italy and Germany and their satellite countries ceased their anti-Communist propaganda. They emphasized their own revolutionary and proletarian origins and attacked the so-called plutocratic western democracies. The fact that fascist countries sought to control national life by methods identical to those of communist governments make such nations vulnerable to communism after the fascist regime is destroyed.

In theory at least, the chief distinction between fascism and communism is that fascism is **nationalist**, exalting the interests of the state and glorifying war between nations, whereas, communism is **internationalist**, exalting the interests of a specific economic class (the proletariat) and glorifying world wide class warfare. In practice, however, this fundamental distinction loses some of its validity. For in its heyday, fascism was also an internationalist movement. A movement dedicated to world conquest, (like communism), as evidenced by the events prior to and during the Second World War. At the same time, many elements in communism as it evolved came to be very nationalistic as well.

Skill 1.3j **Analyze the origins, course, and consequences of World War II, including the human cost of the war, the resulting redrawing of boundaries, and the movement of peoples in Europe, Asia, Africa, and the Middle East.**

World War I had seriously damaged the economies of the European countries, both the victors and the defeated, leaving them deeply in debt. There was difficulty on both sides paying off war debts and loans. It was difficult to find jobs and some countries like Japan and Italy found themselves without enough resources and more than enough people. Solving these problems by expanding the territory merely set up conditions for war later. Germany suffered horribly with runaway inflation ruining the value of its money and wiping out the savings of millions. Even though the U.S. made loans to Germany, which helped the government to restore some order and which provided a short existence of some economic stability in Europe, the Great Depression only served to undo any good that had been done. Mass unemployment, poverty, and despair greatly weakened the democratic governments that had been formed and greatly strengthened the increasing power and influence of extreme political movements, such as communism, fascism, and national-socialism. These ideologies promised to put an end to the economic problems.

The extreme form of patriotism called nationalism that had been the chief cause of World War I grew even stronger after the war ended in 1918. The political, social, and economic unrest fueled nationalism and it became an effective tool enabling dictators to gain and maintain power from the 1930s to the end of World War II in 1945. In the Soviet Union, **Joseph Stalin** succeeded in gaining political control and establishing a strong harsh dictatorship. **Benito Mussolini** and the Fascist party, promising prosperity and order in Italy, gained national support and set up a strong government. In Japan, although the ruler was considered Emperor **Hirohito,** actual control and administration of government came under military officers. In Germany, the results of war, harsh treaty terms, loss of territory, great economic chaos and collapse all enabled **Adolf Hitler** and his National Socialist, or **Nazi,** party to gain complete power and control.

Germany, Italy, and Japan initiated a policy of aggressive territorial expansion with Japan being the first to conquer. In 1931, Japanese forces seized control of **Manchuria**, a part of China containing rich natural resources, and in 1937 began an attack on the rest of China, occupying most of its eastern part by 1938. Italy invaded **Ethiopia** in Africa in 1935, having complete control by 1936. The Soviet Union did not invade or take over any territory but along with Italy and Germany, actively participated in the **Spanish Civil War**, using it as a proving ground to test tactics and weapons setting the stage for World War II.

In Germany, almost immediately after taking power, in direct violation of the World War I peace treaty, Hitler began the buildup of the armed forces. He sent troops into the Rhineland in 1936, then invaded Austria in 1938 and united it with Germany. In 1938, he seized control of the Sudetenland, part of western Czechoslovakia and containing mostly Germans, followed by the rest of Czechoslovakia in March 1939. Despite his territorial designs, the other nations of Europe made no moves to stop Hitler.

Preferring not to embark on another costly war, the European powers opted for a policy of **Appeasement**, believing that once Hitler had satisfied his desire for land he would be satisfied, and war could be averted. Then, on September 1, 1939, Hitler began World War II in Europe by invading **Poland**.

By 1940, Germany had invaded and controlled Norway, Denmark, Belgium, Luxembourg, the Netherlands, and France. Germany military forces struck in what came to be known as the **blitzkrieg**, or "lightning war." A shock attack, it relied on the use of surprise, speed, and superiority in firepower. The German blitzkrieg coordinated land and air attacks to paralyze the enemy by disabling its communications and coordination capacities.

When France fell in June 1940, the Franco-German armistice divided France into two zones: one under German military occupation and one under nominal French control (the southeastern two-fifths of the country). The National Assembly, summoned at Vichy, France ratified the armistice and granted **Philippe Pétain** control of the French State. The **Vichy** government then collaborated with the Germans, eventually becoming little more than a rubber stamp for German policies. Germany would occupy the whole of France in 1942, and by early 1944 a **Resistance** movement created a period of civil war in France. The Vichy regime was abolished after the liberation of Paris.

With Europe safely conquered, Hitler turned his sights to England. The **Battle of Britain** (June 1940 – April 1941) was a series of intense raids directed against Britain by the **Luftwaffe**, Germany's air force. Intended to prepare the way for invasion, the air raids were directed against British ports and Royal Air Force (**RAF**) bases. In September 1940, London and other cities were attacked in the "**blitz**," a series of bombings that lasted for 57 consecutive nights. Sporadic raids until April 1941. The RAF was outnumbered but succeeded in blocking the German air force, and eventually Hitler was forced to abandon his plans for invasion, Germany's first major setback in the war.

After success in North Africa and Italy, and following the D-Day Invasion, the Allied forces faced a protracted campaign across Europe. Each gain was hard won, and both the weather and local terrain at times worked against them. The **Battle of the Bulge**, also known as Battle of the Ardennes (December 16, 1944-January 28, 1945) was the largest World War II land battle on the Western Front, and the last major German counteroffensive of the war. Launched by Adolf Hitler himself, the German army's goal was to cut Allied forces in half and to retake the crucial port of Antwerp. Secretly massed Panzer tank-led units launched their assault into the thinnest part of the Allied forces.

Though surprised and suffering tremendous losses, Allied forces still managed to slow the Germans. American tanks moved swiftly to counterattack and cut German supply lines. The attack resulted in a bulge seventy miles deep into Allied lines, but all forward momentum for the Germans was essentially stopped by Christmas. It took another month before the Allies could push back to the original line. Both sides suffered great casualties, but the Germans' losses were a crushing blow, as the troops and equipment lost were irreplaceable.

During the war, Allied forces flew extensive bombing raids deep into German territory. Launched from bases in England, both American and RAF bomber squadrons proceeded to massively bomb German factories and cities. Although the raids were dangerous, with many planes and lives lost both to the Luftwaffe and ant-aircraft artillery, the raids continued throughout the war. German cities were reduced to virtually rubble by war's end, and the impact on Germany's production capacity and transportation lines helped swing the tide of war.

Before war in Europe had ended, the Allies had agreed on a military occupation of Germany. It was divided into four zones each one occupied by Great Britain, France, the Soviet Union, and the United States with the four powers jointly administering Berlin. After the war, the Allies agreed that Germany's armed forces would be abolished, the Nazi Party outlawed, and the territory east of the Oder and Neisse Rivers taken away. Nazi leaders were accused of war crimes and brought to trial at **Nuremburg**.

Major consequences of the war included horrendous death and destruction, millions of displaced persons, the gaining of strength and spread of Communism and Cold War tensions as a result of the beginning of the nuclear age. World War II ended more lives and caused more devastation than any other war. Besides the losses of millions of military personnel, the devastation and destruction directly affected civilians, reducing cities, houses, and factories to ruin and rubble and totally wrecking communication and transportation systems. Millions of civilian deaths, especially in China and the Soviet Union, were the results of famine. More than 12 million people were uprooted by wars end and had no place to live. Included in those numbers were prisoners of war, those that survived Nazi concentration camps and slave labor camps, orphans, and people who escaped war-torn areas and invading armies. Changing national boundary lines also caused the mass movement of displaced persons.

Germany and Japan were completely defeated; Great Britain and France were seriously weakened; and the Soviet Union and the United States became the world's leading powers. Although allied during the war, the alliance fell apart as the Soviets pushed Communism in Europe and Asia. In spite of the tremendous destruction it suffered, the Soviet Union was stronger than ever. During the war, it took control of Lithuania, Estonia, and Latvia and by mid-1945 parts of Poland, Czechoslovakia, Finland, and Romania. It helped Communist governments gain power in Bulgaria, Romania, Hungary, Czechoslovakia, Poland, and North Korea. China fell to **Mao Zedong**'s Communist forces in 1949. Until the fall of the Berlin Wall in 1989 and the dissolution of Communist governments in Eastern Europe and the Soviet Union, the United States and the Soviet Union faced off in what was called a Cold War. The possibility of the terrifying destruction by nuclear weapons loomed over both nations.

The world after World War II was a complicated place. The Axis powers, Nazi German, Fascist Italy and the Empire of Japan were defeated, but the Cold War had sprung up in its place. Many countries struggled to get out of the debt and devastation that their Nazi occupiers had wrought. The American **Marshall Plan** helped the nations of Western Europe get back on their feet. The Soviet Union helped the Eastern European nations return to greatness, with Communist governments at the helm. The nations of Asia were rebuilt as well, with Communism taking over China and Americanization taking over Japan and Taiwan. East and West struggled for control in this arena, especially in Korea and Southeast Asia. When Communism fell in the USSR and Eastern Europe, it remained in China, North Korea, and Vietnam. Vietnam's neighbors, however set their own path to government.

The kind of nationalism that Europe saw in the nineteenth century spilled over into the mid-twentieth century, with former colonies of European powers declaring themselves independent all the time, especially in Africa. India, a longtime British protectorate, also achieved independence at this time. With independence, these countries continued to grow. Some of these nations now experience severe overcrowding and dearth of precious resources. Some who can escape do; others have no way to escape.

The Middle East has been an especially violent part of the world since the war and the inception of the State of Israel. The struggle for supremacy in the Persian Gulf area has brought about a handful of wars as well. Oil, needed to power the world's devastatingly large transportation and manufacturing engines, is king of all resources.

The **United Nations**, a more successful successor to the League of Nations (which couldn't prevent World War II), began in the waning days of the war. It brought the nations of the world together to discuss their problems, rather than fight about them. Another successful method of keeping the peace since the war has been the atomic bomb. On a more specific note, UNICEF, a worldwide children's fund, has been able to achieve great things in just a few decades of existence. Other peace-based organizations like the Red Cross and Doctors Without Borders have seen their membership and their efficacy rise during this time as well.

Skill 1.3k   Analyze the international developments of the post-World War II era, including decolonization, nationalism, nation-building, the development of international organizations, and global migration.

Decolonization refers to the period after World War II when many African and Asian colonies and protectorates gained independence from the powers that had colonized them. The independence of India and Pakistan from Britain in 1945 marked the beginning of an especially important period of decolonization that lasted through 1960. Several British colonies in eastern Africa and French colonies in western Africa and Asia also formed as independent countries during this period.

Colonial powers had found it efficient to draw political boundaries across traditional ethnic and national lines, thereby dividing local populations and making them easier to control. With the yoke of colonialism removed, many new nations found themselves trying to reorganize into politically stable and economically viable units. The role of nationalism was important in this reorganization, as formerly divided peoples had opportunity to reunite. **Nationalism** is most simply defined as the belief that the nation is the basic unit of human association, and that a nation is a well-defined group of people sharing a common identity. This process of organizing new nations out of the remains of former colonies was called nation building.

Nation building in this fashion did not always result in the desired stability. Pakistan, for example, eventually split into Bangladesh and Pakistan along geographic and religious lines. Ethnic conflicts in newly formed African nations arose, and are still flaring in some areas. As the United States and the Soviet Union emerged as the dominant world powers, these countries encouraged dissent in post-colonial nations such as Cuba, Vietnam and Korea, which became arenas for Cold War conflict.

With the emergence of so many new independent nations, the role of **international organizations** such as the newly formed United Nations grew in importance. The United Nations was formed after World War II to establish peaceful ties between countries. Dismayed by the failure of the former League of Nations to prevent war, the organizers of the United Nations provided for the ability to deploy peacekeeping troops and to impose sanctions and restrictions on member states. Other international organizations arose to take the place of former colonial connections. The British Commonwealth and the French Union, for example, maintained connections between Britain and France and their former colonies.

Global migration saw an increase in the years during and following World War II. During the war years, many Jews left the hostile climate under Nazi Germany for the United States and Palestine.

Following the war, the Allied countries agreed to force German people living in Eastern Europe to return to Germany, affecting over 16 million people. In other parts of the world, instability in post-colonial areas often led to migration. Colonial settlers who had enjoyed the protection of a colonial power sometimes found themselves in hostile situations as native peoples gained independence and ascended to power, spurring migration to more friendly nations. Economic instability in newly forming countries created incentive for people to seek opportunity in other countries.

Skill 1.3I   Analyze the Cold War from its origins in the post-World War II 1940s to the dissolution of the Soviet Union in 1991, including its impact on social, cultural, political, economic, technological, and geographic developments in the world.

The major thrust of U.S. foreign policy from the end of World War II to 1990 was the post-war struggle between non-Communist nations, led by the United States, and the Soviet Union and the Communist nations who were its allies. It was referred to as a **Cold War** because its conflicts did not lead to a major war of fighting, or a "hot war." Both the Soviet Union and the United States embarked on an arsenal buildup of atomic and hydrogen bombs as well as other nuclear weapons. Both nations had the capability of destroying each other but because of the continuous threat of nuclear war and accidents, extreme caution was practiced on both sides. The efforts of both sides to serve and protect their political philosophies and to support and assist their allies resulted in a number of events during this 45-year period.

After 1945, social and economic chaos continued in Western Europe, especially in Germany. Secretary of State George C. Marshall came to realize that Europe's problems were serious and could affect the U.S. To aid in the recovery, he proposed a program known as the European Recovery Program or the **Marshall Plan**. Although the Soviet Union withdrew from any participation, the U.S. continued the work of assisting Europe in regaining its economic stability. In Germany in particular the situation was critical, with the American Army shouldering the staggering burden of relieving the serious problems of the German economy. In February 1948, Britain and the U.S. combined their two zones, with France joining in June.

In 1946, Josef Stalin stated publicly that the presence of capitalism and its development of the world's economy made international peace impossible. This led an American diplomat in Moscow named **George F. Kennan** to propose the idea of **containment**, as a response to Stalin and as a statement of U.S. foreign policy. The goal of the U.S. would be to limit the extension or expansion of Soviet Communist policies and activities. After Soviet efforts to make trouble in Iran, Greece, and Turkey, U.S. President Harry Truman stated what is known as the **Truman Doctrine** which committed the U.S. to a policy of intervention in order to contain or stop the spread of communism throughout the world.

The Soviets were opposed to German unification and in April 1948 took serious action to either stop it or to force the Allies to give up control of West Berlin to the Soviets. The Soviets blocked all road traffic access from West Germany to West Berlin, which lay wholly within Soviet-controlled East German,. To avoid any armed conflict, it was decided to airlift into West Berlin the needed food and supplies. During the **Berlin Airlift**, from June 1948 to mid-May 1949 Allied air forces flew in all that was needed for the West Berliners, forcing the Soviets to lift the blockade and permit vehicular traffic access to the city.

The Cold War was, more than anything else, an ideological struggle between proponents of democracy and those of communism. The two major players were the United States and the Soviet Union, but other countries were involved as well. It was a "cold" war because no large-scale fighting took place directly between the two big protagonists. It wasn't just form of government that was driving this war, either. Economics were a main concern as well. A concern in both countries was that the precious resources (such as oil and food) from other like-minded countries wouldn't be allowed to flow to "the other side." These resources didn't much flow between the U.S. and Soviet Union, either.

The Soviet Union kept much more of a tight leash on its supporting countries, including all of Eastern Europe, which made up a military organization called the **Warsaw Pact**. The Western nations responded with a military organization of their own, **NATO** or **North American Treaty Organization**. Another prime battleground was Asia, where the Soviet Union had allies in China, North Korea, and North Vietnam and the U.S. had allies in Japan, South Korea, Taiwan, and South Vietnam. The Korean War and Vietnam War were major conflicts in which both protagonists played big roles but didn't directly fight each other.

The main symbol of the Cold War was the **arms race**, a continual buildup of missiles, tanks, and other weapons that became ever more technologically advanced and increasingly more deadly. The ultimate weapon, which both sides had in abundance, was the nuclear bomb. Spending on weapons and defensive systems eventually occupied great percentages of the budgets of the U.S. and the USSR, and some historians argue that this high level of spending played a large part in the end of the latter.

The war was a cultural struggle as well. Adults brought up their children to hate "the Americans" or "the Communists." Cold War tensions spilled over into many parts of life in countries around the world. The ways of life in countries on either side of the divide were so different that they seemed entirely foreign to outside observers.

The Cold War continued to varying degrees from 1947 to 1991, when the Soviet Union collapsed. Other Eastern European countries had seen their communist governments overthrown by this time as well, marking the shredding of the "Iron Curtain." The "**Iron Curtain**" referred to the ideological, symbolic and physical separation of Europe between East and West.

Skill 1.3m   **Analyze the emergence of a global economy and its impact on the environment, epidemiology, and demographics, and the development and impact of the information, technology, and communications revolutions.**

Globalism is defined as the principle of the interdependence of all the world's nations and their peoples. Within this global community, every nation, in some way to a certain degree, is dependent on other nations. Since no one nation has all of the resources needed for production, trade with other nations is required to obtain what is needed for production, to sell what is produced or to buy finished products, to earn money to maintain and strengthen the nation's economic system. Developing nations receive technical assistance and financial aid from developed nations. Many international organizations have been set up to promote and encourage cooperation and economic progress among member nations. Through the elimination of such barriers to trade as tariffs, trade is stimulated resulting in increased productivity, economic progress, increased cooperation and understanding on diplomatic levels.

Those nations not part of an international trade organization not only must make those economic decisions of what to produce, how and for whom, but must also deal with the problem of tariffs and quotas on imports. Regardless of international trade memberships, economic growth and development are vital and affect all trading nations. Businesses, labor, and governments share common interests and goals in a nation's economic status. International systems of banking and finance have been devised to assist governments and businesses in setting the policy and guidelines for the exchange of currencies.

The global economy had its origins in the early twentieth century, with the advent of the **airplane**, which made travel and trade easier and less time-consuming than ever. Airplanes travel the fastest of any mode of transportation on the planet. They can reduce days long trips to hours long adventures, resulting in not only shorter tourist trips but also shorter trade trips, meaning that goods (especially perishable foods) can travel farther and wider than ever before. Being able to ship goods quickly and efficiently means that businesses can conduct business overseas much more efficiently than they ever could.

Trucks, trains, and ships carry cargo all over the world. Trains travel faster than ever, as do ships. Roads are more prevalent and usually in better repair than they have ever been, making truck and even car travel not the dead-end option that it once was.

With all of this capability has come increasing demand. People traditionally had gotten their goods using their own means or from traders who lived nearby. As technology improved, trade routes got longer and demand for things from overseas grew. This demand feeds the economic imperative of creating more supply, and vice versa. As more people discovered goods from overseas, the demand for those foreign goods increased. Because people could get goods from overseas with relative ease, they continued to get them and demand more. Suppliers were only too happy to supply the goods.

An incredible increase in demand for something is not always a good thing, however, especially if what is being demanded s in limited supply. A good example is wood, paper, and other goods that are made from trees. The demand for paper especially these days is staggering. In order to fulfill that demand, companies are cutting down more and more trees. Forests around the world are disappearing at an alarming rate, especially in the precious rainforests of South America. Recycling of paper is very much a focus for many people today, but it can't keep up with clear-cutting.

An example of **nonrenewable resources** like coal and oil are in worldwide demand these days, and the supplies won't last forever. Making it easier to ship goods all over the world has made demand grow at an unbelievable rate, raising concerns about supply. Because resources like this have a limited supply (even though the day when that limit is reached seems far away still), they are in danger of becoming extinct without being replaced.

Globalization has also brought about welcome and unwelcome developments in the field of epidemiology. Vaccines and other cures for diseases can be shipped relatively quickly all around the world. For example, this has made it possible for HIV vaccines to reach the remotest areas of the world, for example. Unfortunately, the preponderance of global travel has also meant that the threat of spreading a disease to the world by an infected person traveling on an international flight is quite real.

The most recent example of technology contributing to globalization is the development of the **Internet**. Instant communication between people millions of miles apart is possible just by plugging in a computer and connecting to the Net. The Internet is an extension of the telephone and cell phone revolutions; all three are developments that have brought faraway places closer together. All three allow people to communicate no matter the distance. This communication can facilitate friendly chatter and, of course, trade. A huge number of businesses use cell phones and the Internet to do business these days, also using computers to track goods and receipts quickly and efficiently. With the recent advent of the Internet, the world might be better termed a global neighborhood.

Globalization has also brought financial and cultural exchange on a worldwide scale. A large number of businesses have investments in countries around the world. Financial transactions are conducted using a variety of currencies. The cultures of the countries of the world are increasingly viewed by people elsewhere in the world through the wonders of television and the Internet. Not only goods but also belief systems, customs, and practices are being exchanged.

With this exchange of money, goods, and culture has come an increase in immigration. Many people who live in less-developed nations see what is available in other places and want to move there, in order to fully take advantage of all that those more-developed nations have to offer. This can conceivably create an increase in immigration. Depending on the numbers of people who want to immigrate and the resources available, this could become a problem. The technological advances in transportation and communications have made such immigration easier than ever.

Skill 1.3n   Describe the causes and effects of genocide in the 20th century, including, but not limited to, the Armenian genocide, the Holocaust, and post-World War II "ethnic cleansing."

Genocide, or the intended extinction of one people by another, is not a new concept. However, in the twentieth century, it has reached great heights—and depths.

The first organized genocide in the 1900s was the **Armenian genocide,** an attempted extermination of a huge number of Armenians at the hands of the young Turks who inherited Turkey from the Ottoman Empire. More than one million Armenian people (nearly half of their population) died between 1915 and 1917. The government blamed the Armenians for early defeats at the hands of Russia and its allies. Armenians were forcibly moved and kept in harsh conditions elsewhere. A total of twenty-five concentration camps are believed to have existed. Turkish authorities claimed that the Armenian people had agitated for separation from the Ottoman Empire and that the relocation was pursuant to the goals of both peoples. Others disagree. Some sources blame other causes for these deaths; most scholars, however, agree that it was a determined attempt to exterminate an entire group of people.

The most well-known genocide of the twentieth century is the **Holocaust** of Jews before and during World War II. Much of this took place in Germany, although the practice increased throughout German-occupied countries throughout the war. German authorities capitalized on hundreds of years of distrust of Jewish people and invented what they saw as "the **Final Solution** of the Jewish Question": extermination of the Jewish people. Germans in charge of this "Final Solution" constructed a vast, complicated system of transport systems and concentration camps, where Jews were imprisoned, forced to work, and killed in increasingly large numbers. This Holocaust was known especially for its efficiency and its record-keeping, which was extensive. Thousands of pages of documents describe in excruciating detail how thorough and determined Nazi authorities were in pursuing their goals.

German doctors also carried out experiments on their Jewish prisoners, pursuing radical cures for diseases and, more often than not, new methods of torture and mistreatment of prisoners of war. The deadly fingers of torture and killing were not at all restricted to able-bodied people. Youngsters, the elderly, the disabled, the mentally ill, and the near-dead were all subject to the harshest treatment imaginable. One common practice was the forced march from one location to another, miles away, without food or sustenance. These "**death marches**" left many of the prisoners dead or near death.

The number of Jews killed during the Holocaust is generally said to be six million. This figure includes people from all over Europe. The Holocaust didn't kill just Jews, however. Gypsies, communists, homosexuals, Jehovah's Witnesses, Catholics, psychiatric patients, and even common criminals were systematically incarcerated and, in many cases, killed for being "enemies of the state."

The number of concentration camps in Nazi-controlled lands during World War II was more than 40. Not all of them were death camps, altough the most famous ones, including Auschwitz, were. The Holocaust ended with Germany's defeat in World War II. The liberating troops of the West and East uncovered the concentration camps and all of the killing that the Nazis wrought. Much of the meticulous record-keeping was intact, preserving for all the world the horrors that these people had wrought.

Ethnic cleansing in Yugoslavia occurred in Kosovo in the 1990s. The country was a melting pot of ethnic peoples, all of whom were struggling for meager resources and living space. The people who had the most power, including control of the government and the army, were the Serbs. In 1989 the Serbian president, **Slobodan Milosevic**, abrogated the constitutional autonomy of Kosovo. He and the minority of Serbs in Kosovo had long bristled at the fact that Muslim Albanians were in control of an area considered sacred to Serbs. The Serbian government expelled ethnic Albanians from the province. The Serbian officials also confiscated all identity documentation from those who were expelled so that any attempt to return could be refused by claiming that without documents to prove Serbian citizenship the people must be native Albanians. The effort even went so far as to destroy archival documents that proved citizenship.

Growing tensions led in 1998 to armed clashes between Serbs and the Kosovo Liberation Army (**KLA**), which had begun killing Serbian police and politicians. The Serbs responded with a ruthless counteroffensive, inducing the UN Security Council to condemn the Serbs' excessive use of force, including ethnic cleansing (killing and expulsion), and to impose an arms embargo, but the violence continued. After diplomatic efforts broke down, **NATO** responded with an 11-week bombing campaign that extended to Belgrade and significantly damaged Serbia's infrastructure. NATO and Yugoslavia signed an accord in June 1999 outlining Serbian troop withdrawal and the return of nearly 1,000,000 ethnic Albanian refugees as well as 500,000 displaced within the province. Bosnia is now its own country, as is Croatia and Serbia and Montenegro. The leaders of this genocide have been convicted of their crimes, as were the Nazi perpetrators before them.

Rwandan Genocide was the 1994 mass extermination of hundreds of thousands of ethnic **Tutsis** and moderate **Hutu** sympathizers in Rwanda and was the largest atrocity during the Rwandan Civil War. This genocide was mostly carried out by two extremist Hutu militia groups April 6 through mid-July 1994. Hundreds of thousands of people were slaughtered.

In the wake of the Rwandan Genocide, the United Nations and the international community drew severe criticism for its inaction. Despite international news media coverage of the violence as it unfolded, most countries, including France, Belgium, and the United States, declined to intervene or speak out against the massacres. Canada continued to lead the UN peacekeeping force in Rwanda. However, the UN Security Council did not authorize direct intervention or the use force to prevent or halt the killing.

The genocide ended when a Tutsi-dominated expatriate rebel overthrew the Hutu government and seized power. Fearing reprisals, hundreds of thousands of Hutu and other refugees fled into eastern Zaire (now the Democratic Republic of the Congo). People who had actively participated in the genocide hid among the refugees, fueling the First and Second Congo Wars. Rivalry between Hutu and Tutsi tribal factions is also a major factor in the Burundi Civil War.

Skill 1.3o   Explain and evaluate the strategic importance of the Middle East and the volatile political relations within the region.

The Middle East is defined by its name and its geographic position. It is in the middle of the globe, a position that enables it to exert tremendous influence on not only the trade that passes through its realm of influence but also the political relations between its countries and those of different parts of the world.

From the beginnings of civilization, the Middle East has been a destination: for attackers, for adventure-seekers, for those starving for food and a progressively more technologically advanced series of other resources, from iron to oil. Now, as then, the countries of the Middle East play an important role in the economics of the world.

First and foremost is the importance of **oil**. Saudi Arabia most notably but also Iran, Iraq, Kuwait, Qatar, Dubai, and the United Arab Emirates are huge exporters of oil. The Middle East is not the only place to get oil by any means; Russia, for example, is another excellent source of oil. The appeal of the Middle East countries as sources of oil is that it is much easier to get at and put on tankers than it is to procure from the wilds of central Russia. In some cases, the amount of oil that one of these countries exports exceeds 90 percent of its total economic outflow. Most of the world requires oil in huge numbers, to run its machines and especially its transportation vehicles—cars, trucks, airplanes, and buses.

The vast majority of the world's developed nations would be helpless without this oil, and so the governments of these nations will pay nearly any price to keep that oil flowing from the Middle East into their countries. The oil-rich exporters of the Middle East can hold the rest of the world hostage by increasing the price of oil even slightly, since the consumption for even a small developed nation numbers in the billions of gallons every month.

It can be argued that whoever controls a country in the Middle East controls the oil. With few exceptions, all of these countries have strong central governments, which control the collection and export of oil. If a country were to take over one of these big exporters, the infrastructure would already be in place to control the flow of oil. The recent American occupation of Iraq illustrates this, since the existing oil companies were taken over by American operations.

The countries of the Middle East, despite their economic similarities, have important differences in their government, belief systems, and global outlooks. Iran and Iraq fought a devastating war in the 1980s. **Iraq** invaded **Kuwait** in the late 1990s. It is not outside the realm of possibility that other conflicts will arise in the future.

The **Iranian Revolution** in 1979 transformed a constitutional monarchy, led by the Shah, into an Islamic populist theocratic republic. The new ruler was Ayatollah Ruhollah Khomeini. This revolution occurred in two essential stages. In the first, religious, liberal and leftist groups cooperated to oust the **Shah** (king). In the second stage, the Ayatollah rose to power and created an Islamic state.

The Shah had faced intermittent opposition from the middle classes in the cities and from Islamic figures. These groups sought a limitation of the Shah's power and a constitutional democracy. The Shah enforced censorship laws and imprisoned political enemies. At the same time, living conditions of the people improved greatly and several important democratic rights were given to the people. Islamic **Mullahs** fiercely opposed giving women the right to vote.

The Shah was said to be a puppet of the U.S. government. A series of protests in 1978 escalated until December of that year when more than two million people gathered in Tehran in protest against the Shah. In a very short period of time, the Ayatollah Khomeini had gathered his revolutionaries and completed the overthrow of the monarchy.

The revolution accomplished certain goals: reduction of foreign influence and a more even distribution of the nation's wealth. It did not change repressive policies or levels of government brutality. It reversed policies toward women, restoring ancient policies of repression. Religious repression became rife, particularly against members of the Bahai Faith. The revolution has also isolated Iran from the rest of the world, being rejected by both capitalist and communist nations. This isolation, however, allowed the country to develop its own internal political system, rather than having a system imposed by foreign powers.

Another large factor of the instability in the Middle East is ethnic strife. It's not just Muslims who occupy these countries. Each country has its own ethnic mix. A good example of this is Iraq, which has a huge minority of **Kurdish** people. Saddam Hussein, the former dictator of Iraq, made a habit of persecuting Kurds just because of who they were. Iraq is an also an example of a religious conflict, with the minority Shiites now in power and Hussein's Sunnis out of power. These two people agree very little outside the basics of Islamic faith The prospect of a civil war in Iraq looms large, as it does in other neighboring countries, which have their own ethnic problems.

Religious conflict is the name of the game in Israel as well, as **Israelis** and **Palestinians** continue a centuries-old fight over religion and geography. This conflict goes back to the beginnings of Islam, in the seventh century. Muslims claimed Jerusalem, capital of the ancient civilization of Israel, as a holy city, in the same way that Jews and Christians did. Muslims seized control of Palestine and Jerusalem and held it for a great many years, prompting Christian armies from Europe to muster for the Crusades, in a series of attempts to "regain the Holy Land." For hundreds of years after Christendom's failure, these lands were ruled by Muslim leaders and armies. In recent centuries, Palestine was made a British colony and then eliminated in favor of the modern state of Israel. Since that last event, in 1948, the conflict has escalated to varying degrees.

The addition of Israel to the Middle East equation presents a religious conflict not only with the Palestinians but also with the Arab peoples of neighboring Egypt and Syria. The armed forces of all of these countries have so many advanced weapons that they would seem to be a deterrent to further bloodshed, yet the attacks continue. In the last 40 years, Israel has won two major wars with its neighbors. Nearly daily conflict continues, much as it has for thousands of years. This conflict is not so much an economic one, but a full-blown war in this region would certainly involve Israel's neighbors and, by extension, other large countries in the world, most notably the United States.

DOMAIN 2:   U.S. HISTORY

COMPETENCY 2.1   PRE-REVOLUTIONARY ERA AND THE WAR FOR INDEPENDENCE

Skill 2.1a   Describe the major American Indian cultural groups and their contributions to early American society.

Native American tribes lived throughout what we now call the United States in varying degrees of togetherness. They adopted different customs, pursued different avenues of agriculture and food gathering, and made slightly different weapons. They fought among themselves and with other peoples. To varying degrees, they had established cultures long before Columbus or any other European explorer arrived on the scene.

Perhaps the most famous of the Native American tribes is the **Algonquians**. We know so much about this tribe because they were one of the first to interact with the newly arrived English settlers in Plymouth and elsewhere. The Algonquians lived in wigwams and wore clothing made from animal skins. They were proficient hunters, gatherers, and trappers who also knew quite a bit about farming. Beginning with a brave man named **Squanto**, they shared this agricultural knowledge with the English settlers, including how to plant and cultivate corn, pumpkins, and squash. Other famous Algonquians included **Pocahontas** and her father, Powhatan, both of whom are immortalized in English literature, and **Tecumseh** and Black Hawk, known foremost for their fierce fighting ability. To the overall Native American culture, they contributed wampum and dream catchers.

Another group of tribes who lived in the Northeast were the **Iroquois**, who were fierce fighters but also forward thinkers. They lived in long houses and wore clothes made of buckskin. They, too, were expert farmers, growing the "**Three Sisters**" (corn, squash, and beans). Five of the Iroquois tribes formed a Confederacy which was a shared form of government. The Iroquois also formed the False Face Society, a group of medicine men who shared their medical knowledge with others but kept their identities secret while doing so. These masks are one of the enduring symbols of the Native American era.

Living in the Southeast were the **Seminoles** and **Creeks**, a huge collection of people who lived in **chickees** (open, bark-covered houses) and wore clothes made from plant fibers. They were expert planters and hunters and were proficient at paddling dugout canoes, which they made. The bead necklaces they created were some of the most beautiful on the continent. They are best known, however, for their struggle against Spanish and English settlers, especially led by the great Osceola.

SOCIAL SCIENCE   72

The **Cherokee** also lived in the Southeast. They were one of the most advanced tribes, living in domed houses and wearing deerskin and rabbit fur. Accomplished hunters, farmers, and fishermen, the Cherokee were known the continent over for their intricate and beautiful basketry and clay pottery. They also played a game called lacrosse, which survives to this day in countries around the world.

In the middle of the continent lived the Plains tribes, such as the **Sioux, Cheyenne, Blackfeet, Comanche,** and **Pawnee**. These peoples lived in teepees and wore buffalo skins and feather headdresses. (It is this image of the Native American that has made its way into most American movies depicting the period.) They hunted wild animals on the Plains, especially the buffalo. They were well known for their many ceremonies, including the Sun Dance, and for the peace pipes that they smoked. Famous Plains people include **Crazy Horse** and **Sitting Bull**, authors of Custer's defeat at Little Big Horn; **Sacagawea**, leader of the Lewis & Clark expedition; and **Chief Joseph**, the famous Nez Perce leader.

Dotting the deserts of the Southwest were a handful of tribes, including the famous **Pueblo**, who lived in houses that bear their tribe's name, wore clothes made of wool and woven cotton, farmed crops in the middle of desert land, created exquisite pottery and Kachina dolls, and had one of the most complex religions of all the tribes. They are perhaps best known for the challenging vista-based villages that they constructed from the sheer faces of cliffs and rocks and for their **adobes**, mud-brick buildings that housed their living and meeting quarters.
Another well-known Southwestern tribe were the **Apache**, with their famous leader **Geronimo**. The Apache lived in homes called wickiups, which were made of bark, grass, and branches. They wore cotton clothing and were excellent hunters and gatherers. Adept at basketry, the Apache believed that everything in Nature had special powers and that they were honored just to be part of it all.

The **Navajo**, also residents of the Southwest, lived in **hogans** (round homes built with forked sticks) and wore clothes of rabbit skin. Their major contribution to the overall culture of the continent was in sand painting, weapon-making, silversmithing, and weaving. Some of the most beautiful woven rugs ever were crafted by Navajo hands.

Living in the Northwest were the **Inuit**, who lived in tents made from animal skins or, in some cases, **igloos**. They wore clothes made of animal skins, usually seals or caribou. They were excellent fishermen and hunters and crafted efficient kayaks and umiaks to take them through waterways and harpoons with which to hunt animals. The Inuit are perhaps best known for the great carvings that they left behind. Among these are ivory figures and tall totem poles.

Skill 2.1b   **Explain and analyze the struggle for the control of North America among European powers and the emergence of the 13 colonies under English rule.**

Columbus' first trans-Atlantic voyage was an attempt to prove the idea that Asia could be reached by sailing west. And to a certain extent, this idea was true. It could be done but only after figuring how to go around or across or through the landmass in between. Long after Spain dispatched explorers and her famed conquistadors to gather the wealth for the Spanish monarchs and their coffers, the British were still searching valiantly for the **Northwest Passage**, an open-water route across North America, from the Atlantic to the Pacific, to the wealth of Asia. Not until after the Lewis and Clark Expedition, when Captains Meriwether Lewis and William Clark proved conclusively that there simply was no Northwest Passage, did this idea cease to hold sway.

However, lack of an open-water passage did not deter exploration and settlement. **Spain, France,** and **England** - along with some participation by the **Dutch** - led the way in expanding Western European civilization in the New World. These three nations had strong monarchial governments and were struggling for dominance and power in Europe. With the defeat of Spain's mighty Armada in 1588, England became undisputed ruler of the seas. Spain lost its power and influence in Europe and it was left to France and England to carry on the rivalry, leading to eventual British control in Asia as well.

Spain's influence extended across Florida, along the Gulf Coast of Texas all the way west to California and south to the tip of South America. French control centered from New Orleans north to what is now northern Canada including the entire Mississippi Valley, the St. Lawrence Valley, the Great Lakes, and the land that was part of the Louisiana Territory. England settled the eastern seaboard of North America, including parts of Canada and the US from Maine to Georgia. Each of the three nations controlled various islands of the West Indies. The Dutch had New Amsterdam for a period but later ceded it into British hands.

One interesting aspect of all of this was that each of these nations, especially England, laid claim to land that extended partly or all the way across the continent, regardless of the fact that the others claimed the same land. The wars for dominance and control of power and influence in Europe would undoubtedly and eventually extend to the Americas, especially North America.

The part of North America claimed by **France** was called New France and consisted of the land west of the Appalachian Mountains. This area of claims and settlement included the St. Lawrence Valley, the Great Lakes, the Mississippi Valley, and the entire region of land westward to the Rockies. They established the permanent settlements of Montreal and New Orleans, thus giving them control of the two major gateways into the heart of North America, the vast, rich interior. The St. Lawrence River, the Great Lakes, and the Mississippi River along with its tributaries made it possible for the French explorers and traders to roam at will, virtually unhindered in exploring, trapping, trading, and furthering the interests of France.

Most of the French settlements were in Canada along the **St. Lawrence River**. Only scattered forts and trading posts were found in the upper Mississippi Valley and Great Lakes region. The rulers of France originally intended New France to have vast estates owned by nobles and worked by peasants with the peasants living on the estates in compact farming villages - the New World version of the Old World's medieval system of feudalism. However, it didn't work out that way. Each of the nobles wanted his estate to be on the river for ease of transportation. The peasants working the estates wanted the prime waterfront location, also. The result of all this real estate squabbling was that New France's settled areas wound up mostly as a string of farmhouses stretching from Quebec to Montreal along the St. Lawrence and Richelieu Rivers.

In the non-settled areas in the interior were the **French fur traders.** They made friends with the friendly tribes of Indians, spending the winters with them getting the furs needed for trade. In the spring, they would return to Montreal in time to take advantage of trading their furs for the products brought by the cargo ships from France, which usually arrived at about the same time. Most of the wealth for New France and its "Mother Country" was from the fur trade, which provided a livelihood for many, many people. Manufacturers and workmen back in France, ship-owners and merchants, as well as the fur traders and their Indian allies all benefited. However, the freedom of roaming and trapping in the interior was a strong enticement for the younger, stronger men and resulted in the French not strengthening the areas settled along the St. Lawrence.

Into the eighteenth century, French rivalry with the **British** grew stronger. New France was united under a single government and enjoyed the support of many Indian allies. The French traders were very diligent in not destroying the forests and driving away game upon which the Indians depended for life. It was difficult for the French to defend all of their settlements as they were scattered over half of the continent. However, by the early 1750s, in Western Europe, France was the most powerful nation. Its armies were superior to all others and its navy was giving the British stiff competition for control of the seas. The stage was set for confrontation in both Europe and America.

Spanish settlement had its beginnings in the Caribbean with the establishment of colonies on Hispaniola at Santo Domingo which became the capital of the West Indies, Puerto Rico, and Cuba. The first permanent settlement in what is now the United States was in 1565 at **St. Augustine**, Florida. A later permanent settlement in the southwestern United States was in 1609 at Santa Fe, New Mexico. At the peak of Spanish power, the area in the United States claimed, settled, and controlled by Spain included Florida and all land west of the Mississippi River. There were a number of reasons for Spanish involvement in the Americas, among them:

- the spirit of adventure
- the desire for land
- expansion of Spanish power, influence, and empire
- the desire for great wealth
- expansion of Roman Catholic influence and conversion of native peoples

Of course, France and England also laid claim to the same areas. Nonetheless, ranches and missions were built and the Indians who came in contact with the Spaniards were introduced to animals, plants, and seeds from the Old World that they had never seen before. Animals brought in included horses, cattle, donkeys, pigs, sheep, goats, and poultry.

Barrels were cut in half and filled with earth to transport and transplant trees bearing apples, oranges, limes, cherries, pears walnuts, olives, lemons, figs, apricots and almonds. Even sugar cane and flowers made it to America along with bags bringing seeds of wheat, barley, rye, flax, lentils, rice, and peas.

All Spanish colonies belonged to the King of Spain. He was considered **an absolute monarch** with complete or absolute power who claimed rule by divine right, the belief being that God had given him the right to rule and he answered only to God for his actions. His word was final, was the law. The people had no voice in government. The land, the people, the wealth all belonged to him to use as he pleased. He appointed personal representatives, or **viceroys**, to rule for him in his colonies. They ruled in his name with complete authority. Since the majority of them were friends and advisers, they were richly rewarded with land grants, gold and silver, privileges of trading, and the right to operate the gold and silver mines.

For the needed labor in the mines and on the plantations, Indians were used first as slaves. However, they either rapidly died out due to a lack of immunity from European diseases or escaped into nearby jungles or mountains. As a result, African slaves were brought in, especially to the islands of the West Indies. Some historians state that Latin American slavery was less harsh than in the later English colonies in North America.

Three reasons for that statement are given:

1. The following of a slave code based on ancient Roman laws
2. The efforts of the Roman Catholic Church to protect and defend slaves because of efforts to convert them;
3. The lack of prejudice due to racial mixtures in Spain, which was once controlled by dark-skinned Moors from North Africa.

Regardless, slavery was still slavery and was very harsh - cruelly denying dignity and human worth.

Spain's control over its New World colonies lasted more than 300 years, longer than England or France. To this day, Spanish influence remains in the names of places, art, architecture, music, literature, law, and cuisine. The Spanish settlements in North America were not commercial enterprises but were for protection and defense of the trading and wealth from their colonies in Mexico and South America. The treasure and wealth found in Spanish New World colonies went back to Spain to be used to buy whatever goods and products were needed instead of setting up industries to make what was needed. As the amount of gold and silver was depleted, Spain could not pay for the goods needed and was unable to produce goods for themselves.

Also, at the same time, Spanish treasure ships at sea were being seized by English and Dutch "pirates" taking the wealth to fill the coffers of their own countries. On land, Russian seal-hunters came down the Pacific coast; the English moved into Florida and west into and beyond the Appalachians; and French traders and trappers made their way from Louisiana and other parts of New France into Spanish territory. Facing encroachment on all sides, and without self-sustaining economic development and colonial trade, the Spanish settlements in the U.S. never really prospered.

By the 1750s in Europe, Spain was "out of the picture," no longer the most powerful nation and not even a contender. The remaining rivalry was between Britain and France. For nearly 25 years, between 1689 and 1748, a series of "armed conflicts" involving these two powers had been taking place. These conflicts had spilled over into North America. The War of the League of Augsburg in Europe, 1689 to 1697, had been King William's War. The War of the Spanish Succession, 1702 to 1713, had been Queen Anne's War. The War of the Austrian Succession, 1740 to 1748, was called King George's War in the colonies. The two nations fought for possession of colonies, especially in Asia and North America, and for control of the seas, but none of these conflicts was decisive.

The final conflict, which decided once and for all who was the most powerful, began in North America in 1754, in the Ohio River Valley. It was known in America as the **French and Indian War** and in Europe as the Seven Years' War, since it began there in 1756. In America, both sides had advantages and disadvantages.

The British colonies were well established and consolidated in a smaller area. British colonists outnumbered French colonists 23 to 1. Except for a small area in Canada, French settlements were scattered over a much larger area (roughly half of the continent) and were smaller. However, the French settlements were united under one government and were quick to act and cooperate when necessary. In addition, the French had many more Indian allies than the British. The British colonies had separate, individual governments and very seldom cooperated, even when needed. In Europe, at that time, France was the more powerful of the two nations.

Both sides had stunning victories and humiliating defeats. If there was one person who could be given the credit for British victory, it would have to be **William Pitt**. He was a strong leader, enormously energetic, supremely self-confident, and determined on a complete British victory. Despite the advantages and military victories of the French, Pitt succeeded. He got rid of the incompetents in the army and replaced them with men who could do the job. He sent more troops to America, strengthened the British navy, gave to the officers of the colonial militias equal rank to the British officers - in short, he saw to it that Britain took the offensive and kept it to victory. Of all the British victories, perhaps the most crucial and important was winning Canada.

The French depended on the St. Lawrence River for transporting supplies, soldiers, and messages-the link between New France and the Mother Country. Tied into this waterway system were the connecting links of the Great Lakes, Mississippi River and its tributaries along which were scattered French forts, trading posts, and small settlements. When, in 1758, the British captured Louisburg on Cape Breton Island, New France was doomed. Louisburg gave the British navy a base of operations preventing French reinforcements and supplies getting to their troops. Other forts fell to the British: Frontenac, Duquesne, Crown Point, Ticonderoga, Niagara, those in the upper Ohio Valley, and, most importantly, Quebec and finally Montreal. Spain entered the war in 1762 to aid France but it was too late. British victories occurred all around the world: in India, in the Mediterranean, and in Europe.

In 1763 in Paris, Spain, France, and Britain met to draw up the **Treaty of Paris** to end the Seven Years' War. Great Britain got most of India and all of North America east of the Mississippi River, except for New Orleans. Britain received from Spain control of Florida and returned to Spain Cuba and the islands of the Philippines, taken during the war. France lost nearly all of its possessions in America and India and was allowed to keep four islands: Guadeloupe, Martinique, Haiti on Hispaniola, and Miquelon and St. Pierre. France gave Spain New Orleans and the vast territory of Louisiana, west of the Mississippi River. Britain was now the most powerful nation--period.

Skill 2.1c   Analyze the effects of English, French, Dutch, and Spanish colonial rule on social, economic, and governmental structures in North America, and the relationships of these colonies with American Indian societies.

Colonists from England, France, Holland, Sweden, and Spain all settled in North America, on lands once frequented by Native Americans. Spanish colonies were mainly in the south, French colonies were mainly in the extreme north and in the middle of the continent, and the rest of the European colonies were in the northeast and along the Atlantic coast. These colonists got along with their new neighbors with varying degrees of success.

Of all of them, the French colonists seemed the most willing to work with the Native Americans. Even though their pursuit of animals to fill the growing demand for the fur trade was overpowering, they managed to find a way to keep their new neighbors happy. The French and Native Americans even fought on the same side of the war against England.

The Dutch and Swedish colonists were interested mainly in surviving in their new homes. The Dutch West India Company founded a colony in what is now New York, establishing it as New Holland. It was eventually captured by English settlers and named New York, but many of the Dutch families that had been granted large segments of land by the Dutch government were allowed to keep their estates. As hostility built between England and the colonies over the taxation of tea, colonists turned to the Dutch to supply them with this important import.

The English and Spanish colonists had the worst relations with the Native Americans, mainly because the Europeans made a habit of taking land, signing and then breaking treaties, massacring, and otherwise abusing their new neighbors. The Native Americans were only too happy to share their agriculture and jewel-making secrets with the Europeans; what they got in return was grief and deceit. The term "Manifest Destiny" meant nothing to the Native Americans, who believed that they lived on land granted access to them by the gods above.

The colonies were divided generally into the three regions of New England, Middle Atlantic, and Southern. The culture of each was distinct and affected attitudes, ideas towards politics, religion, and economic activities. The geography of each region also contributed to its unique characteristics.

The **New England** colonies consisted of **Massachusetts, Rhode Island, Connecticut,** and **New Hampshire**. Life in these colonies was centered on the towns. Each family farmed its own plot of land but a short summer growing season and limited amount of good soil gave rise to other economic activities such as manufacturing, fishing, shipbuilding, and trade. The vast majority of the settlers shared similar origins, coming from England and Scotland. Towns were carefully planned and laid out the same way. The form of government was the **town meeting** where all adult males met to make the laws. The legislative body, the General Court, consisted of an upper and lower house.

The **Middle or Middle Atlantic** colonies included **New York, New Jersey, Pennsylvania, Delaware,** and **Maryland**. New York and New Jersey were at one time the Dutch colony of New Netherland and Delaware at one time was New Sweden. These five colonies, from their beginnings were considered "melting pots" with settlers from many different nations and backgrounds. The main economic activity was farming with the settlers scattered over the countryside cultivating rather large farms. The Indians were not as much of a threat as in New England so they did not have to settle in small farming villages. The soil was very fertile, the land was gently rolling, and a milder climate provided a longer growing season. These farms produced a large surplus of food, not only for the colonists themselves but also for sale. This colonial region became known as the "breadbasket" of the New World and the New York and Philadelphia seaports were constantly filled with ships being loaded with meat, flour, and other foodstuffs for the West Indies and England.

There were other economic activities such as shipbuilding, iron mines, and factories producing paper, glass, and textiles. The legislative body in Pennsylvania was unicameral or consisted of one house. In the other four colonies, the legislative body had two houses. Also units of local government were in counties and towns.

The **Southern** colonies were **Virginia, North and South Carolina,** and **Georgia.** Virginia was the first permanent successful English colony and Georgia was the last. The year 1619 was a very important year in the history of Virginia and the United States with three very significant events. First, sixty women were sent to Virginia to marry and establish families; second, twenty Africans, the first of thousands, arrived; and third, most importantly, the Virginia colonists were granted the right to self-government and they began by electing their own representatives to the **House of Burgesses**, their own legislative body.

The major economic activity in this region was farming. Here too the soil was very fertile and the climate was very mild with an even longer growing season. The large plantations eventually requiring large numbers of slaves were found in the coastal or tidewater areas. Although the wealthy slave-owning planters set the pattern of life in this region, most of the people lived inland away from coastal areas. They were small farmers and very few, it any, owned slaves.

The settlers in these four colonies came from diverse backgrounds and cultures. Virginia was colonized mostly by people from England while Georgia was started as a haven for debtors from English prisons. Pioneers from Virginia settled in North Carolina while South Carolina welcomed people from England and Scotland, French Protestants, Germans, and emigrants from islands in the West Indies. Products from farms and plantations included rice, tobacco, indigo, cotton, some corn and wheat. Other economic activities included lumber and naval stores (tar, pitch, rosin, and turpentine) from the pine forests and fur trade on the frontier. Cities such as Savannah and Charleston were important seaports and trading centers.

In the colonies, the daily life of the colonists differed greatly between the coastal settlements and the inland or interior. The Southern planters and the people living in the coastal cities and towns had a way of life similar to that in towns in England. The influence was seen and heard in the way people dressed and talked; the architectural styles of houses and public buildings; and the social divisions or levels of society. Both the planters and city dwellers enjoyed an active social life and had strong emotional ties to England.

On the other hand, life inland on the frontier had marked differences. All facets of daily living--clothing, food, home, economic and social activities--were all connected to what was needed to sustain life and survive in the wilderness. Everything was produced practically themselves. They were self-sufficient and extremely individualistic and independent. There were little, if any, levels of society or class distinctions as they considered themselves to be the equal to all others, regardless of station in life. The roots of equality, independence, individual rights and freedoms were extremely strong and well developed. People were not judged by their fancy dress, expensive house, eloquent language, or titles following their names.

Skill 2.1d   Describe the institutionalization of African slavery in the Western Hemisphere and analyze its consequences in sub-Saharan Africa.

Slavery in the English colonies began in 1619 when twenty Africans arrived in the colony of Virginia at Jamestown. From then on, slavery had a foothold, especially in the agricultural South, where a large amount of slave labor was needed for the extensive plantations. Free men refused to work for wages on the plantations when land was available for settling on the frontier. Therefore, slave labor was the only recourse left. If it had been profitable to use slaves in New England and the Middle Colonies, then without doubt slavery would have been more widespread. However, it came down to whether or not slavery was profitable. It was in the South, but not in the other two colonial regions.

Slavery began in the Western Hemisphere in 1619 and ended in 1865. During that time, thousands and thousands of African people were brought against their will from their homes to America and elsewhere, as property of other people. The practice of slavery in America ended only after the South's final defeat in the Civil War and the passage of the Thirteenth Amendment, which outlawed slavery. America's Caribbean neighbor, Haiti, had ended slavery a half-century before, thanks to the heroics of Toussaint L'Ouverture.

The effect of this Western Hemisphere slavery on sub-Saharan Africa was traumatic. First and foremost, a tremendous number of people were forcibly removed from their homes. In some cases, entirely families were taken prisoner; in other cases, only the adults or only the men were taken. In the latter cases, families were split asunder, with those left behind struggling to make a new life for themselves, often without those who could work the hardest to do so. A decrease in population might have meant less people to consume the natural resources, but it also meant fewer hands to do the work that needed to be done to produce goods that could be traded for food and money.

Some people in Africa made quite a good living selling others to be enslaved in America. They were not always popular with their fellow Africans, but they did make a lot of money. When the Civil War ended and slavery was outlawed in America, this lucrative practice was no longer available. A money-making practice that had endured for more than 200 years had suddenly ended.

Skill 2.1e   Analyze the causes for the War for Independence, the conduct of the war, and its impact on Americans.

The war for independence occurred due to a number of changes, the two most important ones being economic and political. By the end of the French and Indian War in 1763, Britain's American colonies were thirteen out of a total of thirty-three scattered around the earth. Like all other countries, Britain strove for having a strong economy and a favorable balance of trade. That delicate required wealth, self-sufficiency, and a powerful army and navy. This is why the overseas colonies developed.

The English colonies, with only a few exceptions, were considered commercial ventures founded to make a profit for the crown, or the company, or whoever financed its beginnings. The colonies would provide raw materials for the industries in the Mother Country, be a market for finished products by buying them and assist the Mother Country in becoming powerful and strong. In the case of Great Britain, a strong merchant fleet would provide training for the Royal Navy as well as provide places as bases of operation.

Trade explains the major reason for British encouragement and support of colonization, especially in North America. So between 1607 and 1763, at various times for various reasons, the British Parliament enacted different laws to assist the government in getting and keeping this trade balance. One series of laws required that most of the manufacturing be done only in England, such as the prohibition on exporting any wool or woolen cloth from the colonies, and no manufacture of beaver hats or iron products. The didn't concern the colonists as they had no money and no highly skilled labor to set up any industries, anyway. Other acts had greater impact.

The **Navigation Acts of 1651** put restrictions on shipping and trade within the British Empire by requiring that it was allowed only on British ships. This increased the strength of the British merchant fleet and greatly benefited the American colonists. Since they were British citizens, they could have their own vessels, and build and operate them as well. By the end of the war in 1763, the shipyards in the colonies were building one third of the merchant ships under the British flag. There were quite a number of wealthy, American, colonial merchants.

The **Navigation Act of 1660** restricted the shipment and sale of colonial products to England only. In 1663 another Navigation Act stipulated that the colonies had to buy manufactured products only from England and that any European goods going to the colonies had to go to England first. These acts were a protection from enemy ships and pirates and from competition from European rivals.

The New England and Middle Atlantic colonies at first felt threatened by these laws as they had started producing many of the same products being produced in Britain. But they soon found new markets for their goods and began their own **"triangular trade."** Colonial vessels started the first part of the triangle by sailing for Africa loaded with kegs of rum from colonial distilleries. On Africa's West Coast, the rum was traded for either gold or slaves. The second part of the triangle was from Africa to the West Indies where slaves were traded for molasses, sugar, or money. The third part of the triangle was home, bringing sugar or molasses (to make more rum), gold, and silver.

The major concern of the British government was that the trade violated the 1733 **Molasses Act**. Planters had wanted the colonists to buy all of their molasses in the British West Indies but these islands could give the traders only about one eighth of the amount of molasses needed for distilling the rum. The colonists were forced to buy the rest of what they needed from the French, Dutch, and Spanish islands, thus evading the law by not paying the high duty on the molasses bought from these islands. If Britain had enforced the Molasses Act, economic and financial chaos and ruin would have occurred. So for this act and all the other mercantile laws, the government followed the policy of "salutary neglect," deliberately failing to enforce the laws.

In 1763, after the war, money was needed to pay the British war debt, for the defense of the empire, and to pay for the governing of thirty-three colonies scattered around the earth. It was decided to adopt a new colonial policy and pass laws to raise revenue. It was reasoned that the colonists were subjects of the king, and since the king and his ministers had spent a great deal of money defending and protecting them (this especially for the American colonists), it was only right and fair that the colonists should help pay the costs of defense, especially theirs. The earlier laws passed had been for the purposes of regulating production and trade which generally put money into colonial pockets. These new laws would take some of that rather hard-earned money out of their pockets and it would be done, in colonial eyes, unjustly and illegally.

As the proportion of English-born colonists decreased and the diversity of settlers increased, fewer and fewer colonists felt a cultural tie to the country that held so much influence over the colonies' trade and government. Divisions between the colonies became more pronounced as settlers of differing religious and national groups established themselves.

Government of the colonies differed depending on the type of colony. Each colony had a lower legislative assembly that was elected and a higher council and governor that were elected or appointed in different ways depending on the how the colony was organized initially. In most colonies, the councils and governors were appointed by the King of England or by British property owners or agencies. In corporate colonies, the council and governors were elected by colonial property owners who maintained a close connection to England.

Thus, while the colonies were allowed to tax themselves and regulate much of their daily lives through representation in the colonial assemblies, Britain maintained control of international affairs and international trade by controlling the upper levels of colonial government. In practice, Britain allowed the colonies to go about their business without interference, largely because the colonies were providing important raw materials to the home country.

The first glimmers of dissent from the colonies came during the French and Indian War, in which **colonial militias** were raised to fight the French in America. Conflict arose with Britain over who should control these militias, with the colonies wanting the assemblies to have authority. Following the British victory over the French, Britain found itself in debt from the war and looked to the colonies to provide revenue. Britain began enforcing taxes on colonial trade that it had ignored prior to the war and began passing new regulations.

The thirteen colonies also began to realize that cooperating with each other was the only way to defend themselves. That last lesson wouldn't be fully implemented until the time came for the war for independence and establishing a national government, but a start had been made. Shortly after the start of the war in 1754, the French and their Indian allies had defeated Major George Washington and his militia at Fort Necessity. This left the entire northern frontier of the British colonies vulnerable and open to attack. In the wake of this, Benjamin Franklin proposed to the thirteen colonies that they unite permanently to be able to defend themselves.

Delegates from seven of the thirteen colonies met at Albany, New York, along with the representatives from the Iroquois Confederation and British officials. Franklin's proposal, known as the Albany Plan of Union, was rejected by the colonists, along with a similar proposal from the British. Delegates simply did not want each of the colonies to lose its right to act independently. However, the seed was planted.

Before 1763, except for trade and supplying raw materials, the colonies had mostly been left to themselves. England looked on them merely as part of an economic or commercial empire. Little consideration was given as to how they were to conduct their daily affairs, so the colonists became very independent, self-reliant, and extremely skillful at handling those daily affairs. This, in turn, gave rise to leadership, initiative, achievement, and vast experience. In fact, there was a far greater degree of independence and self-government in America than could be found in Britain or the major countries on the Continent or any other colonies anywhere.

In America, as new towns and counties were formed, there began the practice' of representation in government. Representatives to the colonial legislative assemblies were elected from the district in which they lived, chosen by qualified property-owning male voters, and representing the interests of the political district from which they were elected. Each of the thirteen colonies had a royal governor appointed by the king, representing his interests in the colonies. Nevertheless, the colonial legislative assemblies controlled the purse strings by having the power to vote on all issues involving money to be spent by the colonial governments.

Contrary to this was the established government in England. Members of Parliament were not elected to represent their own districts. They were considered representative of classes, not individuals. If some members of a professional or commercial class or some landed interests were able to elect representatives, then those classes or special interests were represented. It had nothing at all to do with numbers or territories. Some large population centers had no direct representation at all, yet the people there considered themselves represented by men elected from their particular class or interest somewhere else. Consequently, it was extremely difficult for the English to understand why the American merchants and landowners claimed they were not represented because they themselves did not vote for members of Parliament.

The colonists' protest of, "**No taxation without representation**" was meaningless to the English. Parliament represented the entire nation, was completely unlimited in legislation, and had become supreme. The colonists were incensed at this English attitude and considered their colonial legislative assemblies equal to Parliament, a position which was totally unacceptable in England. There were now two different environments: the older, traditional British system in the Mother Country, and the American system with its new ideas and different ways of doing things. In a new country, a new environment has little or no tradition, institutions or vested interests. New ideas and traditions grew extremely fast, pushing aside what was left of the old ideas and old traditions. By 1763, Britain had changed its perception of its American colonies to their being a "territorial" empire. The stage was set and the conditions were right for a showdown.

In 1763, Parliament decided to have a standing army in North America to reinforce British control. In 1765, the **Quartering Act** was passed requiring the colonists to provide supplies and living quarters for the British troops. In addition, efforts by the British were made to keep the peace by establishing good relations with the Indians. Consequently, a proclamation was issued which prohibited any American colonists from making any settlements west of the Appalachians until provided for through treaties with the Indians.

The **Sugar Act of 1764** required efficient collection of taxes on any molasses that were brought into the colonies and gave British officials free license to conduct searches of the premises of anyone suspected of violating the law. The colonists were taxed on newspapers, legal documents, and other printed matter under the **Stamp Act of 1765**. Nine colonies assembled in New York to call for the repeal of the Act. At the same time, a group of New York merchants organized a protest to stop the importation of British goods. Similar protests arose in Philadelphia and Boston and other merchant cities, often erupting in violence. As Britain's representatives in the colonies, the governors and members of the cabinet and council were sometimes the targets of these protests. Although a stamp tax was already in use in England, the colonists would have none of it and after the ensuing uproar of rioting and mob violence, Parliament repealed the tax.

Of course, great exultation resulted when news of the repeal reached America. However, what no one noticed was the small, quiet Declaratory Act attached to the repeal. This act plainly, unequivocally stated that Parliament still had the right to make all laws for the colonies and denied their right to be taxed only by their own colonial legislatures - a very crucial, important piece of legislation, virtually overlooked and unnoticed at the time. Other acts leading up to armed conflict included the **Townshend Acts** passed in 1767 taxing lead, paint, paper, and tea brought into the colonies. This, too, increased anger and tension resulting in the British sending troops to New York City and Boston. In Boston, mob violence provoked retaliation by the troops thus bringing about the deaths of five people and the wounding of eight others. The so-called **Boston Massacre** shocked Americans and British alike.

Meanwhile, increased contact between colonials had allowed a growing patriot movement to gain foothold and the issue of independence arose in common thought. When Britain proposed that the East India Company be allowed to import tea to the colonies without customs duty, the colonists were faced with a dilemma. They could purchase the tea at a much lower price than the smuggled Dutch tea they had been drinking, however tea was still subject to the Townshend Act, and to purchase it would be an acceptance of this act. The **Boston Tea Party** was the result, where a group of colonists seized a shipment of British tea in Boston Harbor and dumped it into the sea.

Britain responded with a series of even more restrictive acts, driving the colonies to come together in the **First Continental Congress** to make a unified demand that Britain remove these **Intolerable Acts**, as they were called by the colonists.

In 1774, the passage of the **Quebec Act** extended the limits of that Canadian colony's boundary southward to include territory located north of the Ohio River. However, the punishment for Boston's Tea Party came in the same year with the Intolerable Acts. Boston's port was closed; the royal governor of the colony of Massachusetts was given increased power, and the colonists were compelled to house and feed the British soldiers. The propaganda activities of the patriot organizations **Sons of Liberty** and **Committees of Correspondence** kept the opposition and resistance before everyone.

Delegates from twelve colonies met in Philadelphia September 5, 1774, in the **First Continental Congress**. They definitely opposed acts of lawlessness and wanted some form of peaceful settlement with Britain. They still maintained American loyalty to the Mother Country, however, and affirmed Parliament's power over colonial foreign affairs. They did insist on repeal of the **Intolerable Acts** and demanded ending all trade with Britain until this took place. The reply from George III, the last king of America, was an insistence of colonial submission to British rule or be crushed.

Britain stood firm and sought to dissolve the colonial assemblies that were coming forth in opposition to British policies, and were stockpiling weapons and preparing militias. When the British military in America were ordered to break up the illegal meeting of the Massachusetts' assembly outside Boston, they were met with armed resistance at **Lexington and Concord** on April 19, 1775, and the Revolutionary War was underway. The Second Continental Congress met a month later in Philadelphia on May 10th to conduct the business of war and government for the next six years. Many of the delegates recommended a declaration of independence from Britain. The group established an army and commissioned George Washington as its commander.

British forces attacked patriot strongholds at Breed's Hill and **Bunker Hill**. Although the colonists withdrew, the loss of life for the British was nearly fifty percent of the army. The next month King George III declared the American colonies to be in a state of rebellion. The war quickly began in earnest.

Although the colonial army was quite small in comparison to the British army, and although it was lacking in formal military training, the colonists had learned a new method of warfare from the Indians. To be sure, many battles were fought in the traditional style of two lines of soldiers facing off and firing weapons. But the advantage the patriots had was the understanding of guerilla warfare – fighting from behind trees and other defenses, and more importantly, fighting on the run.

By 1776, the colonists and their representatives in the Second Continental Congress realized that things were past the point of no return. On July 3, 1776, British General Howe arrived in New York harbor with 10,000 troops to prepare for an attack on the city. The next day, the **Declaration of Independence** was drafted and declared July 4, 1776.
The first American victory of the Revolutionary War followed a surprise attack of Continental troops under the command of George Washington on British and Hessian troops at **Trenton**, New Jersey. Washington and his men crossed the icy **Delaware River** on Christmas Day, 1776, and attacked the next day, completely surprising the British. It helped to restore American morale.

Washington labored against tremendous odds to wage a victorious war. Although the suffering of troops during the winter of 177-1778 at **Valley Forge** is part of American folklore, other winter ordeals were probably worse; Valley Forge is well known because Washington stressed his army's suffering in order to gain political support. However, the army's discipline and efficiency improved during the winter, which marked a turning point in the war, and the encampment became a symbol of endurance in adversity.

The turning point in the Americans' favor occurred in 1777 with the American victory at **Saratoga**. This victory led to the French to aligning themselves with the Americans against the British. With the aid of Admiral deGrasse and French warships blocking the entrance to Chesapeake Bay, British General Cornwallis trapped at **Yorktown**, Virginia, surrendered in 1781 and the war was over. The Treaty of Paris officially ending the war was signed in 1783.

When the war began, the colonies began to establish state governments. To a significant extent, the government that was defined for the new nation was intentionally weak. The colonies/states feared centralized government. But the lack of continuity between the individual governments was confusing and economically damaging.

COMPETENCY 2.2 THE DEVELOPMENT OF THE CONSTITUTION AND THE EARLY REPUBLIC

Skill 2.2a **Describe and evaluate the impact of the Enlightenment and the unique colonial experiences on the writing of the Declaration of Independence, Articles of Confederation, the Federalist Papers, the Constitution, and the Bill of Rights.**

Democracy is loosely defined as "rule by the people," either directly or through representatives. Associated with the idea of democracy are freedom, equality, and opportunity. The basic concept of democracy existed in the thirteen English colonies with the practice of independent self-government. The right of qualified persons to vote, hold office and actively participate in his or her own government is sometimes referred to as "political" democracy. "Social" and "economic" democracy pertain to the idea that all have the opportunity to get an education, choose their own careers, and live as free men everyday all equal in the eyes of the law to everyone.

These three concepts of democracy were basic reasons why people came to the New World and the practices of these concepts continued through the colonial and revolutionary periods and were extremely influential in the shaping of the new central government under the Constitution.

The Declaration of Independence is an outgrowth of both ancient Greek ideas of democracy and individual rights and the ideas of the European Enlightenment and the Renaissance, especially the ideology of the political thinker **John Locke**. **Thomas Jefferson** (1743-1826) the principle author of the Declaration borrowed much from Locke's theories and writings. John Locke was one of the most influential political writers of the 17th century who put great emphasis on human rights and put forth the belief that when governments violate those rights people should rebel. He wrote the book "*Two Treatises of Government*" in 1690, which had tremendous influence on political thought in the American colonies and helped shaped the U.S. Constitution and Declaration of Independence.

Essentially, Jefferson applied Locke's principles to the contemporary American situation. Jefferson argued that the reigning King George III had repeatedly violated the rights of the colonists as subjects of the British Crown. Disdaining the colonial petition for redress of grievances (a right guaranteed by the Declaration of Rights of 1689), the King seemed bent upon establishing an "absolute tyranny" over the colonies. Such disgraceful behavior itself violated the reasons for which government had been instituted. The American colonists were left with no choice, *"it is their right, it is their duty, to throw off such a government, and to provide new guards for their future security"* so wrote Thomas Jefferson.

Yet, though his fundamental principles were derived from Locke's, Jefferson was bolder than his intellectual mentor was. He went farther in that his view of natural rights was much broader than Locke's and less tied to the idea of property rights.

For instance, though both Jefferson and Locke believed very strongly in property rights, especially as a guard for individual liberty, the famous line in the Declaration about people being endowed with the inalienable right to "life, liberty and the pursuit of happiness," was slightly different from Locke's original idea. That was "life, liberty, and *private property.*" Jefferson didn't want to tie the idea of rights to any one particular circumstance however, thus, he changed Locke's original specific reliance on property and substituted the more general idea of human happiness as being a fundamental right that is the duty of a government to protect.

Locke and Jefferson both stressed that the individual citizen's rights are prior to and more important than any obligation to the state. Government is the servant of the people. The officials of government hold their positions at the sufferance of the people. Their job is to ensure that the rights of the people are preserved and protected by that government. The citizen comes first, the government comes second. The Declaration thus produced turned out to be one of the most important and historic documents that expounded the inherent rights of all peoples; a document still looked up to as an ideal and an example.

The Declaration was intended to demonstrate the reasons that the colonies were seeking separation from Great Britain. Conceived by and written for the most part by Thomas Jefferson, it is not only important for what it says, but also for how it says it. The Declaration is in many respects a poetic document. Instead of a simple recitation of the colonists' grievances, it set out clearly the reasons why the colonists were seeking their freedom from Great Britain. They had tried all means to resolve the dispute peacefully. It was the right of a people, when all other methods of addressing their grievances have been tried and failed, to separate themselves from that power that was keeping them from fully expressing their rights to "**life, liberty, and the pursuit of happiness**".

The **Articles of Confederation** was the first political system under which the newly independent colonies tried to organize themselves. It was drafted after the Declaration of Independence, in 1776, was passed by the Continental Congress on November 15, 1777, ratified by the thirteen states, and took effect on March 1, 1781.

The newly independent states were unwilling to give too much power to a national government. They were already fighting Great Britain. They did not want to replace one harsh ruler with another. After many debates, the form of the Articles was accepted. Each state agreed to send delegates to the Congress. Each state had one vote in the Congress. The Articles gave Congress the power to declare war, appoint military officers, and coin money. The Congress was also responsible for foreign affairs. The Articles of Confederation limited the powers of Congress by giving the states final authority. Although Congress could pass laws, at least nine of the thirteen states had to approve a law before it went into effect. Congress could not pass any laws regarding taxes. To get money, Congress had to ask each state for it, no state could be forced to pay.

Thus, the Articles created a loose alliance among the thirteen states. The national government was weak, in part, because it didn't have a strong chief executive to carry out laws passed by the legislature. This weak national government might have worked if the states were able to get along with each other. However, many different disputes arose and there was no way of settling them. Thus, the delegates went to meet again to try to fix the Articles; instead they ended up scrapping them and created a new Constitution that learned from these earlier mistakes.

The central government of the new United States of America consisted of a Congress of two to seven delegates from each state with each state having just one vote. The government under the Articles solved some of the postwar problems but had serious weaknesses. Some of its powers included: borrowing and coining money, directing foreign affairs, declaring war and making peace, building and equipping a navy, regulating weights and measures, asking the states to supply men and money for an army. The delegates to Congress had no real authority as each state carefully and jealously guarded its own interests and limited powers under the Articles. Also, the delegates to Congress were paid by their states and had to vote as directed by their state legislatures. The serious weaknesses were the lack of power: to regulate finances, over interstate trade, over foreign trade, to enforce treaties, and military power. Something better and more efficient was needed.

In May of 1787, delegates from all states except Rhode Island began meeting in Philadelphia. At first, they met to revise the Articles of Confederation as instructed by Congress; but they soon realized that much more was needed. Abandoning the instructions, they set out to write a new Constitution, a new document, the foundation of all government in the United States and a model for representative government throughout the world.

The first order of business was the agreement among all the delegates that the convention would be kept secret. No discussion of the convention outside of the meeting room would be allowed. They wanted to be able to discuss, argue, and agree among themselves before presenting the completed document to the American people.

The delegates were afraid that if the people were aware of what was taking place before it was completed the entire country would be plunged into argument and dissension. It would be extremely difficult, if not impossible, to settle differences and come to an agreement. Between the official notes kept and the complete notes of future President James Madison, an accurate picture of the events of the Convention is part of the historical record.

The delegates went to Philadelphia representing different areas and different interests. They all agreed on a strong central government but not one with unlimited powers. They also agreed that no one part of government could control the rest. It would be a republican form of government (sometimes referred to as representative democracy) in which the supreme power was in the hands of the voters who would elect the men who would govern for them.

One of the first serious controversies involved the small states versus the large states over representation in Congress. Virginia's Governor Edmund Randolph proposed that state population determine the number of representatives sent to Congress, also known as the **Virginia Plan**. New Jersey delegate William Paterson countered with what is known as the **New Jersey Plan**, each state having equal representation.

After much argument and debate, the **Great Compromise** was devised, known also as the Connecticut Compromise, as proposed by Roger Sherman. It was agreed that Congress would have two houses. The Senate would have two Senators, giving equal powers in the Senate. The House of Representatives would have its members elected based on each state's population. Both houses could draft bills to debate and vote on with the exception of bills pertaining to money, which must originate in the House of Representatives.

Another controversy involved economic differences between North and South. One concerned the counting of the African slaves for determining representation in the House of Representatives. The southern delegates wanted this but didn't want it to determine taxes to be paid. The northern delegates argued the opposite: count the slaves for taxes but not for representation. The resulting agreement was known as the **"three-fifths" compromise**. Three-fifths of the slaves would be counted for both taxes and determining representation in the House.

The last major compromise, also between North and South, was the **Commerce Compromise**. The economic interests of the northern part of the country were ones of industry and business whereas the south's economic interests were primarily in farming. The Northern merchants wanted the government to regulate and control commerce with foreign nations and with the states. Southern planters opposed this idea as they felt that any tariff laws passed would be unfavorable to them.

The acceptable compromise to this dispute was that Congress was given the power to regulate commerce with other nations and the states, including levying tariffs on imports. However, Congress did not have the power to levy tariffs on any exports. This increased Southern concern about the effect it would have on the slave trade. The delegates finally agreed that the importation of slaves would continue for 20 more years with no interference from Congress. Any import tax could not exceed 10 dollars per person. After 1808, Congress would be able to decide whether to prohibit or regulate any further importation of slaves.

Once work was completed and the document was presented, nine states needed to approve for it to go into effect. There was no little amount of discussion, arguing, debating, and haranguing. The opposition had three major objections:

1. The states felt they were being asked to surrender too much power to the national government.
2. The voters did not have enough control and influence over the men who would be elected by them to run the government.
3. A lack of a "bill of rights" guaranteeing hard-won individual freedoms and liberties.

Eleven states finally ratified the document and the new national government went into effect. It was no small feat that the delegates were able to produce a workable document that satisfied all opinions, feelings, and viewpoints. The separation of powers of the three branches of government and the built-in system of checks and balances to keep power balanced were a stroke of genius. It provided for the individuals and the states as well as an organized central authority to keep a new inexperienced young nation on track.

They created a government that as Benjamin Franklin said, *"though it may not be the best there is";* he said that he, *"wasn't sure that it could be possible to create one better".* A fact that might be true considering that the Constitution has lasted, through civil war, foreign wars, depression, and social revolution for over 200 years.

It is truly a living document because of its ability to remain strong while allowing itself to be changed with changing times.

Skill 2.2b   **Examine the issues regarding ratification of the Constitution, and compare and contrast the positions of the Federalists and Anti-Federalists.**

Ratification of the U.S. Constitution was by no means a foregone conclusion. The representative government had powerful enemies, especially those who had seen firsthand the failure of the Articles of Confederation. The strong central government had powerful enemies, including some of the guiding lights of the American Revolution.

Those who wanted to see a strong central government were called **Federalists**, because they wanted to see a federal government reign supreme Among the leaders of the Federalists were Alexander Hamilton and John Jay. These two, along with James Madison, wrote a series of letters to New York newspapers, urging that that state ratify the Constitution. These became known as the **Federalist Papers**.

In the Anti-Federalist camp were Thomas Jefferson and Patrick Henry. These men and many others like them were worried that a strong national government would descend into the kind of tyranny that they had just worked so hard to abolish. In the same way that they took their name from their foes, they wrote a series of arguments against the Constitution called the **Anti-Federalist Papers.**

In the end, both sides got most of what they wanted. The Federalists got their strong national government, which was held in place by the famous "checks and balances." The Anti-Federalists got the Bill of Rights, the first ten Amendments to the Constitution and a series of laws that protect some of the most basic of human rights. The states that were in doubt for ratification of the Constitution signed on when the Bill of Rights was promised.

COMPETENCY 2.3   THE EMERGENCE OF A NEW NATION

Skill 2.3a   Describe the differing visions of the early political parties and explain the reasons for the respective successes and failures of those parties.

In regards to the American political system, it is important to realize that political parties are never mentioned in the United States Constitution. In fact, George Washington himself warned against the creation of "factions" in American politics that cause "jealousies and false alarms" and the damage they could cause to the body politic. Thomas Jefferson echoed this warning, yet he would come to lead a party himself.

In 1789 the Electoral College unanimously elected George Washington as the first President and the new nation was on its way. The early presidential administrations established much of the form and many of the procedures still present today, including the development of the party system. George Washington, the first US President, established a cabinet form of government, with individual advisors overseeing the various functions of the executive branch and advising the President, who makes a final decision. Divisions within his cabinet and within Congress during his administration eventually led to the development of political parties, which Washington himself opposed.

By the time Washington retired from office in 1796, the new political parties would come to play an important role in choosing his successor. Each party would put up its own candidates for office. The election of 1796 was the first one in which political parties played a role. A role that, for better or worse, they have continued to play in various forms for all of American history.

Washington's Vice President, **John Adams**, was elected to succeed him. Adams' administration was marked by the new nation's first entanglement in international affairs. Britain and France were at war, with Adams' Federalist Party supporting the British and Vice President Thomas Jefferson's Republican Party supporting the French. The nation was brought nearly to the brink of war with France, but Adams managed to negotiate a treaty that avoided full conflict. In the process, however, he lost the support of his party and was defeated after one term by Thomas Jefferson.

Americans had good reason to fear the emergence of political parties. They had witnessed how parties worked in Great Britain. Parties, called "factions" in Britain, thus Washington's warning, were made up of a few people who schemed to win favors from the government. They were more interested in their own personal profit and advantage than in the public good. Thus, the new American leaders were very interested in keeping factions from forming. It was, ironically, disagreements between two of Washington's chief advisors, **Thomas Jefferson** and **Alexander Hamilton**, that spurred the formation of the first political parties in the newly formed United States of America.

The two parties that developed through the early 1790s were led by Jefferson as the Secretary of State and Alexander Hamilton as the Secretary of the Treasury. Jefferson and Hamilton were different in many ways. Not the least was their views on what should be the proper form of government of the United States. This difference helped to shape the parties that formed around them.

Hamilton wanted the federal government to be stronger than the state governments. Jefferson believed that the state governments should be stronger. Hamilton supported the creation of the first Bank of the United States. Jefferson opposed it because he felt that it gave too much power to wealthy investors who would help run it.

Jefferson interpreted the Constitution strictly; he argued that nowhere did the Constitution give the federal government the power to create a national bank. He believed that the common people, especially the farmers, were the backbone of the nation. He thought that the rise of big cities and manufacturing would corrupt American life.

Hamilton interpreted the Constitution much more loosely. He pointed out that the Constitution gave Congress the power to make all laws "necessary and proper" to carry out its duties. He reasoned that since Congress had the right to collect taxes, then Congress had the right to create the bank. Hamilton wanted the government to encourage economic growth. He favored the growth of trade, manufacturing, and the rise of cities as the necessary parts of economic growth. He favored the business leaders and mistrusted the common people.

Finally, Hamilton and Jefferson had their disagreements only in private. But when Congress began to pass many of Hamilton's ideas and programs, Jefferson and his friend, James Madison, decided to organize support for their own views. They moved quietly and very cautiously in the beginning. In 1791, they went to New York telling people that they were going to just study its wildlife.

Actually, Jefferson was more interested in meeting with several important New York politicians such as it' governor George Clinton and Aaron Burr, a strong critic of Hamilton. Jefferson asked Clinton and Burr to help defeat Hamilton's program by getting New Yorkers to vote for Jefferson's supporters in the next election. Before long, leaders in other states began to organize support for either Jefferson or Hamilton. Jefferson's supporters called themselves **Democratic-Republicans** (often this was shortened just to Republicans, though in actuality it was the forerunner of today's Democratic Party). Hamilton and his supporters were known as **Federalists**, because they favored a strong federal government. The Federalists had the support of the merchants and ship owners in the Northeast and some planters in the South. Small farmers, craft workers, and some of the wealthier landowners supported Jefferson and the Democratic-Republicans.

By the beginning of the 1800s, the Federalist Party, torn by internal divisions, began suffering a decline. The election in 1800 of Thomas Jefferson as President, Hamilton's bitter rival, and after its leader Alexander Hamilton was killed in 1804 in a duel with Aaron Burr, the Federalist Party began to collapse. By 1816, after losing a string of important elections, (Jefferson was reelected in 1804, and James Madison, a Democratic-Republican was elected in 1808), the Federalist Party ceased to be an effective political force, and soon passed off the national stage.

By the late 1820s, new political parties had grown up. The **Democratic-Republican** Party, or simply the **Republican** Party, had been the major party for many years, but differences within it about the direction the country was headed in caused a split after 1824. Those who favored strong national growth took the name **Whigs** after a similar party in Great Britain and united around then President John Quincy Adams. Many business people in the Northeast as well as some wealthy planters in the South, supported it.

Those who favored slower growth and were more worker and small farmer oriented, went on to form the new Democratic Party, with Andrew Jackson being its first leader as well as becoming the first President from it. It is the forerunner of today's present party of the same name.

In the mid-1850s, the slavery issue was beginning to heat up and in 1854, those opposed to slavery, the Whigs, and some Northern Democrats opposed to slavery, united to form the Republican Party. Before the Civil War, the Democratic Party was more heavily represented in the South and was thus pro-slavery for the most part.

Thus, by the time of the Civil War, the present form of the major political parties had been formed. Though there would sometimes be drastic changes in ideology and platforms over the years, no other political parties would manage to gain enough strength to seriously challenge the "Big Two" parties.

In fact, they have shown themselves adaptable to changing times. In many instances, they have managed to shut out other parties by simply adapting their platforms, such as in the 1930s during the Great Depression and in the years immediately preceding. The Democratic Party adapted much of the Socialist Party platform and, under Franklin Roosevelt, put much of it into effect thus managing to eliminate it as any serious threat. Since the Civil War, no other political party has managed to gain enough support to either elect substantial members to Congress or elect a President. Some have come closer than others, but barring any unforeseen circumstances, the absolute monopoly on national political debate seems very secure in the hands of the Republican and Democratic Parties.

Time will tell if this is to remain so. For history and political science both teach us that the American people are quite willing to change their support from one area or group to another. Especially if it means a better way of doing things or will give them more opportunity and freedoms. As conservative as some might think Americans have become, there has always been and always will be, something of the revolutionary spirit about them.

Skill 2.3b   Compare the significant political and socioeconomic ideas and issues during the Jeffersonian and Jacksonian periods and contrast how they were implemented in policy and practice.

European events had profoundly shaped U.S. policies, especially foreign policies. After 1815, the U.S. became much more independent from European influence and began to be treated with growing respect by European nations who were impressed by the fact that the young United States showed no hesitancy in going to war with the world's greatest naval power.

The election of Andrew Jackson as President signaled a swing of the political pendulum from government influence of the wealthy, aristocratic Easterners to the interests of the Western farmers and pioneers and the era of the "common man." Jacksonian democracy was a policy of equal political power for all.

After the War of 1812, Henry Clay and supporters favored economic measures that came to be known as the American System. This involved tariffs protecting American farmers and manufacturers from having to compete with foreign products, stimulating industrial growth and employment. With more people working, more farm products would be consumed, prosperous farmers would be able to buy more manufactured goods, and the additional monies from tariffs would make it possible for the government to make the needed internal improvements. To get all of this going, in 1816, Congress not only passed a high tariff, but also chartered a second Bank of the United States. Upon becoming President, Jackson fought to get rid of the bank.

One of the many duties of the bank was to regulate the supply of money for the nation. The President believed that the bank was a monopoly that favored the wealthy. Congress voted in 1832 to renew the bank's charter but Jackson vetoed the bill, withdrew the government's money, and the bank finally collapsed.

Jackson also faced the "null and void," or nullification issue from South Carolina. Congress, in 1828, passed a law placing high tariffs on goods imported into the United States. Southerners, led by South Carolina's then Vice-President of the U.S., John C. Calhoun, felt that the tariff favored the manufacturing interests of New England, denounced it as an abomination, and claimed that any state could nullify any of the federal laws it considered unconstitutional. The tariff was lowered in 1832, but not low enough to satisfy South Carolina, which promptly threatened to secede from the Union. Although Jackson agreed with the rights of states, he also believed in preservation of the Union. A year later, the tariffs were lowered and the crisis was averted.

Skill 2.3c   Describe American foreign policy prior to the Civil War.

In the early years of the American nation, three primary ideas determined American foreign policy. The first of these, **isolationism,** was perhaps also the most long-lasting. The founding fathers and the earliest Americans (after the Revolution) tended to believe that the U.S. had been created and destined for a unique role as what Thomas Jefferson called the "City on the Hill." They understood personal and religious freedom as a unique blessing given by God to the people of the nation. Although many hoped the nation would grow, this expectation did not extend to efforts to plant colonies in other parts of the world.

The second idea was that of **"No Entangling Alliances."** George Washington's farewell address had initially espoused the intention of avoiding permanent alliances in any part of the world. This was echoed in Jefferson's inaugural address. In fact, when James Madison led the nation into the War of 1812, he refrained from entering an alliance with France, which was also at war with England at the time.

The United States' unintentional and accidental involvement in what was known as the **War of 1812** came about due to the political and economic struggles between France and Great Britain. Napoleon's goal was complete conquest and control of Europe, including and especially Great Britain. Although British troops were temporarily driven off the mainland of Europe, the navy still controlled the seas, the seas across which France had to bring the products needed. America traded with both nations, especially with France and its colonies. The British decided to destroy the American trade with France, mainly for two reasons. First, products and goods from the U.S. gave Napoleon what he needed to keep up his struggle with Britain. He and France was the enemy and it was felt that the Americans were aiding the Mother Country's enemy. Second, Britain felt threatened by the increasing strength and success of the U.S. merchant fleet. They were becoming major competitors with the ship owners and merchants in Britain.

The British issued the **Orders in Council** which was a series of measures prohibiting American ships from entering any French ports, not only in Europe but also in India and the West Indies. At the same time, Napoleon began efforts for a coastal blockade of the British Isles. He issued a series of Orders prohibiting all nations, including the United States, from trading with the British. He threatened seizure of every ship entering French ports after they stopped at any British port or colony, even threatening to seize every ship inspected by British cruisers or that paid any duties to their government. The British were stopping American ships and impressing American seamen to service on British ships. Americans were outraged.

In 1807, Congress passed the **Embargo Act** forbidding American ships from sailing to foreign ports. It couldn't be completely enforced and it also hurt business and trade in America so it was repealed in 1809. Two additional acts passed by Congress after James Madison became president attempted to regulate trade with other nations and to get Britain and France to remove the restrictions they had put on American shipping. The catch was that whichever nation removed restrictions, the U.S. agreed not to trade with the other one. Napoleon was the first to do this, prompting Madison to issue orders prohibiting trade with Britain, ignoring warnings from the British not to do so. Although Britain eventually rescinded the Orders in Council, war came in June of 1812.

During the war, Americans were divided over not only whether or not it was necessary to even fight, but also over what territories should be fought for and taken. The nation was still young and just not prepared for war. The primary American objective to conquer Canada ended in failure. Two naval victories and one military victory stand out for the United States. Oliver Perry gained control of Lake Erie and Thomas MacDonough fought on Lake Champlain. Both of these naval battles successfully prevented the British invasion of the United States from Canada. Nevertheless, British troops did land below Washington on the Potomac, marched into the city, and burned the public buildings, including the White House. Andrew Jackson's victory at New Orleans was a great morale booster to Americans, giving them the impression the U.S. had won the war. The battle actually took place after Britain and the United States had reached an agreement and it had no impact on the war's outcome.

The war ended Christmas Eve, 1814, with the signing of the Treaty of Ghent. The peace treaty did little for the United States other than bringing peace, releasing prisoners of war, restoring all occupied territory, and setting up a commission to settle boundary disputes with Canada. Interestingly, the war proved to be a turning point in American history.

Previously, European events had profoundly shaped U.S. policies, especially foreign policies. In President Monroe's message to Congress on December 2, 1823, he delivered what we have always called the **Monroe Doctrine**. The United States was informing the powers of the Old World that the American continents were no longer open to European colonization, and that any effort to extend European political influence into the New World would be considered by the United States "as dangerous to our peace and safety." The United States would not interfere in European wars or internal affairs, and expected Europe to stay out of American affairs.

Thus the third primary idea, that of **nationalism.** The American experience had created a profound wariness of any encroachment onto the continent by European countries. The Monroe Doctrine was a clear warning: no new colonies in the Americas.

The nineteenth century was the age of "Manifest Destiny" – the belief in the divinely given right of the nation to expand westward and incorporate more of the continent into the nation. This belief had been expressed, at the end of the Revolutionary War, in the demand that Britain cede all lands east of the Mississippi River to America. The goal of expanding westward was further confirmed with the Northwest Ordinance (1787) and the Louisiana Purchase (1803). Manifest Destiny was the justification of the Mexican-American War (1846-48) which resulted in the annexation of Texas and California, as well as much of the southwest.

Skill 2.3d **Identify and describe the political, social, religious, economic, and geographic factors that led to the formation of distinct regional and sectional identities and cultures.**

Regionalism can be defined as the political division of an area into partially autonomous regions or to loyalty to the interests of a particular region. **Sectionalism** is generally defined as excessive devotion to local interests and customs.

When the United States declared independence from England, the founding fathers created a political point of view that created a national unity while respecting the uniqueness and individual rights of each of the thirteen colonies or states. The colonies had been populated and governed by England and other countries. Some came to America in search of religious freedom, others for a fresh start, and others for economic opportunity. Each colony had a particular culture and identity.

As the young nation grew, territories came to be defined as states. The states began to acquire their own particular cultures and identities. In time regional interests and cultures also began to take shape. Religious interests, economic life, and geography began to be understood as definitive of particular regions. The northeast tended toward industrial development. The south tended to rely upon agriculture. The west was an area of untamed open spaces where people settled and practiced agriculture and animal husbandry.

Each of these regions came to be defined, at least to some extent, on the basis of the way people made their living and the economic and social institutions that supported them. In the industrialized north, the factory system tended to create a division between the tycoons of business and industry and the poor industrial workers. The conditions in which the labor force worked were far from ideal – the hours were long, the conditions bad, and the pay was small.

The south was characterized by cities that were centers of social and commercial life. The agriculture that supported the region was practiced on "plantations" that were owned by the wealthy and worked by slaves or indentured servants.

The west was a vast expanse to be explored and tamed. Life on a western ranch was distinctly different from either life in the industrial north or the agricultural south. The challenges of each region were also distinctly different. The role of children in the economy was different; the role of women was different; the importance of trade was different. And religion was called upon to support each unique regional lifestyle.

The regional differences between North and South came to a head over the issue of slavery. The rise of the abolitionist movement in the North, the publication of **Uncle Tom's Cabin**, and issues of trade and efforts by the national government to control trade for the regions coalesced around the issue of slavery in a nation that was founded on the principle of the inalienable right of every person to be free. As the South defended its lifestyle and its economy and the right of the states to be self-determining, the North became stronger in its criticism of slavery. The result was a growing sectionalism.

As the nation extended its borders into the lands west of the Mississippi, thousands of settlers streamed into this part of the country bringing with them ideas and concepts adapting them to the development of the unique characteristics of the region. Equality for everyone, as stated in the Declaration of Independence, did not yet apply to minority groups, black Americans or American Indians. Voting rights and the right to hold public office were restricted in varying degrees in each state. All of these factors decidedly affected the political, economic, and social life of the country and all three were focused in the attitudes of the three sections of the country on slavery.

Skill 2.3e **Describe the purpose, challenges, and economic incentives associated with settlements of the West, including the concept of Manifest Destiny.**

In the United States, territorial expansion occurred in the expansion westward under the banner of "**Manifest Destiny**." In addition, the U.S. was involved in the War with Mexico, the Spanish-American War, and support of the Latin American colonies of Spain in their revolt for independence. In Latin America, the Spanish colonies were successful in their fight for independence and self-government

After the U.S. purchased the Louisiana Territory, Jefferson appointed Captains Meriwether Lewis and William Clark to explore it, to find out exactly what had been bought.With the help of local guides, including a Native American woman named **Sacagawea**, the expedition called the **Corps of Discovery** went all the way to the Pacific Ocean. Having been presumed long since dead, they returned two years later with maps, journals, and artifacts. This led the way for future explorers to make available more knowledge about the territory and resulted in the Westward Movement and the later belief in the doctrine of Manifest Destiny.

It was the belief of many that the United States was destined to control all of the land between the two oceans or as one newspaper editor termed it, "Manifest Destiny." This mass migration westward put the U.S. government on a collision course with the Indians, Great Britain, Spain, and Mexico. The fur traders and missionaries ran up against the Indians in the northwest and the claims of Great Britain for the Oregon country.

The Red River cession was the next acquisition of land and came about as part of a treaty with Great Britain in 1818. It included parts of North and South Dakota and Minnesota. In 1819, Florida, both east and West, was ceded to the U.S. by Spain along with parts of Alabama, Mississippi, and Louisiana. Texas was annexed in 1845 and after the war with Mexico in 1848, the government paid $15 million for what would become the states of California, Utah, and Nevada and parts of four other states.

The U.S. and Britain had shared the Oregon country. By the 1840s, with the increase in the free and slave populations and the demand of the settlers for control and government by the U.S., the conflict had to be resolved. In a treaty, signed in 1846, the **Oregon Country** was ceded to the U.S., which extended the western border to the Pacific Ocean. The northern U.S. boundary was established at the 49th parallel. The states of Idaho, Oregon, and Washington were formed from this territory. In 1853, the **Gadsden Purchase** rounded out the present boundary of the 48 conterminous states with payment to Mexico of $10 million for land that makes up the present states of New Mexico and Arizona.

In the American southwest, the results were exactly the opposite. Spain had claimed this area since the 1540s, had spread northward from Mexico City, and, in the 1700s, had established missions, forts, villages, towns, and very large ranches. After the purchase of the Louisiana Territory in 1803, Americans began moving into Spanish territory. A few hundred American families in what is now Texas were allowed to live there but had to agree to become loyal subjects to Spain. In 1821, Mexico successfully revolted against Spanish rule, won independence, and chose to be more tolerant towards the American settlers and traders. The Mexican government encouraged and allowed extensive trade and settlement, especially in Texas. Many of the new settlers were southerners who brought their slaves with them. Slavery was outlawed in Mexico and technically illegal in Texas, although the Mexican government rather looked the other way.

Friction increased between land-hungry Americans swarming into western lands and the Mexican government, which controlled these lands. The clash was not only political but also cultural and economic. The Spanish influence permeated all parts of southwestern life: law, language, architecture, and customs. By this time, the doctrine of Manifest Destiny was in the hearts and on the lips of those seeking new areas of settlement and a new life. Americans were demanding U.S. control of not only the Mexican Territory but also Oregon. Peaceful negotiations with Great Britain secured Oregon but it took two years of war to gain control of the southwestern U.S.

In addition, the Mexican government owed debts to U.S. citizens whose property was damaged or destroyed during its struggle for independence from Spain. By the time war broke out in 1845, Mexico had not paid its war debts. The government was weak, corrupt, irresponsible, tom by revolutions, and not in decent financial shape. Mexico was also bitter over American expansion into Texas and the 1836 revolution, which resulted in Texas independence. In the 1844 Presidential Election, the Democrats pushed for annexation of Texas and Oregon and after winning, they started the procedure to admit Texas to the Union.

When statehood occurred, diplomatic relations between the U.S. and Mexico was ended. President Polk wanted U.S. control of the entire southwest, from Texas to the Pacific Ocean. He sent a diplomatic mission with an offer to purchase New Mexico and Upper California but the Mexican government refused to even receive the diplomat. Consequently, in 1846, each nation claimed aggression on the part of the other and war was declared. The treaty signed in 1848 and a subsequent one in 1853 completed the southwestern boundary of the United States, reaching to the Pacific Ocean, as President Polk wished.

The impact of the entire westward movement resulted in the completion of the borders of the present-day conterminous United States. Contributing factors include the bloody war with Mexico, the ever-growing controversy over slave versus free states affecting the balance of power or influence in the U.S. Congress, especially the Senate and finally to the Civil War itself.

Skill 2.3f **Map and analyze the expansion of U.S. borders and the settlement of the West, and describe how geographic features influenced this expansion.**

Westward expansion occurred for a number of reasons, the most important being economic. Cotton had become most important to most of the people who lived in the southern states. The effects of the Industrial Revolution, which began in England, were now being felt in the United States. With the invention of power-driven machines, the demand for cotton fiber greatly increased for the yarn needed in spinning and weaving. Eli Whitney's cotton gin made the separation of the seeds from the cotton much more efficient and faster. This, in turn, increased the demand and more and more farmers became involved in the raising and selling of cotton.

The innovations and developments of better methods of long-distance transportation moved the cotton in greater quantities to textile mills in England as well as the areas of New England and Middle Atlantic States in the U.S. As prices increased along with increased demand, southern farmers began expanding by clearing increasingly more land to grow more cotton. Movement, settlement, and farming headed west to utilize the fertile soils. This, in turn, demanded increased need for a large supply of cheap labor. The system of slavery expanded, both in numbers and in the movement to lands "west" of the South.

Cotton farmers and slave owners were not the only ones heading west. Many, in other fields of economic endeavor, began the migration: trappers, miners, merchants, ranchers, and others were all seeking their fortunes. The Lewis and Clark expedition stimulated the westward push. Fur companies hired men, known as "Mountain Men", to go westward, searching for the animal pelts to supply the market and meet the demands of the East and Europe. These men in their own way explored and discovered the many passes and trails that would eventually be used by settlers in their trek to the west. The California gold rush also had a very large influence on the movement west.

The availability of cheap land and the expectation of great opportunity prompted thousands, including immigrants, to travel across the Mississippi River and settle the Great Plains and California. The primary basis of the new western economy was farming, mining, and ranching. Both migration and the economy were facilitated by the expansion of the railroad and the completion of the transcontinental railroad in 1869.

There were also religious reasons for westward expansion. Increased settlement was encouraged by missionaries who traveled west with the fur traders. They sent word back east for more settlers and the results were tremendous. By the 1840s, the population increases in the Oregon country alone were at a rate of about a thousand people a year. People of many different religions and cultures as well as Southerners with black slaves made their way west which leads to a third reason: political.

Skill 2.3g   Analyze the evolution of American Indian policy up to the Civil War.

During the American Revolution there was competition with the British for the allegiance of Native Americans east of the Mississippi River. Many Native Americans sided with the British in the hope of stopping the expansion of the American colonies into the lands they occupied.

By the terms of the **Treaty of Paris** which ended the Revolutionary War, a large amount of land occupied and claimed by American Indians was ceded to the United States. The British, however, did not inform the Native People of the change. The government of the new nation first tried to treat the tribes who had fought with the British as conquered people and claimed their land. This policy was later abandoned because it could not be enforced.

During the nineteenth century the nation expanded westward. This expansion and settlement of new territory forced the Native Americans to continue to move farther west. The Native Americans were gradually giving up their homelands, their sacred sites, and the burial grounds of their ancestors. Some of the American Indians chose to move west. Many, however, were relocated by force.

The Indian Removal Act of 1830 authorized the government to negotiate treaties with Native Americans to provide land west of the Mississippi River in exchange for lands east of the river. This policy resulted in the relocation of more than 100,000 Native Americans. Theoretically, the treaties were expected to result in voluntary relocation of the native people. In fact, however, many of the native chiefs were forced to sign the treaties.

One of the worst examples of "Removal" was the Treaty of New Echota. This treaty was signed by a faction of the Cherokees rather than the actual leaders of the tribe. When the leaders attempted to remain on their ancestral lands, the treaty was enforced by President Martin Van Buren. The removal of the Cherokees came to be known as "**The Trail of Tears**" and resulted in the deaths of more than 4000 Cherokees, mostly due to disease.

The next phase of the government's policy toward the American Indians was to purchase their land in treaties in order to continue national expansion. This created tension with the states and with settlers. Migration and settlement were not easy. As the settlers moved west they encountered Native American tribes who believed they had a natural right to the lands upon which their ancestors had lived for generations. Resentment of the encroachment of new settlers was particularly strong among the tribes that had been ordered to relocate to "Indian Country" prior to 1860.

Skill 2.3h   **Describe and analyze the impact of slavery on American society, government, and economy, and the contributions of enslaved Africans to America, and trace the attempts to abolish slavery in the first half of the 19th century.**

In between the growing economy, expansion westward of the population, and improvements in travel and mass communication, the federal government did face periodic financial depressions. Contributing to these downward spirals were land speculations, availability and soundness of money and currency, failed banks, failing businesses, and unemployment. Sometimes conditions outside the nation would help trigger it; at other times, domestic politics and presidential elections affected it. The growing strength and influence of two major political parties with opposing philosophies and methods of conducting government did not ease matters at times.

The drafting of the Constitution, its ratification and implementation, united thirteen different, independent states into a Union under one central government. The two crucial compromises of the convention delegates concerning slaves pacified Southerners, especially the slave owners, but the issue of slavery was not settled and from then on, **sectionalism** became stronger and more apparent each year putting the entire country on a collision course.

Slavery in the English colonies began in 1619 when twenty Africans arrived in the colony of Virginia at Jamestown. From then on, slavery had a foothold, especially in the agricultural South, where a large amount of slave labor was needed for the extensive plantations. Free men refused to work for wages on the plantations when land was available for settling on the frontier. Therefore, slave labor was the only recourse left. If it had been profitable to use slaves in New England and the Middle Colonies, then without doubt slavery would have been more widespread. Profit, or the lack thereof, confined slavery to the South.

The West was involved in the controversy as well as the North and South. By 1860, the country was made up of these three major regions. The people in all three sections or regions had a number of beliefs and institutions in common. Of course, there were major differences with each region having its own unique characteristics. The basic problem was their development along very different lines.

The North was industrial with towns and factories growing and increasing at a very fast rate. The South had become agricultural, eventually becoming increasingly dependent on the one crop of cotton. In the West, restless pioneers moved into new frontiers seeking land, wealth, and opportunity. Many were from the South and were slave owners, bringing their slaves with them. So between these three different parts of the country, the views on tariffs, public lands, internal improvements at federal expense, banking and currency, and the issue of slavery were decidedly different to say the least.

This period of U.S. history was a period of compromises, breakdowns of the compromises, desperate attempts to restore and retain harmony among the three sections, short-lived intervals of the uneasy balance of interests, and ever-increasing conflict.

At the Constitutional Convention, one of the slavery compromises concerned counting slaves for deciding the number of representatives for the House and the amount of taxes to be paid. Southerners pushed for counting the slaves for representation but not for taxes. The Northerners pushed for the opposite. The resulting compromise, sometimes referred to as the **"three-fifths compromise,"** was that both groups agreed that three-fifths of the slaves would be counted for both taxes and representation.

The other compromise over slavery was part of the disputes over how much regulation the central government would control over commercial activities such as trade with other nations and the slave trade. It was agreed that Congress would regulate commerce with other nations including taxing imports. Southerners were worried about taxing slaves coming into the country and the possibility of Congress prohibiting the slave trade altogether. The agreement reached allowed the states to continue importation of slaves for the next twenty years until 1808, at which time Congress would make the decision as to the future of the slave trade. During the 20-year period, no more than $10 per person could be levied on slaves coming into the country.

These two slavery compromises were a necessary concession to have Southern support and approval for the new document and new government. Many Americans felt that the system of slavery would eventually die out in the U.S., but by 1808, cotton was becoming increasingly important in the primarily agricultural South and the institution of slavery had become firmly entrenched in Southern culture. It is also evident that as early as the Constitutional Convention, active anti-slavery feelings and opinions were very strong, leading to extremely active groups and societies.

As the nation extended its borders into the lands west of the Mississippi, thousands of settlers streamed into the West brought their ideas and adapted them to the development of the unique characteristics of the region. Equality for everyone, as stated in the Declaration of Independence, did not yet apply to minority groups, black Americans or American Indians. Voting rights and the right to hold public office were restricted in varying degrees in each state. All of these factors decidedly affected the political, economic, and social life of the country and all three were focused in the attitudes of the three sections of the country on slavery.

The first serious clash between North and South occurred during 1819-1820 when James Monroe was in office as President and it was concerning admitting Missouri as a state. In 1819, the U.S. consisted of 21 states: 11 free states and 10 slave states. The Missouri Territory allowed slavery and if admitted would cause an imbalance in the number of U.S. Senators. Alabama had already been admitted as a slave state and that had balanced the Senate with the North and South each having 22 senators. The first **Missouri Compromise** resolved the conflict by approving admission of Maine as a free state along with Missouri as a slave state, thus continuing to keep a balance of power in the Senate with the same number of free and slave states.

An additional provision of this compromise was that with the admission of Missouri, slavery would not be allowed in the rest of the Louisiana Purchase territory north of latitude 36 degrees 30'. This was acceptable to the Southern Congressmen since it was not profitable to grow cotton on land north of this latitude line anyway. It was thought that the crisis had been resolved but in the next year, it was discovered that in its state constitution, Missouri discriminated against the free blacks. Anti-slavery supporters in Congress went into an uproar, determined to exclude Missouri from the Union. Henry Clay, known as the **Great Compromiser**, then proposed a second Missouri Compromise which was acceptable to everyone. His proposal stated that the Constitution of the United States guaranteed protections and privileges to citizens of states and Missouri's proposed constitution could not deny these to any of its citizens. The acceptance in 1820 of this second compromise opened the way for Missouri's statehood--a temporary reprieve only.

The slavery issue flared again not to be done away with until the end of the Civil War. It was obvious that the newly acquired territory would be divided up into territories and later become states. In addition to the two factions of Northerners who advocated prohibition of slavery and of Southerners who favored slavery existing there, a third faction arose supporting the doctrine of "**popular sovereignty**" which stated that people living in territories and states should be allowed to decide for themselves whether or not slavery should be permitted. In 1849, California applied for admittance to the Union and the furor began.

The result was the **Compromise of 1850**, a series of laws designed as a final solution to the issue. Concessions made to the North included the admission of California as a free state and the abolition of slave trading in Washington, D.C. The laws also provided for the creation of the New Mexico and Utah territories. As a concession to Southerners, the residents there would decide whether to permit slavery when these two territories became states. In addition, Congress authorized implementation of stricter measures to capture runaway slaves.

A few years later, Congress took up consideration of new territories between Missouri and present-day Idaho. Again, heated debate over permitting slavery in these areas flared up. Those opposed to slavery used the Missouri Compromise to prove their point showing that the land being considered for territories was part of the area the Compromise had designated as banned to slavery. But on May 25, 1854, Congress passed the infamous **Kansas-Nebraska Act** which nullified this provision, created the territories of Kansas and Nebraska, and provided for the people of these two territories to decide for themselves whether or not to permit slavery to exist there. Feelings were so deep and divided that any further attempts to compromise would meet with little, if any, success. Political and social turmoil swirled everywhere. Kansas was called "**Bleeding Kansas**" because of the extreme violence and bloodshed throughout the territory because two governments existed there, one pro-slavery and the other anti-slavery.

The Supreme Court in 1857 handed down a decision guaranteed to cause explosions throughout the country. **Dred Scott** was a slave whose owner had taken him from slave state Missouri, then to free state Illinois, into Minnesota Territory, free under the provisions of the Missouri Compromise, then finally back to slave state Missouri. Abolitionists pursued the dilemma by presenting a court case, stating that since Scott had lived in a free state and free territory, he was in actuality a free man. Two lower courts had ruled before the Supreme Court became involved, one ruling in favor and one against. The Supreme Court decided that residing in a free state and free territory did not make Scott a free man because Scott (and all other slaves) was not a U.S. citizen or a state citizen of Missouri. Therefore, he did not have the right to sue in state or federal courts. The Court went a step further and ruled that the old Missouri Compromise was now unconstitutional because Congress did not have the power to prohibit slavery in the Territories.

Anti-slavery supporters were stunned. They had just recently formed the new Republican Party and one of its platforms was keeping slavery out of the Territories. Now, according to the decision in the Dred Scott case, this basic party principle was unconstitutional. The only way to ban slavery in new areas was by a Constitutional amendment, requiring ratification by three-fourths of all states. At this time, this was out of the question because the supporters would be unable to get a majority due to Southern opposition.

In 1858, **Abraham Lincoln** and Stephen A. Douglas were running for the office of U.S. Senator from Illinois and participated in a series of debates, which directly affected the outcome of the 1860 Presidential election. Douglas, a Democrat, was up for re-election and knew that if he won this race, he had a good chance of becoming President in 1860. Lincoln, a Republican, was not an abolitionist but he believed that slavery was wrong morally and he firmly believed in and supported the Republican Party principle that slavery must not be allowed to extend any further.

Douglas, on the other hand, originated the doctrine of "popular sovereignty" and was responsible for supporting and getting through Congress the inflammatory Kansas-Nebraska Act. In the course of the debates, Lincoln challenged Douglas to show that popular sovereignty reconciled with the Dred Scott decision. Either way he answered Lincoln, Douglas would lose crucial support from one group or the other. If he supported the Dred Scott decision, Southerners would support him but he would lose Northern support. If he stayed with popular sovereignty, Northern support would be his but Southern support would be lost. His reply to Lincoln, stating that Territorial legislatures could exclude slavery by refusing to pass laws supporting it, gave him enough support and approval to be re-elected to the Senate. But it cost him the Democratic nomination for President in 1860.

Southerners came to the realization that Douglas supported and was devoted to popular sovereignty but not necessarily to the expansion of slavery. On the other hand, two years later, Lincoln received the nomination of the Republican Party for President.

In 1859, abolitionist **John Brown** and his followers seized the federal arsenal at Harper's Ferry in what is now West Virginia. His purpose was to take the guns stored in the arsenal, give them to slaves nearby, and lead them in a widespread rebellion. He and his men were captured by Colonel Robert E. Lee of the United States Army and after a trial with a guilty verdict, he was hanged. Most Southerners felt that the majority of Northerners approved of Brown's actions but in actuality, most of them were stunned and shocked. Southern newspapers took great pains to quote a small but well-known minority of abolitionists who applauded and supported Brown's actions. This merely served to widen the gap between the two sections.

The final straw came with the election of Lincoln to the Presidency the next year. Due to a split in the Democratic Party, there were four candidates from four political parties. With Lincoln receiving a minority of the popular vote and a majority of electoral votes, the Southern states, one by one, voted to secede from the Union as they had promised they would do if Lincoln and the Republicans were victorious. The die was cast.

The slavery issue was at the root of every problem, crisis, event, decision, and struggle from then on. The next crisis involved the issue concerning Texas. By

1836, Texas was an independent republic with its own constitution. During its fight for independence, Americans were sympathetic to and supportive of the Texans and some recruited volunteers who crossed into Texas to help the struggle. Problems arose when the state petitioned Congress for statehood. Texas wanted to allow slavery but Northerners in Congress opposed admission to the Union because it would disrupt the balance between free and slave states and give Southerners in Congress increased influence.

Skill 2.3i   Describe and compare and contrast early 19th-Century social and reform movements and their impact on antebellum American society.

During the nineteenth century there arose a great spirit of reform. This spirit of reform found expression in the effort to protect the rights and opportunities of all. The beginning of the labor organization movement in the 1830s – 1850s resulted in the establishment of a ten-hour workday in several states. A new understanding of education led to movements for public education for all children. The public school system became common in the North. Many other social reform movements began during this period, including education, women's rights, labor, and working conditions, temperance, prisons and insane asylums.

But the most intense and controversial was the abolitionists' efforts to end slavery, an effort alienating and splitting the country, hardening Southern defense of slavery, and leading to four years of bloody war. The abolitionist movement had political fallout, affecting admittance of states into the Union and the government's continued efforts to keep a balance between total numbers of free and slave states. Congressional legislation after 1820 reflected this.

The **Industrial Revolution** had spread from Great Britain to the United States. Before 1800, most manufacturing activities were done in small shops or in homes. However, starting in the early 1800s, factories with modern machines were built making it easier to produce goods faster. The eastern part of the country became a major industrial area although some developed in the West. At about the same time, improvements began to be made in building roads, railroads, canals, and steamboats. The increased ease of travel facilitated the westward movement as well as boosted the economy with faster and cheaper shipment of goods and products, covering larger and larger areas. Some of the innovations include the Erie Canal connecting the interior and Great Lakes with the Hudson River and the coastal port of New York. Many other natural waterways were connected by canals.

Robert Fulton's **Clermont**, the first commercially successful steamboat, led the way in the fastest way to ship goods, making it the most important way to do so. Later, steam-powered railroads soon became the biggest rival of the steamboat as a means of shipping, eventually being the most important transportation method opening the West. With expansion into the interior of the country, the United States became the leading agricultural nation in the world. The hardy pioneer farmers produced a vast surplus and emphasis went to producing products with a high-sale value. Implements such as the cotton gin and reaper aided in production efficiencies. Travel and shipping were greatly assisted in areas not yet touched by railroad or, by improved or new roads, such as the National Road in the East and in the West the Oregon and Santa Fe Trails.

People were exposed to works of literature, art, newspapers, drama, live entertainment, and political rallies. With better communication and travel, more information was desired about previously unknown areas of the country, especially the West. The discovery of gold and other mineral wealth resulted in a literal surge of settlers and even more interest.

More industries and factories required more and more labor. Women, children, and, at times, entire families worked the long hours and days, until the 1830s. By that time, the factories were getting even larger and employers began hiring immigrants who were coming to America in huge numbers. Before then, efforts were made to organize a labor movement to improve working conditions and increase wages. It never really caught on until after the Civil War, but the seed had been sown.

Utopianism is the dream of or the desire to create the perfect society. However by the nineteenth century few believed this was possible. One of the major "causes" of utopianism is the desire for moral clarity. Against the backdrop of the efforts of a young nation to define itself and to ensure the rights and freedoms of its citizens, and within the context of the second great awakening, it becomes quite easy to see how the reform movements, the religious sentiment, and the gathering national storm would lead to the rise of expressions of desire to create the perfect society. Robert Owen was one of the movements major proponents.

The Second Great Awakening was an evangelical Protestant revival that preached personal responsibility for one's actions both individually and socially. This movement was led by preachers such as Charles Finney who traveled the country preaching the gospel of social responsibility. This point of view was taken up by the "mainline Protestant denominations" (Episcopal, Methodist, Presbyterian, Lutheran, Congregational). Part of the social reform movement that led to an end to child labor, to better working conditions, and to other changes in social attitudes, arose from this new recognition that the Christian faith should be expressed for the good of society.

Closely allied to the Second Great Awakening was **the temperance movement**. This movement to end the sale and consumption of alcohol, arose from religious beliefs, the violence many women and children experienced from heavy drinkers, and from the effect of alcohol consumption on the work force. The Society for the Promotion of Temperance was organized in Boston in 1826.

Public schools were established in many of the states with more and more children being educated. With more literacy and more participation in literature and the arts, the young nation was developing its own unique culture becoming less and less influenced by and dependent on that of Europe.

Horace Mann grew up a poor child with little opportunity for education except for his small community library. He took full advantage of it, however, and was admitted to Brown University, from which he graduated in 1819. Mann practiced law for several years and served in the Massachusetts House of Representatives. He served on the committee of the first school funded by public tax dollars in Dedham, Massachusetts, and in 1837 was appointed secretary to the newly formed State Board of Education. Mann became an outspoken proponent of educational reform, and fought for better resources for schools and teachers. Mann planned the Massachusetts Normal School system for training new teachers. The compulsory public education that is taken for granted today was a new idea in antebellum America, and Mann faced opposition to his ideas. Shortly after Massachusetts adopted this system, New York followed suit, laying the foundation for the present state-based educational system.

Dorothea Dix was an advocate for public treatment and care for the mentally ill. In the early 1840s, Dix called attention to the deplorable treatment and conditions to which the mentally ill in Massachusetts were subjected in a pamphlet entitled *Memorial*. Her efforts resulted in a bill that expanded the state hospital. Dix traveled to several other states, encouraging and overseeing the founding of state mental hospitals. Dix proposed federal legislation that would have sold public land with the proceeds being distributed to the states to fund care for the mentally ill. The legislation was approved by Congress, however, using public money for social welfare was a contentious issue, and President Franklin Pierce vetoed it on these grounds.

Other social issues were also addressed. It was during this period that efforts were made to transform the prison system and its emphasis on punishment into a penitentiary system that attempted rehabilitation.

A group of women emerged in the 1840s that was the beginning of the first women's rights movement in the nation's history. Among the early leaders of the movement were **Elizabeth Cady Stanton, Lucretia Mott,** and **Ernestine Rose**. At this time very few states recognized women's rights to vote, own property, sue for divorce, or execute contracts. In 1869, **Susan B. Anthony**, Ernestine Rose and Elizabeth Cady Stanton founded the National Woman Suffrage Association.

The **Seneca Falls Convention** was a gathering of women and men in 1848, in the New York mill town of Seneca Falls, to address the rights of women in the United States. The growing momentum of the anti-slavery movement and discussion over the rights of black citizens had drawn attention to the rights of female citizens, who could not vote or hold important positions in American government. Some 300 people attended the convention, which culminated in the publication of a "Declaration of Sentiments," which was modeled on the Declaration of Independence and called for equal participation for women. The Seneca Falls Convention is considered and early milestone in the feminist movement.

The following is just a partial list of well-known Americans who contributed their leadership and talents in various fields and reforms:

Emma Hart Willard, Catharine Esther Beecher, and Mary Lyon for **education for women**

Dr. Elizabeth Blackwell, the **first woman doctor**

Antoinette Louisa Blackwell, the **first female minister**

Elihu Burritt and William Ladd for **peace movements**

Horace Mann, Henry Barmard, Calvin E. Stowe, Caleb Mills, and John Swett for **public education**

Benjamin Lundy, David Walker, William Lloyd Garrison, Isaac Hooper, Arthur and Lewis Tappan, Theodore Weld, Frederick Douglass, Harriet Tubman, James G. Birney, Henry Highland Garnet, James Forten, Robert Purvis, Harriet Beecher Stowe, Wendell Phillips, and John Brown for **abolition of slavery and the Underground Railroad**

Louisa Mae Alcott, James Fenimore Cooper, Washington Irving, Walt Whitman, Henry David Thoreau, Ralph Waldo Emerson, Herman Melville, Richard Henry Dana, Nathaniel Hawthorne, Henry Wadsworth Longfellow, John Greenleaf Whittier, Edgar Allan Poe, Oliver Wendell Holmes, **famous writers**

John C. Fremont, Zebulon Pike, Kit Carson, **explorers**

Henry Clay, Daniel Webster, Stephen Douglas, John C. Calhoun, American **statesmen** Robert Fulton, Cyrus McCormick, Eli Whitney, **inventors**

Noah Webster, American **dictionary and spellers**

The list goes on but the contributions of these and many, many others greatly enhanced the unique American culture.

COMPETENCY 2.4   CIVIL WAR AND RECONSTRUCTION

Skill 2.4a   Interpret the debates over the doctrines of nullification and state secession.

The doctrine of nullification states that the states have the right to "nullify" – declare invalid – any act of Congress they believed to be unjust or unconstitutional.

The nullification crisis of the mid nineteenth century climaxed over a new tariff on imported manufactured goods that was enacted by the Congress in 1828. While this tariff protected the manufacturing and industrial interests of the North, it placed an additional burden of cost on the South, which was only affected by the tariff as consumers of manufactured goods. The north had become increasingly economically dependent on industry and manufacturing, while the south had become increasingly agricultural. Despite the fact that the tariff was primarily intended to protect Northern manufacturing interests in the face of imports from other countries, the effect on the south was to simply raise the prices of needed goods.

This issue of disagreement reached its climax when John C. Calhoun, Jackson's vice president, led South Carolina to adopt the Ordinance of Nullification which declared the tariff null and void within state borders. Although this issue came to the brink of military action, it was resolved by the enactment of a new tariff in 1832.

The question of a state's right to nullify any law of the nation which was contrary to local interests was based on the assumption that the United States was a union of independent commonwealths, and that the general government was merely their agent. This was the Southern view. The North, however, assumed the Federal government to be supreme and that the Union was inseparable.

When economic issues and the issue of slavery came to a head, the North declared slavery illegal. The South acted on the principles of the doctrine of nullification, declared the new laws null, and acted upon their presumed right as states to secede from the union and form their own government. The North saw secession as a violation of the national unity and contract.

Skill 2.4b   Compare and contrast the strengths and weaknesses of the Union and Confederacy.

It is ironic that **South Carolina** was the first state to **secede** from the Union and the first shots of the war were fired on Fort Sumter in Charleston Harbor. Both sides quickly prepared for war. The North had more in its favor: a larger population; superiority in finances and transportation facilities; manufacturing, agricultural, and natural resources. The North possessed most of the nation's gold, had about 92% of all industries, and almost all known supplies of copper, coal, iron, and various other minerals. Since most of the nation's railroads were in the North and mid-West, men and supplies could be moved wherever needed; food could be transported from the farms of the mid-West to workers in the East and to soldiers on the battlefields. Trade with nations overseas could go on as usual due to control of the navy and the merchant fleet. The Northern states numbered 24 and included western (California and Oregon) and border (Maryland, Delaware, Kentucky, Missouri, and West Virginia) states.

The Southern states numbered eleven and included South Carolina, Georgia, Florida, Alabama, Mississippi, Louisiana, Texas, Virginia, North Carolina, Tennessee, and Arkansas, making up the **Confederacy**. Although outnumbered in population, the South was completely confident of victory. They knew that all they had to do was fight a defensive war, protecting their own territory until the North, who had to invade and defeat an area almost the size of Western Europe, tired of the struggle and gave up. Another advantage of the South was that a number of its best officers had graduated from the U.S. Military Academy at West Point and had had long years of army experience, some even exercising varying degrees of command in the Indian wars and the war with Mexico. Men from the South were conditioned to living outdoors and were more familiar with horses and firearms than many men from northeastern cities. Since cotton was such an important crop, Southerners felt that British and French textile mills were so dependent on raw cotton that they would be forced to help the Confederacy in the war.

The South had specific reasons and goals for fighting the war, more so than the North. The major aim of the Confederacy never wavered: to win independence, the right to govern themselves as they wished, and to preserve slavery. The Northerners were not as clear in their reasons for conducting war. At the beginning, most believed, along with Lincoln, that preservation of the Union was paramount. Only a few extremely fanatical abolitionists looked on the war as a way to end slavery. However, by war's end, more and more northerners had come to believe that freeing the slaves was just as important as restoring the Union.

Skill 2.4c   Describe the major military and political turning points of the war.

The war strategies for both sides were relatively clear and simple. The South planned a defensive war, wearing down the North until it agreed to peace on Southern terms. The exception was to gain control of Washington, D.C., go North through the Shenandoah Valley into Maryland and Pennsylvania in order to drive a wedge between the Northeast and mid-West, interrupt the lines of communication, and end the war quickly. The North had three basic strategies:

1. Blockade the Confederate coastline in order to cripple the South;
2. Seize control of the Mississippi River and interior railroad lines to split the Confederacy in two;
3. Seize the Confederate capital of Richmond, Virginia, then driving southward to join up with Union forces coming east from the Mississippi Valley.

The South won decisively until the Battle of Gettysburg, July 1 - 3, 1863. Prior to Gettysburg, Lincoln's commanders, **McDowell and McClellan**, were less than desirable, and **Burnside and Hooker** had not been what was needed. **Lee**, on the other hand, had many able officers, **Jackson and Stuart** were depended on heavily by him. Jackson died at Chancellorsville and was replaced by **Longstreet**. Lee decided to invade the North and depended on **J.E.B. Stuart** and his cavalry to keep him informed of the location of Union troops and their strengths. Four things worked against Lee at Gettysburg:

1. The Union troops gained the best positions and the best ground first, making it easier to make a stand there.
2. Lee's move into Northern territory put him and his army a long way from food and supply lines. They were more or less on their own.
3. Lee thought that his Army of Northern Virginia was invincible and could fight and win under any conditions or circumstances.
4. Stuart and his men did not arrive at Gettysburg until the end of the second day of fighting and by then, it was too little too late. He and the men had had to detour around Union soldiers and he was delayed getting the information Lee needed.

Consequently, he made the mistake of failing to listen to Longstreet and following the strategy of regrouping back into Southern territory to the supply lines. Lee felt that regrouping was retreating and almost an admission of defeat. He was convinced the army would be victorious. Longstreet was concerned about the Union troops occupying the best positions and felt that regrouping to a better position would be an advantage. He was also very concerned about the distance from supply lines.

It was not the intention of either side to fight there but the fighting began when a Confederate brigade stumbled into a unit of Union cavalry while looking for shoes.

The third and last day Lee launched the final attempt to break Union lines. **General George Pickett** sent his division of three brigades under Generals Garnet, Kemper, and Armistead against Union troops on Cemetery Ridge under command of General Winfield Scott Hancock. Union lines held and Lee and the defeated Army of Northern Virginia made their way back to Virginia. Although Lincoln's commander George Meade successfully turned back a Confederate charge, he and the Union troops failed to pursue Lee and the Confederates. This battle was the turning point for the North. After this, Lee never again had the troop strength to launch a major offensive.

The day after Gettysburg, on July 4, Vicksburg, Mississippi surrendered to Union **General Ulysses Grant**, thus severing the western Confederacy from the eastern part. In September 1863, the Confederacy won its last important victory at Chickamauga. In November, the Union victory at Chattanooga made it possible for Union troops to go into Alabama and Georgia, splitting the eastern Confederacy in two. Lincoln gave Grant command of all Northern armies in March of 1864. Grant led his armies into battles in Virginia while Phil Sheridan and his cavalry did as much damage as possible. In a skirmish at a place called Yellow Tavern, Virginia, Sheridan's and Stuart's forces met, with Stuart being fatally wounded. The Union won the Battle of Mobile Bay and in May 1864, **William Tecumseh Sherman** began his march to successfully demolish Atlanta, then on to Savannah. He and his troops turned northward through the Carolinas to Grant in Virginia. On April 9, 1865, Lee formally surrendered to Grant at **Appamattox Courthouse**, Virginia.

Skill 2.4d   Describe and analyze the physical, social, political, and economic impact of the war on combatants, civilians, communities, states, and the nation.

The Civil War took more American lives than any other war in history, the South losing one-third of its soldiers in battle compared to about one-sixth for the North. More than half of the total deaths were caused by disease and the horrendous conditions of field hospitals. Both sections paid a tremendous economic price but the South suffered more severely from direct damages. Destruction was pervasive with towns, farms, trade, industry, lives and homes of men, women, children all destroyed and an entire Southern way of life was lost. The deep resentment, bitterness, and hatred that remained for generations gradually lessened as the years went by but legacies of it surface and remain to this day. The South had no voice in the political, social, and cultural affairs of the nation, lessening to a great degree the influence of the more traditional Southern ideals. The Northern Yankee Protestant ideals of hard work, education, and economic freedom became the standard of the United States and helped influence the development of the nation into a modern, industrial power.

The effects of the Civil War were tremendous. It changed the methods of waging war and has been called the first modern war. It introduced weapons and tactics that, when improved later, were used extensively in wars of the late 1800s and 1900s. Civil War soldiers were the first to fight in trenches, first to fight under a unified command, first to wage a defense called "major cordon defense", a strategy of advance on all fronts. They were also the first to use repeating and breech loading weapons. Observation balloons were first used during the war along with submarines, ironclad ships, and mines. Telegraphy and railroads were put to use first in the Civil War. It was considered a modern war because of the vast destruction and was "total war", involving the use of all resources of the opposing sides. There was probably no way it could have ended other than total defeat and unconditional surrender of one side or the other.

By executive proclamation and constitutional amendment, slavery was officially and finally ended, although there remained deep prejudice and racism, still raising its ugly head today. Also, the Union was preserved and the states were finally truly united. **Sectionalism**, especially in the area of politics, remained strong for another 100 years but not to the degree and with the violence as existed before 1861. It has been noted that the Civil War may have been American democracy's greatest failure for, from 1861 to 1865, calm reason, basic to democracy, fell to human passion. Yet, democracy did survive.

The victory of the North established that no state has the right to end or leave the Union. Because of unity, the U.S. became a major global power. Lincoln never proposed to punish the South. He was most concerned with restoring the South to the Union in a program that was flexible and practical rather than rigid and unbending. In fact he never really felt that the states had succeeded in leaving the Union but that they had left the 'family circle' for a short time. His plans consisted of two major steps:

All Southerners taking an **oath of allegiance** to the Union promising to accept all federal laws and proclamations dealing with slavery would receive a full pardon. The only ones excluded from this were men who had resigned from civil and military positions in the federal government to serve in the Confederacy, those who were part of the Confederate government, those in the Confederate army above the rank of lieutenant, and Confederates who were guilty of mistreating prisoners of war and blacks.

A state would be able to write a new constitution, elect new officials, and return to the Union fully equal to all other states on certain conditions: a minimum number of persons (at least 10% of those who were qualified voters in their states before secession from the Union who had voted in the 1860 election) must take an oath of allegiance.

.

Lincoln and Johnson had considered the conflict of Civil War as a "rebellion of individuals," but Congressional Radicals, such as Charles Sumner in the Senate, considered the Southern states as complete political organizations and were now in the same position as any unorganized Territory and should be treated as such. Radical House leader Thaddeus Stevens considered the Confederate States, not as Territories, but as conquered provinces and felt they should be treated that way. President Johnson refused to work with Congressional moderates, insisting on having his own way. As a result, the Radicals gained control of both houses of Congress and when Johnson opposed their harsh measures, they came within one vote of impeaching him.

Skill 2.4e   Compare and contrast plans for Reconstruction with its actual implementation.

Following the Civil War, the nation was faced with repairing the torn Union and readmitting the Confederate states. **Reconstruction** refers to this period between 1865 and 1877 when the federal and state governments debated and implemented plans to provide civil rights to freed slaves and to set the terms under which the former Confederate states might once again join the Union.

Planning for Reconstruction began early in the war, in 1861. Abraham Lincoln's Republican Party in Washington favored the extension of voting rights to black men, but was divided as to how far to extend the right. Moderates, such as Lincoln, wanted only literate blacks and those who had fought for the Union to be allowed to vote. Radical Republicans wanted to extend the vote to all black men. Conservative Democrats did not want to give black men the vote at all. In the case of former Confederate soldiers, moderates wanted to allow all but former leaders to vote, while the radicals wanted to require an oath from all eligible voters that they had never borne arms against the US, which would have excluded all former rebels. On the issue of readmission into the Union, moderates favored a much lower standard, with the radicals demanding nearly impossible conditions for rebel states to return.

Lincoln's moderate plan for Reconstruction was actually part of his effort to win the war. Lincoln and the moderates felt that if it remained easy for states to return to the Union, and if moderate proposals on black suffrage were made, that Confederate states involved in the hostilities might be swayed to re-join the Union rather than continue fighting. The radical plan was to ensure that reconstruction did not actually start until after the war was over.

In 1863 Abraham Lincoln was assassinated leaving his Vice President Andrew Johnson to oversee the beginning of the actual implementation of Reconstruction. Johnson struck a moderate pose, and was willing to allow former confederates to keep control of their state governments. Unfortunately, after Johnson became President the radical Republicans gained control of Congress in 1866 and the harsh measures of radical Reconstruction were implemented.

The economic and social chaos in the South after the war was unbelievable with starvation and disease rampant, especially in the cities. The U.S. Army provided some relief of food and clothing for both white and blacks but the major responsibility fell to the Freedmen's Bureau. Though the bureau agents to a certain extent helped southern whites, their main responsibility was to the freed slaves. They were to assist the freedmen to become self-supporting and protect them from being taken advantage of by others. Northerners looked on it as a real, honest effort to help the South out of the chaos it was in. Most white Southerners charged the bureau with causing racial friction, deliberately encouraging the freedmen to consider former owners as enemies.

As a result, as southern leaders began to be able to restore life as it had once been, they adopted a set of laws known as "black codes", containing many of the provisions of the prewar "slave codes." There were certain improvements in the lives of freedmen, but the codes denied the freedmen their basic civil rights. In short, except for the condition of freedom and a few civil rights, white Southerners made every effort to keep the freedmen in a way of life subordinate to theirs.

Radicals in Congress pointed out these illegal actions by white Southerners as evidence that they were unwilling to recognize, accept, and support the complete freedom of black Americans and could not be trusted. Therefore, Congress drafted its own program of Reconstruction, including laws that would protect and further the rights of blacks. Three amendments were added to the Constitution: the **13th Amendment** of 1865 outlawed slavery throughout the entire United States. The **14th Amendment** of 1868 made blacks American citizens. The **15th Amendment** of 1870 gave black Americans the right to vote and made it illegal to deny anyone the right to vote based on race.

In 1866, the radical Republicans in control of Congress passed the Reconstruction Acts, which placed the governments of the southern states under the control of the federal military. With this backing, the Republicans began to implement their radical policies such as granting all black men the vote, and denying the vote to former confederate soldiers. Congress made ratification of the 13th, 14th and 15th amendments a condition of readmission into the Union by the rebel states. The Republicans found support in the south among Freedmen, as former slaves were called, white southerners who had not supported the Confederacy, called **Scalawags**, and northerners who had moved to the south, known as **Carpetbaggers**.

Military control continued throughout Grant's administration, despite growing conflict both inside and outside the Republican Party. Conservatives in Congress and in the states opposed the liberal policies of the Republicans. Some Republicans became concerned over corruption issues among Grant's appointees and dropped support for him.

Under President Rutherford B. Hayes, the federal troops were removed from the South. Without this support, the Republican governments were replaced by so-called **Redeemer** governments, who promised the restoration of the vote those whites who had been denied it and limitations on civil rights for blacks.

The rise of the Redeemer governments marked the beginning of the **Jim Crow** laws and official segregation. Blacks were still allowed to vote, but ways were found to make it difficult for them to do so, such as literacy tests and poll taxes. Reconstruction, which had set as its goal the reunification of the South with the North and the granting of civil rights to freed slaves was a limited success, at best, and in the eyes of blacks was considered a failure.

Federal troops were stationed throughout the South and protected Republicans who took control of Southern governments. Bitterly resentful, white Southerners fought the new political system by joining a secret society called the **Ku Klux Klan**, using violence to keep black Americans from voting and getting equality. However, before being allowed to rejoin the Union, the Confederate states were required to agree to all federal laws. Between 1866 and 1870, all of them had returned to the Union, but Northern interest in Reconstruction was fading. Reconstruction officially ended when the last Federal troops left the South in 1877. It can be said that Reconstruction had a limited success as it set up public school systems and expanded legal rights of black Americans. Nevertheless, white supremacy came to be in control again and its bitter fruitage is still with us today.

Skill 2.4f   Explain and assess the development and adoption of segregation laws, the influence of social mores on the passage and implementation of these laws, and the rise of white supremacist organizations.

After the Civil War, the **Emancipation Proclamation** in 1863 and the 13th Amendment in 1865 ended slavery in the United States, but these measures did not erase the centuries of racial prejudices among whites that held blacks to be inferior in intelligence and morality. These prejudices, along with fear of economic competition from newly freed slaves, led to a series of state laws that permitted or required businesses, landlords, school boards and others to physically segregate blacks and whites in their everyday lives.

Segregation laws were foreshadowed in the **Black Codes**, strict laws proposed by some southern states during the Reconstruction period which sought to essentially recreate the conditions of pre-war servitude. Under these codes, blacks were to remain subservient to their white employers, and were subject to fines and beatings if they failed to work. Freedmen, as newly freed slaves were called, were afforded some civil rights protection during the Reconstruction period, however beginning around 1876, so called Redeemer governments began to take office in southern states after the removal of Federal troops that had supported Reconstruction goals. The Redeemer state legislatures began passing segregation laws which came to be known as **Jim Crow** laws.

The Jim Crow laws varied from state to state, but the most significant of them required separate school systems and libraries for blacks and whites and separate ticket windows, waiting rooms and seating areas on trains and, later, other public transportation. Restaurant owners were permitted or sometimes required to provide separate entrances and tables and counters for blacks and whites, so that the two races did not see one another while dining. Public parks and playgrounds were constructed for each race. Landlords were not allowed to mix black and white tenants in apartment houses in some states.

The Jim Crow laws were given credibility in 1896 when the Supreme Court handed down its decision in the case *Plessy vs. Ferguson*. In 1890, Louisiana had passed a law requiring separate train cars for blacks and whites. To challenge this law, in 1892 Homer Plessy, a man who had a black great grandparent and so was considered legally "black" in that state, purchased a ticket in the white section and took his seat. Upon informing the conductor that he was black, he was told to move to the black car. He refused and was arrested. His case was eventually elevated to the Supreme Court.

The Court ruled against Plessy, thereby ensuring that the Jim Crow laws would continue to proliferate and be enforced. The Court held that segregating races was not unconstitutional as long as the facilities for each were identical. This became known as the **"separate but equal"** principle. In practice, facilities were seldom equal. Black schools were not funded at the same level, for instance. Streets and parks in black neighborhoods were not maintained. This trend continued throughout the following decades. Even the federal government adopted segregation as official policy when President Woodrow Wilson segregated the civil service in the 1910s.

Legal segregation was a part of life for generations of Americans until the separate but equal fallacy was finally challenged in 1954, in another Supreme Court case, *Brown vs. Board of Education*. This case arose when a Topeka, Kansas man attempted to enroll his third-grade daughter in a segregated white elementary school and was refused. In the Court decision, the policy of maintaining separate schools was found to be inherently unequal and unconstitutional.

Even with the new legal interpretation, some states refused to integrate their schools. In Virginia, the state closed some schools rather than integrate them. In Arkansas, the Governor Orville Faubus mobilized the National Guard to prevent the integration of Little Rock High School. President Eisenhower sent federal troops to enforce the integration.

Opposition to Jim Crow laws became an important part of the civil rights movement, led by **Martin Luther King, Jr**. and others, which culminated in the **Civil Rights Act of 1964**. This act ended legal segregation in the United States, however some forms of de facto segregation continued to exist, particularly in the area of housing.

Paralleling the development of segregation legislation in the mid-nineteenth century was the appearance of organized groups opposed to any integration of blacks into white society. The most notable of these was the **Ku Klux Klan**. First organized in the Reconstruction south, the KKK was a loose group made up mainly of former Confederate soldiers who opposed the Reconstruction government and espoused a doctrine of white supremacy. KKK members intimidated and sometimes killed their proclaimed enemies. The first KKK was never completely organized, despite having nominal leadership. In 1871, President Grant took action to use federal troops to halt the activities of the KKK, and actively prosecuted them in federal court. Klan activity waned, and the organization disappeared.

In 1915, the Klan was resurrected following the glorification of the Reconstruction era Klan in the film "**The Birth of a Nation**." The new clan added an anti-immigrant and anti-Catholic slant to its platform, and was organized on a national level. Reaching its peak in the 1920s, this new Klan obtained widespread political and social influence especially throughout the south and midwest. Members continued to intimidate and murder their opponents. The Klan saw membership decline through the Great Depression and the Second World War, when they emerged as sympathizers with Nazi sentiment and lost public support. The Klan still exists, although several independent groups are simply using the name.

Skill 2.4g **Analyze the relationship of the 13th, 14th, and 15th Amendments to Reconstruction, and compare and contrast their initial and later interpretations.**

The **13th Amendment** abolished slavery and involuntary servitude, except as punishment for crime. The amendment was proposed on January 31, 1865. It was declared ratified by the necessary number of states on December 18, 1865. The Emancipation Proclamation had freed slaves held in states that were considered to be in rebellion. This amendment freed slaves in states and territories controlled by the Union. The Supreme Court has ruled that this amendment does not bar mandatory military service.

The **14ᵗʰ Amendment** provides for **Due Process and Equal Protection** under the Law. It was proposed on June 13, 1866 and ratified on July 28, 1868. The drafters of the Amendment took a broad view of national citizenship. The law requires that states provide equal protection under the law to all persons (not just all citizens). This amendment also came to be interpreted as overturning the Dred Scott case (which said that blacks were not and could not become citizens of the U.S.). The full potential of interpretation of this amendment was not realized until the 1950s and 1960s, when it became the basis of ending segregation in the Supreme Court case *Brown v. Board of Education*. This amendment includes the stipulation that all children born on American soil, with very few exceptions, are U.S. citizens. There have been recommendations that this guarantee of citizenship be limited to exclude the children of illegal immigrants and tourists, but this has not yet occurred. There is no provision in this amendment for loss of citizenship.

After the Civil War, many Southern states passed laws that attempted to restrict the movements of blacks and prevent them from bringing lawsuits or testifying in court. In the *Slaughterhouse Cases* (1871) the Supreme Court ruled that the Amendment applies only to rights granted by the federal government. In the *Civil Rights Cases*, the Court held that the guarantee of rights did not outlaw racial discrimination by individuals and organizations. In the next few decades the Court overturned several laws barring blacks from serving on juries or discriminating against the Chinese immigrants in regulating the laundry businesses.

In the case of *Plessy v. Ferguson*, the Court ruled that segregation could be imposed provided blacks were provided equivalent facilities. This was the basis of the "separate but equal" doctrine. This doctrine held sway until the case of *Brown v. Board of Education* nearly 50 years later. Since this ruling, the Court has extended the equal protection clause to a number of other historically disadvantaged groups.

This amendment enabled the federal courts to intervene when necessary to guarantee due process and equal protection under the law and to reinforce it with other rights such as free speech, freedom of religion, protection from unreasonable search, and protection from cruel and unusual punishment.

The second section of the amendment establishes the "one man, one vote" apportionment of congressional representation. This ended the counting of blacks as three fifths of a person. Section III prevents the election to Congress or the Electoral College of anyone who has engaged in insurrection, rebellion or treason. Section IV stipulated that the government would not pay "damages" for the loss of slaves or for debts incurred by the Confederate government (e.g., with English or French banks).

The **15th Amendment** grants voting rights regardless of race, color or previous condition of servitude. It was ratified on February 3, 1870.

All three of these Constitutional Amendments were part of the Reconstruction effort to create stability and rule of law to provide, protect, and enforce the rights of former slaves throughout the nation.

COMPETENCY 2.5   THE "GILDED AGE"

Skill 2.5a   Describe and analyze the role of entrepreneurs and industrialists and their impact on the United States economy.

There was a marked degree of industrialization before and during the Civil War, but at war's end, industry in America was small. After the war, dramatic changes took place. Machines replaced hand labor, extensive nationwide railroad service made possible the wider distribution of goods, invention of new products made available in large quantities, and large amounts of money from bankers and investors for expansion of business operations. American life was definitely affected by this phenomenal industrial growth. Cities became the centers of this new business activity resulting in mass population movements there and tremendous growth. This new boom in business resulted in huge fortunes for some Americans and extreme poverty for many others. The discontent this caused resulted in a number of new reform movements from which came measures controlling the power and size of big business and helping the poor.

Of course, industry before, during, and after the Civil War was centered mainly in the North, especially the tremendous industrial growth after. The late 1800s and early 1900s saw the increasing buildup of military strength and the U.S. becoming a world power.

The use of machines in industry enabled workers to produce a large quantity of goods much faster than by hand. With the increase in business, hundreds of workers were hired, assigned to perform a certain job in the production process. This was a method of organization called **"division of labor"** and by its increasing the rate of production, businesses lowered prices for their products making the products affordable for more people. As a result, sales and businesses were increasingly successful and profitable.

A great variety of new products or inventions became available such as: the typewriter, the telephone, barbed wire, the electric light, the phonograph, and the gasoline automobile. From this list, the one that had the greatest effect on America's economy was the **automobile**.

As business grew, methods of sales and promotion were developed. Salespersons went to all parts of the country promoting the various products, opening large department stores in the growing cities, offering the varied products at reasonable affordable prices. People who lived too far from the cities, making it impossible to shop there, had the advantage of using a mail order service, buying what they needed from catalogs furnished by the companies. The developments in communication, such as the telephone and telegraph, increased the efficiency and prosperity of big business.

Investments in corporate stocks and bonds resulted from business prosperity. As individuals began investing heavily in an eager desire to share in the profits, their investments made available the needed capital for companies to expand their operations. From this, banks increased in number throughout the country, making loans to businesses and significant contributions to economic growth. At the same time, during the 1880s, government made little effort to regulate businesses. This gave rise to **monopolies** where larger businesses were rid of their smaller competitors and assumed complete control of their industries.

Some owners in the same business would join or merge to form one company. Others formed what were called "**trusts**," a type of monopoly in which rival businesses were controlled but not formally owned. Monopolies had some good effects on the economy. Out of them grew the large, efficient corporations, which made important contributions to the growth of the nation's economy. Also, the monopolies enabled businesses to keep their sales steady and avoid sharp fluctuations in price and production. At the same time, the downside of monopolies was the unfair business practices of the business leaders. Some acquired so much power that they took unfair advantage of others. Those who had little or no competition would require their suppliers to supply goods at a low cost, sell the finished products at high prices, and reduce the quality of the product to save money.

The industrial boom produced several very wealthy and powerful "**captains of industry**" such as **Andrew Carnegie, John D. Rockefeller**, Jay Gould, J.P Morgan and Philip Armour. While they were envied and respected for their business acumen and success, they were condemned for exploitation of workers and questionable business practices and they were feared because of their power.

While these "captains of industry" were becoming wealthy, the average worker enjoyed some increase in the standard of living. Most workers were required to put in long hours in dangerous conditions doing monotonous work for low wages. Most were not able to afford to participate in the new comforts and forms of entertainment that were becoming available. Farmers believed they were also being exploited by the bankers, suppliers and the railroads. This produced enough instability to fuel several recessions and two severe depressions.

Skill 2.5b   Describe and analyze the effects of industrialization on the American economy and society, including increased immigration, changing working conditions, and the growth of early labor organizations.

The nation witnessed significant industrial growth during the Civil War. This continued after the war. Steam power generation, sophisticated manufacturing equipment, the ability to move about the country quickly by railroad, and the invention of the steam powered tractor, resulted in a phenomenal growth in industrial output. The new steel and oil industries provided a significant impetus to industrial growth and added thousands of new jobs.

Between 1870 and 1916, more than 25 million immigrants came into the United States adding to the phenomenal population growth taking place. This tremendous growth aided business and industry in two ways. First, the number of consumers increased creating a greater demand for products thus enlarging the markets for the products, and second, with increased production and expanding business, more workers were available for newly created jobs. The completion of the nation's **transcontinental railroad** in 1869 contributed greatly to the nation's economic and industrial growth. Some examples of the benefits of using the railroads include raw materials were shipped quickly by the mining companies and finished products were sent to all parts of the country. Many wealthy industrialists and railroad owners saw tremendous profits steadily increasing due to this improved method of transportation.

The "inventive spirit" of the time was a major force propelling the industrial revolution forward. This spirit led to improvement in products, development of new production processes and equipment, and even to the creation of entirely new industries. During the last 40 years of the nineteenth century inventors registered almost 700,000 new patents. Innovations in new industrial processes and technology grew at a pace unmatched at any other time in American history. **Thomas Edison** was the most prolific inventor of that time, using a systematic and efficient method to invent and improve on current technology in a profitable manner

One result of industrialization was the growth of the **Labor Movement**. There were numerous boycotts and strikes which often became violent when the police or the militia were called in to stop the strikes. Labor and farmer organizations were created and became a political force. Industrialization also brought an influx of immigrants from Asia (particularly Chinese and Japanese) and from Europe (particularly European Jews, the Irish, and Russians). High rates of immigration led to the creation of communities in various cities like "little Russia" or "little Italy." Industrialization also led to overwhelming growth of cities as workers moved closer to their places of work. The economy was booming, but that economy was based on basic needs and luxury goods, for which there was to be only limited demand, especially during times of economic recession or depression.

Skilled laborers were organized into a labor union called the **American Federation of Labor** in an effort to gain better working conditions and wages for its members. Farmers joined organizations such as the **National Grange** and Farmers Alliances. Farmers were producing more food than people could afford to buy. This was the result of both new farmlands rapidly sprouting on the plains and prairies, and the development and availability of new farm machinery and newer and better methods of farming. They tried selling their surplus abroad but faced stiff competition from other nations selling the same farm products. Other problems contributed significantly to their situation. Items they needed for daily life were priced exorbitantly high. Having to borrow money to carry on farming activities kept them constantly in debt. Higher interest rates, shortage of money, falling farm prices, dealing with the so-called middlemen, and the increasingly high charges by the railroads to haul farm products to large markets all contributed to the desperate need for reform to relieve the plight of American farmers.

Skill 2.5c   Explain and analyze the causes for, and the impact of, Populism and Progressivism.

Populism is the philosophy that is concerned with the common sense needs of average people. Populism often finds expression as a reaction against perceived oppression of the average people by the wealthy elite in society. The prevalent claim of populist movements is that they will put the people first. Populism is often connected with religious fundamentalism, racism, or nationalism. Populist movements claim to represent the majority of the people and call them to stand up to institutions or practices that seem detrimental to their well-being.

Populism flourished in the late nineteenth and early twentieth centuries. Several political parties were formed out of this philosophy, including: the Greenback Party, the Populist Party, the Farmer-Labor Party, the Single Tax movement of Henry George, the Share Our Wealth movement of **Huey Long**, the Progressive Party, and the Union Party. In the 1890s, the People's Party won the support of millions of farmers and other working people. This party challenged the social ills of the monopolists of the "Gilded Age."

The tremendous change that resulted from the industrial revolution led to a demand for reform that would control the power wielded by big corporations. The gap between the industrial moguls and the working people was growing. This disparity between rich and poor resulted in a public outcry for reform at the same time that there was an outcry for governmental reform that would end the political corruption and elitism of the day.

The late 1800s and early 1900s were a period of the efforts of many to make significant reforms and changes in the areas of politics, society, and the economy. There was a need to reduce the levels of poverty and to improve the living conditions of those affected by it. Regulations of big business, ridding governmental corruption and making it more responsive to the needs of the people were also on the list of reforms to be accomplished. Until 1890, there was very little success, but from 1890 on the reformers gained increased public support and were able to achieve some influence in government. Since some of these individuals referred to themselves as "**progressives**," the period of 1890 to 1917 is referred to by historians as the **Progressive Era**.

This fire was fueled by the writings on investigative journalists – the "**muckrakers**" of "**yellow journalism**" – who published scathing exposes of political and business wrongdoing and corruption. The result was the rise of a group of politicians and reformers who supported a wide array of populist causes. Although these leaders came from many different backgrounds and were driven by different ideologies, they shared a common fundamental belief that government should be eradicating social ills and promoting the common good and the equality guaranteed by the Constitution.

The reforms initiated by these leaders and the spirit of Progressivism were far-reaching. Politically, many states enacted the initiative and the referendum. The adoption of the recall occurred in many states. Several states enacted legislation that would undermine the power of political machines. On a national level the two most significant political changes were the ratification of the **17th Amendment**, which required that all U.S. Senators be chosen by popular election, and the ratification of the **19th Amendment**, which granted women the right to vote.

Major economic reforms of the period included aggressive enforcement of the **Sherman Antitrust Act**; passage of the Elkins Act and the Hepburn Act, which gave the Interstate Commerce Commission greater power to regulate the railroads; the **Pure Food and Drug Act** prohibited the use of harmful chemicals in food; The Meat Inspection Act regulated the meat industry to protect the public against tainted meat; over two thirds of the states passed laws prohibiting child labor; workmen's compensation was mandated; and the **Department of Commerce and Labor** was created.

Responding to concern over the environmental effects of the timber, ranching, and mining industries, Roosevelt set aside 238 million acres of federal lands to protect them from development. Wildlife preserves were established, the national park system was expanded, and the **National Conservation Commission** was created. The Newlands Reclamation Act also provided federal funding for the construction of irrigation projects and dams in semi-arid areas of the country.

The Wilson Administration carried out additional reforms. The **Federal Reserve Act** created a national banking system, providing a stable money supply. The Sherman Act and the Clayton Antitrust Act defined unfair competition, made corporate officers liable for the illegal actions of employees, and exempted labor unions from antitrust lawsuits. The Federal Trade Commission was established to enforce these measures. Finally, the **16th Amendment was ratified**, establishing an income tax. This measure was designed to relieve the poor of a disproportionate burden in funding the federal government and make the wealthy pay a greater share of the nation's tax burden.

Skill 2.5d **Explain the development of federal Indian policy – including the environmental consequences of forced migration into marginal regions – and its consequences for American Indians.**

This forced migration of the Native Americans to lands that were deemed marginal, combined with the near-extermination of the buffalo, caused a downturn in Prairie Culture that relied on the horse for hunting, trading, and traveling.Pree-Civil War conflict was intense and frequent until 1867 when the government established two large tracts of land called "reservations" in Oklahoma and the Dakotas to which all tribes would be confined. With the war over, troops were sent west to enforce the relocation and reservation containment policies. There were frequent wars, particularly as white settlers attempted to move onto Indian lands and as the tribes resisted this confinement.

Numerous conflicts, often called the "**Indian Wars**," broke out between the U.S. army and many different native tribes. Many treaties were signed with the various tribes, but most were broken by the government for a variety of reasons. Two of the most notable battles were the **Battle of Little Bighorn** in 1876, in which native people defeated General Custer and his forces, and the massacre of Native Americans in 1890 at **Wounded Knee**. In 1876, the U.S. government ordered all surviving Native Americans to move to reservations.

Continuing conflict led to passage of the **Dawes Act of 1887**. This was a recognition that confinement to reservations was not working. The law was intended to break up the Indian communities and bring about assimilation into white culture by deeding portions of the reservation lands to individual Indians who were expected to farm their land. The policy continued until 1934.

In addition, during the late nineteenth century, the avid reformers of the day instituted a practice of trying to "civilize" Indian children by educating them in Indian Boarding Schools. The children were forbidden to speak their native languages, they were forced to convert to Christianity, and generally forced to give up all aspects of their native culture and identity. There are numerous reports of abuse of the Indian children at these schools.

Armed resistance essentially came to an end by 1890. The surrender of **Geronimo** and the massacre at Wounded Knee, led to a change of strategy by the Indians. Thereafter, the resistance strategy was to preserve their culture and traditions.

During World War I, a large number of Native Americans were drafted into military service. Most served heroically. This fact, combined with a growing desire to see the native peoples effectively merged into mainstream society, led to the enactment of the **Indian Citizenship Act of 1924**, by which Native Americans were granted U.S. citizenship.

Still, until recent years the policy of the federal government was to segregate and marginalize Native Americans. Their religion, arts, and culture had been largely ignored up until a revival in Indian culture and issues in the late 1960's and 70's. Safely restricted to reservations in the "Indian territory," various attempts were made to strip them of their inherited culture, just as they were stripped of their ancestral lands. Life on the reservations has been difficult for most Native Americans. The policies of extermination and relocation, as well as the introduction of disease among them significantly decimated their numbers by the end of the nineteenth century.

Skill 2.5e   Analyze the impact of industrialism and urbanization on the physical and social environments of the United States.

The increase in business and industry was greatly affected by the many rich natural resources that were found throughout the nation. The industrial machines were powered by the abundant water supply. The construction industry as well as products made from wood depended heavily on lumber from the forests. Coal and iron ore in abundance were needed for the steel industry, which profited and increased from the use of steel in such things as skyscrapers, automobiles, bridges, railroad tracks, and machines. Other minerals such as silver, copper, and petroleum played a large role in industrial growth, especially petroleum, from which gasoline was refined as fuel for the increasingly popular automobile.

The abundance of resources, together with growth of industry and the pace of capital investments led to the growth of cities. Populations were shifting from rural agricultural areas to urban industrial areas and by the early 1900s a third of the nation's population lived in cities. Industry needed workers in its factories, mills and plants and rural workers were being displaced by advances in farm machinery and their increasing use and other forms of automation.

The dramatic growth of population in cities was fueled by growing industries, more efficient transportation of goods and resources, and the people who migrated to those new industrial jobs, either from rural areas of the United States or immigrants from foreign lands. Increased urban populations, frequently packed into dense tenements, often without adequate sanitation or clean water, led to public health challenges that required cities to establish sanitation, water and public health departments to cope with and prevent epidemics. Political organizations also saw the advantage of mobilizing the new industrial working class and created vast patronage programs that sometimes became notorious for corruption in big-city machine politics, like **Tammany Hall** in New York.

(See also Skills 2.5b and 2.5c)

COMPETENCY 2.6   THE U.S. AS A WORLD POWER

Skill 2.6a   Evaluate the debate about American imperialistic policies before, during and following the Spanish-American War.

Once the American West was subdued and firmly under United States control did the United States start looking beyond its shores. When Great Britain finally acknowledged American independence in 1783, the country claimed about 900,000 square miles of territory. By 1899, the purchase of the Louisiana Territory from France and Florida from Spain, the addition of Texas, California and the southwest, and the Oregon Country, and the purchase of Alaska from Russia had more than quadrupled the size of the nation. The American "Empire" was now the fifth largest in the world, and it was time to look elsewhere.

Overseas markets were becoming important as American industry produced goods more efficiently and manufacturing capacity grew. Out of concern for the protection of shipping, the United States modernized and built up the Navy, which by 1900 ranked third in the world. This gave the U.S. the means to become an imperial power. The first overseas possession was **Midway Island** annexed in 1867.

By the 1880s, Secretary of State James G. Blaine pushed for expanding U.S. trade and influence to Central and South America and in the 1890s, President Grover Cleveland invoked the **Monroe Doctrine** to intercede in Latin American affairs when it looked like Great Britain was going to exert its influence and power in the Western Hemisphere. In the Pacific, the United States lent its support to American sugar planters who overthrew the Kingdom of **Hawaii** and eventually annexed it as U.S. territory.

During the 1890s, Spain controlled such overseas possessions as Puerto Rico, the Philippines, and Cuba. Cubans rebelled against Spanish rule and the U.S. government found itself besieged by demands from Americans to assist the Cubans in their revolt. The event that proved a turning point was the **Spanish-American War** in 1898.

When the revolution began in Cuba, it aroused the interest and concern of Americans who were aware of what was happening "at their doorstep." When the Spanish attempted to put down the revolt, the women and children of Cuba were treated with great cruelty. They were gathered into camps surrounded by armed guards and given little food. Much of the food that kept them alive came from supplies sent by the U.S. Americans were already concerned over years of anarchy and misrule by the Spanish. When reports of gross atrocities reached America, public sentiment clearly favored the Cuban people.

President McKinley had refused to recognize the rebellion, but had affirmed the possibility of American intervention. Spain resented this attitude of the Americans.

In February 1898, the American battleship *Maine* was blown up in Havana harbor. Although there was no incontrovertible evidence that the Spanish were responsible, popular sentiment accused Spanish agents and war became inevitable.

Two months later, Congress declared war on Spain and the U.S. quickly defeated them. The peace treaty gave the U.S. possession of Puerto Rico, the Philippines, Guam and Hawaii, which was annexed during the war. Victory over the Spanish proved fruitful for American territorial ambitions. Although Congress passed legislation renouncing claims to annex Cuba in a rare moment of idealism, the United States gained control of the island of **Puerto Rico**, a permanent deep-water naval harbor at Guantanamo Bay, Cuba, the Philippines and various other Pacific islands formerly possessed by Spain. The decision to occupy the **Philippines**, rather than grant it immediate independence, led to a guerrilla war, the "Philippines Insurrection" that lasted until 1902. U.S. rule over the Philippines lasted until 1942, but unlike the guerrilla war years, American rule was relatively benign. The peace treaty gave the U.S. possession of **Puerto Rico, the Philippines, Guam and Hawaii**, which was annexed during the war.

Skill 2.6b   **Analyze the political, economic, and geographic significance of the Panama Canal, the "Open Door" policy with China, Theodore Roosevelt's "Big Stick" Diplomacy, William Howard Taft's "Dollar" Diplomacy, and Woodrow Wilson's Moral Diplomacy.**

Until the middle of the nineteenth century, American foreign policy and expansionism was essentially restricted to the North American Continent. America had shown no interest in establishing colonies in other lands. Specifically, the U.S. had stayed out of the rush to claim African territories. The variety of imperialism that found expression under the administrations of McKinley and Theodore Roosevelt was not precisely comparable to the imperialistic goals of European nations. There was a type of idealism in American foreign policy that sought to use military power in territories and other lands only in the interest of human rights and the spread of democratic principles. Much of the concern and involvement in Central and South America, as well as the Caribbean, was to link the two coasts of the nation and to protect the American economy from European encroachment.

Although the idea of a canal in Panama goes back to the early sixteenth century, work did not begin until 1880 by the French. The effort collapsed and the U.S. completed the task, opening the **Panama Canal** in 1914. Construction was an enormous task of complex engineering. The significance of the canal is that it connects the Gulf of Panama in the Pacific Ocean with the Caribbean Sea and the Atlantic Ocean. It eliminated the need for ships to skirt the southern boundary of South America, effectively reducing the sailing distance from New York to San Francisco by 8,000 miles (over half of the distance). The Canal results in a shorter and faster voyage, thus reducing shipping time and cost.

The U.S. helped Panama win independence from Colombia in exchange for control of the Panama Canal Zone. A large investment was made in eliminating disease from the area, particularly yellow fever and malaria. After WWII, control of the Canal became an issue of contention between the U.S. and Panama. Negotiations toward a settlement began in 1974, resulting in the Torrijos-Carter Treaties of 1977. Thus began the process of handing the Canal over to Panama. On December 31, 1999, control of the Canal was handed over to the Panama Canal Authority. Tolls for the use of the Canal have ranged from $0.36, when Richard Halliburton swam the canal, to about $226,000.

The **Open Door Policy** refers to maintaining equal commercial and industrial rights for the people of all countries in a particular territory. The Open Door policy generally refers to China, but it has also been used in application to the Congo basin. The policy was first suggested by the U.S., but its basis is the typical nation clause of the treaties made with China after the **Opium War** (1829-1842). The essential purpose of the policy was to permit equal access to trade for all nations with treaties with China while protecting the integrity of the Chinese empire. This policy was in effect from about 1900 until the end of WWII. After the war, China was recognized as a sovereign state. There was no longer opportunity for other nation to attempt to carve out regions of influence or control. When the Communist Party came to power in China, the policy was rejected. This continued until the late 1970s, when China began to adopt a policy of again encouraging foreign trade.

Big Stick Diplomacy was a term adopted from an African proverb, "speak softly and carry a big stick," to describe President Theodore Roosevelt's policy of the U.S. assuming international police power in the Western Hemisphere. The phrase implied the power to retaliate if necessary. The intention was to safeguard American economic interests in Latin America. The policy led to the expansion of the U.S. Navy and to greater involvement in world affairs. Should any nation in the Western Hemisphere become vulnerable to European control because of political or economic instability, the U.S. had both the right and the obligation to intervene.

Dollar Diplomacy describes U.S. efforts under President Taft to extend its foreign policy goals in Latin America and East Asia via economic power. The designation derives from Taft's claim that U.S. interests in Latin America had changed from "warlike and political" to "peaceful and economic." Taft justified this policy in terms of protecting the Panama Canal. The practice of dollar diplomacy was from time to time anything but peaceful, particularly in Nicaragua. When revolts or revolutions occurred, the U.S. sent troops to resolve the situation. Immediately upon resolution, bankers were sent in to loan money to the new regimes. The policy persisted until the election of Woodrow Wilson to the Presidency in 1913.

Wilson repudiated the dollar diplomacy approach to foreign policy within weeks of his inauguration. Wilson's "moral diplomacy" became the model for American foreign policy to this day. Wilson envisioned a federation of democratic nations, believing that democracy and representative government were the foundation stones of world stability. Specifically, he saw Great Britain and the United States as the champions of self-government and the promoters of world peace. Wilson's beliefs and actions set in motion an American foreign policy that was dedicated to the interests of all humanity rather than merely American national interests. Wilson promoted the power of free trade and international commerce as the key to enlarging the national economy into world markets as a means of acquiring a voice in world events. This approach to foreign policy was based on three elements. First, maintain a combat-ready military to meet the needs of the nation, second, promote democracy abroad, and third, improve the U.S. economy through international trade. Wilson believed that democratic states would be less inclined to threaten U.S. interests.

Skill 2.6c   Evaluate the political, economic, social, and geographic consequences of World War I in terms of American foreign policy and the war's impact on the American home front.

U.S. involvement in the war did not occur until 1916. When the war began in 1914, triggered by the assassination of Austrian Archduke Francis Ferdinand and his wife in Sarajevo, President Woodrow Wilson declared that the U.S. was neutral. Most Americans were opposed to any involvement anyway and were content to stay out of the matter as Europe marched off to war.

In 1916, Wilson was reelected to a second term based on a slogan proclaiming his efforts at keeping America out of the war. For a few months after, he put forth most of his efforts to stopping the war but German submarines began unlimited warfare against American merchant shipping. The development of the German *unterseeboat* or **U-boat** allowed them to efficiently attack merchant ships that were supplying their European enemies from Canada and the US. In 1915, a German U-boat sunk the passenger liner RMS **Lusitania**, killing over 1,000 civilians including over 100 Americans. This attack outraged the American public and turned public opinion against Germany. The attack on the Lusitania became a rallying point for those advocating US involvement in the European conflict.

Great Britain intercepted and decoded a secret message from Germany to Mexico urging Mexico to go to war against the U.S. The publishing of this information, known as the **Zimmerman Note,** along with continued German destruction of American ships resulted in the eventual entry of the U.S. into the conflict, the first time the country prepared to fight in a conflict not on American soil. Though unprepared for war, governmental efforts and activities resulted in massive defense mobilization with America's economy directed to the war effort. Though America made important contributions of war materials, its greatest contribution to the war was manpower, soldiers desperately needed by the Allies.

The United States war effort included over four million who served in the military in some capacity, over two million of whom served overseas. The cost of the war up to April 30, 1919 was over 22.5 billion dollars. Nearly 50,000 Americans were killed in battle and an additional 221,000 were wounded. On the home front, people energetically supported the war effort in every way necessary. The menace of German submarines was causing the loss of ships faster than new ships could be built. At the beginning of the war, the U.S. had little overseas shipping. Scores of shipyards were quickly constructed to build both wooden and steel ships. At the end of the war the United States had more than 2,000 ships.

Some ten months before the war ended, President Wilson had proposed a program called the **Fourteen Points** as a method of bringing the war to an end with an equitable peace settlement. In these Points he had five points setting out general ideals; there were eight pertaining to immediately working to resolve territorial and political problems; and the fourteenth point counseled establishing an organization of nations to help keep world peace.

When Germany agreed in 1918 to an armistice, it assumed that the peace settlement would be drawn up on the basis of these Fourteen Points. However, the peace conference in Paris ignored these points and Wilson had to be content with efforts at establishing the **League of Nations**. Italy, France, and Great Britain, having suffered and sacrificed far more in the war than America, wanted retribution. The treaties punished severely the Central Powers, taking away arms and territories and requiring payment of reparations. Germany was punished more than the others and, according to one clause in the treaty, was forced to assume the responsibility for causing the war.

President Wilson lost in his efforts to get the U.S. Senate to approve the peace treaty. The Senate at the time was a reflection of American public opinion and its rejection of the treaty was a rejection of Wilson. The approval of the treaty would have made the U.S. a member of the League of Nations but Americans had just come off a bloody war to ensure that democracy would exist throughout the world. Americans just did not want to accept any responsibility that resulted from its new position of power and were afraid that membership in the League of Nations would embroil the U.S. in future disputes in Europe.

After the war President Woodrow Wilson announced the willingness of the United States to become a partner in international alliances that were committed to peace and national self-determination and prevention of violation of those principles by the forcible intervention of other nations. Wilson's unwillingness to compromise at home on the issue of limiting U.S. sovereignty resulted in a failure to lead the U.S. into the League of Nations. Franklin Roosevelt learned from this experience and was able to ensure that the United Nations charter incorporated a mechanism by which a nation could refuse to accede to the will of the majority in the Security Council.

Herbert Hoover had chaired the Belgian Relief Commission previously. He was named "food commissioner," later called the U.S. Food Administration Board. His function was to manage conservation and distribution of the food supply to ensure that there was adequate food to supply every American both at home and overseas, as well as providing additional food to people who were suffering in Europe.

In December of 1917, the government assumed control of all of the railroads in the nation and consolidated them into a single system with regional directors. The goal of this action was to increase efficiency and enable the rail system to meet the needs of both commerce and military transportation. This was done with the understanding that private ownership would be restored after the war. The restoration occurred in 1920. In 1918, telegraph, telephone and cable services were also taken over by the federal government; they were returned to original management and ownership in 1919.

The American Red Cross and the volunteers who supported their effort knitted garments for both the Army and the Navy. In addition, they prepared surgical dressings, hospital garments and refugee garments. More than eight million people participated in this effort.

To secure the huge sums of money needed to finance the war, the government sold "**Liberty Bonds**" to the people. Nearly $25 billion worth of bonds were sold in four issues of bonds. After the war "Victory Bonds" were sold. The first Liberty loan was issues at 3.5%, the second at 4%, the remaining ones at 4.25%. A strong appeal was made to the people to buy bonds. The total response meant that more than one fifth of the inhabitants of the U.S. bought bonds. For the first time in their lives, millions of people had begun saving money.

The war effort required massive production of weapons, ammunition, radios, and other equipment of war and the support of war. During wartime, work hours were shortened, wages were increased, and working conditions improved. But when the war ended, and business and industrial owners and managers attempted a return to pre-war conditions, the workers revolted. These conditions contributed to the Red Scare and the establishment of new labor laws.

COMPETENCY 2.7   **THE 1920s**

Skill 2.7a   **Analyze domestic events that resulted in, or contributed to, the Red Scare, Marcus Garvey's Back to Africa movement, the Ku Klux Klan, the American Civil Liberties Union, the National Association for the Advancement of Colored People, and the Anti-Defamation League.**

The 1920s was a period of relative prosperity, under the leadership of Warren G. Harding and Calvin Coolidge. Harding had promised a return to "normalcy" in the aftermath of World War I and the radical reactions of labor. During most of the decade, the output of industry boomed and the automobile industry put almost 27 million cars on the road. Per capita income rose for almost everyone except farmers.

The decade was also characterized by profound change. **Jazz** was the popular musical form. Professional boxing, radio and silent movies provided new entertainment for the public. The Charleston (dance) and the "flapper look" were popular. The National Origins Act of 1924 ended immigration for the first time in history. In Tennessee, the "**Monkey Trial**" convicted John Scopes for teaching evolution in science classes. The Bolshevik Revolution in Russia was also in the minds of the populace.

Part of the return to "normalcy" promised by Harding, was to restore order in the aftermath of a wave of radicalism. During the war, patriotism prevailed. Many believed that this strong patriotism was the fertile ground from which the Red Scare grew. During the war, about nine million people in the nation were employed in war-related industries. An additional four million were serving in the military. When the war ended, most of these people were without jobs and the war industries were without work. There was a small depression in 1920-21, which gave rise to worker unrest. Two groups were highly visible at the time: the **International Workers of the World (IWW)** and the Socialist party, led by Eugene Debs. Because both groups had opposed the war, the intensely patriotic population viewed them as unpatriotic and dangerous.

A huge wave of labor strikes sought a return to war-time working conditions when the work day was shorter, wages were higher, and conditions were better. Many of these labor strikes turned violent. The majority of the population viewed the early strikes as the work of radicals, who were labeled "reds" (communists). As the news spread and other strikes occurred, the "**red scare**" swept the country. Americans feared a Bolshevik-type revolution in America. As a result, people were jailed for expressing views that were considered anarchist, communist or socialist. In an attempt to control the potential for revolution, civil liberties were ignored and thousands were deported. The Socialist Party also came to be viewed as a group of anarchist radicals. Several state and local governments passed a variety of laws designed to reduce radical speech and activity. Congress considered more than 70 anti-sedition bills, though none was passed.

Within a year, the Red Scare had essentially run its course. Although many they returned to their normal pursuits, there was a response that gave rise to a variety of groups and organizations that hoped to restore order.

Marcus Garvey, an English-educated Jamaican, established an organization called the *Universal Negro Improvement and Conservation Association and African Communities League* (usually called the Universal Negro Improvement Association). In 1919 this "Black Moses" claimed followers numbering about twi million. He spoke of a "new Negro" who was proud to be black. He published a newspaper in which he taught about the "heroes" of the race and the strengths of African culture. He told blacks that they would be respected only when they were economically strong. He created a number of businesses by which he hoped to achieve this goal. He then called blacks to work with him to build an all-black nation in Africa. His belief in racial purity and black separatism was not shared by a number of black leaders. In 1922 he and other members of the organization were jailed for mail fraud. His sentence was commuted and he was deported to Jamaica as an undesirable alien.

The **Ku Klux Klan** (KKK) is a name that has been used by several white supremacist organizations through history. Their beliefs encompass white supremacy, anti-Semitism, racism, anti-Catholicism and nativism. Their typical methods of intimidation have included terrorism, violence, cross burning and the like. The birth of the organization was in 1866. At that time, members were veterans of the Confederate Army seeking to resist Reconstruction and the "**carpetbaggers**. "

The Klan entered a second period beginning in 1915. Using the new film medium, this group tried to spread its message with *The Birth of a Nation*. They also published a number of anti-Semitic newspaper articles. The group became a structured membership organization. Its membership did not begin to decline until the Great Depression. Although the KKK began in the South, its membership at its peak extended into the Midwest, the Northern states, and even into Canada. Membership during the 1920s reached approximately four million – 20% of the adult white male population in many regions and as high as 40% in some areas. The political influence of the group was significant. They essentially controlled the governments of Tennessee, Indiana, Oklahoma and Oregon as well as some Southern legislatures.

Within the context of fear of radicalism and rampant racism and efforts to repress various groups within the population, it is not surprising that several groups were formed to protect the civil rights and liberties guaranteed to all citizens by the U.S. Constitution. The **American Civil Liberties Union** was formed in 1920. It was originally an outgrowth of the American Union Against Militarism, which had opposed American involvement in WWI, and provided legal advice and assistance for conscientious objectors and those who were being prosecuted under the Espionage Act of 1917 and the Sedition Act of 1918. With the name change there was attention to additional concerns and activities. The agency began to try to protect immigrants threatened with deportation and citizens threatened with prosecution for communist activities and agendas. They also opposed efforts to repress the Industrial Workers of the World and other labor unions.

Today, the ACLU is a non-profit organization whose mission is "to defend and preserve the individual rights and liberties guaranteed to every person in this Country by the Constitution and laws of the United States." [American Civil Liberties Union website], The organization accomplishes its goals through community education, litigation and legislation.

The National Association for the Advancement of Colored People (NAACP) was founded in 1909 to assist African Americans. In the early years, the work of the organization focused on working through the courts to overturn "Jim Crow" statutes that legalized racial discrimination. The group organized voters to oppose Woodrow Wilson's efforts to weave racial segregation into federal government policy. Between WWI and WWII, much energy was devoted to stopping the lynching of blacks throughout the country.

The Anti-Defamation League was created in 1913 to stop discrimination against the Jewish people. Its charter states, "Its ultimate purpose is to secure justice and fair treatment to all citizens alike and to put an end forever to unjust and unfair discrimination against ridicule of any sect or body of citizens. The organization has historically opposed all groups considered anti-Semitic and/or racist. This has included the Ku Klux Klan, the Nazis, and a variety of others.

Skill 2.7b **Analyze the significance of the passage of the 18th and 19th Amendments as they related to the changing political and economic roles of women in society.**

The end of World War I and the decade of the 1920s saw tremendous changes in the United States, signifying the beginning of its development into its modern society today. The shift from farm to city life was occurring in tremendous numbers. Social changes and problems were occurring at such a fast pace that it was extremely difficult and perplexing for many Americans to adjust to them. Politically the 18th Amendment to the Constitution, the so-called Prohibition Amendment, prohibited selling alcoholic beverages throughout the U.S. resulting in problems affecting all aspects of society. The passage of the 19th Amendment gave women the right to vote in all elections. The decade of the 1920s also showed a marked change in roles and opportunities for women with more and more of them seeking and finding careers outside the home. They began to think of themselves as the equal of men and not as much as housewives and mothers.

The influence of the automobile, the entertainment industry, and the rejection of the morals and values of pre-World War I life, resulted in the fast-paced "**Roaring Twenties.**" There were significant effects on events leading to the Depression-era 1930s and another world war. Many Americans greatly desired the pre-war life and supported political policies and candidates in favor of the return to what was considered normal. It was desired to end government's strong role and adopt a policy of isolating the country from world affairs, a result of the war.

Prohibition of the sale of alcohol had caused the increased activities of bootlegging and the rise of underworld gangs and the illegal speakeasies, the jazz music and dances they promoted. The customers of these clubs were considered "modern," reflected by extremes in clothing, hairstyles, and attitudes towards authority and life. Movies and other types of entertainment, along with increased interest in sports figures and the accomplishments of national heroes, such as aviator **Charles Lindbergh**, influenced Americans to admire, emulate, and support individual accomplishments.

As wild and uninhibited modern behavior became, this decade witnessed an increase in a religious tradition known as "revivalism," emotional preaching. Although law and order were demanded by many Americans, the administration of President Warren G. Harding was marked by widespread corruption and scandal, not unlike the administration of Ulysses S. Grant, except Grant was honest and innocent. The decade of the 1920s also saw the resurgence of such racist organizations as the Ku Klux Klan.

Skill 2.7c   Assess changes in American immigration policy in the 1920s.

Immigration has played a crucial role in the growth and settlement of the United States from the start. With a large interior territory to fill and ample opportunity, the US encouraged immigration throughout most of the nineteenth century, maintaining an almost completely open policy. Famine in Ireland and Germany in the 1840s resulted in over 3.5 million immigrants from these two countries alone between the years of 1830 and 1860.

Following the Civil War, rapid expansion in rail transportation brought the interior states within easy reach of new immigrants who still came primarily from Western Europe and entered the US on the east coast. As immigration increased, several states adopted individual immigration laws, and in 1875 the US Supreme Court declared immigration a federal matter. Following a huge surge in European immigration in 1880, the United States began to regulate immigration, first by passing a tax to new immigrants, then by instituting literacy requirements and barring those with mental or physical illness. A large influx of Chinese immigration to the western states had resulted in the complete exclusion of immigrants from that country in 1882. In 1891, the Federal Bureau of Immigration was established. Even with these new limits in place, immigration remained relatively open in the US to those from European countries, and increased steadily until World War I.

With much of Europe left in ruins after WWI, immigration to the US exploded in the years following the war. In 1920 and 1921, some 800,000 new immigrants arrived. Unlike previous immigrants who came mainly from western European countries, the new wave of immigrants was from southern and eastern Europe. The US responded to this sudden shift in the makeup of new immigrants with a **quota system**, first enacted by Congress in 1921. This system limited immigration in proportion to the ethnic groups that were already settled in the US according to previous census records. This national-origins policy was extended and further defined by Congress in 1924.

This policy remained the official policy of the US for the next forty years. Occasional challenges to the law from non-white immigrants re-affirmed that the intention of the policy was to limit immigration primarily to white, western Europeans, who the government felt were most likely to assimilate into American culture. Strict limitations on Chinese immigration was extended throughout the period, and only relaxed in 1940. In 1965, Congress overhauled immigration policy, removing the quotas and replacing them with a preference based system. Now, immigrants reuniting with family members and those with special skills or education were given preference. As a result, immigration from Asian and African countries began to increase. The 40-year legacy of the 1920s immigration restrictions had a direct and dramatic impact on the makeup of modern American society. Had Congress not imposed what amounted to racial limits on new arrivals to the country, the US would perhaps be a larger more diverse nation today.

Skill 2.7d   Describe new tends in literature, music, and art, including the Harlem Renaissance and the Jazz Age.

As African Americans left the rural South and migrated to the North in search of opportunity, many settled in Harlem in New York City. By the 1920s Harlem had become a center of life and activity for persons of color. The music, art, and literature of this community gave birth to a cultural movement known as **the Harlem Renaissance**. The artistic expressions that emerged from this community in the 1920s and 1930s celebrated the black experience, black traditions, and the voices of black America. Major writers and works of this movement included: Langston Hughes (The Weary Blues), Nella Larsen (Passing), Zora Neale Hurston (Their Eyes Were Watching God), Claude McKay, Countee Cullen, and Jean Toomer.

Many refer to the decade of the 1920s as **The Jazz Age**. The decade was a time of optimism and exploration of new boundaries. It was a clear movement in many ways away from conventionalism. Jazz music, uniquely American, was the country's popular music at the time. The jazz musical style perfectly typified the mood of society. Jazz is essentially free-flowing improvisation on a simple theme with a four-beat rhythm. Jazz originated in the poor districts of New Orleans as an outgrowth of the Blues. The leading jazz musicians of the time included: Buddy Bolden, Joseph "King" Oliver, Duke Ellington, Louis Armstrong, and Jelly Roll Morton.

As jazz grew in popularity and in the intricacy of the music, it gave birth to **Swing** and the era of **Big Band** by the mid 1920s. Some of the most notable musicians of the Big Band era were: Bing Crosby, Frank Sinatra, Don Redman, Fletcher Henderson, Count Basie, Benny Goodman, Billie Holiday, Ella Fitzgerald, and The Dorsey Brothers among others.

In painting and sculpture, the new direction of the decade was **realism**. In the early years of the twentieth century, American artists had developed several realist styles, some of which were influenced by modernism, others that reacted against it. Several groups of artists of this period are particularly notable.

The Eight or **The Ashcan School** developed around the work and style of Robert Henri. Their subjects were everyday urban life that was presented without adornment or glamour. **The American Scene Painters** produced a tight, detailed style of painting that focused on images of American life that were understandable to all. In the Midwest, a school within this group was called **regionalism**. One of the leading artists of regionalism was Grant Wood, best known for *American Gothic.* Other important realists of the day were Edward Hopper and Georgia O'Keeffe.

Skill 2.7e   **Assess the impact of radio, mass production techniques, and the growth of cities on American society.**

Although the British patent for the **radio** was awarded in 1896, it was not until WWI that the equipment and capability of the use of radio was recognized. The first radio program was broadcast August 31, 1920. The first entertainment broadcasts began in 1922 from England. One of the first developments in the twentieth century was the use of commercial AM radio stations for aircraft navigation. In addition, radio was used to communicate orders and information between army and navy units on both sides of the war during WWI. Broadcasting became practical in the 1920s. Radio receivers were introduced on a wide scale.

The relative economic boom of the 1920s made it possible for many households to own a radio. The beginning of broadcasting and the proliferation of receivers revolutionized communication. The news was transmitted into every home with a radio. In addition, news and information could be transmitted very quickly. Rather than the newsreels at movie theaters or awaiting the printing of stories sent to newspapers by mail, the news was now immediate. With the beginning of entertainment broadcasting, people were able to remain in their homes for entertainment. Rather than obtaining filtered information, people were able to hear the actual speeches and information that became news. By the time of the Stock Market Crash in 1929, approximately 40% of households had a radio.

Another innovation of the 1920s was the introduction of **mass production**. This is the production of large amounts of standardized products on production lines. The method became very popular when Henry Ford used mass production to build the Model T Ford. The process facilitates high production rates per worker. Thus, it created very inexpensive products. The process is, however, capital intensive. It requires expensive machinery in high proportion to the number of workers needed to operate it.

From an economic perspective, mass production decreases labor costs, increases the rate of production, and thus increases profit. The equipment and start-up costs of implementing mass production techniques is very high. Mass production reduces the amount of non-productive effort. It also reduces the chance of human error and variation. The downside of mass production is its inflexibility. Once a process is established, it is difficult to modify a design or a production process. From the viewpoint of labor, however, mass production can create job shortages.

During the period before and after 1900, a large number of people migrated to the cities of America. Throughout the nineteenth century city populations grew faster than rural populations. The new immigrants were not farmers. Polish immigrants became steelworkers in Pittsburgh; Serbian immigrants became meatpackers in Chicago; Russian Jewish immigrants became tailors in New York City; Slovaks assembled cars in Detroit; Italians worked in the factories of Baltimore.

Several factors promoted urbanization during the decade of the 1920s. The decline of agriculture, the drop in prices for grain and produce, and the end of financial support for farming after WWI caused many farmers to go under during the 1920s. Many sold or lost their farms and migrated to cities to find work. Continuing industrialization drew increasing numbers of workers to the areas near or surrounding industrial or manufacturing centers. Cities were becoming the locus of political, cultural, financial and economic life. Transportation to the place of work or shopping for necessities facilitated the growth of cities.

As the population grew in cities, the demographic composition of those areas began to change. Workers flocked to the cities to be closer to the factories that employed them. As the populations of poorer workers increased, the wealthy moved from the city into the suburbs. The availability of automobiles and the extension of public transportation beyond the city limits enabled the middle and upper classes to leave city centers.

Urbanization brings certain needs in its wake, including: adequate water supply, management of sewage and garbage, the need for public services, such as fire and police, road construction and maintenance, building of bridges to connect parts of cities, and taller buildings were needed. This last led to the invention of steel-framed buildings and of the elevator. In addition, electricity and telephone lines were needed, department stores and supermarkets grew, and the need for additional schools were related to urbanization. With the large migration and low wages came overcrowding, often in old buildings. **Slums** began to appear. Soon public health issues began to arise.

COMPETENCY 2.8 THE GREAT DEPRESSION AND THE NEW DEAL

Skill 2.8a **Analyze the differing explanation for the 1929 stock market crash, Herbert Hoover's and Congress' responses to the crisis, and the implementation of Franklin Delano Roosevelt's New Deal policies.**

The 1929 Stock Market crash was the powerful event that is generally interpreted as the beginning of the Great Depression in America. Although the crash of the Stock Market was unexpected, it was not without identifiable causes. The 1920s had been a decade of social and economic growth and hope. But the attitudes and actions of the 1920s regarding wealth, production, and investment created several trends that quietly set the stage for the 1929 disaster.

Uneven distribution of wealth: In the 1920s, the distribution of wealth between the rich and the middle-class was grossly disproportionate. In 1929, the combined income of the top 0.1% of the population was equal to the combined income of the bottom 42%. The top 0.1% of the population controlled 34% of all savings, while 80% of American had no savings. Capitalism was enriching the wealthy at the expense of the workers. Between 1920 and 1929, the amount of disposable income per person rose 9%. The top 0.1% of the population, however, enjoyed an increase in disposable income of 75%. One reason for this disparity was increased manufacturing productivity during the 1920s. Average worker productivity in manufacturing increased 32% during this period. Yet wages in manufacturing increased only 8%. The wages of the workers rose very slowly, failing to keep pace with increasing productivity. As production costs fell and prices remained constant, profits soared. But profits were retained by the companies and the owners.

The legislative and executive branches of the Coolidge administration tended to favor business and the wealthy. The **Revenue Act of 1926** reduced income taxes for the wealthy significantly. This bill lowered taxes such that a person with a million-dollar income saw his/her taxes reduced from $600,000 to $200,000. Despite the rise of labor unions, even the Supreme Court ruled in ways that further widened the gap between the rich and the middle class. In the case of Adkins v. Children's Hospital (1923), the Court ruled that minimum wage legislation was unconstitutional.

This kind of disparity in the distribution of wealth weakens the economy. Demand was unable to equal supply. The surplus of manufactured goods was beyond the reach of the poor and the middle class. The wealthy, however, could purchase all they wanted with a smaller and smaller portion of their income. This meant that in order for the economy to remain stable, the wealthy must invest their money and spend money on luxury items and others must buy on credit.

The majority of the population did not have enough money to buy what was necessary to meet their needs. The concept of buying on credit caught on very quickly. Buying on credit, however, creates artificial demand for products people cannot ordinarily afford. This has two effects: first, at some point there is less need to purchase products (because they have already been bought), and second, at some point paying for previous purchases makes it impossible to purchase new products. This exacerbated the problem of a surplus of goods.

The economy also relied on investment and luxury spending by the rich in the 1920s. **Luxury spending**, however, only occurs when people are confident with regard to the economy and the future. Should these people lose confidence, that luxury spending would come to an abrupt halt. This is precisely what happened when the stock market crashed in 1929. Investing in business produces returns for the investor. During the 1920s, investing was very healthy. Investors, however, began to expect greater returns on their investments. This led many to make speculative investments in risky opportunities.

The disproportionate distribution of wealth between the rich and the middle-class mirrors the uneven distribution of wealth between industries. In 1929, half of all corporate wealth was controlled by just 200 companies. The automotive industry was growing exceptionally quickly, but agriculture was steadily declining. In fact, in 1921 food prices dropped about 70% due to surplus. The average income in agriculture was only about one-third of the national average across all industries.

Two industries, automotive and radio, drove the economy in the 1920s. During this decade, the government tended to support new industries rather than agriculture. During WWI, the government had subsidized farms and paid ridiculously high prices for grains. Farmers had been encouraged to buy and farm more land and to use new technology to increase production. The nation was feeding much of Europe during and in the aftermath of the war. But when the war ended, these farm policies were cut off. Prices plummeted, farmers fell into debt, and farm prices declined. The agriculture industry was on the brink of ruin before the stock market crash.

The concentration of production and economic stability in the automotive industry and the production and sale of radios was expected to last forever. But there comes a point when the growth of an industry slows due to market saturation. When these two industries declined, due to decreased demand, they caused the collapse of other industries upon which they were dependent (e.g., rubber tires, glass, fuel, construction, etc.).

The other factor contributing to the Great Depression was the economic condition of Europe. The U.S. was lending money to European nations to rebuild. Many of these countries used this money to purchase U.S. food and manufactured goods. But they were not able to pay off their debts. While the U.S. was providing money, food, and goods to Europe, however, it was not willing to buy European goods. **Trade barriers** were enacted to maintain a favorable trade balance.

Risky speculative investments in the stock market was the second major factor contributing to the stock market crash of 1929 and the ensuing Depression. Stock market speculation was spectacular throughout the 1920s. In 1929, shares traded on the New York Stock Exchange reached 1,124,800,410. In 1928 and 1929 stock prices doubled and tripled (RCA stock prices rose from 85 to 420 within one year). The opportunity to achieve such profits was irresistible. In much the same way that buying goods on credit became popular, buying stock on margin allowed people to invest a very small amount of money in the hope of receiving exceptional profit. This created an investing craze that drove the market higher and higher. But brokers were also charging higher interest rates on their margin loans (nearly 20%). If, however, the price of the stock dropped, the investor owed the broker the amount borrowed plus interest.

Several other factors are cited by some scholars as contributing to the Great Depression. First, in 1929, the Federal Reserve increased interest rates. Second, some believe that as interest rates rose and the stock market began to decline, people began to hoard money. This was certainly the case after the crash.

In September 1929, stock prices began to slip somewhat, yet people remained optimistic. On Monday, October 21, prices began to fall quickly. The volume traded was so high that the tickers were unable to keep up. Investors were frightened, and they started selling very quickly. This caused further collapse. For the next two days prices stabilized somewhat. On **Black Thursday**, October 24, prices plummeted again. By this time investors had lost confidence. On Friday and Saturday an attempt to stop the crash was made by some leading bankers. But on Monday the 28th, prices began to fall again, declining by 13% in one day. The next day, **Black Tuesday, October 29**, saw 16.4 million shares traded. Stock prices fell so far, that at many times no one was willing to buy at any price.

Much of the stock speculation of the 1920's involved paying a small part of the cost and borrowing the rest. This led eventually to the stock market crash of 1929, financial ruin for many investors, a weakening of the nation's economy, and the **Great Depression** of the 1930s. The Depression hit the United States tremendously hard resulting in bank failures, loss of jobs due to cut-backs in production and a lack of money leading to a sharp decline in spending which in turn affected businesses, factories and stores, and higher unemployment. Farm products were not affordable so the farmers suffered even more. Foreign trade sharply decreased and in the early 1930s, the U.S. economy was effectively paralyzed. Europe was affected even more so.

In the immediate aftermath of the stock market crash, many urged President Herbert Hoover to provide government relief. Hoover responded by urging the nation to be patient. By the time he signed relief bills in 1932, it was too late, and Hoover's bid for re-election in 1932 failed.

The new president, **Franklin D. Roosevelt** won the White House on his promise to the American people of a "new deal." The revival of political liberalism in the twentieth century can be traced to the policies of **Franklin Roosevelt** beginning in the Great Depression of the 1930s. Roosevelt's **"New Deal"** programs aimed in part to provide relief to hard-hit workers by providing government sponsored work programs such as the Civilian Conservation Corps. This step was in stark contrast to prior administrations, particularly that of President Herbert Hoover, who believed that the government should not provide direct aid to citizens or be directly involved in the economy.

Many of Roosevelt's policies faced strong opposition, and some programs were struck down by the Supreme Court. Roosevelt was a tremendously popular president, however, and was elected to four terms. Numerous like-minded Democrats were swept into office in the wake of Roosevelt's popularity.

The election of Franklin Roosevelt, largely on his promise to the American people of a "new deal," was the start of the social and economic recovery and reform legislative acts designed to gradually ease the country back to more prosperity. Upon assuming the office, Roosevelt and his advisers immediately launched a massive program of innovation and experimentation to try to bring the Depression to an end and get the nation back on track. Congress gave the President unprecedented power to act to save the nation. During the next eight years, the most extensive and broadly-based legislation in the nation's history was enacted. The legislation was intended to accomplish three goals: **relief, recovery, and reform.**

The first step in the **New Deal** was to relieve suffering. This was accomplished through a number of job-creation projects. The second step, the recovery aspect, was to stimulate the economy. The third step was to create social and economic change through innovative legislation.

To provide economic stability and prevent another crash, Congress passed the **Glass-Steagall Act**, which separated banking and investing. The Securities and Exchange Commission was created to regulate dangerous speculative practices on Wall Street. The Wagner Act guaranteed a number of rights to workers and unions in an effort to improve worker-employer relations. The **Social Security Act of 1935** established pensions for the aged and infirm as well as a system of unemployment insurance.

Much of the recovery program was emergency, but certain permanent national policies emerged. The intention of the public through its government was to supervise and, to an extent, regulate business operations, from corporate activities to labor problems. This included protecting bank depositors and the credit system of the country, employing gold resources and currency adjustments to aid permanent restoration of normal living, and, if possible, establishing a line of subsistence below which no useful citizen would be permitted to sink.

The National Recovery Administration attempted to accomplish several goals:

- Restore employment
- Increase general purchasing power
- Provide character-building activity for unemployed youth
- Encourage decentralization of industry and thus divert population from crowded cities to rural or semi-rural communities
- To develop river resources in the interest of navigation and cheap power and light
- To complete flood control on a permanent basis
- To enlarge the national program of forest protection and to develop forest resources
- To control farm production and improve farm prices
- To assist home builders and home owners
- To restore public faith in banking and trust operations
- To recapture the value of physical assets, whether in real property, securities, or other investments

These objectives and their accomplishment implied a restoration of public confidence and courage.

Among the "alphabet organizations" set up to work out the details of the recovery plan, the most prominent were:

- **Agricultural Adjustment Administration** (AAA), designed to readjust agricultural production and prices thereby boosting farm income
- **Civilian Conservation Corps** (CCC), designed to give wholesome, useful activity in the forestry service to unemployed young men
- **Civil Works Administration** (CWA) and the **Public Works Administration** (PWA), designed to give employment in the construction and repair of public buildings, parks, and highways
- **Works Progress Administration** (WPA), whose task was to move individuals from relief rolls to work projects or private employment

The **Tennessee Valley Authority** (TVA) was of a more permanent nature, designed to improve the navigability of the Tennessee River and increase productivity of the timber and farm lands in its valley, this program built 16 dams that provided water control and hydroelectric generation.

The **Public Works Administration** employed Americans on over 34,000 public works projects at a cost of more than $4 billion. Among these projects was the construction of a highway that linked the Florida Keys and Miami, the Boulder Dam (now the Hoover Dam) and numerous highway projects.

Many of the steps taken by the Roosevelt administration have had far-reaching effects. They alleviated the economic disaster of the Great Depression, they enacted controls that would mitigate the risk of another stock market crash, and they provided greater security for workers. The nation's economy, however, did not fully recover until America entered World War II.

Skill 2.8b	**Describe and assess the human toll of the Great Depression, including the impact of natural disasters and agricultural practices on the migration from rural Southern and Eastern regions to urban and Western areas.**

Unemployment quickly reached 25% nation-wide. People thrown out of their homes created makeshift domiciles of cardboard, scraps of wood and tents. With unmasked reference to President Hoover, who was quite obviously overwhelmed by the situation and incompetent to deal with it, these communities were called "**Hoovervilles**." Families stood in bread lines, rural workers left the dust bowl of the plains to search for work in California, and banks failed. More than 100,000 businesses failed between 1929 and 1932. The despair that swept the nation left an indelible scar on all who endured the Depression.

When the stock market crashed, businesses collapsed. Without demand for products other businesses and industries collapsed. This set in motion a domino effect, bringing down the businesses and industries that provided raw materials or components to these industries. Hundreds of thousands became jobless. Then the jobless often became homeless. Desperation prevailed. Little had been done to assess the toll hunger, inadequate nutrition, or starvation took on the health of those who were children during this time. Indeed, food was cheap, relatively speaking, but there was little money to buy it.

Everyone who lived through the Great Depression was permanently affected in some way. Many never trusted banks again. Many people of this generation later hoarded cash so they would not risk losing everything again. Some permanently rejected the use of credit.

In several parts of the country, economic disaster was exacerbated by natural disaster. The Florida Keys were hit by the "**Labor Day Hurricane**" in 1935. This was one of only three hurricanes in history to make landfall as a Category 5 storm. More than 400 died in the storm, including 200 WWI veterans who were building bridges for a public works project. In the Northeast, The **Great Hurricane of 1938** struck Long Island, causing more than 600 fatalities, decimating Long Island, and resulting in millions of dollars in damage to the coast from New York City to Boston.

By far the worst natural disaster of the decade came to be known as the **Dust Bowl.** Due to severe and prolonged drought in the Great Plains and previous reliance on inappropriate farming techniques, a series of devastating dust storms occurred in the 1930s that resulted in destruction, economic ruin for many, and dramatic ecological change.

Plowing the plains for agriculture removed the grass and exposed the soil. When the drought occurred, the soil dried out and became dust. Wind blew away the dust. Between 1934 and 1939 winds blew the soil to the east, all the way to the Atlantic Ocean. The dust storms, called "black blizzards" created huge clouds of dust that were visible all the way to Chicago. Topsoil was stripped from millions of acres. Crops were ruined, the land was destroyed, and people either lost or abandoned homes and farms.

In Texas, Arkansas, Oklahoma, New Mexico, Kansas and Colorado over half a million people were homeless. Many of these people journeyed west in the hope of making a new life in California. Fifteen percent of Oklahoma's population left. Because so many of the migrants were from Oklahoma, the migrants came to be called "**Okies**" no matter where they came from. Estimates of the number of people displaced by this disaster range from 300,000 or 400,000 to 2.5 million.

During the first 100 days in office, the Roosevelt Administration responded to this crisis with programs designed to restore the ecological balance. One action was the formation of the **Soil Conservation Service** (now the Natural Resources Conservation Service). The story of this natural disaster and its toll in human suffering is poignantly preserved in the photographs of Dorothea Lange.

Skill 2.8c   Analyze the effects of, and controversies arising from, New Deal policies, including the social and physical consequences of regional programs.

To be sure, there were negative reactions to some of the measures taken to pull the country out of the Depression. There was a major reaction to the deaths of the WWI veterans in the Labor Day Hurricane, ultimately resulting in a Congressional investigation into possible negligence. The Central Valley Project ruffled feathers of farmers who lost tillable land and some water supply to the construction of the aqueduct and the Hoover Dam. Tennesseans were initially unhappy with the changes in river flow and navigation when the Tennessee Valley Authority began its construction of dams and the directing of water to form reservoirs and to power hydroelectric plants. Some businesses and business leaders were not happy with the introduction of minimum wage laws and restrictions and controls on working conditions and limitations of work hours for laborers. The numerous import/export tariffs of the period were the subject of controversy.

In the long view, however, much that was accomplished under the New Deal had positive long-term effects on economic, ecological, social and political issues for the next several decades. The Tennessee Valley Authority and the Central Valley Project in California provided a reliable source and supply of water to major cities, as well as electrical power to meet the needs of an increasingly electricity-dependent society. For the middle class and the poor, the labor regulations, the establishment of the Social Security Administration, and the separation of investment and banking have served the nation admirably for more than six decades.

Skill 2.8d   Trace and evaluate the gains and losses or organized labor in the 1930s.

The charter of the National Recovery Administration included a statement defending the right of labor unions to exist and to negotiate with employers. This was interpreted by thousands as support for unions. But the Supreme Court declared this unconstitutional, and there would be several major events or actions that were particularly important to the history of organized labor during the decade.

The **Wagner Act** (The National Labor Relations Act) established a legal basis for unions, set collective bargaining as a matter of national policy required by the law, provided for secret ballot elections for choosing unions, and protected union members from employer intimidation and coercion. This law was later amended by the Taft-Hartley Act (1947) and by the Landrum Griffin Act (1959). The Wagner Act itself was upheld by the Supreme Court in 1937.

One of the most common tactics of the union was the **strike**. Half a million Southern mill workers walked off the job in the Great Uprising of 1934, establishing the precedent that without workers, industry could not move forward. Then, in 1936, the United Rubber Workers staged the first **sit-down strike** where instead of walking off the job, they stayed at their posts but refused to work. The United Auto Workers used the sit-down strike against General Motors in 1936.

Strikes were met with varying degrees of resistance by the companies. Sometimes, "**scabs**" were brought in to replace the striking workers. In 1936, the Anti-Strikebreaker Act (the Byrnes Act) made it illegal to transport or aid strikebreakers in interstate or foreign trade. In part this was an attempt to stem the violence often associated with management's attempts to bully the workers back into their jobs.

As the leaders of industry were often powerful community figures, they sometimes employed law enforcement to disrupt the strikes. During a strike in 1937 of the Steel Workers Organizing Committee against Republic Steel, police attacked a crowd gathered in support of the strike, killing ten and injuring eighty. This came to be called **The Memorial Day Massacre**.

A number of acts were designed to provide fair compensation and other benefits to workers. The Davis-Bacon Act was passed in 1931 and provided that employers of contractors and subcontractors on public construction should be paid the prevailing wages. The states sometimes took matters into their own hands. Wisconsin created the first unemployment insurance act in the country in 1932. The Public Contracts Act (the **Walsh-Healey Act**) of 1936 established labor standards, including minimum wages, overtime pay, child and convict labor provisions and safety standards on federal contracts. The **Fair Labor Standards** Act created a $0.25 minimum wage, stipulated time-and-a-half pay for hours over 40 per week. The Social Security Act was approved in 1935.

There were also efforts to clean up or unionize particular industries. The Supreme Court upheld the Railway Labor Act in 1930, including its prohibition of employer interference or coercion in the choice of bargaining representatives which was later applied to other organize labor unions. The Guffey Act stabilized the coal industry and improved labor conditions in 1935, though a year later it was declared unconstitutional. General Motors recognized the **United Auto Workers** and US Steel recognized the **Steel Workers Organizing Committee**, both in 1937. Then in 1938 Merchant Marine Act created a Federal Maritime Labor Board.

One of labor's biggest unions was formed in 1935. The Committee for Industrial Organization (**CIO**) was formed within the AFL to carry unionism to the industrial sector. By 1937, however, the CIO had been expelled from the AFL over charges of dual unionism or competition. It then became known as the Congress of Industrial Organizations.

Federal labor efforts included:
- The Anti-Injunction Act of 1932 which prohibited Federal injunctions in most labor disputes.
- The Wagner-Peyser Act which created the United States Employment Service within the Department of Labor in 1933.
- The Secretary of Labor calling for the first National Labor Legislation Conference to get better cooperation between the Federal Government and the States in defining a national labor legislation program in 1934.
- The U.S. joining the International Labor Organization, also in 1934.
- And the National Apprenticeship Act establising the Bureau of Apprenticeship within the Department of Labor in 1937.

COMPETENCY 2.9   WORLD WAR II

Skill 2.9a   Explain the origins of American involvement in World War II, including reactions to events in Europe, Africa, and Asia.

World War II: 1939 to 1945
After war began in Europe in 1939, U.S. **President Franklin D. Roosevelt** announced that the United States was neutral. Most Americans, although hoping for an Allied victory, wanted the U.S. to stay out of the war. President Roosevelt and his supporters, called "interventionists," favored all aid except war to the Allied nations fighting Axis aggression. They were fearful that an Axis victory would seriously threaten and endanger all democracies. On the other hand, the "isolationists" were against any U.S. aid being given to the warring nations, accusing President Roosevelt of leading the U.S. into a war very much unprepared to fight. Roosevelt's plan was to defeat the Axis nations by sending the Allied nations the equipment needed to fight; ships, aircraft, tanks, and other war materials.

In Asia, the U.S. had opposed Japan's invasion of Southeast Asia, an effort to gain Japanese control of that region's rich resources. Consequently, the U.S. stopped all important exports to Japan, whose industries depended heavily on petroleum, scrap metal, and other raw materials. Later Roosevelt refused the Japanese withdrawal of its funds from American banks. General Tojo became the Japanese premier in October 1941 and quickly realized that the U.S. Navy was powerful enough to block Japanese expansion into Asia. Deciding to cripple the Pacific Fleet, the Japanese aircraft, without warning, bombed the Fleet December 7, 1941, while at anchor in **Pearl Harbor** in Hawaii. Temporarily it was a success. It destroyed many aircraft and disabled much of the U.S. Pacific Fleet. In the end, it was a costly mistake as it quickly motivated the Americans to prepare for and wage war.

Skill 2.9b   Analyze American foreign policy before and during WWII.

By the 1930s, after a period of strong economic growth, the United States and the rest of the world, entered a period of economic decline known as the Depression. The new American President, Franklin Roosevelt, as well as the country as a whole were more concerned initially with domestic affairs. Roosevelt thus tried to pursue peace and cooperation, especially in regards to the American continent and the nations of Central and South America. His policy was called the "**Good Neighbor Policy**". However, in Europe matters were becoming more difficult because the worldwide economic downturn had more serious effects there.

Because of the problems in Europe, the isolationist mood in the United States continued with ever increasing support well into the late 1930s. With the rise to power of dictatorships in Germany and Italy the general trend toward war in the 1930s progressed. Many in the United States, most notably President Franklin Roosevelt, came to see that it was in America's interest to promote peace and democracy in the world. A country as big and as powerful as the United States could not realistically continue to remove itself from world affairs. Nevertheless, since the general mood in the nation at that time was away from world involvement and in favor of isolation, not much could be done internationally. Memories of the slaughter of the First World War were too strong for many to even consider getting involved in another European conflict. George Washington's warning against "entangling alliances in the problems and conflicts of Europe" was very much in mind.

After the outbreak of war in 1939, the American government had to proclaim a public stance of neutrality. While covertly and carefully doing what it could to aid its friends and allies. This involved the process that came to be known as **Lend-Lease**, in which the United States would give, on what was presumed a temporary basis, certain war supplies to the forces fighting Germany and its' allies. This helped them to maintain themselves during Nazi Germany's attacks. At first, Lend-Lease went only to Great Britain. When Germany attacked the Soviet Union in June 1941, it went there as well.

Skill 2.9c **Evaluate and analyze significant events, issues, and experiences during World War II and the experiences and contributions of American fighting forces, including the role of minorities.**

Military strategy in the European theater of war as developed by **Roosevelt, Churchill, and Stalin** was to concentrate on Germany's defeat first, then Japan's. The start was made in North Africa, pushing Germans and Italians off the continent, beginning in the summer of 1942 and ending successfully in May, 1943. Before the war, Hitler and Stalin had signed a non-aggression pact in 1939, which Hitler violated in 1941 by invading the Soviet Union. The German defeat at Stalingrad, which marked a turning point in the war, was brought about by a combination of entrapment of German troops by Soviet troops and the death of many more Germans by starvation and freezing due to the horrendous winter conditions. All of this occurred at the same time the Allies were driving them out of North Africa.

The liberation of Italy began in July 1943 and ended May 2, 1945. The third part of the strategy was **D-Day, June 6, 1944,** with the Allied invasion of France at Normandy. At the same time, starting in January, 1943, the Soviets began pushing the German troops back into Europe greatly assisted by supplies from Britain and the United States. By April, 1945, Allies occupied positions beyond the Rhine and the Soviets moved on to Berlin, surrounding it by April 25. Germany surrendered May 7 and the war in Europe was finally over.

The **Yalta Conference** took place in Yalta in February 1945, between the Allied leaders Winston Churchill, Franklin Roosevelt and Joseph Stalin. With the defeat of Nazi Germany within sight, the three allies met to determine the shape of post-war Europe. Germany was to be divided into four zones of occupation, as was the capital city of Berlin. Germany was also to undergo demilitarization and to make reparations for the war. Poland was to remain under control of Soviet Russia. Roosevelt also received a promise from Stalin that the Soviet Union would join the new United Nations.

Following the surrender of Germany in May, 1945, the Allies called the Potsdam Conference in July, between Clement Attlee, Harry Truman and Stalin. **The Potsdam Conference** addressed the administration of post-war Germany and provided for the forced migration of millions of Germans from previously occupied regions.

Meanwhile, in the Pacific, in the six months after the attack on Pearl Harbor, Japanese forces moved across Southeast Asia and the western Pacific Ocean. By August, 1942, the Japanese Empire was at its largest size and stretched northeast to Alaska's Aleutian Islands, west to Burma, south to what is now Indonesia. Invaded and controlled areas included Hong Kong, Guam, Wake Island, Thailand, part of Malaysia, Singapore, the Philippines, and bombed Darwin on the north coast of Australia.

The raid of **General Doolittle**'s bombers on Japanese cities and the American naval victory at **Midway** along with the fighting in the **Battle of the Coral Sea** helped turn the tide against Japan. **Island-hopping** by U.S. Seabees and Marines and the grueling bloody battles fought resulted in gradually pushing the Japanese back towards Japan. After victory was attained in Europe, concentrated efforts were made to secure Japan's surrender, but it took dropping two atomic bombs on the cities of **Hiroshima** and **Nagasaki** to finally end the war in the Pacific.

Japan formally surrendered on September 2, 1945, aboard the U.S. battleship Missouri, anchored in Tokyo Bay. The war was finally ended.

After Japan's defeat, the Allies began a military occupation directed by American **General Douglas MacArthur**, who introduced a number of reforms eventually ridding Japan of its military institutions transforming it into a democracy. A constitution was drawn up in 1947 transferring all political rights from the emperor to the people, granting women the right to vote, and denying Japan the right to declare war. War crimes trials of twenty-five war leaders and government officials were also conducted. The U.S. did not sign a peace treaty until 1951. The treaty permitted Japan to rearm but took away its overseas empire.

Internment of people of Japanese ancestry. From the turn of the twentieth century, there was tension between Caucasians and Japanese in California. A series of laws had been passed discouraging Japanese immigration and prohibiting land ownership by Japanese. The Alien Registration Act of 1940 (the Smith Act) required the fingerprinting and registration of all aliens over the age of fourteen. Aliens were also required to report any change of address within five days. Almost five million aliens registered under the provisions of this act. The Japanese attack on Pearl Harbor (December 7, 1941) raised suspicion that Japan was planning a full-scale attack on the West Coast. Many believed that American citizenship did not necessarily imply loyalty. Some authorities feared sabotage of both civilian and military facilities within the country. By February 1942, Presidential Executive Orders had authorized the arrest of all aliens suspected of subversive activities and the creation of exclusion zones where people could be isolated from the remainder of the population and kept where they could not damage national infrastructure. These War Relocation Camps were used to isolate about 120,000 Japanese and Japanese Americans (62% were citizens) during World War II.

Allied response to the Holocaust. International organizations received sharp criticism during WWII for their failure to act to save the European Jews. The Allied Powers, in particular, were accused of gross negligence. Many organizations and individuals did not believe reports of the abuse and mass genocide that was occurring in Europe. Many nations did not want to accept Jewish refugees. The International Red Cross was one of the organizations that discounted reports of atrocities. One particular point of criticism was the failure of the Allied Powers to bomb the death camp at Auschwitz-Birkenau or the railroad tracks leading there. Military leaders argued that their planes did not have the range to reach the camp; they argued that they could not provide sufficiently precise targeting to safeguard the inmates. Critics have claimed that even if Allied bombs killed all inmates at Auschwitz at the time, the destruction of the camp would have saved thousands of other Jews. The usual response was that, had the Allies destroyed the camp, the Nazis would have turned to other methods of extermination.

It was not until after the war that genocide was accepted by the United Nations as a crime against humanity. Also after the war, there was recognition that the United Nations charter was insufficiently precise as to the rights it protected. The UN then unanimously passed the Universal Declaration of Human Rights. The Nuremberg Trials redefined morality on a global scale. The phrase "crimes against humanity" attained popular currency, and individuals, rather than governments, were held accountable for war crimes.

Women and minorities accepted remarkable new roles and served them with great distinction during WWII, both in the theater of military operations and at home. Within the military theater, women and minorities filled a number of new roles. Women served in the military as drivers, nurses, communications operators, clerks, etc. The Flight Nurses corps was created at the beginning of the war. Among the most notable minority groups in the military were:

The Tuskegee Airmen were a group of African American aviators who made a major contribution to the war effort. Although they were not considered eligible for the gold wings of a Navy Pilot until 1948, these men completed standard Army flight classroom instruction and the required flying time. This group of fliers was the first blacks permitted to fly for the military. They flew more than 15,000 missions, destroyed over 1,000 German aircraft, earned more than 150 Distinguished Flying Crosses and hundreds of Air Medals.

The 442nd Regimental Combat Team was a unit composed of Japanese Americans who fought in Europe. This unit was the most highly decorated unit of its size and length of service in the history of the U.S. Army. This self-sufficient force served with great distinction in North Africa, Italy, southern France, and Germany. The medals earned by the group include 21 Congressional Medals of Honor (the highest award given). The unit was awarded 9,486 purple hearts (for being wounded in battle). The casualty rate, combining those killed in action, missing in action, and wounded and removed from action, was 93%.

The Navajo Code Talkers have been credited with saving countless lives and accelerating the end of the war. There were over 400 Navajo Indians who served in all six Marine divisions from 1942 to 1945. At the time of WWII, less than 30 non-Navajo's understood the Navajo language. Because it was a very complex language and because it was not a code, it was unbreakable by the Germans or the Japanese. The job of these men was to talk and transmit information on tactics, troop movements, orders and other vital military information. Not only was the enemy unable to understand the language, but it was far faster than translating messages into Morse Code. It is generally accepted that without the Navajo Code Talkers, Iwo Jima could not have been taken.

The statistics on minority representation in the military during WWII are interesting:

Negroes
Chinese
Japanese
Hawaiians
American Indians
Filipinos
Puerto Ricans
1,056,841
13,311
20,080
1,320
19,567
11,506
51,438

The role of women and minority groups at home overturned many expectations and assumptions. Most able-bodied men of appropriate age were called up for military service. Minorities were generally not drafted. Yet many critical functions remained to be fulfilled by those who remained at home.

To a greater extent than any previous war, WWII required industrial production. Those who remained at home were needed to build the planes, tanks, ships, bombs, torpedoes, etc. The men who remained at home were working. But more labor was desperately needed. In particular, a call went out to women to join the effort and enter the industrial work force. A vast campaign was launched to recruit women to these tasks that combined emotional appeals and patriotism. One of the most famous recruiting campaigns featured "**Rosie the Riveter**." Yet all of the recruitment efforts emphasized that the need for women in industry was temporary. By the middle of 1944 more than 19 million women had entered the work force. Women worked building planes and tanks, but they also did more. Some operated large cranes to move heavy equipment; some loaded and fired machine guns and other weapons to ensure that they were in working order; some operated hydraulic presses; some were volunteer fire fighters; some were welders, riveters, drill press operators, and cab drivers. Women worked all manufacturing shifts making everything from clothing to fighter jets. Most women and their families tended "**Victory Gardens**" to produce food items that were in short supply.

Major developments in aviation, weaponry, communications, and medicine were achieved during the war. The years between WWI and WWII had produced significant advancement in aircraft technology. But the pace of aircraft development and production was dramatically increased during WWII. Major developments included flight-based weapon delivery systems such as the long-range bomber, the first jet fighter, the first cruise missile, and the first ballistic missile, although the cruise and ballistic missiles were not widely used during the war. Glider planes were heavily used in WWII because they were silent upon approach. Another significant development was the broad use of paratrooper units. Finally, hospital planes came into use to extract the seriously wounded from the front and transport them to hospitals for treatment.

Weapons and technology in other areas also improved rapidly during the war. These advances were critical in determining the outcome of the war. Used for the first time were: radar, electronic computers, nuclear weapons, and new tank designs. More new inventions were registered for patents than ever before. Most of these new ideas were aimed to either kill or prevent being killed.

The war began with essentially the same weaponry that had been used in WWI. The aircraft carrier joined the battleship; the Higgins boat, the primary landing craft, was invented; light tanks were developed to meet the needs of a changing battlefield; other armored vehicles were developed. Submarines were also perfected during this period. Numerous other weapons were also developed or invented to meet the needs of battle during WWII: the bazooka, the rocket propelled grenade, anti-tank weapons, assault rifles, the tank destroyer, mine-clearing Flail tanks, Flame tanks, submersible tanks; cruise missiles, rocket artillery and air launched rockets, guided weapons, torpedoes, self-guiding weapons and napalm. The Atomic Bomb was also developed and used for the first time during WWII.

The significance and ramifications of the decision to drop the atomic bomb. The development of the atomic bomb was probably the most profound military development of the war years. This invention made it possible for a single plane to carry a single bomb that was sufficiently powerful to destroy an entire city. It was believed that possession of the bomb would serve as a deterrent to any nation because it would make aggression against a nation with a bomb a decision for mass suicide. The development and use of nuclear weapons marked the beginning of a new age in warfare that created greater distance from the act of killing and eliminated the ability to minimize the effect of war on non-combatants.

Two nuclear bombs were dropped in 1945 on the cities of Nagasaki and Hiroshima. They caused the immediate deaths of 100,000 to 200,000 people, and far more deaths over time. This was (and still is) a controversial decision. Those who opposedthe use of the atom bomb argued that was an unnecessary act of mass killing, particularly of non-combatants. Proponents argued that it ended the war sooner, thus resulting in fewer casualties on both sides.

Skill 2.9d   Assess American foreign policy in the aftermath of World War II, using geographic, political, and economic perspectives.

The American isolationist mood was given a shocking and lasting blow in 1941 with the Japanese attack on Pearl Harbor. The nation arose and forcefully entered the international arena as never before. Declaring itself "the arsenal of democracy", it entered the Second World War and emerged not only victorious, but also as the *strongest power* on the Earth. It would now, like it or not, have a permanent and leading place in world affairs.

Since the end of the Second World War, the United States has perceived its greatest threat to be the expansion of Communism in the world. To that end, it has devoted a larger and larger share of its foreign policy, diplomacy, and both economic and military might to combating it.

In the aftermath of the Second World War, with the Soviet Union having emerged as the *second* strongest power on Earth, the United States embarked on a policy known as "**Containment**" of the Communist menace. This involved what came to be known as the "**Marshall Plan**" and the "**Truman Doctrine**". The Marshall Plan involved the economic aid that was sent to Europe in the aftermath of the Second World War aimed at preventing the spread of communism.

The Truman Doctrine offered military aid to those countries that were in danger of communist upheaval. This led to the era known as the **Cold War** in which the United States took the lead along with the Western European nations against the Soviet Union and the Eastern Bloc countries. It was also at this time that the United States finally gave up on George Washington's' advice against "European entanglements" and joined the **North Atlantic Treaty Organization** or **NATO**. This was formed in 1949 and was comprised of the United States and several Western European nations for the purposes of opposing communist aggression.

The **United Nations** was also formed at this time (1945) to replace the defunct League of Nations for the purposes of ensuring world peace. Even with American involvement, would prove largely ineffective in maintaining world peace.

In the 1950s, the United States embarked on what was called the "**Eisenhower Doctrine**", after the then President Eisenhower. This aimed at trying to maintain peace in a troubled area of the world, the Middle East. However, unlike the Truman Doctrine in Europe, it would have little success.

The introduction and possession of nuclear weapons by the United States quickly led to the development of similar weapons by other nations, proliferation of the most destructive weapons ever created, massive fear of the effects of the use of these weapons, including radiation poisoning and **nuclear winter**, and led to the Cold War.

The United States also became involved in a number of world conflicts in the ensuing years. Each had at the core the struggle against communist expansion. Among these were the **Korean War** (1950-1953), the **Vietnam War** (1965-1975), and various continuing entanglements in Central and South America and the Middle East. By the early 1970s under the leadership of then Secretary of State, Henry Kissinger, the United States and its allies embarked on the policy that came to be known as "**Détente**". This was aimed at the easing of tensions between the United States and its allies and the Soviet Union and its allies.

By the 1980s, the United States embarked on what some saw as a renewal of the Cold War. This owed to the fact that the United States was becoming more involved in trying to prevent communist insurgency in Central America. A massive expansion of its armed forces and the development of space-based weapons systems were undertaken at this time. As this occurred, the Soviet Union, with a failing economic system and a foolhardy adventure in Afghanistan, found itself unable to compete. By 1989, events had come to a head. This ended with the breakdown of the Communist Bloc, the virtual end of the monolithic Soviet Union, and the collapse of the communist system by the early 1990s.

Now the United States remains active in world affairs in trying to promote peace and reconciliation, with a new specter rising to challenge it and the world, the specter of nationalism.

COMPETENCY 2.10   POST-WORLD WAR II AMERICA

Skill 2.10a   Describe and evaluate the significance of changes in international migration patterns and their impact on society and the economy.

Until the middle of the twentieth century, voluntary migrations to America were primarily Europeans. After WWII, a large number of Europeans were admitted to the U.S. and Canada. These were considered the most desirable immigrants. Indeed, immigration policies based upon ethnicity or country of origin were not eliminated until the 1960s. The impact of the Cold War on migration patterns was very significant. American policies toward immigration became more open to political escapees from communist countries, partly out of a desire to embarrass these nations. The number of immigrants from third-world nations was also increasing dramatically. The end of the Cold War marked a shift in migration patterns such that migrations from south to north came to predominate global migration.

A significant change in immigration policy occurred after WWII. Both the U.S. and Canada began to distinguish between economically motivated voluntary immigrants and **political refugees**. The conditions that existed after the war made it clear that some immigrants must be treated differently on the basis of humanitarian concerns. Fear of persecution caused massive migrations. The United Nations created the **International Refugee Organization** in 1946. In the next three years this organization relocated over a million European refugees.

Immigration policy in the U.S. was carefully aligned with foreign policy. President Truman introduced the **Displaced Persons Act** in 1948 which facilitated the admission of more than 400,000 persons from Europe. During the 1950s, however, the immigration policy became very restrictive. The McCarran-Walter Immigration Nationality Act of 1952 established a quota system and was clearly anti-Asian. The number of refugees from Eastern Europe far exceeded these quotas. Both President Truman and President Eisenhower urged extension of the quotas, and in time they were abandoned. Refugees from communist Europe were admitted under the President's Escapee Program of 1952 and the Refugee Relief Act of 1953.

Immigration by Asians had been restricted for some time and this policy did not change after WWII. The changes in immigration policies and the great influx of Europeans brought a wide variety of people into the U.S. To be sure, some were farmers and laborers, but many were highly trained and skilled scientists, teachers, inventors, and executives. This migration added to the American "melting pot" experience. The immigrants provided new sources of labor for a booming economy and the introduction of new cultural ideas and contributions to science and technology. The acceptance and assimilation of European immigrants was, for the most part, easier than the prejudiced assimilation of persons of Asian descent, particularly after the recent hostilities with Japan.

Skill 2.10b   Describe the increased role of the federal government in response to World War II and the Cold War and assess the impact of this increased role on regional economic structures, society, and the political system.

During World War II Americans found it advisable to cede to the federal government a greater degree of control over the economy, key institutions and services, and ensuring both their personal welfare and their security. This led to a significant growth in both the reach and the size of the federal government. The nation had faced two major crises: The Great Depression and World War. The government had assumed greater responsibility for ensuring the basic needs of its citizens, promoting economic opportunity for all, and managing economic growth. The government had also taken on the role of providing for the military safety and security of the nation against foreign enemies.

This marked the culmination of a major change in the role of the federal government that many have called "**the rise of the welfare state**." Since the First World War, regulatory agencies had been created to control the actions of big business, to protect labor, to protect the rights and privileges of minorities. In addition, a truly national culture had emerged from the shared hardships, the growth of the railroad and the radio, the introduction of the automobile, and the war effort itself. These factors had smoothed out many of the regional differences that previously divided the social and cultural interests of the American people.

New challenges had led to the growth of the power and control of the federal government. The attempts to bring the nation through both the Depression and the war had utilized much experimentation. Franklin Roosevelt and his administration drew upon past experience and experimentation to bring the nation through crisis. Roosevelt's use of the radio to speak to the American people in his "**fireside chats**" permitted him to rally the populace and persuade the public to consider new ideas and new approaches to the problems of the day. Essentially, Roosevelt convinced the nation that a more active role for the federal government both internationally and at home would prevent another Depression and another world war.

This transition was very important in American history and in the national ethos. Americans had traditionally distrusted a centralization of authority in the federal government. They had also traditionally repudiated international alliances and commitments. Yet both of these changes came about in the years following WWII.

In many ways, the period from 1945 to 1972 was a time of unprecedented prosperity for everyone in the nation. Wages increased, car and home ownership increased, average educational levels increased when the veterans of the war took full advantage of the opportunity to receive a college education paid for by their G.I benefits. People were willing to give the government this major role in perpetuating this prosperous society. Just as WWII had united the people in a common commitment to the purpose of supporting the troops and winning the war, they again rallied together to support the government in the Cold War.

Skill 2.10c   Describe the effects of technological developments on society, politics, and the economy since 1945.

The first decade and a half after WWII was a time of great hope and economic prosperity in America. Europe was redefined and began to recover from the devastating effects of the war. The spirit of people around the world was marked by a commitment to peace and reconstruction. The threat of the spread of communism and the Cold War was a palpable feature of everyday life.

During these years the discoveries and innovations of the war years in both science and technology were simultaneously directed to: (1) peaceful and life-enhancing uses of technology, and (2) the buildup of sufficient military and weaponry to ensure the security of the nation against any future aggression.

The days of empires were over. Nations rose from former colonial holdings. Borders and boundaries were essentially stable. New territories had been explored and civilized. With the available technology and the remaining urge to push boundaries and explore new worlds, attention turned to the remaining uninhabited areas: the North and South Poles, the mountain heights, and to space.

Significant advances in science and medicine made it possible to treat and prevent deadly and crippling diseases. Life expectancy rose, and with it, the desire to develop new enhancements for living. As millions of returning veterans took advantage of the G.I. bill and obtained more education, society gave more attention to education at all levels.

Major technological developments since 1945:
- Discovery of penicillin (1945)
- Detonation of the first atomic bombs (1945)
- Xerography process invented (1946)
- Exploration of the South Pole
- Studies of X-ray radiation
- U.S. airplane first flies at supersonic speed (1947)
- Invention of the transistor (1947)
- Long-playing record invented (1948)
- Studies begin in the science of chemo genetics (1948)
- Mount Palomar reflecting telescope (1948)
- Idlewild Airport opens in New York City
- Cortisone discovered (1949)
- USSR tests first atomic bomb (1949)
- U.S. guided missile launched and traveled 250 miles (1949)
- Plutonium separated (1950)
- Tranquilizer meprobamate comes to wide use (1950)
- Antihistamines become popular in treating colds and allergies (1950)
- Electric power produced from atomic energy (1951)
- First heart-lung machine devised (1951)
- First solo flight over the North Pole (1951)
- Yellow fever vaccine developed (1951)
- Isotopes used in medicine and industry (1952)
- Contraceptive pill produced (1952)
- First hydrogen bomb exploded (1952)
- Nobel Prize in medicine for discovery of streptomycin (1952)
- Cave Cougnac discovered with prehistoric paintings (1953)
- USSR explodes hydrogen bomb (1953)
- Hillary and Tenzing reach the summit of Mount Everest (1953)
- Lung cancer connected to cigarette smoking (1953)
- First U.S. submarine converted to nuclear power (1954)
- Polio vaccine invented (1954)
- Discovery of Vitamin B12 (1955)
- Discovery of the molecular structure of insulin (1955)
- First artificial manufacture of diamonds (1955)
- Beginning of development of "visual telephone" (1956)
- Beginning of Transatlantic cable telephone service (1956)
- USSR launches first earth satellites (Sputnik I and II) (1957)
- Mackinac Straits Bridge in Michigan opens as the longest suspension bridge (1957)
- Stereo recordings introduced (1958)
- NASA created (1958)
- USSR launches rocket with 2 monkeys aboard (1959)
- Nobel Prize for Medicine for synthesis of RNA and DNA (1959)

Skill 2.10d   Analyze the major domestic policies of presidential administrations from Harry S Truman to the present.

Harry S. Truman. Truman became president near the end of WWII. He is credited with some of the most important decisions in history. When Japan refused to surrender, Truman authorized the dropping of atomic bombs on Japanese cities dedicated to war support: Hiroshima and Nagasaki. He then took to the Congress a 21-point plan that came to be known as the **Fair Deal**. It included: expansion of Social Security, a full-employment program, public housing and slum clearance, and a permanent Fair Employment Practices Act.

The **Truman Doctrine** provided support for Greece and Turkey when they were threatened by the Soviet Union. The **Marshall Plan** (implemented by Truman's Secretary of State) stimulated amazing economic recovery for Western Europe. Truman participated in the negotiations that resulted in the formation of the NATO. He and his administration believed it necessary to support South Korea when it was threatened by the communist government of North Korea. But he contained American involvement in Korea so as not to risk conflict with China or Russia.

Dwight David Eisenhower succeeded Truman. Eisenhower obtained a truce in Korea and worked during his two terms to mitigate the tension of the Cold War. When Stalin died, he was able to negotiate a peace treaty with Russia that neutralized Austria. His domestic policy was a middle road. He continued most of the programs introduced under both the New Deal and the Fair Deal. When desegregation of schools began, he sent troops to Little Rock, Arkansas to enforce desegregation of the schools. He ordered the complete **desegregation** of the military. During his administration, the Department of Health, Education and Welfare was established and the National Aeronautics and Space Administration was formed.

John F. Kennedy is widely remembered for his Inaugural Address in which the statement was made, "Ask not what your country can do for you – ask what you can do for your country." His campaign pledge was to get America moving again. During his brief presidency, his economic programs created the longest period of continuous expansion in the country since WWII. He wanted the U.S. to again take up the mission as the first country committed to the revolution of human rights. Through the Alliance for Progress and the **Peace Corps**, the hopes and idealism of the nation reached out to assist developing nations. He was deeply and passionately involved in the cause of equal rights for all Americans and he drafted new civil rights legislation. He also drafted plans for a broad attack on the systemic problems of privation and poverty. He believed the arts were critical to a society and instituted programs to support the arts.

Lyndon B. Johnson assumed the presidency after the assassination of Kennedy. His vision for America was called "**A Great Society**." He won support in Congress for the largest group of legislative programs in the history of the nation. These included programs Kennedy had been working on at the time of his death, including a new civil rights bill and a tax cut. He defined the "great society" as "a place where the meaning of man's life matches the marvels of man's labor." The legislation enacted during his administration included: an attack on disease, urban renewal, Medicare, aid to education, conservation and beautification, development of economically depressed areas, a war on poverty, voting rights for all, and control of crime and delinquency. Johnson managed an unpopular military action in Vietnam and encouraged the exploration of space. During his administration the Department of Transportation was formed and the first black, Thurgood Marshall, was nominated and confirmed to the Supreme Court.

Richard Nixon inherited racial unrest and the Vietnam War, from which he extracted the American military. His administration is probably best known for improved relations with both China and the USSR. However, the **Watergate** scandal divided the country and led to his resignation. His major domestic achievements were: the appointment of conservative justices to the Supreme Court, passed new anti-crime legislation, introduced a broad environmental program, sponsored revenue sharing legislation and ended the draft.

Gerald Ford was the first Vice President selected under the 25th Amendment. The challenges that faced his administration were a depressed economy, inflation, energy shortages, and the need to champion world peace. Once inflation slowed and recession was the major economic problem, he instituted measures that would stimulate the economy. He tried to reduce the role of the federal government. He reduced business taxes and lessened the controls on business. His international focus was on preventing a major war in the Middle East. He negotiated with Russia for limitations on nuclear weapons.

Jimmy Carter strove to make the government "competent and compassionate" in response to the American people and their expectations. The economic situation of the nation was intensely difficult when he took office. Although significant progress was made by his administration in creating jobs and decreasing the budget deficit, inflation and interest rates were nearly at record highs. There were several notable achievements, including the establishment of a national energy policy to deal with the energy shortage, decontrolling petroleum prices to stimulate production, civil service reform that improved government efficiency, deregulation of the trucking and airline industries, and the creation of the Department of Education. He expanded the national park system, supported the Social Security system, and appointed a record number of women and minorities to government jobs. The last year of Carter's presidential term was taken up with the fifty-three American hostages held in Iran.

Ronald Reagan introduced an innovative program that came to be known as the Reagan Revolution. The goal of this program was to reduce the reliance of the American people upon government. The Reagan administration restored the hope and enthusiasm of the nation. His legislative accomplishments include economic growth stimulation, curbing inflation, increasing employment, and strengthening the national defense. He won Congressional support for a complete overhaul of the income tax code in 1986. By the time he left office there was prosperity in peacetime with no depression or recession. His foreign policy was "peace through strength." Reagan nominated Sandra Day O'Connor as the first female justice on the Supreme Court.

George H. W. Bush was committed to "traditional American values" and to making America a "kinder and gentler nation". During the Reagan administration, Bush held responsibility for anti-drug programs and Federal deregulation. When the Cold War ended and the Soviet Union broke apart, he supported the rise of democracy, but took a position of restraint toward the new nations. Bush also dealt with defense of the Panama Canal and Iraq's invasion of Kuwait, which led to the first Gulf War, known as **Desert Storm**. Although his international affairs record was strong, he was not able to turn around increased violence in the inner cities and a struggling economy.

William Clinton led the nation in a time of greater peace and economic prosperity than has been experienced at any other time in history. His domestic accomplishments include: the lowest inflation in thirty years, the lowest unemployment rate in modern days, the highest home ownership rate in history, lower crime rates in many places, and smaller welfare rolls. He proposed and achieved a balanced budget and achieved a budget surplus.

COMPETENCY 2.11   POST-WORLD WAR II U.S. FOREIGN POLICY

Skill 2.11a   Trace the origins of the Cold War.

The major thrust of U.S. foreign policy from the end of World War II to 1990 was the post-war struggle between non-Communist nations, led by the United States, and the Soviet Union and the Communist nations who were its allies. It was referred to as a "Cold War" because its conflicts did not lead to a major war of fighting, or a "hot war." Both the Soviet Union and the United States embarked on an arsenal buildup of atomic and hydrogen bombs as well as other nuclear weapons. Both nations had the capability of destroying each other but because of the continuous threat of nuclear war and accidents, extreme caution was practiced on both sides. The efforts of both sides to serve and protect their political philosophies and to support and assist their allies resulted in a number of events during this 45-year period.

In 1946, Josef Stalin stated publicly that the presence of capitalism and its development of the world's economy made international peace impossible. This resulted in an American diplomat in Moscow named George F. Kennan to propose in response to Stalin, a statement of U.S. foreign policy. The idea and goal of the U.S. was to contain or limit the extension or expansion of Soviet Communist policies and activities. After Soviet efforts to make trouble in Iran, Greece, and Turkey, U.S. President Harry Truman stated what is known as the **Truman Doctrine** which committed the U.S. to a policy of intervention in order to contain or stop the spread of communism throughout the world.

Skill 2.11b   Analyze the roles of the Truman Doctrine, the Marshall Plan, and military alliances, including the North American Treaty Organization (NATO), the South East Asian Treaty Organization (SEATO), and the Warsaw Pact.

In the aftermath of the Second World War, with the Soviet Union having emerged as the *second* strongest power on Earth, the United States embarked on a policy known as "**Containment**" of the Communist menace. This involved what came to be known as the "**Marshall Plan**" and the "**Truman Doctrine**". The Marshall Plan involved the economic aid that was sent to Europe in the aftermath of the Second World War aimed at preventing the spread of communism.

After 1945, social and economic chaos continued in Western Europe, especially in Germany. Secretary of State George C. Marshall came to realize that the U.S. had serious problems and to assist in the recovery, he proposed a program known as the European Recovery Program or the Marshall Plan. Although the Soviet Union withdrew from any participation, the U.S. continued the work of assisting Europe in regaining economic stability. In Germany, the situation was critical with the American Army shouldering the staggering burden of relieving the serious problems of the German economy. In February 1948, Britain and the U.S. combined their two zones, with France joining in June.

The **Truman Doctrine** offered military aid to those countries that were in danger of communist upheaval. This led to the era known as the **Cold War** in which the United States took the lead along with the Western European nations against the Soviet Union and the Eastern Bloc countries. It was also at this time that the United States finally gave up on George Washington's' advice against "European entanglements" and joined the **North Atlantic Treaty Organization** or **NATO**. This was formed in 1949 and was comprised of the United States and several Western European nations for the purpose of opposing communist aggression.

Skill 2.11c   Trace the origins and consequences of the Korean War.

The first "hot war" in the post-World War II era was the Korean War, begun June 25, 1950 and ending July 27, 1953. Troops from Communist North Korea invaded democratic South Korea in an effort to unite both sections under Communist control. The United Nations organization asked its member nations to furnish troops to help restore peace. Many nations responded and President Truman sent American troops to help the South Koreans. The war dragged on for three years and ended with a truce, not a peace treaty. Korea remains divided to this day.

Korea was under control of Japan from 1895 to the end of the Second World War in 1945. At war's end, the Soviet and U.S. military troops moved into Korea with the U.S. troops in the southern half and the Soviet troops in the northern half with the **38 degree North Latitude** line as the boundary.

The General Assembly of the UN in 1947 ordered elections throughout all of Korea to select one government for the entire country. The Soviet Union would not allow the North Koreans to vote, so they set up a Communist government there. The South Koreans set up a democratic government but both claimed the entire country. At times, there were clashes between the troops from 1948 to 1950. After the U.S. removed its remaining troops in 1949 and announced in early 1950 that Korea was not part of its defense line in Asia, the Communists decided to act and invaded the south.

Participants were: North and South Korea, United States of America, Australia, New Zealand, China, Canada. France, Great Britain, Turkey, Belgium, Ethiopia, Colombia, Greece, South Africa, Luxembourg, Thailand, the Netherlands, and the Philippines. It was the first war in which a world organization played a major military role and it presented quite a challenge to the UN, which had only been in existence five years.

The war began June 25, 1950 and ended July 27, 1953. A truce was drawn up and an armistice agreement was signed ending the fighting. A permanent treaty of peace has never been signed and the country remains divided between the Communist North and the Democratic South. It was a very costly and bloody war destroying villages and homes, displacing and killing millions of people.

Skill 2.11d   Explain and analyze the relationship between domestic and foreign policy during the Cold War.

After 1945, social and economic chaos continued in Western Europe, especially in Germany. Secretary of State George C. Marshall came to realize that the U.S. had greatly underestimated serious problems and to assist in the recovery, he proposed a program known as the European Recovery Program or the **Marshall Plan**. Although the Soviet Union withdrew from any participation, the U.S. continued the work of assisting Europe in regaining economic stability. In Germany, the situation was critical with the American Army shouldering the staggering burden of relieving the serious problems of the German economy. In February 1948, Britain and the U.S. combined their two zones, with France joining in June.

The Soviets were opposed to German unification and in April 1948 took serious action to either stop it or to force the Allies to give up control of West Berlin to the Soviets. The Soviets blocked all road traffic access to West Berlin from West Germany. To avoid any armed conflict, it was decided to airlift into West Berlin the needed food and supplies. From June 1948 to mid-May 1949 during the **Berlin Airlift** Allied air forces flew in all that was needed for the West Berliners, forcing the Soviets to lift the blockade and permit vehicular traffic access to the city.

In 1954, the French were forced to give up their colonial claims in Indochina, the present-day countries of Vietnam, Laos, and Cambodia. Afterwards, the Communist northern part of Vietnam began battling with the democratic southern part over control of the entire country. In the late 1950s and early 1960s, U.S. Presidents Eisenhower and Kennedy sent to Vietnam a number of military advisers and military aid to assist and support South Vietnam's non-Communist government.

During Lyndon Johnson's presidency, the war escalated with thousands of American troops being sent to participate in combat with the South Vietnamese. The war was extremely unpopular in America and caused such serious divisiveness among its citizens that Johnson decided not to seek reelection in 1968. It was in President Richard Nixon's second term in office that the U.S. signed an agreement ending war in Vietnam and restoring peace. This was done January 27, 1973, and by March 29, the last American combat troops and American prisoners of war left Vietnam for home. It was the longest war in U.S. history and to this day carries the perception that it was a "lost war."

Skill 2.11e   Analyze the foreign policies of post-World War II presidential administrations and their effect on the Cold War.

In 1962, during the administration of **President John F. Kennedy**, Premier Khrushchev and the Soviets decided, as a protective measure for Cuba against an American invasion, to install nuclear missiles on the island. In October, American U-2 spy planes photographed over Cuba what were identified as missile bases under construction, touching off the **Cuban Missile Crisis**. The decision in the White House was how to handle the situation without starting a war. The only recourse was removal of the missile sites and preventing more being set up. Kennedy announced that the U.S. had set up a "quarantine" of Soviet ships heading to Cuba. It was in reality a blockade but the word itself could not be used publicly as a blockade was actually considered an act of war.

The Soviets were concerned about American missiles installed in Turkey aimed at the Soviet Union and about a possible invasion of Cuba. If successful, Khrushchev would demonstrate to the Russian and Chinese critics of his policy of peaceful coexistence that he was tough and not to be intimidated. At the same time, the Americans feared that if Russian missiles were put in place and launched from Cuba to the U.S., the short distance of 90 miles would not allow enough time for adequate warning. Furthermore, it would originate from a direction that radar systems could not detect. It was felt that if America gave in and allowed a Soviet presence practically at the back door that the effect on American security and morale would be devastating.

A week of incredible tension and anxiety gripped the entire world until Khrushchev capitulated. Soviet ships carrying missiles for the Cuban bases turned back and the crisis eased. What precipitated the crisis was Khrushchev's underestimation of Kennedy. The President made no effort to prevent the erection of the Berlin Wall and was reluctant to commit American troops to invade Cuba and overthrow Fidel Castro. The Soviets assumed this was a weakness and decided they could install the missiles without any interference. As tensions eased in the aftermath of the crisis, several agreements were made. The missiles in Turkey were removed, as they were obsolete. A telephone "hot line" was set up between Moscow and Washington to make it possible for the two heads of government to have instant contact with each other. The U.S. agreed to sell its surplus wheat to the Soviets.

During **Lyndon Johnson**'s presidency, the war in Vietnam escalated with thousands of American troops being sent to participate in combat with the South Vietnamese. The war was extremely unpopular in America and caused such serious divisiveness among its citizens that Johnson decided not to seek reelection in 1968

Probably the highlight of the foreign policy of **President Richard Nixon**, after the end of the Vietnam War and withdrawal of troops, was his 1972 trip to **China**. When the Communists gained control of China in 1949, the policy of the U.S. government was refusal to recognize the Communist government. It regarded as the legitimate government of China to be that of Chiang Kai-shek, exiled on the island of Taiwan.

In 1971, Nixon sent Henry Kissinger on a secret trip to Peking to investigate whether or not it would be possible for America to give recognition to China. In February 1972, President and Mrs. Nixon spent a number of days in the country visiting well-known Chinese landmarks, dining with the two leaders, Mao Tse-tung and Chou En-lai. Agreements were made for cultural and scientific exchanges, eventual resumption of trade, and future unification of the mainland with Taiwan. In 1979, formal diplomatic recognition was achieved. With this one visit, the pattern of the Cold War was essentially shifted.

Under the administration of **President Jimmy Carter,** Egyptian President Anwar el-Sadat and Israeli Prime Minister Menachem Begin met at presidential retreat **Camp David** and agreed, after a series of meetings, to sign a formal treaty of peace between the two countries. In 1979, the Soviet invasion of Afghanistan was perceived by Carter and his advisers as a threat to the rich oil fields in the Persian Gulf but at the time U.S. military capability to prevent further Soviet aggression in the Middle East was weak. The last year of Carter's presidential term was taken up with the 53 American hostages held in Iran. The Shah had been deposed and control of the government and the country was in the hands of Muslim leader, Ayatollah Ruhollah Khomeini.

Khomeini's extreme hatred for the U.S. was the result of the 1953 overthrow of Iran's Mossadegh government, sponsored by the CIA. To make matters worse, the CIA proceeded to train the Shah's ruthless secret police force. So when the terminally ill exiled Shah was allowed into the U.S. for medical treatment, a fanatical mob stormed into the American embassy taking the fifty-three Americans as prisoners, supported and encouraged by Khomeini.

President Carter froze all Iranian assets in the U.S., set up trade restrictions, and approved a risky rescue attempt, which failed. He had appealed to the UN for aid in gaining release for the hostages and to European allies to join the trade embargo on Iran. Khomeini ignored UN requests for releasing the Americans and Europeans refused to support the embargo so as not to risk losing access to Iran's oil. American prestige was damaged and Carter's chances for reelection were doomed. The hostages were released on the day of Ronald Reagan's inauguration as President when Carter released Iranian assets as ransom.

The foreign policy of **President Ronald Reagan** was, in his first term, focused primarily on the Western Hemisphere, particularly in Central America and the West Indies. U.S. involvement in the domestic revolutions of El Salvador and Nicaragua continued into Reagan's second term when Congress held televised hearings on what came to be known as the **Iran-Contra Affair**. A cover-up was exposed showing that profits from secretly selling military hardware to Iran had been used to give support to rebels, called Contras, who were fighting in Nicaragua.

In 1983, in Lebanon, 241 American Marines were killed when an Islamic suicide bomber drove an explosive-laden truck into the United States Marines headquarters located at the airport in Beirut. This tragic event came as part of the unrest and violence between the Israelis and the Palestinian Liberation Organization (PLO) forces in southern Lebanon. In the same month, 1,900 U.S. Marines landed on the island of **Grenada** to rescue a small group of American medical students at the medical school and depose the leftist government.

Perhaps the most intriguing and far-reaching event towards the end of Reagan's second term was the arms-reduction agreement Reagan reached with Soviet General Secretary **Mikhail Gorbachev**. Gorbachev began easing East-West tensions by stressing the importance of cooperation with the West and easing the harsh and restrictive life of the people in the Soviet Union. Though regarded as a fierce Cold Warrior, having compared the Soviet Union to an "evil empire," Reagan proved willing to talk repeatedly with the Soviets, and a new level of accord was reached.

President George Bush, in December of 1989, sent U.S. troops to invade **Panama** and arrest the Panamanian dictator Manuel Noriega. Although he had periodically assisted CIA operations with intelligence information, at the same time, Noriega laundered money from drug smuggling and gunrunning through Panama's banks. When a political associate tried unsuccessfully to depose him and an off-duty U.S. Marine was shot and killed at a roadblock, Bush acted. Noriega was brought to the U.S. where he stood trial on charges of drug distribution and racketeering.

During the time of the American hostage crisis, Iraq and Iran fought a war in which the U.S. and most of Iraq's neighbors supported Iraq. In a five-year period, **Saddam Hussein** received from the U.S. $500 million worth of American technology, including lasers, advanced computers, and special machine tools used in missile development. The Iraq-Iran war was a bloody one resulting in a stalemate with a UN truce ending it. Deeply in debt from the war and totally dependent on oil revenues, Saddam invaded and occupied Kuwait. The U.S. made extensive plans to put into operation strategy to successfully carry out **Operation Desert Storm**, the liberation of Kuwait. In four days, February 24-28, 1991, the war was over and Iraq had been defeated, its troops driven back into their country. Saddam remained in power although Iraq's economy was seriously damaged.

President William Clinton sent U.S. troops to Haiti to protect the efforts of Jean-Bertrand Aristide to gain democratic power and to Bosnia to assist UN peacekeeping forces. He also inherited from the Bush administration the problem of Somalia in East Africa, where U.S. troops had been sent in December 1992 to support UN efforts to end the starvation of the Somalis and restore peace. The efforts were successful at first, but eventually failed due to the severity of the intricate political problems within the country. After U.S. soldiers were killed in an ambush along with 300 Somalis, American troops were withdrawn and returned home.

Skill 2.11f   Trace the causes, controversies, and consequences of the Vietnam War, its effects on American combatants and civilians, and its continued impact on American society.

Though ostensibly an American war, conflict in the region began with what is often called the French Indochina War, which waged from 1946-1954. This conflict involved France, which had ruled Vietnam as its colony (French Indochina), and the newly independent Democratic Republic of Vietnam under **Ho Chi Minh**. On May 7, 1954, at a French military base known as **Dien Bien Phu**, Vietminh troops emerged victorious after a 56-day siege, leading to the end of France's involvement in Indochina. The war ended in Vietnamese victory and the country was then divided into the communist-dominated north and the U.S.-supported south. Almost inevitably, war soon broke out between the two.

U.S. involvement in the **Vietnam War** from 1957 to 1973 was the second phase of three in Vietnam's history. The first phase began in 1946 when the Vietnamese fought French troops for control of the country. Vietnam prior to 1946 had been part of the French colony of Indochina since 1861 along with Laos and Kampuchea or Cambodia. In 1954, the defeated French left and the country became divided into Communist North and Democratic South. The United States' aid and influence continued as part of the U.S. "Cold War" foreign policy to help any nation threatened by Communism.

The second phase involved a much more direct U.S. commitment. The Communist Vietnamese considered the war one of national liberation, a struggle to avoid continual dominance and influence of a foreign power. Participants were the United States of America, Australia, New Zealand, South and North Vietnam, South Korea, Thailand, and the Philippines. With active U.S. involvement from 1957 to 1973, it was the longest war participated in by the U.S. to date. It was tremendously destructive and completely divided the American public in their opinions and feelings about the war. Many were frustrated and angered by the fact that it was the first war fought on foreign soil in which U.S. combat forces were totally unable to achieve their goals and objectives.

The Vietnam War also divided the Democratic Party, and the **1968 Democratic National Convention** in Chicago turned out to be a highly contentious and bitterly fought, both on the floor of the convention and outside, where thousands had gathered to protest the Vietnam War. Vice President Hubert H. Humphrey became the party's nominee, but he led a divided party.

In Vietnam, the forces of the **Viet Cong** and the **North Vietnamese Army (NVA)** launched a coordinated and devastating offensive on January 30, on the eve of Tet, the Lunar New Year, disproving the Johnson Administration officials who claimed that the Vietnamese Communists were no longer a viable military force. Although the **Tet Offensive** was a tactical defeat for the Viet Cong, it no longer could field a large enough military force to match American firepower in a set-piece engagement, it was a strategic defeat for the Americans, in public relations and the political will to continue in a seemingly endless conflict.

A cease-fire was arranged in January 1973 and a few months later, U.S. troops left for good. The third and final phase consisted of fighting between the Vietnamese but ended April 30, 1975, with the surrender of South Vietnam, the entire country being united under Communist ruler.

Poverty remained a serious problem in the central sections of large cities resulting in riots and soaring crime rates, which ultimately found its way to the suburbs. The escalation of the war in Vietnam and the social conflict and upheaval of support vs opposition to U.S. involvement led to antiwar demonstrations, escalation of drug abuse, weakening of the family unit, homelessness, poverty, mental illness, along with increasing social, mental, and physical problems experienced by the Vietnam veterans returning to families, marriages, and a country all divided and tom apart.

Returning veterans faced not only readjustment to normal civilian life but also bitterness, anger, rejection, and no heroes' welcomes. Many suffered severe physical and deep psychological problems. The war set a precedent where both Congress and the American people actively challenged U.S. military and foreign policy. The conflict, though tempered markedly by time, still exists and still has a definite effect on people.

COMPETENCY 2.12   CIVIL RIGHTS MOVEMENT

Skill 2.12a   Examine and analyze the key people, events, policies, and court cases in the field of civil rights from varying perspectives.

The economic boom following the war led to prosperity for many Americans in the 1950s. This prosperity did not extend to the poor blacks of the south, however, and the economic disparities between the races became more pronounced. After World War II and the Korean War, efforts began to relieve the problems of millions of African-Americans, including ending discrimination in education, housing, and jobs and the grinding widespread poverty.

Taking inspiration from similar struggles in India at the time led by Mahatma Ghandi, a burgeoning civil rights movement began to gain momentum under such leaders as **Dr. Martin Luther King, Jr**. The phrase "the civil rights movement" generally refers to the nation-wide effort made by black people and those who supported them to gain equal rights to whites and to eliminate segregation. Discussion of this movement is generally understood in terms of the period of the 1950s and 1960s.

The **key people** in the civil rights movement are:

Rosa Parks - A black seamstress from Montgomery Alabama who, in 1955, refused to give up her seat on the bus to a white man. This event is generally understood as the spark that lit the fire of the Civil Rights Movement. She has been generally regarded as the "mother of the Civil Rights Movement."

Martin Luther King, Jr. - the most prominent member of the Civil Rights movement. King promoted nonviolent methods of opposition to segregation. The "**Letter from Birmingham Jail**" explained the purpose of nonviolent action as a way to make people notice injustice. He led the march on Washington in 1963, at which he delivered the "**I Have a Dream**" speech. He received the 1968 Nobel Prize for Peace.

James Meredith – the first African American to enroll at the University of Mississippi.

Emmett Till – a teenage boy who was murdered in Mississippi while visiting from Chicago. The crime of which he was accused was "whistling at a white woman in a store." He was beaten and murdered, and his body was dumped in a river. His two white abductors were apprehended and tried. They were acquitted by an all-white jury. After the acquittal, they admitted their guilt, but remained free because of double jeopardy laws. His death became one of the key events in the movement.

Ralph Abernathy – A major figure in the Civil Rights Movement who succeeded Martin Luther King, Jr. as head of the Southern Christian Leadership Conference

Malcolm X – a political leader and part of the Civil Rights Movement. Unlike Dr King, Malcolm X did not take a pacifist stance and maintained the view that African Americans should do everything that was necessary to secure their rights. He was a prominent Black Muslim.

Stokeley Carmichael – one of the leaders of the Black Power movement that called for independent development of political and social institutions for blacks. Carmichael called for black pride and maintenance of black culture. He was head of the Student Nonviolent Coordinating Committee.

Key events of the Civil Rights Movement include:

Brown vs. Board of Education, 1954

Rosa Parks and the Montgomery Bus Boycott, 1955-56 – After refusing to give up her seat on a bus in Montgomery, Alabama, Parks was arrested, tried, and convicted of disorderly conduct and violating a local ordinance. When word reached the black community a bus boycott was organized to protest the segregation of blacks and whites on public buses. The boycott lasted 381 days, until the ordinance was lifted.

Strategy shift to "direct action" – nonviolent resistance and civil disobedience, 1955 – 1965. This action consisted mostly of bus boycotts, sit-ins, freedom rides.

Formation of the Southern Christian Leadership Conference, 1957. This group was formed by Martin Luther King, Jr., John Duffy, Rev. C. D. Steele, Rev. T. J. Jemison, Rev. Fred Shuttlesworth, Ella Baker, A. Philip Randolph, Bayard Rustin and Stanley Levison. The group provided training and assistance to local efforts to fight segregation. Non-violence was its central doctrine and its major method of fighting segregation and racism.

The Desegregation of Little Rock, 1957. Following up on the decision of the Supreme Court in Brown vs. Board of Education, the Arkansas school board voted to integrate the school system. The NAACP chose Arkansas as the place to push integration because it was considered a relatively progressive Southern state. However, the governor called up the National Guard to prevent nine black students from attending Little Rock's Central High School.

Sit-ins – In 1960, students began to stage "sit-ins" at local lunch counters and stores as a means of protesting the refusal of those businesses to desegregate. The first was in Greensboro, NC. This led to a rash of similar campaigns throughout the South. Demonstrators began to protest parks, beaches, theaters, museums, and libraries. When arrested, the protesters made "jail-no-bail" pledges. This called attention to their cause and put the financial burden of providing jail space and food on the cities.

Freedom Rides – Activists traveled by bus throughout the deep South to desegregate bus terminals (required by federal law). These protesters undertook extremely dangerous protests. Many buses were firebombed, and protestors were attacked by the KKK and beaten. They were crammed into small, airless jail cells and mistreated in many ways. Key figures in this effort included John Lewis, James Lawson, Diane Nash, Bob Moses, James Bevel, Charles McDew, Bernard Lafayette, Charles Jones, Lonnie King, Julian Bond, Hosea Williams, and Stokeley Carmichael.

The Birmingham Campaign, 1963-64. A campaign was planned to use sit-in, kneel-ins in churches, and a march to the county building to launch a voter registration campaign. The City obtained an injunction forbidding all such protests. The protesters, including Martin Luther King, Jr., believed the injunction was unconstitutional, and defied it. They were arrested. While in jail, King wrote his famous "Letter from Birmingham Jail." When the campaign began to falter, the "Children's Crusade" called students to leave school and join the protests. The events became news when more than 600 students were jailed. The next day more students joined the protest.

The media was present and broadcast vivid pictures to the nation, showing fire hoses being used to knock down children and dogs attacking some of them. The resulting public outrage led the Kennedy administration to intervene. About a month later, a committee was formed to end hiring discrimination, arrange for the release of jailed protesters, and establish normative communication between blacks and whites. Four months later, the KKK bombed the **Sixteenth Street Baptist Church**, killing four girls.

The March on Washington, 1963. This was a march on Washington for jobs and freedom. It was a combined effort of all major civil rights organizations. The goals of the march were: meaningful civil rights laws, a massive federal works program, full and fair employment, decent housing, the right to vote, and adequate integrated education. It was at this march that Martin Luther King, Jr. made the famous "I Have a Dream" speech.

Mississippi Freedom Summer, 1964. Students were brought from other states to Mississippi to assist local activists in registering voters, teaching in "Freedom Schools" and in forming the Mississippi Freedom Democratic Party. Three of the workers disappeared – murdered by the KKK. It took six weeks to find their bodies. The national uproar forced President Johnson to send in the FBI. Johnson was able to use public sentiment to effect passage in Congress of the Civil Rights Act of 1964.

Selma to Montgomery marches, 1965. Attempts to obtain voter registration in Selma, Alabama had been largely unsuccessful due to opposition from the city's sheriff. M.L. King came to the city to lead a series of marches. He and over 200 demonstrators were arrested and jailed. Each successive march was met with violent resistance by police. In March, a group of over 600 intended to walk from Selma to Montgomery (54 miles). News media were on hand when, six blocks into the march, state and local law enforcement officials attacked the marchers with billy clubs, tear gas, rubber tubes wrapped in barbed wire and bull whips. They were driven back to Selma. National broadcast of the footage provoked a nation-wide response. President Johnson again used public sentiment to achieve passage of the Voting Rights Act of 1965.

Key policies, legislation and court cases included the following:

Brown v. Board of Education, 1954 – the Supreme Court declared that Plessy v. Ferguson was unconstitutional. This was the ruling that had established "Separate but Equal" as the basis for segregation. With this decision, the Court ordered immediate desegregation.

Civil Rights Act of 1964 – bars discrimination in public accommodations, employment and education

Voting Rights Act of 1965 – suspended poll taxes, literacy tests and other voter tests for voter registration. This law irrevocably changed the political landscape of the South.

Tragically, the Reverend Martin Luther King, Jr., an influential leader of the Civil Rights Movement and its most eloquent spokesman, was assassinated in Memphis, Tennessee, sparking racial riots in many American cities. Also, Senator Robert F. Kennedy of New York, the late President John F. Kennedy's younger brother, was assassinated in Los Angeles after winning the California Democratic Primary. Before he died, it looked very possible that he would have won the party's nomination, running on an anti-war platform.

Skill 2.12b **Describe the civil rights movements of African Americans and other minority groups and their impacts on government, society, and the economy.**

"**Minority rights**" encompasses two ideas: the first is the normal individual rights of members of ethnic, racial, class, religious or sexual minorities; the second is collective rights of minority groups. Various civil rights movements have sought to guarantee that the individual rights of persons are not denied on the basis of being part of a minority group. The effects of these movements may be seen in guarantees of minority representation, affirmative action quotas, etc.

Since 1941 a number of anti-discrimination laws have been passed by the Congress. These acts have protected the civil rights of several groups of Americans. These laws include:

- Fair Employment Act of 1941
- Civil Rights Act of 1964
- Immigration and Nationality Services Act of 1965
- Voting Rights Act of 1965
- Civil Rights Act of 1968
- Age Discrimination in Employment Act of 1967
- Age Discrimination Act of 1975
- Pregnancy Discrimination Act of 1978
- Americans with Disabilities Act of 1990
- Civil Rights Act of 1991
- Employment Non-Discrimination Act

Numerous groups have used various forms of protest, attempts to sway public opinion, legal action, and congressional lobbying to obtain full protection of their civil rights under the Constitution. The **disability rights** movement was a successful effort to guarantee access to public buildings and transportation, equal access to education and employment, and equal protection under the law in terms of access to insurance, and other basic rights of American citizens. As a result of these efforts, public buildings and public transportation must be accessible to persons with disabilities, discrimination in hiring or housing on the basis of disability is also illegal.

A "**prisoners' rights**" movement has been working for many years to ensure the basic human rights of persons incarcerated for crimes. Immigrant rights movements have provided for employment and housing rights, as well as preventing abuse of immigrants through hate crimes. In some states, **immigrant rights** movements have led to bi-lingual education and public information access. Another group movement to obtain equal rights is the lesbian, gay, bisexual and transgender social movement. This movement seeks equal housing, freedom from social and employment discrimination, and equal recognition of relationships under the law.

Skill 2.12c   Analyze the development of the women's rights movement and its connections to other social and political movements.

The **women's rights** movement is concerned with the freedoms of women as differentiated from broader ideas of human rights. These issues are generally different from those that affect men and boys because of biological conditions or social constructs. The rights the movement has sought to protect throughout history include:

- The right to vote
- The right to work
- The right to fair wages
- The right to bodily integrity and autonomy
- The right to own property
- The right to an education
- The right to hold public office
- Marital rights
- Parental rights
- Religious rights
- The right to serve in the military
- The right to enter into legal contracts

The movement for women's rights has resulted in many social and political changes. Many of the ideas that seemed very radical merely 100 years ago are now normative.

Some of the most famous leaders in the women's movement throughout American history are:

- Abigail Adams
- Susan B. Anthony
- Gloria E. Anzaldua
- Betty Friedan
- Olympe de Gouges
- Gloria Steinem
- Harriet Tubman
- Mary Wollstonecraft
- Virginia Woolf
- Germaine Greer

Many within the women's movement are primarily committed to justice and the natural rights of all people. This has led many members of the women's movement to be involved in the Black Civil Rights Movement, the gay rights movement, and the recent social movement to protect the rights of fathers. It should be noted that many of these groups often support one another (though not always) as they seek similar goals of protection of rights and justice for minority or under-represented groups.

DOMAIN 3:   CALIFORNIA HISTORY

COMPETENCY 3.1   PRE-COLUMBIAN PERIOD THROUGH THE END
**   OF MEXICAN RULE**

Skill 3.1a   Describe the geography, economic life, and culture of
**   California's American Indian peoples, as well as their**
**   relationship with the environment.**

Geographically California can be understood in terms of four primary sections: the coast, the mountains, the central valley, and the deserts. California offers a wide variety of habitats and many species of plants and animals, as well as climates. As a result, there was great cultural diversity among the early people of California. These differences included housing, dress, kinship systems, political organizations, and religious beliefs and practices.

The native peoples of California believe that they were created in their homelands and have lived there forever. Each culture has its own story of creation. But most anthropologists believe that the early native population is descended from ancient people who crossed the **Bering Land Bridge** that once connected Asia and North America. There is no certainty about when the first people reached California, but there is widespread belief that Native Americans were living in this region for 15,000 years before the first European explorers visited the California coast.

Most California Native Americans subsisted by hunting and gathering. But they also managed the natural resources. Some groups pruned plants and trees, culled animal populations, and periodically burned groundcover to enrich the earth. The **Cahuilla** dug wells in the deserts. They created pools by building up the sand around the wells. They cultivated melons, squash, beans and corn. The **Yumas,** who lived around the lower Colorado River, planted corn, pumpkins and beans in the mud after the annual floods of the river. The primary food for most tribes was the acorn. Hunters had access to deer, antelope, elk, sheep and bears. Fish were plentiful in the lakes, rivers, streams and in the ocean.

It is believed (though it cannot be proven with certainty) that the population of California before the arrival of Europeans was about 300,000. The number of tribes, cultures and languages of the early Native Californians was vast. The languages have been classified into seven groups: Penutian, Hokan, Utian, Yukian, Algic, Uto-Aztecan, and Na-Dene. Over 100 tribes have been identified. The tribes, however, were further subdivided into "tribelets" or groups of villages. It is believed that there were as many as 500 of these communities.

Due to the great diversity of the native communities, the state is generally divided into six "culture areas."

The Southern Culture Area was home to some of the most populous tribes. Some of these communities had as many as 2,000 residents. The **Kumeyaay** migrated each year as plants in their territory ripened. The **Cahuilla** hunted with bows and arrows, nets, traps, or by throwing sticks at small animals. The women gathered nuts and fruits. They also planted corn, squash, beans and melons when there was sufficient water. The **Tongva** tribe had a structured society that was divided into distinct classes. The villages of the **Chumash** sometimes included as many as 2,000 people. The villages generally included a storehouse, sweathouse, cemetery, ceremonial enclosure and playing field. They were skilled fishermen and navigators. They made canoes of planks caulked with asphaltum. They harpooned seals, sea otters, and porpoises and traveled between the coast and the many islands off shore. They also produced spectacular colorful rock paintings.

The Central Culture Area included about 60% of all of the Native people of California. The climate was mild and hunting and gathering was easy. Tools and weapons made by these tribes were not very sophisticated, but basketry was quite advanced. These groups were organized into tribelets and small villages. The people of the villages were quite territorial and did not tolerate trespassing. However, clashes between the tribes were minor. The **Yokuts** were hunters and gatherers, as well as fishermen. They are notable for the development of hunting strategies such as wearing animal disguises and for building traps for quail. The **Miwok** groups were spread over a large area and constructed dwellings differently in these areas ranging from earth-covered homes that were partly underground to thatched huts, to bark slab structures. Each of the triblets was autonomous. The **Pomo**, actually several groups of native peoples, were particularly known for their basketry.

The Northwestern Culture Area was notable for tribes that valued material wealth. The possession of certain prized items determined social status. Political leadership belonged to the wealthiest. The **Yurok** lived along the Klamath River in permanent villages of distinctive dwellings built of split planks. Their proximity to the redwood forests provided for wood which was made into numerous household items and dugout canoes. The **Hupa** lived near the Trinity River. Wealth determined social rank. They subsisted primarily on salmon and acorns. Their religion included the "world-renewal rituals" of the White Deerskin and Jumping Dances. The **Shasta** lived in the mountain area of northwestern California. They settled in river valleys or at the mouths of rivers. In these villages, individual families owned hunting and fishing grounds, tobacco plots and oak trees. They practiced trade with their neighbors.

The Northeastern Culture Area was sparsely settled. Some of the tribes in this area occupied rich lands and lived much like tribes in other areas. Other tribes, however, lived in more desolate areas and subsisted on small game and gathered seeds and roots. The **Achumawi** lived along the Pit River. These people dug pits to trap deer and other animals. They used the deer skins to make caps, capes, belts, moccasins, leggings, skirts and quivers. They had elaborate puberty rituals for girls, extensive mourning rites, and respected their Shamans. About half of their shamans were women. The **Atsugewi** lived in rugged valleys and barren plains. Hard work was highly valued and respected. They fished with baskets and nets. Small game was hunted in groups; large game was usually hunted by individuals and was shared by the community. They set aside every sixth day for rest, and held an annual celebration to which they invited people of neighboring villages.

The Great Basic Culture Area included the areas along the current eastern border and the eastern deserts of the southern part of the state. This is an area in which food and water are scarce. The **Tubatulabal** lived in the southern foothills of the Sierra Nevada. They were divided into three groups, each speaking a different dialect of the language. These tribes were led by a headman (timiwal) who was elected for life by a council of elders. His function was primarily dispute resolution and representation of the group when dealing with other groups. They subsisted by hunting, fishing and gathering. The **Owens Valley Paiute** lived in an area that received very little rainfall and, hence, had little vegetation. The small groups tended to migrate frequently seeking food and water. The men hunted and the women gathered. This group was notable for its development of a system of agriculture that utilized communal labor. They built dams and ditches to irrigate wild plants.

The Colorado River Culture Area, on the western edge of the Southwest Culture Area. These Native Americans also hunted and gathered and grew beans, corn, and pumpkins. They considered themselves more unified than the tribes that divided themselves into tribelets. They traveled extensively outside their own regions. The people of this area include the **Quechan (Yuma)**, the **Halchidhoma**, and the **Mohave**.

Skill 3.1b   Define and assess the impact of Spanish exploration and colonization, including the establishment of the missionsystem, ranchos, and pueblos, and their influences on the development of the agricultural economy of early California.

The first explorers visited California in search of riches and a route to Asia. **Hernan Cortes** led an expedition north from Acapulco to the Baja peninsula in 1535. He established a colonial outpost on the coast of the Bay of La Paz, but it was abandoned in 1536. The coastal areas of California were first explored by Europeans in 1542 by the Portuguese explorer Jouan Rodriguez Cabrillo, who was working for the Spaniard Cortes. This expedition resulted in the discovery of Alta California. But **Francis Drake**, an Englishman, was the first to explore the entire coast and claim possession of the territory.

The strategy of the Spanish empire in California was to exploit, transform and include the native people of the Americas in the new settlements called missions. The founding of **missions** was the key to transplanting the empire and converting the native people to Roman Catholicism. Beginning in 1769, California missions were established along the coast by Spanish Catholic Missionaries in a program called "the Sacred Expedition." The Franciscan order founded the first mission at San Diego. Others followed until there were 21 by 1823. The Franciscan leader of this mission was Father Junipero Serra. After Serra's death, Fermin Francisco de Lasuen became the leader of the missionary effort.

Missions were generally established with the distance of a day's walk between them. Once the native people were brought into the missions, they were given religious instruction and they were taught various practical skills. The secondary goal of the missions was to thoroughly transition the native people to the life of the Spanish empire. This included language, work habits, social organization, attire, etc. The missions were surrounded by orange groves, grape plantations and cattle ranches.

Some of the California native people cooperated with the missionaries. Some chose a course of passive resistance. Still others attempted to resist more actively. In general, revolts were put down quite quickly.

The missions were intended to be temporary schools that would convert the native people and acculturate them as Spaniards. Once this was accomplished, the missions were to be disbanded. When Mexico declared independence from Spain, the missions became possessions of the Mexican government. By 1832 they were essentially abandoned and dissolved.

The impact of the missions on the native people of California is a matter of considerable debate. Some believe they had a destructive effect on the native people. Others believe the native people benefited from the missions. It is clear that the change in lifestyle, the compression of the people in a small area, and the introduction of new diseases resulted in an exceptionally high death rate. The life of the native people at the missions, while occasionally good, was generally described as very severe.

Beginning in the 1820s, trappers and settlers from Canada and the United States began to reach California, bringing tremendous change. There was a weak attempt during this period to claim part of California for Russia, but these were short-lived. The territory was sparsely settled during this period due to frequent endemic outbreaks of malaria, plague and yellow fever.

Spanish colonial officials also built four military forts, **presidios**, along the coast of California. These were built near the best ports, where the harbors could be defended against attack. The forts were also in close proximity to the missions so that soldiers could be dispatched quickly in the event of an Indian uprising.

To ensure an adequate food supply for the soldiers, civilian towns were also founded. These were called **pueblos**. Settlers were attracted to these settlements with offers of free land, farming equipment, livestock, and an annual stipend. In return, they were required to sell their surplus agricultural products to the presidios.

For the next twenty-five years, California was considered a Mexican province. Cattle and horses were introduced in the late eighteenth century. These doubled in number about every five years, giving rise to cattle ranches (**ranchos**). These ranches quickly became the primary expressions of the lifestyle of Mexican California. The families that owned and operated these ranches were the elite of Mexican California. These ranches, however, used native labor, in return for which the natives received only food, clothing and shelter. This resulted in a society that closely resembled European feudalism.

Skill 3.1c   Describe the causes of the Mexican-American War and assess its impact on California.

The immediate cause of the **Mexican-American War** was the annexation of Texas by the United States in 1845. In 1836, Texas had revolted from Mexico and established an independent republic. The **Republic of Texas** was recognized by the U.S. in 1837. Despite the fact that several European countries had recognized The Republic of Texas, Mexico never acknowledged its independence. In the face of constant friction between Texas and Mexico, the U.S. had been warned that Mexico would consider an attempt to annex Texas to the American Union a declaration of war.

The Texas issue was a major consideration in the Presidential election of 1844. The Democrats favored annexation, the Whigs opposed it. The Democrat, **James K. Polk**, was elected and made the annexation of Texas the first major action of his administration. A more conciliatory approach to the issue probably could have averted war. Nonetheless, there was a dispute about the western boundary of Texas. Texas claimed the Rio Grande River as its western boundary. Mexico claimed the Nueces River, about 100 miles east, as the boundary. The dispute over this approximately 2,000 square mile area further antagonized Mexico.

President Polk did not try diplomatic negotiation, but ordered General Zachary Taylor and his troops to the Rio Grande. This was met by a counter-advance by the Mexican army. On April 25, 1846 the war began. On May 13, Congress declared war.

Although the annexation of Texas was the direct cause of the Mexican-American War, there were also indirect causes. By the terms of the **Missouri Compromise,** slavery was banned north of the boundary 36° 30'. Texas was the last potential slave-holding state that could be admitted to the Union. The balance of power in the Senate on the slavery debate was at issue.

In California, Lt. **John C. Fremont** (an officer with the Army Corps of Topographical Engineers) and a troop of about sixty armed men arrived in California. All of the men were expert marksmen. Mexican officials ordered them out of California. After initially refusing to leave, Fremont relented and started moving north toward Oregon. He later returned to California and helped instigate what came to be called the **Bear Flag Revolt.** Fremont joined forces with a group of Anglo-American settlers in northern California who had seized Colonel Mariano Guadalupe Vallejo and other Mexicans in Sonoma on June 14, 1846. The combined force (called the **California Battalion**) declared California an independent republic.

When the settlers declared independence, they raised a flag that showed a crude drawing of a bear, a single star, and the words "California Republic." From this flag, the event came to be known as the Bear Flag Revolt. The Revolt had the main result of creating tension and bitterness between the Anglo-Americans and the Spanish-speaking *Californios.*

U.S. naval forces landed on the coast of California in July 1846 and proclaimed California part of the United States. Mexico responded with military force that included the *Californios*. Fighting in California ended on January 13, 1847 when Andres Pico surrendered to John C. Fremont. Fighting continued elsewhere for another year.

The Mexican-American War officially ended with the signing of the **Treaty of Guadalupe Hidalgo** on February 2, 1848. The U.S. agreed to pay Mexico $15 million and to assume unpaid claims against Mexico. Mexico agreed to transfer to the United States more than 525,000 square miles of land. This area is now the states of California, Nevada and Utah, most of Arizona and New Mexico, and parts of Colorado and Wyoming. Mexico lost half of its land, and the American people believed they had achieved their Manifest Destiny. A small strip of land north of the Rio Grande remained in Mexican control. This was later purchased by the U.S. in the **Gadsden Purchase**. Slavery was prohibited in this area.

The major results of the Mexican-American War were the addition of more than 525,000 square miles of territory to the United States and tthe reorganization of the political parties along the lines of anti-slavery and pro-slavery. Indirect results included an incease in the prestige of the United States with the acquisition of an extended coastline on the Pacific. In addition, the development of California was facilitated by the discovery of gold in California, which led to various additions to the nation's resources. Also introduced was the doctrine of squatter sovereignty, which became one of the underlying causes of the Civil War. Finally, there was military training obtained in the war by officers who would assume a major role in the Civil War.

COMPETENCY 3.2   FROM THE GOLD RUSH TO THE PRESENT

Skill 3.2a   **Describe the discovery of gold and assess its consequences on the cultures, societies, politics, and economies of California, including its impact on California Indians and Californios.**

On January 24, 1848, James Marshall, an employee of Captain John A. Sutter, observed the glitter of gold in sands he had picked up in a mill race at Sutter's Coloma sawmill. By August, word of the discovery of gold had reached the East. In December, more than 300 ounces of pure gold reached Washington, D.C. Gold fever swept the nation. Men left farms, businesses and families to become part of the **Gold Rush**. The population of California rose from 14,000 to over 100,000 within a year and to more than 220,000 by 1852. **Mark Twain** and **Bret Harte** later wrote of the Gold Rush. They wrote of the roughness, the sentiment and the unexpected heroism of the "forty-niners."

People came from all over the world. Most came from the East by "**prairie schooner**," proclaiming the motto "**California or bust.**" They made their way over mountains, through mountain passes and through canyons no one believed a wagon could cross. Many made the journey in ships, enduring the dangers of rounding Cape Horn.

Expectedly, most of the people who came were men without families. Widespread disorder was the result of this influx of men who experienced the sudden rise to wealth or the dark despair of failure. The land had just been ceded from Mexico and had no established government and no laws. What law there was varied from camp to camp. Nugget stealing and horse stealing were considered worse than murder and was punished accordingly.

One of the most important tasks for the early settlers was to establish communication with the rest of the world. Steamship lines began to make the 19,000 mile trip around Cape Horn. Equally important were the overland routes that carried mail and freight from Missouri to San Francisco. The most notable overland routes were:

- The Merchant's Express, with 2,000 wagons and 20,000 yoke of oxen to move freight across the continent; and
- The **Pony Express** relayed mail from Missouri to San Francisco in just ten days.
- Stage lines traveled twice a week from Saint Louis to San Francisco and made it possible to travel from coast to coast in only three weeks.
- The **Union Pacific Railroad** was completed in 1869, eliminating the need for stage travel.

The successful miners were building the famous palaces along the crest of **Nob Hill** in San Francisco. The unsuccessful were drifting down into the valley and filling it with wheat fields and orchards, and beginning the remarkable agricultural development that would define California well into the future. To a large extent, California's economic and social character can be traced to both the successful and unsuccessful miners of the Gold Rush.

The gold rush gave rise to several notable **boom towns**. The largest in the central part of the state were Sacramento, which was the gateway to the mines in the central and northern part of the state, and Stockton, which was the supply center for the southern mines. **San Francisco**, however, was the greatest of the boom towns, being the port through which those who traveled to California by sea entered the state and as the center of banking and manufacturing.

In addition to those who discovered their wealth in gold mines and stream beds, the second group that amassed great wealth was the people who provided supplies and services for the miners.

The earliest mining methods (panning, rockers, "long tom") were essentially innocuous in environmental terms. But as the supply of readily available gold was exhausted, miners turned to more destructive methods of finding and extracting gold from the earth. Some dug deep shafts or tunnels into the earth. Most destructive was "**hydraulicking**." This method used high-pressure water to erode banks and hills. This uniquely California innovation was the predominant type of mining for about 30 years.

Skill 3.2b   **Describe the international migration to California in the 19th century, the social, economic, and political responses to this migration, and the contributions of immigrants to the development of California.**

In the mining towns, regional mining districts were established that essentially operated on the basis of democratic principles. But they were discriminatory. Not only did the miners ignore the tribal governments of the California native peoples, they also ignored the practices that remained in place from the days of Mexican rule. These mining districts generally excluded **African Americans, Asians,** and **Latinos,** and resorted to **vigilante justice** when people were suspected of wrongdoing.

The discrimination practiced by the Anglo-American settlers had far-reaching effects on an increasingly and uniquely diverse and predominantly immigrant society. The lure of gold attracted people from all parts of America, from Mexico, Chile, Peru, and other South and Central American countries, from various European countries, and from China and the Pacific islands. In fact, the region became notorious for frequent ethnic conflicts.

The **Native people** of California responded in several ways. Some simply got out of the way and moved into the central part of the state. Some, particularly the Miwok and Yokuts, raided the settlements for horses and livestock. Some became miners, or worked for white miners. Some mined gold and traded it to white merchants for goods. In their ignorance of the value of the gold, still others traded gold for beads on an equal weight basis, until they began to understand the value the white men placed on the gold.

Within four years of the beginning of the gold rush, the Native American population declined from about 150,000 to 30,000. Much of this was due to malnutrition and **disease** introduced by the white men (for which the native people had no immunity). Thousands of Native people died in campaigns of **extermination** carried out by the whites. Miners and ranchers joined forces, with the support of local sentiment, to carry out raids on native villages. Some frontier communities even paid **bounties** for Indian scalps and heads. Even the federal government assisted in funding these extermination efforts.

The Treaty of Guadalupe Hidalgo, which ended the Mexican American War provided for the property rights of **Mexicans** who owned property in the lands claimed by the United States. At the time, the ranchos covered about 13 million acres. Gold frenzy, however, ignored the property rights of the rancho owners. Miners settled on rancho lands as "**squatters**." There was vast confusion about ownership of the land. In 1851 Congress passed a land law that outlined an extensive process by which rancho owners could prove their title to the land and have the squatters removed. Resolution of these claims took about seventeen years. About 200 of the claim owners lost land amounting to nearly four million acres. About 600 of the claim owners demonstrated their ownership of about nine million acres. But by the time the claims were won, the owners were usually bankrupt and lost the land anyway. Their bitterness was profound.

African Americans accounted for about one percent of the non-Indian population during the gold rush. These were both escaped slaves and free persons. The free blacks came to mine for themselves. Slaves were brought by their southern owners, despite the fact that California was a free state (no slavery). They were also victims of discrimination. The state constitution restricted voting rights to "free white males." Membership in the state militia was also restricted to whites. The state enacted a harsh fugitive slave law. And the state passed a law that made it illegal for "blacks, negroes, mulattoes" and Indians from testifying either for or against a "white man."

Latin American immigrants made up the largest group of foreign miners. There was great hostility between the Latino miners and the Anglo miners. Some of this hostility was a residual effect of the recent war. But a large part of the animosity was due to economic competition. Most of the Latino miners were more experienced and more knowledgeable in mining.

In 1850 the state legislature passed the **Foreign Miners License Tax**. All miners who were not U.S. citizens were required to pay a monthly tax of $20. After the tax was passed, about two-thirds of the Mexican miners returned to Mexico.

In 1853 one newspaper estimated that there were 32,000 French gold miners in the state. The French also suffered discrimination by U.S. citizens. Two specific elements of the persecution of the French (who it was feared were taking too much of the nation's wealth) were:

- The Americans called the French "Keskydees". This was a derogatory imitation of the question frequently asked by the French miners, "Qu'est-ce qu'il dit?" ("What does he say?").
- Anglo-Americans required the French to pay the special monthly tax of $20 for the privilege of mining gold in California. Some of the French miners joined forces with Germans and some Mexicans and staged a peaceful protest at Sonora. This came to be called "**The French Revolution.**"

Natives of the **Hawaiian Islands** (called Kanakas) began to immigrate to California fifty years earlier to hunt sea otter and work in other coastal areas. Hundreds more came to work in the gold mines. They were treated no better.

Thousands of **Chinese** came during the gold rush. At least one estimate indicates that one-fourth of the miners in the state in 1870 were Chinese. Anglo-American miners feared that they, too, would take too much of the gold. Others hated them because they were willing to work for very low wages. But, in general, their "foreignness" was considered dangerous to the state. The state legislature enacted another Foreign Miners License Tax of $3 per month in 1852 that was particularly directed against the Chinese. For 18 years this tax generated almost 25% of the state's annual revenue. It was not until 1870 that it was declared unconstitutional.

Despite discrimination and hostility, California's development resulted to a great extent from the labor and struggle of these immigrants. The Chinese, in particular, working in the mines, and with their superior knowledge of explosives, and working on the railroads, were the major source of labor that built the mechanisms of wealth and communication upon which the state has been built.

The completion of the **transcontinental railroad** in 1869 ended the problem of California's isolation from the rest of the country. The four men who provided the vision and much of the initial financial backing for the construction of the railroad were known as the **Big Four (Leland Stanford, Collis P. Huntington, Mark Hopkins, and Charles Crocker)**. They became the wealthiest and most powerful men of their generation. The majority of the work in constructing the railroad was done by Chinese workers. The Chinese were paid minimal wages and given very dangerous tasks. Construction took more than six years. There was a great celebration when the tracks of the **Central Pacific Railroad** met the tracks of the **Union Pacific Railroad**. The track was attached to the final tie with three commemorative spikes, one was silver and two were gold.

The immediate benefit of the completion of the railroad and the invention of the refrigerated car was that the cars could not only deliver California produce to the east quickly, but the produce could be kept ripe and cool during shipment. Yet the first ten years after the completion of the railroad were disappointing. The expected new prosperity did not arrive.

In fact, what followed was ten years of depression. Expecting a large influx of new settlers, merchants bought goods in anticipation. When new settlers did not arrive, the market was over-supplied and the prices of the goods declined. Land prices rose as the railroad neared completion, also in anticipation of new settlers. Completion of the railroad actually resulted in decreases in land prices. The completion of the work also returned thousands of workers back to the California labor pool. This reduced wages and caused extensive unemployment.

The expected boom, however, did come in the 1880s, partly due to the railroad. The owners of the railroad advertised California throughout the nation. A second railroad line (the Atchison, Topeka, and Santa Fe) reached Los Angeles in the middle of the decade. A rate war between the two railroads ensued. Over 200,000 new residents came to California in 1887 alone. New towns were built and over half a million home sites were designated.

When construction of the railroad began, the investors recruited the Chinese laborers, even in China, because they were willing to work for low wages (usually a dollar a day) and to do dangerous work. More than 10,000 Chinese laborers, as well as many Irish immigrants, built the railroad. But when construction was complete and the Chinese returned to California, the resulting depression was blamed on them. Anti-Chinese activities included riots, looting and burning of Chinese settlements and the like. Several cities passed laws that were intended to drive out the Chinese. Unemployed whites frequently destroyed Chinese businesses. In 1877, unemployed white men of San Francisco formed a new political party called **The Workingmen's Party**. They demanded that "the Chinese must go."

California voters adopted a new state constitution in 1878, during the height of anti-Chinese hostility. The new constitution was approved by voters a year later. The new constitution included several anti-Chinese provisions.

- "No Chinese shall be employed on any state, county, municipal, or other public work, except in punishment for crime."
- The cities and towns were instructed by the legislature to either confine Chinese residents to certain parts of the city or town or to force them to live outside city or town limits.
- Chinese immigrants were determined to be ineligible for U.S. citizenship because of race.
- The state was instructed to discourage further immigration by Chinese by any means necessary.

The **Chinese Exclusion Act**, approved by the U.S. Congress in 1882 was the ultimate expression of anti-Chinese feeling. It prohibited Chinese immigration for ten years. In 1892, it was extended for another ten years. In 1902, it became permanent. It was not repealed until China and the U.S. became allies against the Japanese during World War II. This law also produced further difficulties for the Chinese, including boycotts of Chinese-produced goods.

Skill 3.2c   Analyze key principles in California's constitutional and political development (including the Progressive Era reforms of initiative, referendum, and recall), and compare and contrast the California and U.S. Constitutions.

Between the end of the Mexican American War and California's admission to the Union in 1850, the political situation was quite unstable and confused. The U.S. Congress was consumed with the issue of slavery in the areas ceded to the U.S. by the treaty that ended the war. For this reason, no formal government was established for California until 1850.

Recognizing the need for some form of government, forty-eight prominent men met in September of 1849 to draft a constitution for the new state. The most pressing issue was whether to petition for admission as a state. Due to the great influx of new settlers and gold fever, the delegates decided to apply for statehood immediately. The second major issue facing the delegates was the question of slavery. Admission to the Union was requested as a free (non-slaveholding) state. The constitution also included a provision that permitted **married women** to own property independently of their husbands. Any property owned by a woman prior to marriage or during marriage would remain her personal property. This was the first such provision in the nation. This provision was taken over from the same practice in Mexican California. The eastern boundary of the state was also established as the eastern slope of the Sierra Nevada.

One of the most notable debates in the history of the Congress occurred over the admission of California as a free state because admission would upset the equal balance of slave and free states in the Congress. The issue was resolved by passing a very strict new fugitive slave law. The bill for admission was signed by the President, Millard Fillmore, on September 9. 1850. This news did not reach California for almost five weeks.

One of the very critical issues not addressed in the original constitution was the location of the state capital. The convention allowed that the location should be determined on the basis of bids from the various towns. The intention was to acquire the land and buildings needed without cost to the state. For about six years, the capital moved between San Jose, Vallejo, and Benicia. A permanent capital of **Sacramento** was selected in 1854.

This pre-statehood constitution was superseded by the current California Constitution which was ratified in 1879. Unlike most constitutions, it is very long – 110 pages. It has been amended more than 425 times. Its length is generally attributed to a lack of faith in elected officials and to the fact that many of its provisions and initiatives are in the form of constitutional amendments.

Executive power is vested in a **governor, lieutenant-governor, secretary of state, controller, treasurer, attorney-general** and **surveyor-general,** each elected for a four-year term. The legislature is **bi-cameral**. The senate is made up of a representative of each county, elected for four years, and an assembly made up of representatives of districts of equal population elected for two years. The judiciary consists of a **supreme court** (a chief justice and six associates) elected for a twelve-year term, a **superior court** for each county, and **inferior courts** established by the legislature.

There are several notable provisions:

- Lobbying is a felony.
- In civil cases, a finding can be established by agreement of three-fourths of the jury.
- Trial by jury may be waived in minor criminal cases.

Among the numerous amendments to the California State Constitution are:

- The initiative and referendum,
- The recall,
- A minimum wage law for women, and
- Women's right to vote on an equal basis with men (prior to the national constitutional amendment).

Comparison of the Constitution of the State of California with the U.S. Constitution:

1. Both documents establish three branches of government: executive, legislative and judicial.
2. Both documents establish a bi-cameral legislature.
3. In California, representation in **both houses** of the legislature is based on **population**. In the US. Government, the composition of the House of Representatives is based on population, the Senate consists of two Senators from each state.
4. California Senators are elected for a **four-year term** with a **two-term limit**. U.S. Senators are elected for a six-year term with no term limits.
5. In both the California Assembly and the U.S. House of Representatives, terms are two years. California **limits** members of the Assembly to two terms; members of the U.S. House of Representatives have no term limits.
6. While the U.S. President and Vice President are elected together, in California the Governor and Lieutenant Governor are **elected separately**.
7. The California Attorney General, Controller, Secretary of State, Superintendent of Public Instruction, and Treasurer are **elected** by the voters. The equivalent functions in the Federal Government are presidential appointments.
8. In California, Judges of the Supreme Court are **elected** at large to 12-year terms. Judges of the U.S. Supreme Court are nominated by the President and approved by the Senate. Judges of the Courts of Appeal are **elected** in their districts for twelve year terms. Federal Judges are nominated by the President and approved by the Senate. All Federal Justices serve for life.
9. Both documents establish a system of checks and balances between the branches of government.
10. The President of the United States can utilize a pocket veto. The Governor of California can utilize a **line-item veto**.
11. California added the **initiative, referendum,** and **recall** to its constitution during the era of Progressive Reforms at the turn of the twentieth century.
12. Many of the individual **rights clauses** in the California Constitution have been understood and interpreted to provide broader individual rights than the Bill of Rights in the U.S. Constitution.

Several very important amendments to the constitution were championed by the Progressive Party shortly after the turn of the twentieth century. In 1911, the Progressives introduced three measures intended to guarantee that government truly expressed the will of the people. **The initiative** allowed voters to directly create laws or constitutional amendments. **The referendum** allowed voters to veto acts of the legislature. **The recall** permitted voters to remove from office any elected official.

Among the many other reforms adopted by the progressives were several laws that benefited California workers. The legislature in 1911 enacted a system of workers' compensation, establishing the employers' liability for industrial accidents. Also in 1911 the legislature adopted an eight-hour work day for women and the establishment of a **minimum wage for women and children**.

Skill 3.2d   Describe 20th century migration to California from the rest of the U.S. and the world, and analyze its impact on the cultural, economic, social, and political evolution of the state.

In the late nineteenth and twentieth centuries, California experienced dramatic growth. The climate of the central valley area made it perfect for growing wheat. This agricultural industry fostered the development of new approaches to agriculture and the development of new farming technology. The first was the "**Stockton gang plow**" which was made up of a beam to which was attached several plowshares. This was mounted on wheels and pulled by a team of horses or mules. New machines were also developed for planting seeds and for cutting and threshing grain. Steam-powered "**combined harvests**" were invented, as well as the first steam-powered tractor. Also developed in Stockton was the first tractor that ran on an internal combustion engine.

Luther Burbank, who came to California from Massachusetts in the latter part of the nineteenth century, was a horticulturist who created hundreds of new varieties of plants, including new types of plums, lilies, berries, apples, rhubarb, and quince. Although the Spanish missionaries had first introduced oranges to California, it was not until 1870 that **John Wesley North** began planting the orange trees into sandy soil of riverbanks and irrigating the groves with water from the river. He produced winter-ripening "Riverside navel" oranges and shipped them across the country in refrigerated rail cars. A few years later California produced summer-ripening Valencia oranges. The state was then able to provide fresh **oranges** year-round, and soon it was the source of over 65% of the nation's oranges and 90% of its lemons.

The discovery of extensive **oil deposits** in the late nineteenth century, created the California petroleum industry. The deposits were located in the San Joaquin Valley, the Los Angeles basin, and Santa Barbara County. New discoveries of oil in the 1920s led to a second major economic boom for California. Petroleum refining became the state's major manufacturing industry and the Los Angeles harbor became the leading oil-exporting port in the world.

At about the same time as the discovery of oil in California the **automobile** was becoming more popular in California than anywhere else in the nation. By the middle of the 1920s the car was a mainstay of the California lifestyle. It facilitated numerous other changes, as well. First, workers could live some distance from the workplace. The suburbs grew, connected to the cities by networks of new roads. The suburbs began to experience the rise of shopping centers, supermarkets and single-family homes. And tourism became a major industry for California, which in turn gave rise to motels, auto camps, tourist cabins, and even drive-ins.

Soon after this the **motion picture industry** made its home in southern California. Most of the early movies were brief. But in 1913, Samuel Goldfish and Archibald Selwyn formed the feature motion picture company Goldwyn. They then partnered with Louis B. Mayer to form **Metro-Goldwyn Mayer**, the leading studio in Hollywood for more than a quarter of a century. The industry grew, and with it the need for mansions for the stars and all of the workers who were needed.

Of particular significance in the early twentieth century were the labor struggle and the growth of **labor unions**. Labor was gaining strength and challenging the power of corporate America. This struggle was very intense, particularly in San Francisco. Throughout the first two decades of the twentieth century, San Francisco was in fact a **closed-shop** city (i.e., one in which employers hired only union members). In Los Angeles, largely through the efforts of Harrison Gray Otis and the Los Angeles Times, the **open shop** (employers refuse to agree to require their employees to be union members) carried the day.

California agriculture depended on migratory farm workers. Most of them were foreign-born, unorganized, and non-white. They were organized in the early part of the century into the IWW (**Industrial Workers of the World**). This union was more radical than many other unions of the day. The union's goal was to put an end to capitalism by any means that would achieve that end. Farm owners tended to regard the union as dangerous and threatening to the American way of life. Many local governments tried to pass laws that banned the activities of the union. In the long run, the union won new members out of desperation over the horrific conditions under which they were forced to work.

In 1916, the San Francisco waterfront area was shaken by an explosion and the nation was shaken by a debate that continued for many years. A bomb exploded during a patriotic parade. **Thomas J. Mooney** was blamed, tried, and convicted of murder. He was sentenced to hang. But labor leaders throughout the nation believed Mooney had been framed by an anti-labor conspiracy. Debate was sparked throughout the country. The governor commuted his sentence to life in prison. Twenty-three years later, Mooney was pardoned and released from prison.

There was a steady increase in the number of **Japanese immigrants** in the early part of the twentieth century. As the number of Japanese in California grew, anti-Japanese sentiment also grew. A series of actions were taken against the Japanese immigrants.

Labor leaders in San Francisco formed an "**Asiatic Exclusion League**" in 1905 and demanded public policies against the Japanese. They pressured the city into requiring that Japanese children attend only segregated schools with other Asian children. Protests from Japan led to intervention by President Theodore Roosevelt. The city agreed to suspend the segregation act in exchange for a law that would limit Japanese immigration. Japan agreed in 1907 to prohibit its workers from coming to the U.S.

The Japanese immigrants were capable farmers. White farmers tried to eliminate the competition. In 1913 the state legislature passed a law prohibiting anyone who was not eligible for citizenship from owning land in the state. Asians were ineligible for naturalization (under federal law). In 1924, U.S. Congress passed the "**National Origins Quota Act**." This law prohibited all further immigration from Japan.

This period of rapid economic growth and industrial expansion in California came to an abrupt end with the **Stock Market crash of 1929**. The worst depression in the history of the country and of California ensued. With 20-25% of the population unemployed and losing everything, nativism and a fear of foreigners rose quickly. The first to be subjected to the hostility of the natives were the **Filipinos**. White workers complained that the recent immigrants posed an economic threat to native-born workers. Numerous riots broke out. Congress passed the "**Filipino Repatriation Act**" in 1935. The government offered to pay transportation expenses for any Filipinos who wished to return home.

Then **Mexican** immigrants became the targets. The federal government created a program of repatriation. Some left voluntarily, others were forced to leave. Up to 100,000 deportees left California and returned to Mexico.

But another occurrence in the 1930s created yet another, less desirable influx of people to California. **Dust Bowl refugees** came by the hundreds of thousands in search of a better life in California. The situation in California was not what they expected, and they were unwelcome to many Californians. But these refugees held on to the culture of the Southwest, and created their own subculture in California. They were called "**Okies**" because many came from Oklahoma, although they came from several states.

In the midst of the horrific Depression, Californians continued to build the state. Honoring a decade-old agreement to host the **Olympics in 1932**, in addition to a new coliseum, the city built a 250-acre Olympic village. Also accomplished during this decade of depression was the construction of the **Hoover Dam**. And during the same decade a dream held since the days of the gold rush was fulfilled with the construction of the **San Francisco-Oakland Bay Bridge**. And art did not die during this decade. The very famous and familiar Coit Tower in San Francisco and the murals that present California history were completed in the 1930s, although amid some controversy. Finally, in 1939, San Francisco hosted the **Golden Gate International Exposition** on an island built specifically for the fair.

Skill 3.2e   Identify major environmental issues in California history and their economic, social, and political implications.

Environmental issues have been part of the history of California since the beginning of its civilization. Long before the arrival of Europeans and Mexicans the native tribes in parts of the state subsisted by moving around constantly in search of water and food.

One of the major controversies in California history centered upon the very destructive mining practice called "**hydraulicking**." High-pressure hoses were used to wash away the hills and banks in the search for gold. This "unnatural erosion" damaged more than the hills and banks that were being mined. The runoff deposited tons of mud, gravel, rock and sand into the rivers, burying farms, depositing silt in the rivers, and causing more frequent flooding. It became impossible to navigate several rivers.

Farmers banded together to create the "**Anti-Debris Association**," which wanted the government to outlaw the dumping of mining debris into rivers. The U.S. Circuit Court agreed with the farmers and passed the law. But many miners continued this practice. The final act that protected the rivers and farmlands was the creation of the "**California Debris Commission**," a federal regulatory agency, to enforce the law.

John Muir was responsible for the establishment of Yosemite National Park in 1890. A few years later he founded the Sierra Club. Muir was not, however, able to stop the construction of the Hetch Hetchy dam that provides water to San Francisco.

The water issue in California is that the majority of the precipitation in the state occurs in the northern third of the state while 80% of the need for water is in the southern two-thirds of the state. Moving water is a critical need. As Los Angeles grew, its water supply proved to be inadequate. The decision was made to divert the water of melting snows in the Sierra Nevada that flowed into the Owens River to provide water for Los Angeles with an **aqueduct**. This project was completed in 1913, but it deprived a farming community in the Owens Valley of much-needed water.

The construction of the **Hoover Dam** in the 1930s was an attempt to provide water for San Francisco, as well as hydroelectric power for the region. But the most aggressive approach to moving water in California was the **Central Valley Project.** Construction of the Central Valley Project began in 1937. The original phase of the plan called for the construction of three dams, five canals, and two power transmission lines. This program provides flood control and water for agriculture throughout the Central Valley.

DOMAIN 4:   PRINCIPLES OF AMERICAN DEMOCRACY

COMPETENCY 4.1   PRINCIPLES OF AMERICAN DEMOCRACY

Skill 4.1a   **Analyze the influence of ancient Classical and Enlightenment political thinkers and the pre-Revolutionary colonial and indigenous peoples' experience on the development of the American government, and consider the historical contexts in which democratic theories emerged.**

(See Skill 2.2a)

Skill 4.1b   **Explain and analyze the principles of the Declaration of Independence and how the U.S. Constitution reflects a balance between classical republican and classical liberal thinking.**

The terms "**civil liberties**" and "**civil rights**" are often used interchangeably, but there are some fine distinctions between the two terms. The term **civil liberties** is more often used to imply that the state has a positive role to play in assuring that all its' citizens will have equal protection and justice under the law with equal opportunities to exercise their privileges of citizenship and to participate fully in the life of the nation, regardless of race, religion, sex, color or creed. The term **civil rights** is used more often to refer to rights that may be described as guarantees that are specified as against the state authority implying limitations on the actions of the state to interfere with citizens' liberties. Although the term "civil rights" has thus been identified with the ideal of equality and the term "civil liberties" with the idea of freedom, the two concepts are really inseparable and interacting. Equality implies the proper ordering of liberty in a society so that one individual's freedom does not infringe on the rights of others.

The beginnings of civil liberties and the idea of civil rights in the United States go back to the ideas of the ancient Greeks. The experience of the early struggle for civil rights against the British and the very philosophies that led people to come to the New World in the first place. Religious freedom, political freedom, and the right to live one's life as one sees fit are basic to the American ideal. These were embodied in the ideas expressed in the Declaration of Independence and the Constitution.

All these ideas found their final expression in the United States Constitution's first ten amendments, known as the **Bill of Rights**. In 1789, the first Congress passed these first amendments and by December 1791, three-fourths of the states at that time had ratified them. The Bill of Rights protects certain liberties and basic rights. James Madison who wrote the amendments said that the Bill of Rights does not give Americans these rights. People, Madison said, already have these rights. They are natural rights that belong to all human beings. The Bill of Rights simply prevents the governments from taking away these rights.

Skill 4.1c   Evaluate the Founding Fathers' contribution to theestablishment of a constitutional system as articulated in the Federalist Papers, constitutional debates, and the U.S. Constitution.

Within a few months from the adoption of the Articles of Confederation, it became apparent that there were serious defects in the system of government established for the new republic. There was a need for changes that would create a national government with adequate powers to replace the Confederation, which was actually only a league of sovereign states. In 1786, an effort to regulate interstate commerce ended in what is known as the **Annapolis Convention**. Because only five states were represented, this Convention was not able to accomplish definitive results. The debates, however, made it clear that foreign and interstate commerce could not be regulated by a government with as little authority as the government established by the Confederation. Congress was, therefore, asked to call a convention to provide a constitution that would address the emerging needs of the new nation.

The convention met under the presidency of George Washington, with fifty-five of the sixty-five appointed members present. A constitution was written in four months. The **Constitution of the United States** is the fundamental law of the republic. It is a precise, formal, written document of the extraordinary, or **supreme**, type of constitution. The founders of the Union established it as the highest governmental authority. There is no national power superior to it. The foundations were so broadly laid as to provide for the expansion of national life and to make it an instrument which would last for all time. To maintain its stability, the framers created a difficult process for making any changes to it. No amendment can become valid until it is ratified by three fourths of all of the states. The British system of government was part of the basis of the final document. But significant changes were necessary to meet the needs of a partnership of states that were tied together as a single federation, yet sovereign in their own local affairs. This constitution established a system of government that was unique and advanced far beyond other systems of its day.

There were, to be sure, differences of opinion. The compromises that resolved these conflicts are reflected in the final document. The first point of disagreement and compromise was related to the Presidency. Some wanted a strong, centralized, individual authority. Others feared autocracy or the growth of monarchy. The compromise was to give the President broad powers but to limit the amount of time, through term of office, that any individual could exercise that power. The power to make appointments and to conclude treaties was controlled by the requirement of the consent of the Senate.

The second conflict was between large and small states. The large states wanted power proportionate to their voting strength; the small states opposed this plan. The compromise was that all states should have equal voting power in the Senate, but to make the membership of the House of Representatives determined in proportion to population.

The third conflict was about slavery. The compromise was that (a) fugitive slaves should be returned by states to which they might flee for refuge, and (b) that no law would be passed for 20 years prohibiting the importation of slaves.

The fourth major area of conflict was how the President would be chosen. One side of the disagreement argued for election by direct vote of the people. The other side thought the President should be chosen by Congress. One group feared the ignorance of the people; the other feared the power of a small group of people. The Compromise was the Electoral College.

The Constitution binds the states in a governmental unity in everything that affects the welfare of all. At the same time, it recognizes the right of the people of each state to independence of action in matters that relate only to them. Since the Federal Constitution is the law of the land, all other laws must conform to it.

The debates conducted during the Constitutional Congress represent the issues and the arguments that led to the compromises in the final document. The debates also reflect the concerns of the Founding Fathers that the rights of the people be protected from abrogation by the government itself and the determination that no branch of government should have enough power to override the others. There is, therefore, a system of **checks and balances.**

The **Federalist Papers** were written to win popular support for the new proposed Constitution. In these publications the debates of the Congress and the concerns of the founding fathers were made available to the people of the nation. In addition to providing an explanation of the underlying philosophies and concerns of the Constitution and the compromises that were made, the Federalist Papers conducted what has frequently been called the most effective marketing and public relations campaign in human history.

Skill 4.1d   **Describe the significance of the Bill of Rights and the 14th Amendment as limits on government in the American constitutional process as compared to English Common Law.**

Bill Of Rights - The first ten amendments to the United States Constitution dealing with civil liberties and civil rights. They were written mostly by James Madison. They are in brief:

1. **Freedom of Speech, the Press, Assembly, and Religion.**
2. **Right To Bear Arms.**
3. **Security from the quartering of troops in homes.**
4. **Right against unreasonable search and seizures.**
5. **Right against self-incrimination.**
6. **Right to trial by jury, right to legal council.**
7. **Right to jury trial for civil actions.**
8. **No cruel or unusual punishment allowed.**
9. **These rights shall not deny other rights the people enjoy.**
10. **Powers not mentioned in the Constitution shall be retained by the states or the people.**

The Magna Carta - This charter has been considered the basis of English constitution liberties. It was granted to a representative group of English barons and nobles on **June 15, 1215** by the British King John, after they had forced it on him. The English barons and nobles sought to limit what they had come to perceive as the overwhelming power of the Monarchy in public affairs. The Magna Carta is considered to be the first modern document that sought to try to limit the powers of the given state authority. It guaranteed feudal rights, regulated the justice system, and abolished many abuses of the King's power to tax and regulate trade. It said that the king could not raise new taxes without first consulting a Great Council, made up of nobles, barons, and Church people. Significantly the Magna Carta only dealt with the rights of the upper classes of the nobility and all of its provisions excluded the rights of the common people. However, gradually the rights won by the nobles were given to other English people.

The Great Council grew into a representative assembly called the Parliament. By the 1600s, Parliament was divided into the House of Lords, made up of nobles and the House of Commons. Members of the House of Commons were elected to office. In the beginning, only a few wealthy men could vote. Still English people firmly believed that the ruler must consult Parliament on money matters and obey the law. Thus, it did set a precedent that there was a limit to the allowed power of the state. A precedent, which would have no small effect on the history of political revolution, is notably the American Revolution.

The Petition of Right - In English history, it was the title of a petition that was addressed to the King of England **Charles I,** by the British parliament in **1628**.

The Parliament demanded that the King stop proclaiming new taxes without its' consent. Parliament demanded that he cease housing soldiers and sailors in the homes of private citizens, proclaiming martial law in times of peace, and that no subject should be imprisoned without a good cause being shown. After some attempts to circumvent these demands, Charles finally agreed to them. They later had an important effect on the demands of the revolutionary colonists, as these were some of the rights that as Englishmen, they felt were being denied to them. The Petition of Right was also the basis of specific protections that the designers of the Constitution made a point of inserting in the document.

British Bill of Rights - Also known as the **Declaration of Rights**, it spelled out the rights that were considered to belong to Englishmen. It was granted by **King William III** in 1869. It had previously been passed by a convention of the Parliament and it came out of the struggle for power that took place in Great Britain and at that time was known as **The Glorious Revolution**. It was known as a revolution that was accomplished with virtually no bloodshed and led to King William III and Queen Mary II becoming joint sovereigns.

The Declaration itself was very similar in style to the later American Bill of Rights. It protected the rights of individuals and gave anyone accused of a crime the right to trial by jury. It outlawed cruel punishments; also, it stated that a ruler could not raise taxes or an army without the consent of Parliament. The colonists as Englishmen were protected by these provisions. The colonists considered abridgments of these rights that helped to contribute to the revolutionary spirit of the times.

All of these events and the principles that arose from them are of the utmost importance in understanding the process that eventually led to the ideals that are inherent in the Constitution of the United States. In addition, the fact is that all of these ideals are universal in nature and have become the basis for the idea of human freedoms throughout the world.

Skill 4.1e   Describe the nature and importance of law in U.S. political theory, including the democratic procedures of law making, the rule of adherence to the law, and the role of civil disobedience.

Law is the set of established rules or accepted norms of human conduct in their relationship with other individuals, organizations and institutions. The **rule of law** recognizes that the authority of the government is to be exercised only within the context and boundaries established by laws that are enacted according to established procedure and publicly disclosed. As a Constitutional government and political system, the basis of all laws and all decisions and enforcement of laws is the U.S. Constitution. The Constitution establishes the process by which law can be written and enacted, the basis by which their legitimacy within the context of the principles documented in the Constitution, and the means of interpretation and enforcement of those laws by the police and the courts.

All federal law begins in the Constitution, which grants the Congress of the U.S. the power to enact laws for certain purposes. These statutes are gathered and published in the **United States Code**. Since ratification of the Constitution, laws have been enacted that give agencies of the executive branch of government the power to create regulations that carry the force of law. The meaning of these laws and regulations when challenged or questioned is determined by the courts, those decisions then assuming the force of law.

The process by which laws and regulations can be enacted is defined by the Constitution, within the protection of the balance of powers of the branches of government. Laws are introduced, debated, and passed by the Congress of the United States, with both houses of Congress passing the same version of the law. The law then must be signed by the President of the United States. Once signed, the law is considered enacted and is enforced. Challenges to the constitutionality of the law and questions of interpretation of the law are handled by the federal court system. Each state has the authority to make laws covering anything not reserved to the federal government. These laws cannot negate federal laws.

In order to structure and maintain the functionality of a society and the various safeties of the people, the rule of adherence to the law is considered universal for all who live within the jurisdiction to which laws apply. Failure to adhere to the laws of the state or the nation is punishable under the legal code. **Civil disobedience**, however, is the refusal to obey certain laws, regulations, or requirements of a government because those laws are believed to be detrimental to the freedom or right of the people to exercise government-guaranteed personal and civil liberties. Civil disobedience, in principle, is **nonviolen**t in the steps taken to resist or refuse to obey these laws.

Notable examples of the exercise of civil disobedience have included Henry David Thoreau's refusal to pay taxes in protest against slavery and against the Mexican-American War. Dr Martin Luther King, Jr. led the Civil Rights Movement of the 1960s on the principle and within the established techniques of peaceable civil disobedience.

Skill 4.1f   Analyze the significance and evolving meaning of the principles of American democracy.

The American nation was founded very much with the idea that the people would have a large degree of autonomy and liberty. The famous maxim "no taxation without representation" was a rallying cry for the Revolution, not only because the people didn't want to suffer the increasingly oppressive series of taxes imposed on them by the British Parliament, but also because the people could not in any way influence the lawmakers in Parliament in regard to those taxes. No American colonist had a seat in Parliament, and no American colonist could vote for members of Parliament.

The American people had become used to doing things their own way and solving their own problems, especially during the French and Indian War, during which a large number of soldiers who served and died for the British Army called America home. They had been given the opportunity to choose some of the people who governed them; but the big prizes, the governors of colonies and, of course, the members of Parliament were still out of reach. When the French and Indian War ended, the British Government attempted to levy heavy taxes on the American colonists, since the war had taken place in their own back yard. Not only were these taxes an infringement on the autonomy that the American colonists had become accustomed to, they were also a measure of just how little liberty those people had when it came to things like taxation and representation.

One of the most famous words in the Declaration of Independence is "**liberty**," the pursuit of which all people should be free to attempt. That idea, that a people should be free to pursue their own course, even to the extent of making their own mistakes, has dominated political thought in the 200-plus years of the American republic.

Representation, the idea that a people can vote - or even replace - their lawmakers was not a new idea, except in America. Residents of other British colonies did not have these rights, of course, and America was only a colony, according to the conventional wisdom of the British Government at the time. What the Sons of Liberty and other revolutionaries were asking for was to stand on an equal footing with the Mother Country.

Along with the idea of representation comes the idea that key ideas and concepts can be deliberated and discussed, with theoretically everyone having a chance to voice their views. This applied to both lawmakers and the people who elected them. Lawmakers wouldn't just pass bills that became laws; rather, they would debate the particulars and go back and forth on the strengths and weaknesses of proposed laws before voting on them. Members of both houses of Congress had the opportunity to speak out on the issues, as did the people at large, who could contact their lawmakers and express their views. This idea ran very much counter to the experience that the Founding Fathers had before the Revolution - that of taxation without representation.

Another key concept in the American ideal is **equality**, the idea that every person has the same rights and responsibilities under the law. The Great Britain that the American colonists knew was one of a stratified society, with social classes firmly in place. Not everyone was equal under the law or in the coffers; and it was clear for all to see that the more money and power a person had, the easier it was for that person to avoid things like serving in the army and being charged with a crime. The goal of the Declaration of Independence and the Constitution was to provide equality for all who read those documents. The reality, though, was vastly different for large sectors of society, including women and non-white Americans.

This feeds into the idea of basic opportunity. The so-called "**American Dream**" is that every individual has an equal change to make his or her fortune in a new land and that the country that is the United States will welcome and even encourage that initiative. The history of the country is filled with stories of people who ventured to America and made their fortunes in the Land of Opportunity. Unfortunately for anyone who wasn't a white male, that basic opportunity was sometimes a difficult thing to achieve.

Skill 4.1g   Describe the meaning and importance of each of the rights guaranteed in the Bill of Rights and analyze the reciprocal nature of citizenship.

The first amendment guarantees the basic rights of freedom of religion, freedom of speech, freedom of the press, and freedom of assembly. The next three amendments came out of the colonists' struggle with Great Britain. For example, the third amendment prevents Congress from forcing citizens to keep troops in their homes. Before the Revolution, Great Britain tried to coerce the colonists to house soldiers. Amendments five through eight protect citizens who are accused of crimes and are brought to trial. Every citizen has the right to due process of law, (due process as defined earlier, being that the government must follow the same fair rules for everyone brought to trial.) These rules include the right to a trial by an impartial jury, the right to be defended by a lawyer, and the right to a speedy trial. The last two amendments limit the powers of the federal government to those that are expressly granted in the Constitution, any rights not expressly mentioned in the Constitution, thus, belong to the states or to the people.

In regards to specific guarantees:

Freedom of Religion: Religious freedom has not been seriously threatened in the United States historically. The policy of the government has been guided by the premise that church and state should be separate. However, when religious practices have been at cross-purposes with attitudes prevailing in the nation at particular times, there has been restrictions placed on these practices. Some of these have been restrictions against the practice of polygamy that is supported by certain religious groups. The idea of animal sacrifice that is promoted by some religious beliefs is generally prohibited. The use of mind altering illegal substances that some use in religious rituals has been restricted. In the United States, all recognized religious institutions are tax-exempt in following the idea of separation of church and state, and therefore, there have been many quasi-religious groups that have in the past tried to take advantage of this fact. All of these issues continue, and most likely will continue to occupy both political and legal considerations for some time to come.

Freedom of Speech, Press, and Assembly: These rights historically have been given wide latitude in their practices, though there has been instances when one or the other have been limited for various reasons. The classic limitation, for instance, in regards to freedom of speech, has been the famous precept that an individual is prohibited from yelling fire! in a crowded theatre. This prohibition is an example of the state saying that freedom of speech does not extend to speech that might endanger other people. There is also a prohibition against **slander,** or the knowingly stating of a deliberate falsehood against one party by another. There are many regulations regarding freedom of the press, the most common example are the various laws against **libel,** (or the printing of a known falsehood). In times of national emergency, various restrictions have been placed on the rights of press, speech and sometimes assembly.

The legal system in recent years has also undergone a number of serious changes, some would say challenges, with the interpretation of some constitutional guarantees. America also has a number of organizations that present themselves as champions of the fight for civil liberties and civil rights in this country. Much criticism, however, has been raised at times against these groups as to whether or not they are really protecting rights, or following a specific ideology, perhaps attempting to create "new" rights, or in many cases, looking at the strict letter of the law, as opposed to what the law actually intends. "Rights" come with a measure of responsibility and respect for the public order, all of which must be taken into consideration.

Overall, the American experience has been one of exemplary conduct in regards to the protection of individual rights. Where there has been a lag in its practice, notably the refusal to grant full and equal rights to blacks, the fact of their enslavement, and the second class status of women for much of American history, negates the good that the country has done in other areas. Other than the American Civil War, the country has proved itself to be more or less resilient in being able, for the most part, peacefully, to change when it has not lived up to its' stated ideals in practice. What has been called "the virtual bloodless civil rights revolution" is a case in point.

Though much effort and suffering accompanied the struggle, in the end it did succeed in changing the foundation of society in such a profound way that would have been unheard of in many other countries without the strong tradition of freedom and liberty that was, and is, the underlying feature of American society.

Skill 4.1h   Explain the basis and practice of acquiring American citizenship.

A citizen of the United States may either be native-born or a **naturalized** citizen. **Naturalization** is the process by which one acquires citizenship. Upon a specialized occasion, one may also have dual-citizenship, that is citizenship in the United States as well as in another country.

In order to become a citizen several involved requirements must first be met. Those necessary requirements for citizenship comprise eight specific steps and are as follows:

1. An individual applying for citizenship must be at least 18 years old.
2. The individual must have been lawfully admitted into the United States for permanent residence.
3. The individual must have lived in the United States on a continual basis for at least five years, not counting short trips outside the United States. In addition, one must have resided for at least six months in the state where one is going to file a petition for citizenship. (There are some important exceptions to this residency requirement. One exception is marriage to a spouse who is a citizen, which can shorten the residency requirement to three years. Other exceptions are made for certain spouses of citizens employed overseas and for alien members of the United States armed forces. Still other exceptions to the five-year residency requirement apply to certain refugee groups under various specific federal laws on a case by case basis).
4. The individual must show a good moral character and believe in the principles of the Constitution of the United States of America.
5. The individual must not have been a member of the Communist Party for ten years prior to application for citizenship.
6. The individual must have not broken any immigration laws or to have been ordered to leave the United States.
7. The individual must be able to speak, understand, read and write simple English and must pass an examination about the history and government of the United States.
8. The individual must take an oath promising to give up foreign allegiance to obey the Constitution and laws of the United States and to fight for the United States of America, or do work of importance to the nation if asked lawfully to do so.

The entire naturalization process is accomplished in three separate steps. The first of which is the completion of the required application, this is done only after an individual has met the previous eight requirements.

The "**Application to File Petition for Naturalization**", Form N-400, is used if an individual is applying for their own naturalization. The Immigration and Naturalization Service revises this form periodically, while they will accept the "older" application forms, it is important to obtain the latest one. The form itself consists of three parts, the application, Form N-400 itself, a fingerprint chart, and Form G-325, entitled "**Biographic Information**". All applications must be properly filled out in order to be accepted. Once this is done and filed with the Immigration and Naturalization Service, it is reviewed, and if accepted, an individual will be so informed. They must then go to an appointed court to be officially sworn in by a judge or magistrate as a new citizen.

Once this is done, the individual is considered a citizen of the United States of America with all the privileges, rights and responsibilities that it entails. In addition to those rights that have previously been enumerated, the responsibilities include voting, jury duty, and the proper observance of the laws of the United States.

It is presumed that any citizen of the United States would recognize their responsibilities to the country and that the surest way of protecting their rights is by exercising those rights, which also entail a responsibility. Some examples include the right to vote and the responsibility to be well informed on various issues, the right to a trial by jury and the responsibility to ensure the proper working of the justice system by performing jury duty (rather than avoiding doing so). In the end, it is only by the mutual recognition of the fact that an individual has both rights and responsibilities in society that enables the society to function in order to protect those very rights.

COMPETENCY 4.2   **FUNDAMENTAL VALUES AND PRINCIPLES OF CIVIL SOCIETY**

Skill 4.2a   **Explain and analyze the historical role of religion, religious diversity, and religious discrimination and conflict in American life.**

The second set of English settlers to build a colony in North America are commonly known as the **Pilgrims**. These revolutionaries were fleeing religious persecution not only in their homeland but also their adopted homeland. They wanted to worship their god in the way they wanted, and the state-run religion back home wouldn't let them do that. The Pilgrims found complete freedom of religion in their new homeland and made the most of their opportunity. They also brought with them Christianity's idea of the "Golden Rule": Treat others as you would wish to be treated.

As more and more people settled on the eastern coast of what is now America, they brought with them more and more religions. Protestants and Catholics in many cases lived down the street from one another. The picture was by no means always this rosy. Puritans, the largest group of Protestants to emigrate to America, practiced a rather stern policy of seeking out and targeting people who didn't share their strict religious views and targeting those people for expulsion from the communities where the Puritans held sway. The most famous examples of such discrimination are probably **Anne Hutchison** and **Roger Williams**, both dynamic preachers who were forced to leave Massachusetts for having views different than the Puritan majority there (even though they were both Puritans themselves). Williams founded the neighboring colony of Rhode Island and Hutchinson followed him there before settling in New York.

Another religion to suffer at the hands of Puritans in America was the Society of Friends, or the **Quakers**. Another religion founded in England, the Quakers had sometimes vastly different views than the Puritans did, and this led to trouble in America. The most extreme case of Puritan persecution came in 1660, when the Massachusetts Puritans hanged Quaker leader Mary Dyer for refusing to convert to Puritanism. The Pennsylvania colony was later founded, among other things, as a refuge for Quakers.

Maryland was founded in large part as a colony for **Catholics**, supporters of Mary Stuart, the embattled queen for whom the colony was named. The language of the colony's charter contained absolutely no reference to religion, a significant departure from the charter language of, say, Massachusetts.

The Church of England, or **Anglicanism**, the church founded by Henry VIII and preferred by his daughter Elizabeth, found a haven in Virginia, which was more an economic powerhouse than anything else. The Virginia Anglicans, however, wanted all Virginians to be Anglicans and went out of their way to convince new settlers to embrace the old religion. In this, they inherited the dogmatism of Elizabeth.

With the dawn of the eighteenth century came the **Great Awakening**, a time of intense religious revival in America. The colonies had religion as a prime focus already, but the Great Awakening made religion a main part of their everyday lives. More so than ever before—thanks in part to dynamic sermons by George Whitefield, Cotton Mather, and Jonathan Edwards—settlers in America were thinking about their souls and how to better their chances of going to heaven. Religious discrimination in many parts of the country eased as this century came to a close. Religion was used as a basis for fighting in the French and Indian and the Revolutionary Wars. Americans thought themselves fighting a divinely inspired battle against tyranny.

At the other end of the spectrum from the zealots were the **Deists**, who believed in the general idea of a supreme being but didn't think he took such an active part in human lives. Famous Deists included some of the country's most well-known names, including George Washington and Thomas Jefferson. Another staggeringly famous American, James Madison, didn't have much time for organized religion, either. Jefferson, framer of the Declaration of Independence; Madison, framer of the Bill of Rights; and Washington, a leader that everyone in America followed—none of these men professed a great love of religion and so didn't emphasize it in their writings or in their actions.

The government documents of the newly formed United States sanction no religion whatever. Rather, the First Amendment to the Constitution goes out of its way to say that Congress will not sanction *any* religion. This was certainly a departure from the charters of states like Massachusetts in the seventeenth and eighteenth centuries, which demanded that their citizens believe and behave a certain way.

The federal abandonment of this kind of persecution didn't signal the end of it, however. Religions continued to bump heads with one another, with sometimes disastrous results. Baptists, especially, were on the wrong end of religious arguments in many states. Violence often flared up as the result of religious disagreements. The age-old debates between Catholics and Protestants continued. The difference as the years went by, however, continued to be that the country was large enough to accommodate everyone. If you believed a certain way and people tried to run you out of town, you could let them do it and just pick up and move, to an entirely new place, where you could set the ground rules. A perfect example of this is **Mormonism**, an offshoot of Protantism that had its origins in the visions of its founder, Joseph Smith, and involved a great pilgrimage to the middle of nowhere, not once but twice.

Skill 4.2b **Analyze citizen participation in governmental decision-making in a large modern society and the challenges Americans faced historically to their political participation.**

The sometimes sad reality for most Americans is that they don't play a large role in governmental decision-making, except perhaps at the local level. Only there, in the towns and cities in which they live, can they afford the time and money to personally lobby their lawmakers in the name of passage or defeat of laws. At the state and the national level, the country is just too big for one poor person to have much of a difference individually. Where people make a difference at the higher levels is in joining political parties and, more importantly, **citizen action groups** or **political action committees**. Only in the larger numbers that make up these groups can individual people make a difference in government. In such cases, however, people tend to lose their individual voices and are more easily swayed by the will of their peers.

This is not to say that the avenues of lobbying lawmakers are closed to the average American. Letters are still read, phone calls are still taken, and donations are still appreciated. More cutting-edge methods of communication include e-mail, FAX, and SMS. Personal office visits are definitely appreciated as well. If enough people write or call or visit their lawmakers and say the same thing, those lawmakers will listen. That's why it's still important for people to speak out, not only to their neighbors but also their elected officials. And of course, the ultimate way of expressing one's political views is to elect or oust a lawmaker through the power of the ballot.

This kind of open access and potentially direct role in the political decision-making of the country has not always been with us, though. In the early days of the American colonies, the British settlers could disagree all they wanted with the kind of policies, laws, and taxes that were being impressed on them by the Parliament across the Atlantic. The settlers also couldn't very well decide who their colonial governors were. Those officials were appointed by the British Government.

The colonies weren't totally void of representative government, though. Beginning in 1619, the Virginia colony had such an entity, the **House of Burgesses**. This was one of the most famous governing bodies in colonial American history. Among its members over time were some of the shining lights of the American Revolution, including George Washington, Thomas Jefferson, James Madison, and Patrick Henry. It was Henry who introduced the resolutions that ultimately resulted in the repeal of the dreaded Stamp Act, the devastating tax on paper goods.

A total of 15 of the 22 members of the House of Burgesses were elected by the people of Virginia. (The governor, of course, was appointed.) The Burgesses could make laws, and the governor could veto them. The Burgesses also met just once a year. But the elements of representative government were there.

Other lawmaking bodies followed. Generally, each colony had one. They had various names; most were called the **Assembly**. As with the Virginia House of Burgesses, these Assemblies met just once a year and dealt with financial matters, like taxes and budgets. The governor, however, had the power to dissolve the Assembly, keeping it from meeting even once, which was done relatively frequently during the months leading up to the Revolutionary War.

Representative is a relative term, however. Although it is true that the Assembly had members who were voted in by their peers, those peers were true peers in the sense that they all looked exactly like. Serving in government and voting for those who did was limited to white, property-owning males. Women couldn't vote or even own property. African-American men and women certainly could do either of those things, even if they weren't enslaved. It's one thing to say that the members of the Burgesses or Assembly were elected by the people; it's another thing entirely to say that the people included everyone in the colonies.

Still, the cry for representation was a key rallying point of the Revolution and the War to preserve it, and eventually the Colonial Army had its day in the sun. The Constitution was a blueprint of a representative government such that the world had never seen. The reality, though, was still that white, property-owning males were the ones doing the voting and the legislating.

One holdover from the colonial-appointing days was that Senators, who made up the upper house of Government, were appointed by the Legislature of each state. This practice lasted until the passage of the Seventeenth Amendment, in the early nineteenth century. African-American men, however, had to wait to vote and run for office until the Fourteenth Amendment, ratified in 1868, and women of any color had to wait until the twentieth century to vote for nationwide office.

Skill 4.2c **Analyze the evolving practices of citizen collaboration and deliberation, and special interest influence in American democratic decision-making.**

From the earliest days of political expression in America, efforts were a collaborative affair. One of the first of the democratic movements was the **Sons of Liberty**, an organization that made its actions known but kept the identity of its members a secret. Famous members of this group included John and Samuel Adams. Other patriotic movements sprang up after the success of the Sons of Liberty was assured, and the overall struggle against British oppression was a collaborative effort involving thousands of people throughout the American colonies.

American political discussion built on the example of the British Parliament, which had two houses of its legislative branch of government containing representatives who had great debates on public policy before making laws. Although this process isn't anywhere near as wide open and public and spirited as it is today, the lawmakers nonetheless had their chance to make their views known on the issues of the day. Some laws, like those implementing the infamous taxes following the British and American victory in the French and Indian War, required relatively little debate, since they were so popular and were obviously wanted by the Prime Minister and other heads of the government. Other laws enjoyed spirited debate and took months to pass.

The Assemblies of the American colonies inherited this tradition and enjoyed spirited debate as well, even though they met just one or a few times a year. One of the most famous examples of both collaboration and deliberation was the **Stamp Act Congress**, a gathering of fed-up Americans who drafted resolutions demanding that Great Britain repeal the unpopular tax on paper and documents. The Americans who met at both of the Continental Congresses and the Constitutional Convention built on this tradition as well.

Thanks to the voluminous notes taken diligently by James Madison, we have a clear record of just how contentious at times the debate over the shape and scope of the American federal government was. Still, every interest was advanced, every argument put forward, and every chance given to repeal the main points of the government document. The result was a blueprint for government approved by the vast majority of the delegates and eventually approved by people in all of the American colonies. This ratification process has continued throughout the history of the country, through passage by both houses of Congress to ratification by state legislatures and finally to approval by a majority of the people of a majority of states.

With this sometimes spirited and sometimes virulent debate have come countless opportunities to influence that debate. Even in the earliest times, people having special interests were trying to influence political debates in their favor. Plenty of people who favored a strong central government or its opposite, a weak central government, could be found who were not delegates to the Constitutional Convention. No doubt these people were in communication with the delegates.

Also developing at this time were the nation's first **political parties**, the Federalists and the Democratic-Republicans. It wasn't elected officials who were members of these political parties, although those elected officials were the most famous members. The people who joined these political parties wanted to see their political interests protected and were sometimes very effective in making sure that the people that they voted for did the things that they were elected to do.

As the nation grew, so did the number of political parties and so did the number of people who were pursuing the so-called "**special interests**." Actually, a special interest is nothing more than a subject that a person or people who pursue one issue above all others. As more and more people gained more and more money, they began to pressure their lawmakers more and more to pass laws that favored their interests. Exporters of goods from ports to destinations overseas would not want to see heavy taxes on such exports. People who owned large amounts of land wouldn't want to see a sharp increase in property taxes. The list goes on and on. These special interests can be found today. These days, it's just more money and more ways to influence lawmakers that distinguish special interest pursuits from those made in years past. So, too, can we draw a straight line from the deliberative-collaborative traditions of today to the secret meetings and political conventions of colonial days.

Skill 4.2d Compare and contrast the role of the individual in democratic and authoritarian societies.

A person who lives in a democratic society theoretically has an entire laundry list guaranteed to him or her by the government. In the United States, this is the Constitution and its Amendments. Among these very important rights are:

- the right to speak out in public;
- the right to pursue any religion;
- the right for a group of people to gather in public for *any* reason that doesn't fall under a national security cloud;
- the right *not* to have soldiers stationed in your home;
- the right *not* to be forced to testify against yourself in a court of law;
- the right to a speedy and public trial by a jury of your peers;
- the right *not* to the victim of cruel and unusual punishment;

- and the right to avoid unreasonable search and seizure of your person, your house, and your vehicle.

The average citizen of an authoritarian country has little if any of these rights and must watch his or her words, actions, and even magazine subscriptions and Internet visits in order to avoid the appearance of disobeying one of the many oppressive laws that help the government govern its people.

Both the democratic-society and the authoritarian-society citizens can serve in government. They can even run for election and can be voted in by their peers. One large difference exists, however: In an authoritarian society, the members of government will most likely be of the same political party. A country with this setup, like China, will have a government that includes representatives elected by the Chinese people, but all of those elected representatives will belong to the Communist Party, which runs the government and the country. When the voters vote, they see only Communist Party members on the ballot. in fact, in many cases, only one candidate is on the ballot for each office. China, in fact, chooses its head of government through a meeting of the Party leaders. In effect, the Party is higher in the governmental hierarchy than the leader of the country. Efforts to change this governmental structure and practice are clamped down and discouraged.

On the other side of this spectrum is the citizen of the democratic society, who can vote for whomever he or she wants to and can run for any office he or she wants to. On those ballots will appear names and political parties that run the spectrum, including the Communist Party. Theoretically, any political party can get its candidates on ballots locally, statewide, or nationwide; varying degrees of effort have to be put in to do this, of course. Building on the First Amendment freedom to peacefully assembly, American citizens can have political party meetings, fund-raisers, and even conventions without fearing reprisals from the Government.

Skill 4.2e   Explain how civil society provides opportunities for individuals to promote private or public interests.

In a **civil society**, people are certainly free to pursue business interests both private and public. Private activities are less regulated than public ones, but public activities are not discouraged or dissuaded, as long as they don't violate laws or invade other people's rights.

In America and in other countries as well, a person has the right to pursue any kind of business strategy he or she wants. The age of Internet advertising and marketing has created opportunities abound for new and different businesses. By and large, as long as these businesses don't sell or advertise illegal products or practices, the business owner is left alone by society and its government. If the business succeeds, the business owner is free to reap the rewards of his success; if the business fails, then the business owner will certainly suffer the consequences of that failure. How public that person wants to make his or her business is a personal decision.

The state and federal governments make it a practice of encouraging businesses to succeed, granting them money and time to make that money back, through loans and grants, Most businesses of a significant size are required to file business announcement papers with various local, state, and federal agencies; all businesses are required, of course, to pay taxes on any income that they might earn.

Rather than discourage people from starting businesses, the American government and its various associated entities actually encourage such endeavors. Prospective business owners can find whole libraries of information encouraging them and guiding them through the sometimes rigorous practice of starting a business. Entire organizations exist just to answer questions about this process.

It's not just business that American society encourages. Americans are also free and encouraged to join non-business organizations both public and private. America is a land full of groups—religious groups, political groups, social groups, and economic groups. All these groups meet in public and in private, and the people who belong to these groups are free to associate with any groups that they choose, again as long as the practices of those groups are not illegal or harmful to other people.

Religious participation is a practice that finds extraordinary protection under the law. The First Amendment guarantees every American the right to worship as he or she sees fit, without fear of reprisal by the government. Religious organizations, however, do not, for the most part, receive funding from governments to support their efforts. The First Amendment also denies the Government the right to establish a religion, meaning that it can favor no one religion over others. Entities like parochial schools, which provide both education and religious training, routinely have to seek funding in places other than the federal or state governments.

Social groups are encouraged as well. The First Amendment gives the American people the right to peaceable assembly. This certainly describes the meetings of most social organizations in America, from clubs to interest groups to veterans organizations. Groups, made up of people with similar interests or experiences, may come together on a regular basis to discuss those interests and experiences and to pursue a joint appreciation. So long as those people in those groups assemble peacefully and don't become violent or speak out in the name of fomenting rebellion, they can go on meeting as often as they like.

One very public interest that many people pursue is politics. Theoretically, anyone who is a U.S. citizen can get on a ballot somewhere running for something. Participation in politics is encouraged in America, and more and more people are getting involved—at the local, state, and federal levels—all the time. The federal and state governments, in particular, will provide money and opportunities for candidates who reach certain thresholds of monetary support of their own.

COMPETENCY 4.3   THE THREE BRANCHES OF GOVERNMENT

Skill 4.3a   Analyze Articles I, II, and III as they relate to the legislative, executive, and judicial branches of government.

In the United States, the three branches of the federal government mentioned earlier, the **Executive**, the **Legislative**, and the **Judicial**, divide up their powers thus:

Legislative – Article I of the Constitution established the Lgislative, or law-making branch of the government called the Congress. It is made up of two houses, the House of Representatives and the Senate. Voters in all states elect the members who serve in each respective House of Congress. The Legislative branch is responsible for making laws, raising and printing money, regulating trade, establishing the postal service and federal courts, approving the President's appointments, declaring war and supporting the armed forces. The Congress also has the power to change the Constitution itself, and to *impeach* (bring charges against) the President. Charges for impeachment are brought by the House of Representatives, and are then tried in the Senate.

Executive – Article II of the Constitution created the Executive branch of the government, headed by the President, who leads the country, recommends new laws, and can veto bills passed by the legislative branch. As the chief of state, the President is responsible for carrying out the laws of the country and the treaties and declarations of war passed by the Legislative branch. The President also appoints federal judges and is commander-in-chief of the military when it is called into service. Other members of the Executive branch include the Vice-President, also elected, and various cabinet members as he might appoint: ambassadors, presidential advisors, members of the armed forces, and other appointed and civil servants of government agencies, departments and bureaus. Though the President appoints them, they must be approved by the Legislative branch.

Judicial – Article III of the Constitution established the Judicial branch of government headed by the Supreme Court. The Supreme Court has the power to rule that a law passed by the legislature, or an act of the Executive branch is illegal and unconstitutional. Citizens, businesses, and government officials can also, in an appeal capacity, ask the Supreme Court to review a decision made in a lower court if someone believes that the ruling by a judge is unconstitutional. The Judicial branch also includes lower federal courts known as federal district courts that have been established by the Congress. These courts try law breakers and review cases referred from other courts.

Powers delegated to the federal government: | Powers reserved to the states:

1. To tax.
2. To borrow and coin money
3. To establish postal service.
4. To grant patents and copyrights.
5. To regulate interstate and foreign commerce.
6. To establish courts.
7. To declare war.
8. To raise and support the armed forces.
9. To govern territories.
10. To define and punish felonies and piracy on the high seas.
11. To fix standards of weights and measures.
12. To conduct foreign affairs.

1. To regulate intrastate trade.
2. To establish local governments.
3. To protect general welfare.
4. To protect life and property.
5. To ratify amendments.
6. To conduct elections.
7. To make state and local laws.

Concurrent powers of the federal government and states.

1. Both Congress and the states may tax.
2. Both may borrow money.
3. Both may charter banks and corporations.
4. Both may establish courts.
5. Both may make and enforce laws.
6. Both may take property for public purposes.
7. Both may spend money to provide for the public welfare.

Implied powers of the federal government.

1. To establish banks or other corporations, implied from delegated powers to tax, borrow, and to regulate commerce.
2. To spend money for roads, schools, health, insurance, etc. implied from powers to establish post roads, to tax to provide for general welfare and defense, and to regulate commerce.
3. To create military academies, implied from powers to raise and support an armed force.
4. To locate and generate sources of power and sell surplus, implied from powers to dispose of government property, commerce, and war powers.
5. To assist and regulate agriculture, implied from power to tax and spend for general welfare and regulate commerce.

Skill 4.3b   Analyze how and why the existing roles and practices of the three branches of government have evolved.

See Skill 4.3a.

Skill 4.3c   Describe and analyze the issues that arise as a result of the checks and balances system.

In the United States, **checks and balances** refers to the ability of each branch of government (Executive, Legislative, and Judicial) to "check" or limit the actions of the others. Examples of checks and balances are: The Executive branch limits the Legislature by power of veto over bills and appointments in the court system. The Judicial branch limits the power of the Legislature by judicial review and the ability to rule laws unconstitutional and may also determine executive orders unconstitutional. The Legislature checks the Executive by power of impeachment

Eleven states finally ratified the document and the new national government went into effect. It was no small feat that the delegates were able to produce a workable document that satisfied all opinions, feelings, and viewpoints. The separation of powers of the three branches of government and the built-in system of checks and balances to keep power balanced were a stroke of genius. It provided for the individuals and the states as well as an organized central authority to keep a new inexperienced young nation on track. They created a system of government so flexible that it has continued in its basic form to this day. In 1789, the Electoral College unanimously elected George Washington as the first President and the new nation was on its way.

Skill 4.3d   Explain the process by which the Constitution is amended.

An **amendment** is a change or addition to the United States Constitution. Two-thirds of both houses of Congress must propose and then pass one. Or two-thirds of the state legislatures must call a convention to propose one and then it must be ratified by three-fourths of the state legislatures. To date there are only twenty-seven amendments to the Constitution that have passed. An amendment may be used to cancel out a previous one such as the 18th Amendment (1919) known as Prohibition, canceled by the 21st Amendment (1933). Amending the United States Constitution is an extremely difficult thing to do.

An Amendment must start in Congress. One or more lawmakers propose it, and then each house votes on it in turn. The Amendment must have the support of two-thirds of each house separately in order to progress on its path into law. (It should be noted here that this two-thirds need be only two-thirds of a **quorum**, which is just a simple majority. Thus, it is theoretically possible for an Amendment to be passed and be legal even though it has been approved by less than half of one or both houses.)

The final and most difficult step for an Amendment is the **ratification** of state legislature. A total of three-fourths of those must approve the Amendment. Approvals there need be only a simple majority, but the number of states that must approve the Amendment is 38. Hundreds of Amendments have been proposed through the years, but only 27 have become part of the Constitution.

A key element in some of those failures has been the **time limit** that Congress has the option to put on Amendment proposals. A famous example of an Amendment that got close but didn't reach the threshold before the deadline expired was the Equal Rights Amendment, which was proposed in 1972 but which couldn't muster enough support for passage, even though its deadline was extended from seven to ten years.

The first ten Amendments are called the **Bill of Rights** and were approved at the same time, shortly after the Constitution was ratified. The 11th and 12th Amendments were ratified around the turn of the nineteenth century and, respectively, voided foreign suits against states and revised the method of presidential election. The 13th, 14th, and 15th Amendments were passed in succession after the end of the Civil War. Slavery was outlawed by the 13th Amendment. The 14th & 15th Amendments provided for equal protection and for voting rights, respectively, without consideration of skin color.

The first Amendment of the twentieth century was Number 16, which provided for a federal income tax. Providing for direct election to the Senate was the 17th Amendment. (Before this, Senators were appointed by state leaders, not elected by the public at large.)

The 18th Amendment prohibited the use or sale of alcohol across the country. The long battle for voting rights for women ended in success with the passage of the 19th Amendment. The date for the beginning of terms for the President and the Congress was changed from March to January by the 20th Amendment. With the 21st Amendment came the only instance in which an Amendment was repealed. In this case, it was the 18th Amendment and its prohibition of alcohol consumption or sale.

The 22nd Amendment limited the number of terms that a President could serve to two. Presidents since George Washington had followed Washington's practice of not running for a third term; this changed when Franklin D. Roosevelt ran for re-election a second time, in 1940. He was re-elected that time and a third time, too, four years later. He didn't live out his fourth term, but he did convince Congress and most of the state legislature that some sort of term limit should be in place.

The little-known 23rd Amendment provided for representation of Washington, D.C., in the Electoral College. The 24th Amendment prohibited poll taxes, which people had had to pay in order to vote.

Presidential succession is the focus of the 25th Amendment, which provides a blueprint of what to do if the president is incapacitated or killed. The 26th Amendment lowered the legal voting age for Americans from 21 to 18. The final Amendment, the 27th, prohibits members of Congress from substantially raising their own salaries. This Amendment was one of twelve originally proposed in the late eighteenth century. Ten of those twelve became the Bill of Rights, and one has yet to become law.

A host of potential Amendments have made news headlines in recent years. A total of six Amendments have been proposed by Congress and passed muster in both houses but have not been ratified by enough state legislatures. The aforementioned Equal Rights Amendment is one. Another one, which would grant the District of Columbia full voting rights equivalent to states, has not passed; like the **Equal Rights Amendment**, its deadline has expired. A handful of others remain on the books without expiration dates, including an amendment to regulate child labor.

COMPETENCY 4.4   LANDMARK U.S. SUPREME COURT CASES

Skill 4.4a   Analyze the changing interpretations of the Bill of Rights and later constitutional amendments.

The Bill of Rights consists of the first ten Amendments to the U.S. Constitution. These amendments were passed almost immediately upon ratification of the Constitution by the states. They reflect the concerns that were raised throughout the country and by the Founding Fathers during the ratification process. These Amendments reflect the fears and concerns of the people that the power and authority of the government be restricted from denying or limiting the rights of the people of the nation. The experiences of the founders of the nation as colonists formed the foundation of the concern to limit the power of government.

The Bill of Rights has been interpreted in different ways at different times by different interpreters. These, and other, Constitutional Amendments may be interpreted very strictly or very loosely. The terms of the amendments may be defined in different way to enfranchise or to disenfranchise individuals or groups of persons.

Example: During and after Reconstruction, the interpretation of the Bill of Rights that did not include blacks in the definition of a citizen necessitated the passage of the 14th and 15th amendments. The interpretation of these amendments was broadly interpreted by the Supreme Court in the Plessey case, resulting in the establishment of the doctrine of "separate but equal." It was not until fifty years later, in the case of Brown v. Board of Education, that a narrower interpretation of the amendment resulted in a Supreme Court decision that reversed the previous interpretation.

Skill 4.4b   Evaluate the effects of the Court's interpretations of the Constitution. Give examples.

Marbury v. Madison is perhaps the most famous Supreme Court case of them all. It was the first case to establish what has become the Court's main duty, judicial review.

After George Washington retired, his vice-president, John Adams, succeeded him. Adams ran for election in 1800, and was opposed by his vice-president, Thomas Jefferson. Adams was a Federalist. Jefferson was elected in November 1800. At that time, the new president didn't take office until March 4 of the following year. So Adams had a few months to try to get things done before Jefferson took over. One of the things Adams tried to do was get as many Federalist judges appointed as he could. As March 4 drew near, Adams got more and more concerned with doing this. He kept appointing judges long into the night on March 3. These were known as the "**Midnight Judges**." One of these "Midnight Judges" was **William Marbury**, who was named to be justice of the peace for the District of Columbia.

The normal practice of making such appointments was to deliver a "**commission**," or notice, of appointment. This was normally done by the Secretary of State. Jefferson's Secretary of State at the time was **James Madison**. Jefferson didn't want all those Federalist judges, so he told Madison not to deliver the commission. Marshall and the rest of the Supreme Court decided that the power to deliver commissions to judges, since it was part of the Judiciary Act of 1789 and not part of the Constitution itself, was in conflict with the Constitution and, therefore, illegal. Further, the entire Judiciary Act of 1789 was illegal because it gave to the Judicial Branch powers not granted to it by the Constitution.

It appeared that Marshall sided with his political enemies, but this was not the case. Marbury, a Federalist, didn't get to be Justice of the Peace in the District of Columbia. Adams was probably quite angry because his commission was denied. Jefferson and Madison were probably quite happy because they got to name their own friendly justice of the peace. But Marshall gave to the Supreme Court a whole new power: the power to throw out laws of Congress. So, no matter how many laws Thomas Jefferson and his Democratic-Republicans passed and made into law, the Supreme Court always had the ultimate check on that legislative and executive power. John Marshall, in appearing to lose the political battle, won the political war.

One of the chief political battles of the ninettenth century was between the federal government and state governments. The Supreme Court took this battle to heart and issued a series of decisions that, for the most part, made it clear that any dispute between governments at the state and federal levels would be settled in favor of the federal government. One of the main examples of this was *McCulloch v. Maryland,* which settled a dispute involving the Bank of the United States.

The United States, at this time (1819) still had a federal bank, the Bank of the United States. The State of Maryland voted to tax all bank business not done with state banks. This was meant to be a tax on people who lived in Maryland but who did business with banks in other states. However, the State of Maryland also sought to tax the federal bank. Andrew McCulloch, who worked in the Baltimore branch of the Bank of the United States, refused to pay the tax. The State of Maryland sued, and the Supreme Court accepted the case.

Writing for the Court, Chief Justice John Marshall wrote that the federal government did indeed have the right and power to set up a federal bank. Further, he wrote, a state did not have the power to tax the federal government. "The right to tax is the right to destroy," he wrote, and states should not have that power over the federal government. The Bank of the United States did not survive, but the judicial review of the Supreme Court did.

The Supreme Court reasserted the power of judicial review in **United States v. Nixon**, one of the most dynamic and divisive of the twentieth century. The issue was whether the President had the ability to keep certain items secret. In this case, the items were secret recordings that Richard Nixon, the President at the time, had made of conversations he had had with his advisers. The recordings were thought to implicate Nixon in the cover-up of the Watergate break-in, an attempt by a team of thieves to gain information on the activities of George McGovern, Nixon's opponent in the 1972 election. Nixon claimed that the tapes were the property of the Executive Branch and, more to the point, of Nixon himself. Nixon claimed an "executive privilege" that would keep him from having to relinquish the recordings.

The real issue, though, was that the recordings had been subpoenaed by the Judicial Branch. Thus, the dispute was really whether the Judicial Branch could supersede the authority of the Executive Branch. Like John Marshall before him, Chief Justice Warren Burger declared that the Judicial Branch could trump both other branches in its pursuit of justice and that *no one*, not even the President, was above the law.

Skill 4.4c   Describe and analyze the controversies that have resulted over the changing interpretations of civil rights.

Civil rights came to the fore in a big way with the infamous **Dred Scott v. Sanford** case, in which the Supreme Court famously declared that Scott, a former slave, had no rights even though he was free of his former master. The Civil War changed public opinion, at least in the North, but the struggle for African-Americans especially to achieve basic rights like voting and owning property continued to varying degrees throughout the nineteenth and twentieth centuries.

The court built on the Dred Scott model in 1883, with *The Civil Rights Cases*, a series of five decisions that said, in essence, that the newly minted Fourteenth Amendment and its equal protection clause didn't apply to private individuals or their companies. Little more than a decade later, the Court expanded its denial of the equal protection clause in the infamous **Plessy v. Ferguson** (1896), in which "separate but equal" railway cars were deemed appropriate and legal. The Plessy decision was even more wide-reaching in its ramifications because it applied to state-run organizations. That right to discriminate was extended to schools in 1908 (*Berea College* v. *Kentucky*), and the segregation movement was off and running at high speed.

African-Americans responded with activism and positivism. Led by such public and successful groups as the Universal Negro Improvement Association and the NAACP, African-Americans began to speak out in favor of rights that they were denied in the court of law and in everyday public life. Decades of activism followed and the "separate but equal" doctrine was thrown under more scrutiny.

These activist efforts very often met with virulent opposition, extending to violence in many cases. The Court, ever mindful of public opinion, looked for an opportunity to try to reverse legalized segregation and found it in *Brown* v. *Board of Education*. It was a unanimous decision, and it overturned *Plessy* in ruling that "separate but equal facilities were inherently unequal." It was only the beginning, and at first it applied only to public schools; but the end of legalized segregation had begun. Efforts to hold on to it continued (most famously at Little Rock Central High in 1957), and subsequent Court decisions weren't exactly stern in their rebukes of the various states' (especially Southern) slow speed for complying with those decisions. Still, the efforts continued, and so did the legal support for them. Wide-ranging protests followed, including freedom marches, sit-ins at lunch counters, Freedom Rides, and riots. The Court continued to support desegregation, to varying degrees, and the foot-dragging in the South eventually stopped.

In recent years, however, the phrase "**race-neutral**" has begun to be used. This term seems to be being applied more and more as a response to affirmative action programs, which attempted to grant preferences to African-Americans in order to make up for past injustices. One of the most famous of these series of events culminated in **Regents of the University of California v. Bakke** (1978), in which the Court invalidated the denial of a white student from law school because the school had to meet its mandated quota of minority applicants. In 1995, in **Adarand Constructors, Inc. v. Pena**, the Court mandated that race neutrality be examined in federal agencies under "**strict scrutiny**"; in effect, the Court had validated the idea of race neutrality and ended the raft of affirmative action programs that had dotted the federal government's departments and agencies.

Along with the idea of the government lending a helping hand to those struggling for basic civil rights came the idea of aiding those who were facing a daunting path through the legal system. Prisoners, especially non-white ones, didn't have a whole lot of rights under the law or certainly in practice. The one Court case that resonates throughout the latter half of the twentieth century is ***Miranda* v. *Arizona***, in which the Court set out a series of information that arresting officers had to impart to those they were arresting, including such Bill of Rights-friendly language as the right to an attorney, the right to avoid self-incrimination, and the right to a trial by jury. Other law enforcement cases preceded it and followed it, with the idea that a person who is arrested has the presumption of innocence until guilt has been proven.

Perhaps the most wide-ranging yet personal civil rights case to come about in the last decade is ***Bush* v. *Palm Beach County Canvassing Board***. Presidential candidate George W. Bush sued to invalidate the recount that had begun in the wake of Bush's narrow victory over Al Gore in Florida. Bush claimed, among other things, that his Fifth Amendment due process rights were violated by the various decisions made in the wake of the close vote counts. The result was a decision by the Court to stop all recounting and declare Bush the winner. This was not a classical civil rights case, per se, but it was one that argued as such and involved the sort of protection that had been argued under previous Fifth and Fourteenth Amendment cases.

COMPETENCY 4.5   ISSUES REGARDING CAMPAIGNS FOR NATIONAL, STATE, AND LOCAL ELECTIVE OFFICES

Skill 4.5a   Analyze the origin, development, and role of political parties.

(See Skill 2.3a)

Skill 4.5b   Describe the means that citizens use to participate in the political process.

The most basic way for citizens to participate in the political process is to **vote**. Since the passing of the 23rd Amendment in 1965, US citizens who are at least 18 years old are eligible to vote. Elections are held at regular intervals at all levels of government, allowing citizens to weigh in on local matters as well as those of national scope.

Citizens wishing to engage in the political process to a greater degree have several paths open, such as **participating in local government**. Counties, states, and sometimes even neighborhoods are governed by locally-elected boards or councils which meet publicly. Citizens are usually able to address these boards, bringing their concerns and expressing their opinions on matters being considered. Citizens may even wish to stand for local election and join a governing board, or seek support for higher office.

Supporting a political party is another means by which citizens can participate in the political process. Political parties endorse certain platforms that express general social and political goals, and support member candidates in election campaigns. Political parties make use of much volunteer labor, with supporters making telephone calls, distributing printed material and campaigning for the party's causes and candidates. Political parties solicit donations to support their efforts as well. Contributing money to a political party is another form of participation citizens can undertake.

Another form of political activity is to **support an issue-related political group**. Several political groups work actively to sway public opinion on various issues or on behalf of a segment of American society. These groups may have representatives who meet with state and federal legislators to "lobby" them - to provide them with information on an issue and persuade them to take favorable action.

Skill 4.5c   Explain the function and evolution of the College of Electors and analyze its role in contemporary American politics.

The College of Electors—or the **Electoral College**, as it is more commonly known—has a long and distinguished history of mirroring the political will of the American voters. On some occasions, the results have not been entirely in sync with that political will.

Article II of the Constitution lists the specifics of the Electoral College. The Founding Fathers included the Electoral College as one of the famous "checks and balances" for two reasons: first, to give states with small populations more of an equal weight in the presidential election and second, they didn't trust the common man (women couldn't vote then.) to be able to make an informed decision on which candidate would make the best president.

First of all, the same theory that created the U.S. Senate practice of giving two Senators to each state created the Electoral College. The large-population states had their populations reflected in the House of Representatives. New York and Pennsylvania, two of the states with the largest populations, had the highest number of members of the House of Representatives. But these two states still had only two senators, the exact same number that small-population states like Rhode Island and Delaware had. This was true as well in the Electoral College: Each state had just one vote, regardless of how many members of the House represented that state. So, the one vote that the state of New York cast would be decided by an initial vote of New York's Representatives. (If that initial vote was a tie, then that deadlock would have to be broken.)

Secondly, when the Constitution was being written, not many people knew a whole lot about government, politics, or presidential elections. A large number of people were farmers or lived in rural areas, where they were far more concerned with making a living and providing for their families than they were with who was running for which office. Many of these "common people" could not read or write, either, and wouldn't be able to read a ballot in any case. Like it or not, the Founding Fathers thought that even if these "common people" could vote, they wouldn't necessarily make the best decision for who would make the best president. So, the Electoral College was born.

Technically, the electors do not have to vote for anyone. The Constitution does not require them to do so. And throughout the history of presidential elections, some have indeed voted for someone else. But tradition holds that the electors vote for the candidate chosen by their state, and so the vast majority of electors do just that. The Electoral College meets a few weeks after the presidential election. Mostly, their meeting is a formality. When all the electoral votes are counted, the candidate with the most votes wins. In most cases, the candidate who wins the popular vote also wins in the Electoral College. However, this has not always been the case.

In 1800, **Thomas Jefferson** and **Aaron Burr**, both candidates of the Democratic-Republican Party, got the same number of votes. The election went to the House to decide, and Federalist leader Alexander Hamilton, who hated both Jefferson and Burr, got involved. Choosing to argue for the election of one political rival over another, Hamilton worked behind the scenes to ensure that Burr was not the new president. The House of Representatives eventually, on the 36th ballot, chose Jefferson. Burr became vice-president.

The next challenge to the electoral process came in 1824. James Monroe, a wildly popular president, had retired after two terms, following the example of George Washington. Monroe was so popular that in his re-election bid of 1820, he won every single state and would have received a unanimous electoral vote if not for an elector who cast his vote in an effort to keep Washington as the only president to have been elected unanimously.

In 1824, all of the candidates were members of the Democratic-Republican Party. **John Quincy Adams**, son of President John Adams, was the most experienced. **Andrew Jackson** was a war hero. **Henry Clay** was the Speaker of the House. When the votes were counted, Jackson had the most but not enough to win. Back to the House it was. Clay, as Speaker of the House, had control over the proceedings and, when it became clear that something had to be done, agreed to withdraw from the race if his supporters would instead support Adams. This wasn't about electoral votes anymore, however. Each state had one vote in the House of Representatives. The country had 24 states at the time, and 13 of them voted for Adams. Clay, in turn, was named Secretary of State. Jackson and his supporters, along with many other neutral observers, denounced this turn of events as a "corrupt bargain," but the votes were counted and the son of a president was in the White House.

The third election decided not by the Electoral College was that of 1876. By then, the concept of a popular vote was well established and the electoral vote had become a reflection of that popular vote. In 1876, however, that wasn't the case. The country was still healing from the wounds of the Civil War. Federal troops were still in Southern states, sometimes in large numbers, enforcing the Thirteenth, Fourteenth, and Fifteenth Amendments. Reconstruction was still in effect and many people in the South resented what they saw as the continuation of an occupation by the victorious North.

The two presidential terms of Ulysses S. Grant were marred by political scandal as well, and a constant theme during the election campaigns was political honesty and restoring trust in government. Samuel J. Tilden, the governor of New York, was the Democratic candidate, and the Republicans had nominated Ohio governor **Rutherford B. Hayes**. When the popular votes were counted, Tilden had the most, more than 280,000 more than Hayes. But he didn't have enough electoral votes to win. Florida, Louisiana, South Carolina and Oregon had rather irregular practices that eventually led to a federal commission being formed. The commission's 15 members were 8 Republicans and 7 Democrats, and the resulting final party-line vote was in favor of Hayes, who gained the presidency by getting exactly the number of votes he needed. Hayes took the White House, federal troops left the South, and the republic marched on.

The last election that needed to be decided by means other than the Electoral College took place very recently, in 2000. It all came down to one state and that state's method of counting votes. The state in question was **Florida**, and the election was eventually decided by the Supreme Court. The Democratic Party's nominee was Vice-President Al Gore. A presidential candidate himself back in 1988, Gore had served as vice-president for both of President Bill Clinton's terms. As such, he was both a champion of Clinton's successes and a reflection of his failures. The Republican Party's nominee was George W. Bush, governor of Texas and son of former President George Bush. he campaigned on a platform of a strong national defense and an end to questionable ethics in the White House. The election was hotly contested, and many states went down to the wire, being decided by only a handful of votes. The one state that seemed to be flip-flopping as Election Day turned into Election Night was Florida. In the end, Gore won the popular vote, by nearly 540,000 votes. But he didn't win the electoral vote. The vote was so close in Florida that a recount was necessary under federal law. Eventually, the **Supreme Court** weighed in and stopped all the recounts. The last count had Bush winning by less than a thousand votes. That gave him Florida and the White House.

Because of these irregularities, especially the last one, many have taken up the cry to eliminate the Electoral College, which they see as archaic and capable of distorting the will of the people. After all, they argue, elections these days come down to one or two key states, as if the votes of the people in all the other states don't matter. Proponents of the Electoral College point to the tradition of the entity and all of the other elections in which the electoral vote mirrored the popular vote. Eliminating the Electoral College would no doubt take a constitutional amendment, and those are certainly hard to come by. The debate crops up every four years; in the past decade, though, the debate has lasted longer in between elections.

Skill 4.5d **Describe and evaluate issues of state redistricting and the political nature of reapportionment.**

The struggle over what is to be the fair method to ensure equal political representation for all different groups in the United States continues to dominate the national debate. This has revolved around the problems of trying to ensure proper racial and minority representation. Various civil rights acts, notably the Voting Rights Act of 1965, sought to eliminate the remaining features of unequal suffrage in the United States.

Most recently, the question has revolved around the issue of what is called "**gerrymandering**", which involves the adjustment of various electoral districts in order to achieve a predetermined goal. Usually this is used in regards to the problem of minority political representation. The fact that gerrymandering sometimes creates odd and unusual looking districts (this is where the practice gets its name) and most often the sole basis of the adjustments is racial. This has led to the questioning of this practice being a fair, let alone constitutional, way for society to achieve its desired goals. This alone promises to be the major issue in national electoral politics for some time to come. The debate has centered on those of the "left" (**Liberals**), who favor such methods, and the "right" (**Conservatives**), who oppose them. Overall, most Americans would consider themselves in the "middle" (**Moderates**).

How best to move forward with ensuring civil liberties and civil rights for all continues to dominate the national debate. In recent times, issues seem to revolve not around individual rights, but what has been called "group rights" has been raised. At the forefront of the debate is whether some specific remedies like affirmative action, quotas, gerrymandering and various other forms of preferential treatment are actually fair or just as bad as the ills they are supposed to cure. At the present, no easy answers seem to be forthcoming. It is a testament to the American system that it has shown itself able to enter into these debates, to find solutions and tended to come out stronger.

COMPETENCY 4.6　　POWERS AND PROCEDURES OF THE NATIONAL, STATE, LOCAL AND TRIBAL GOVERNMENTS

Skill 4.6a　Identify the various ways in which federal, state, local, and tribal governments are organized.

The various governments of the United States and of Native American tribes have many similarities and a few notable differences. They are more similar than not; and all in all, they reflect the tendency of their people to prefer a representative that has checks and balances that look after one another and the people that keep them in power.

The United States Government has three distinct branches: the Executive, the Legislative, and the Judicial. Each has its own function and its own "check" on the other two.

The Legislative Branch consists primarily of the House of Representatives and the Senate. Each house has a set number of members, the House having 435 apportioned according to national population trends and the Senate having 100 (two for each state). House members serve two-year terms; Senators serve six-year terms. Each house can initiate a bill, but that bill must be passed by a majority of both houses in order to become a law. The House is primarily responsible for initiating spending bills; the Senate is responsible for ratifying treaties that the President might sign with other countries.

The Executive Branch has the President and Vice-President as its two main figures. The President is the commander-in-chief of the armed forces and the person who can approve or veto all bills from Congress. (Vetoed bills can become law anyway if two-thirds of each house of Congress vote to pass it over the President's objections.) The President is elected to a four-year term by the Electoral College, which usually mirrors the popular will of the people. The President can serve a total of two terms. The Executive Branch also has several departments consisting of advisors to the President. These departments include State, Defense, Education, Treasury, and Commerce, among others. Members of these departments are appointed by the President and approved by Congress.

The Judicial Branch consists of a series of courts and related entities, with the top body being the Supreme Court. The Court decides whether laws of the land are constitutional; any law invalidated by the Supreme Court is no longer in effect. The Court also regulates the enforcement and constitutionality of the Amendments to the Constitution. The Supreme Court is the highest court in the land. Cases make their way to it from federal Appeals Courts, which hear appeals of decisions made by federal District Courts. These lower two levels of courts are found in regions around the country. Supreme Court Justices are appointed by the President and confirmed by the Senate. They serve for life. Lower-court judges are elected in popular votes within their states.

State governments are mirror images of the federal government, with a few important exceptions: Governors are not technically commanders in chief of armed forces; state supreme court decisions can be appealed to federal courts; terms of state representatives and senators vary; judges, even of the state supreme courts, are elected by popular vote; governors and legislators have term limits that vary by state.

Local governments vary widely across the country, although none of them has a judicial branch per se. Some local governments consist of a city council, of which the mayor is a member and has limited powers; in other cities, the mayor is the head of the government and the city council are the chief lawmakers. Local governments also have less strict requirements for people running for office than do the state and federal governments.

The format of the governments of the various Native American tribes varies as well. Most tribes have governments along the lines of the U.S. federal or state governments. An example is the Cherokee Nation, which has a 15-member **Tribal Council** as the head of the Legislative branch, a Principal Chief and Deputy Chief who head up the Executive branch and carry out the laws passed by the Tribal Council, and a Judicial branch made up of the Judicial Appeals Tribunal and the Cherokee Nation District Court. Members of the Tribunal are appointed by the Principal Chief. Members of the other two branches are elected by popular vote of the Cherokee Nation.

Skill 4.6b **Analyze the issues that arise out of the divisions of jurisdiction among federal, state, local, and tribal governments at each level of government; consider their impacts on those different levels of government.**

Historically the functions of government, or people's concepts of government and its purpose and function, have varied considerably. In the theory of political science, the function of government is to secure the common welfare of the members of the given society over which it exercises control. In different historical eras, governments have attempted to achieve the common welfare by various means in accordance with the traditions and ideology of the given society.

Among primitive peoples, systems of control were rudimentary at best. They arose directly from the ideas of right and wrong that had been established in the group and were common in that particular society. Control being exercised most often by means of group pressure, most often in the forms of taboos and superstitions and in many cases by ostracism, or banishment from the group. Thus, in most cases, because of the extreme tribal nature of society in those early times, this led to very unpleasant circumstances for the individual so treated. Without the protection of the group, a lone individual was most often in for a sad and very short, fate. (No other group would accept such an individual into their midst and survival alone was extremely difficult if not impossible).

Among more civilized peoples, governments began to assume more institutional forms. They rested on a well-defined legal basis. They imposed penalties on violators of the social order. They used force, which was supported and sanctioned by their people. The government was charged to establish the social order and was supposed to do so in order to be able to discharge its functions.

Eventually the ideas of government, who should govern and how, came to be considered by various thinkers and philosophers. The most influential of these and those who had the most influence on our present society were the ancient Greek philosophers such as Plato and Aristotle.

Aristotle's conception of government was based on a simple idea. The function of government was to provide for the general welfare of its people. A good government, and one that should be supported, was one that did so in the best way possible, with the least pressure on the people. Bad governments were those that subordinated the general welfare to that of the individuals who ruled. At no time should any function of any government be that of personal interest of any one individual, no matter who that individual was. This does not mean that Aristotle had no sympathy for the individual or individual happiness (as at times Plato has been accused by those who read his "**Republic,**" which was the first important philosophical text to explore these issues). Rather Aristotle believed that a society is greater than the sum of its parts, or that "the good of the many outweighs the good of the few and also of the one".

Skill 4.6c   Analyze the sources of power and influence in democratic politics, such as access to and use of the mass media, money, economic interests, and the ability to mobilize groups.

If there's one thing that drives American politics more than any other, it's money. Much more often than not, the candidate who has the most money at his or her disposal has the best chance of getting or keeping political office. Money can buy so many things that are necessary to a successful campaign that is entirely indispensable. Money drives the utilization of every other factor in the running of a campaign.

First and foremost, money is needed to pay the people who will run a candidate's campaign. A candidate cannot expect people to give up, in some cases, years of their lives without monetary compensation. Volunteers on a political campaign are plentiful, but they are not at the top levels. The faithful lieutenants of a campaign are paid performers.

Money is also needed to buy or rent all of the tangible and intangible *things* that are needed to power a political campaign: office supplies, meeting places, transportation vehicles, and many more. The inventory of these items can add up frighteningly quickly, and money can appear to disappear like water down a drain.

Of course, the expense that gets the most exposure these days is media advertising, specifically television advertising. This is the most expensive kind of advertising, but it also has the potential to reach the widest audience. TV ad prices can run into the hundreds of thousands of dollars, depending on when they run; but they have the potential to reach perhaps millions of viewers. Here, too, money can disappear quickly. A political campaign is also a fashion show and candidates cannot afford to go without showing their friendly faces to as wide an audience as possible on a regular basis. Other forms of advertising include radio and Web ads, signs and billboards, and good old-fashioned flyers.

The sources of all this money that is needed to run a successful political campaign are varied. A candidate might have a significant amount of money in his or her own personal coffers. In rare cases, the candidate finances the entire campaign. However, the most prevalent source of money is **outside donations**. A candidate's friends and family might donate funds to the campaign, as well as the campaign workers themselves. State and federal governments will also contribute to most regional or national campaigns, provided that the candidate can prove that he or she can raise a certain amount of money first. The largest source of campaign finance money, however, comes from so-called "special interests." A large company such as an oil company or a manufacturer of electronic goods will want to keep prices or tariffs down and so will want to make sure that laws lifting those prices or tariffs aren't passed.

To this end, the company will contribute money to the campaigns of candidates who are likely to vote to keep those prices or tariffs down. A candidate is not obligated to accept such a donation, of course, and further is not obligated to vote in favor of the interests of the special interest; however, doing the former might create a shortage of money and doing the latter might ensure that no further donations come from that or any other special interest. An oil company wants to protect its interests, and its leaders don't very much care which political candidate is doing that for them as long as it is being done.

Another powerful source of support for a political campaign is **special interest groups** of a political nature. These are not necessarily economic powers but rather groups whose people want to effect political change (or make sure that such change doesn't take place, depending on the status of the laws at the time). A good example of a special interest group is an anti-abortion group or a pro-choice group. The abortion issue is still a divisive one in American politics, and many groups will want to protect or defend or ban—depending on which side they're on—certain rights and practices. An anti-abortion group, for example, might pay big money to candidates who pledge to work against laws that protect the right for women to have abortions. As long as these candidates continue to assure their supporters that they will keep on fighting the fight, the money will continue to flow. This kind of social group usually has a large number of dedicated individuals who do much more than vote: They organize themselves into political action committees, attend meetings and rallies, and work to make sure that their message gets out to a wide audience. Methods of spreading the word often include media advertising on behalf of their chosen candidates. This kind of expenditure is no doubt welcomed by the candidates, who will get the benefit of the exposure but won't have to spend that money because someone else is signing the checks.

All in all, it's money that makes the political world go around.

COMPETENCY 4.7   THE MEDIA IN AMERICAN POLITICAL LIFE

Skill 4.7a   Describe the significance of a free press, including the role of the broadcast, print, and electronic media in American society and government.

A **free press** is essential to maintaining responsibility and civic-mindedness in government and in the rest of society. The broadcast, print, and electronic media in America serve as societal and governmental **watchdogs**, showcasing for the rest of America and for the world what kinds of brilliant and terrible things the rich, powerful, and elected are doing.

First and foremost, the media report on the actions taken and encouraged by leaders of the government. In many cases, these actions are common knowledge. Policy debates, discussions on controversial issues, struggles against foreign powers in economic and wartime endeavors—all are fodder for media reports. The First Amendment guarantees media in America the right to report on these things, and the media reporters take full advantage of that right and privilege in striving not only to inform the American public but also to keep the governmental leaders in check.

The most extreme kind of action that needs reporting on is an illegal one. Officials who perform illegal actions will, in most cases, find those actions part of the public record. These officials are expected to be models of society or, at the very least, following the very laws that they were elected to pass or erase. This is largely a trust issue as well: If you can't trust your elected leaders, who can you trust?

Many people would answer that question with the skeptical, "No one can be trusted, especially those in government." Others would say, more simply, that greater scrutiny is needed for those in legislative power, since they are more easily able to hide questionable actions. No one is above the law, especially those charged with making those laws. If a lawmaker thinks that he or she is above the law, then in most cases he or she will be sadly mistaken to discover that that assumption is incorrect. In the vast majority of cases, lawmakers who break the law in a big way are caught and informed on, especially because of reporting done by newspapers, radio stations, magazines, and websites.

The flip side of this is that lawmakers often do positive, noteworthy, and newsworthy things that should be reported on as well. The official who spearheads a campaign to get a certain wide-ranging bill passed will want to take the appropriate credit for those efforts, making his actions known to the media so those actions can be reported to his or her constituents. It's the scandals and jail terms that get most of the screaming headlines in mass media today, but praise-worthy actions are no less important in a national understanding of who the lawmakers are and why they take the actions that they do.

Owners of large companies and charities and especially recognizable figures in popular entertainment are continually under scrutiny for signs of questionable actions or behavior. In the same way that lawmakers are responsible for public legislative policy, many company owners are responsible for public economic policy. If a corporation is stealing money from its employees or shareholders, then those employees and shareholders and the American public at large need to know about it. Such reporting is not only informative but also usually leads to indictments, prosecutions, and jail terms for the perpetrators of such economic crimes.

One time when a free press isn't exactly a good idea, however, is when a country is at war. Troop movements and battle plans aren't the sort of thing that need to be broadcast. Such broadcasts have a way of making their way into the hands of the very people that the country's armed forces are attempting to defeat on the battlefield. (An excellent example of this was seen by all in the lead up and prosecution of the Gulf War, when Iraqi leader Saddam Hussein and his allies and followers kept up with Allied actions by watching CNN.) The government, and especially its armed forces, have the right to refuse to provide information that is vital to national security. This right has been validated time and again by the U.S. Supreme Court and is the law of the land.

Of course, the key word in all of this is *free*. American media reporters are *free* to report on such things as lawmakers' actions (good or bad), company owners' practices (good or bad), and goings-on at the local country club or American Legion house because the Constitution—specifically, the First Amendment—guarantees them the right to do so. This freedom of reporting is a right that is enjoyed by reporters in other countries, to varying degrees.

In other countries, most notably China these days, reporters are *not* free to report on everything they see, especially things that the government does not want its people to know. If such reporting is banned, then the government can conceivably conduct all sorts of illegal transactions or escapades without fear of those actions being exposed by the mainstream media. If a country's citizens do not have a handle on how badly their government is behaving on the world stage, then they have no basis for demanding that things change.

It was this idea, after all, which was at the heart of the American Revolution: the idea that a people could stand up and say that they had had enough of their government and its leaders and their actions.

Skill 4.7b   Analyze the interaction between public officials and the media to communicate and influence public opinion.

Public officials have an overwhelming need to communicate. They want other people to know what they're doing and why. They want to make sure that the voters who elected know what great jobs they're doing pursuing the agendas that are closest to their hearts. Ultimately, they want to do as much as they can to get themselves re-elected or, if terms limit won't allow such re-election, to leaving a memorable public legacy.

It used to be that the way to get your picture in the paper if you were a politician running for office was to kiss a baby or help an old lady across the street. Those were the old days. Now, an often cynical public demands much more impressive feats of goodwill and an often fragmented array of media opportunities offers many more ways to communicate with the public.

Again, in the old days, the way to get noticed in the court of public opinion was to get your name in the newspaper or on the radio. Television began to change all that, with its visual record of events. The proliferation of TV channels has made it very difficult for a lawmaker *not* to get noticed if her or she does something remarkable these days. And, of course, we now have the Internet, a vast, heterogeneous world of opportunities. Internet opportunities include not just news websites but personal websites and the eponymous blogs, public opinion pieces that may or may not be true.

This is the key thing to remember if you are reading things on Web pages: They might not have undergone the same sort of scrutiny as comparable efforts released by major media outlets to newspapers, radio, and television. Those media processes have built-in safety measures called editors who will verify information before it is released to the wide world; to be a blogger, all you need is access to a Web-enabled computer and time to write a column. Bloggers routinely do not use editors or run their copy by anyone else before publishing it; as such, they have lower standards of professionalism overall and need to be regarded as such. What they write might be totally true; the blog, however, is known as a *log*, a chronicle of thoughts and opinions about the affairs of the day, not so much a blow-by-blow of facts and figures.

Public officials will hire one or more people or perhaps a whole department or an entire business to conduct **public relations**, which are efforts intended to make the lawmakers look good in the eyes of their constituents. A public relations person or firm will have as its overreaching goal the happiness of the lawmaker who hired her or them and will gladly write press releases, arrange media events (like tours of schools or soup kitchens), and basically do everything else to keep their employer's name in the public eye in a good way. This includes making the lawmaker's position on important issues known to the public. Especially controversial issues will be embraced on the other side by lawmakers, and those lawmakers will want their constituents to know how they intend to vote those issues. It's also a good idea to find out what your constituents think about these issues of the day, since the fastest way to get yourself bad publicity or thrown out at re-election time is to ignore the weight of public opinion.

Another inherent part of the public official-media relationship is the need to appear to be open and above-board. Even if a politician isn't forthcoming with all the details of what he is doing, he or she needs to look like that is what is happening. A lawmaker who communicates with the public is one who appears to be on the level, since an absence of information seems to imply guilt or complicity in the minds of many people. To this end, lawmakers will go out of their way to make their actions, intentions, and political views known to the people who will vote for them and support them by sending them money.

All of these things are true as well for potential lawmakers who are running for office against those already in office. Since incumbents can often call on the **"weight of the office"** to give them free publicity just for doing things like voting on bills or attending local ribbon-cutting or other public functions, challengers routinely face an uphill battle to get their names, views, and deeds into the public debate and will work extra hard to do so.

On the other side of the coin, members of the media will want the public to know what their lawmakers are saying and doing. Many reporters and editors consider it in the best interest of the country to report on the dealings and actions of those in government, especially if those dealings or actions are of a questionable legal or moral nature. It works both ways and the smart politicians understand the nature of that dichotomy and use it to their advantage.

COMPETENCY 4.8   POLITICAL SYSTEMS

Skill 4.8a   Explain and analyze different political systems and the philosophies that underlie them, including the parliamentary system.

Anarchism - Political movement believing in the elimination of all government and its replacement by a cooperative community of individuals. Sometimes it has involved political violence such as assassinations of important political or governmental figures. The historical banner of the movement is a black flag.

Communism - A belief as well as a political system, characterized by the ideology of class conflict and revolution, one party state and dictatorship, repressive police apparatus, and government ownership of the means of production and distribution of goods and services. A revolutionary ideology preaching the eventual overthrow of all other political orders and the establishment of one world Communist government. Same as Marxism. The historical banner of the movement is a red flag and variation of stars, hammer and sickles, representing the various types of workers.

Dictatorship - The rule by an individual or small group of individuals (Oligarchy) that centralizes all political control in itself and enforces its will with a terrorist police force.

Fascism - A belief as well as a political system, opposed ideologically to Communism, though similar in basic structure, with a one party state, centralized political control and a repressive police system. It however tolerates private ownership of the means of production, though it maintains tight overall control. Central to its belief is the idolization of the Leader, a "Cult of the Personality," and most often an expansionist ideology. Examples have been German Nazism and Italian Fascism.

Monarchy - The rule of a nation by a Monarch, (a non-elected usually hereditary leader), most often a king or queen. It may or may not be accompanied by some measure of democratic open institutions and elections at various levels. A modern example is Great Britain, where it is called a Constitutional Monarchy.

Parliamentary System - A system of government with a legislature, usually involving a multiplicity of political parties and often coalition politics. There is division between the head of state and head of government. Head of government is usually known as a Prime Minister who is also usually the head of the largest party. The head of government and cabinet usually both sit and vote in the parliament. Head of state is most often an elected president, (though in the case of a constitutional monarchy, like Great Britain, the sovereign may take the place of a president as head of state). A government may fall when a majority in parliament votes "no confidence" in the government.

Presidential System - A system of government with a legislature, can involve few or many political parties, no division between head of state and head of government. The President serves in both capacities. The President is elected either by direct or indirect election. A President and cabinet usually do not sit or vote in the legislature and the President may or may not be the head of the largest political party. A President can thus rule even without a majority in the legislature. He can only be removed from office before an election for major infractions of the law.

Socialism - Political belief and system in which the state takes a guiding role in the national economy and provides extensive social services to its population. It may or may not own outright means of production, but even where it does not, it exercises tight control. It usually promotes democracy, (Democratic-Socialism), though the heavy state involvement produces excessive bureaucracy and usually inefficiency. Taken to an extreme it may lead to Communism as government control increases and democratic practice decreases. Ideologically the two movements are very similar in both belief and practice, as Socialists also preach the superiority of their system to all others and that it will become the eventual natural order. It is also considered for that reason a variant of Marxism. It also has used a red flag as a symbol.

Skill 4.8b   Analyze problems of new democracies in the 19th and 20th centuries and their internal struggles.

Democratic governments sprouted up around the world in the nineteenth and twentieth centuries, with totals going from a handful to hundreds by the end of the 1990s.

Most countries in **South America** and the **Caribbean** region gained their independence in the nineteenth century, thanks to wars against occupying Spain. By and large, these countries became representative governments eventually, if not right away. In some cases, countries replaced one colonial governor with another authoritarian figure. To varying degrees, these countries suffered internal strife as well, most notably in the twentieth century as the twin demons of the Cold War and horrendous debt threatened to engulf more than one country.

Two of the most notable conversions to democracy in the twentieth century were **India** and **Japan**. India, one of the most ancient of societies, was most recently a colony of Great Britain. Thanks largely to the efforts of **Mohandas Gandhi** and other activists, India achieved its independence by the mid-twentieth century. The country became a democracy, with a president at the head of a representative government. The change in political theory, however, didn't mean an end to the internal strife that India has seemingly always felt.

At the heart of the country's political identity is a religious dichotomy—a struggle between Muslims and Hindus. This religious conflict has continued for hundreds of years and has certainly not been diminished by the fact that the Indian people can elect their own leaders. There is a conflict between India and Pakistan over the Kashmir region. The entire area was known as India at various times under various masters, including Great Britain. But the country was partitioned when it was freed, and the result has been a dangerous dispute over political borders that has resulted in much loss of life and the procurement of atomic weapons by both sides. Another main source of internal strife in India is an economic one. India is the world's second most populous country, and a huge number of these people have little or no resources of their own. A half-century of representative government hasn't made much of a difference in the economic prosperity of these people.

Japan, by contrast, has suffered much less religious and political strife since becoming a democracy after its defeat in World War II. The occupying American army instituted a new Constitution, which provided for a representative government, and also led efforts to rebuild the country. The result has been, for the most part, an economic powerhouse that is now one of the world's strongest and most wide-ranging economies. Japan has had its periods of economic weakness, of course, but has bounced back each time stronger than ever.

The end of World War I brought an end to colonization in Africa. In many cases, these African countries embraced the idea of representative government, with mixed results. In some cases, the idea of democracy found favor; in other countries, democracy lasted only a short time or was on a sort of yo-yo existence between periods of authoritarian takeovers.

Political divisions on the **Korean Peninsula** and in Southeast Asia have created intense internal strife of a mostly economic and political nature. North Korea, an authoritarian state, has lived in relative isolation from the rest of the world and has suffered economically from that isolation. South Korea became a democracy after the end of Japanese occupation after World War II and has prospered economically, although the specter of war with North Korea has loomed large for more than 50 years. The two countries did, in fact, go to war in 1950. The resulting three-year conflict involved forces from a handful of other countries, most notably China and the United States, and resulted in the status quo geographically. The most notable facet of life in either Korean country is the idea that another war could begin tomorrow. Indeed, an intensely patrolled area known as the **Demilitarized Zone** (DMZ) serves as the border between the countries. North Korea has become more and more public in its militancy in recent years, perhaps a sign that the country is finally running out of food.

Southeast Asia has also seen its share of strife since the 1950s, most notably in Vietnam, which was once two countries, a mirror image of Korea with the North being Communist and the South being a more representative government. Those two countries began fighting not long after the end of the WWII, and Communist and the United Nations again became involved. The war consumed the two countries and most of their neighbors for many years, resulting in horrible economic and social conditions throughout the region for many years afterward. North Vietnam ended up winning the war, absorbing all of South Vietnam into one country, which continues under an authoritarian government but is a bit of an economic powerhouse these days.

Another country that has gained a representative government in the twentieth century is France. Even though the French Revolution overthrew the monarchy in 1789, authoritarian rule returned and held sway for more than another century. France in the twentieth century has seen its share of internal strife, notably two devastating wars, but is now recognized as one of the great powers of the world. A growing number of immigrants from former colonies has created a bit of a religious crisis in France, between Christians and Muslims. That seems to be the only looming difficulty, however.

COMPETENCY 4.9   **TENSIONS WITHIN OUR CONSTITUTIONAL DEMOCRACY**

Skill 4.9a   Analyze the constitutional interpretations of the First Amendment's statement about the separation of church and state.

The First Amendment to the Constitution prohibits a state-sponsored religion while also prohibiting the government from interfering with its people's exercise of their religions. These have been two of the most fundamental tenets and faithfully upheld provisions of the Constitution since their inception.

One common term still bandied about is the "wall of **separation between church and state**" that the First Amendment builds. We have this phrase thanks to Thomas Jefferson, himself a committed Deist who wanted no part of an entangling of government and religion. In the 200 years since Jefferson first wrote this phrase, such entanglement has been discouraged numerous times.

From the earliest days of the nineteenth century, this tendency to keep the two entities separate has been challenged, intentionally or not, by parochial school. These schools are run by religious organizations, like churches, and provide their students with not only a secular education but also religious instruction. It would seem to be a straightforward conclusion that the funding of one of these schools by the state or federal government would violate the doctrine of separation between church and state, but churches have tried nonetheless.

The Court has consistently ruled against public funding for parochial schools. And since these things are rarely as straightforward as they assume, it is true as well that the Supreme Court has upheld a series of laws that provided state-sponsored spending for religious schools. In particular, in *Cochran* v. *Louisiana State Board of Educators* (1930), the Court ruled that a law that provided textbook funds for students of secular and parochial schools did not violate the First Amendment because the funds were intended to benefit the students, not the religious entities that sponsored the schools. The effectiveness of that decision has weakened in the seventy years since it was issued, as subsequent Justices found fault with it to one degree or another.

One thing that all Justices seem to agree on, however, is the inadmissibility of prayer in school. The famous *Engle* v. *Vitale* is an excellent example, in which the Court invalidated a school policy of beginning each class day with a school wide prayer. This principle was reaffirmed in *Wallace* v. *Jaffree* (1985), in which the Court invalidated a day-opening moment of silence because the law that mandated it made clear that it was intended as a time for prayer. Students can certainly pray silently any time they wish; the problem was with the state's and the school's mandating a specified prayer time.

Universities have been permitted to allow religious groups' meetings on university property, provided that secular groups have the same meeting opportunity.

Another element of the First Amendment religion phrasing that has come to be contentious is the "Free Exercise Clause," the ability to practice your religion as you see fit. In the twentieth century, many businesses in America closed on Sunday, the traditional day of worship for Christians. This practice was enforced by laws in many states, called "**Blue Laws**," which in many cases required businesses to close on Sunday. Since Jewish people honored their Sabbath on Saturday, not Sunday, they felt disenfranchised by such laws. The case was *Braunfeld* v. *Brown* (1961), and the Court ruled for the Blue Laws, saying that the loss of business that Jewish owners suffered by closing Sunday in addition to Saturday (which they did because of *their* religious beliefs) was not a state-mandated restriction of their religious beliefs but, rather, a secular policy.

Other famous religious beliefs-government mandated cases have involved the Amish religion's prohibition of education beyond eighth grade (*Wisconsin* v. *Yoder*, 1972 and *United States* v. *Lee*, 1982). A particularly contentious issue has arisen in the last 20 years, involving the Native American use of **peyote**, a narcotic in religious ceremonies. Technically, according to American law, the use of such a drug is illegal; Native Americans, however, claim that they use it as part of sacred practices that supersede the laws of the land. The result has been a federal law protecting such practices, extending to the growth and cultivation of said substance but only for religious means.

Perhaps the most contentious church-state conflict has been **public displays** of religious images on state-owned property. In the news recently have been the Ten Commandments, the Christian and Jewish religions' ancient set of laws that happen to include religious elements. Various groups have tried to prevent such displays of these laws and statues from appearing on courthouse walls and lawns, but the Court has consistently treated the Commandments as a part of legal history. Other battles have involved depictions of scenes from the Jesus story on state-owned property, especially at Christmastime. In most cases, the Court has ruled that such displays are permissible as long as the holiday display also included images of Santa Claus and other recognizably secular parts of the Christmas holiday (*Lynch* v. *Donnelly*, 1984).

Skill 4.9b   Debate the adequacy of the solution of majority rule and the role of minority rights in a majority-rules system.

A majority-rules system has some powerful positive attributes and some horrible drawbacks. Strictly speaking, a **majority-rules system** is one that places the responsibility for governing and policy-making in the hands of the group that has at least more than 50 percent of the members. Theoretically, if every member of that group voted the same way, the group would "win" whatever dispute was being contested. Also theoretically, those not in the group would not be able to be on the "winning" side and enjoy the benefits thereof. Theory and practice are sometimes very different things.

As stated above, the main benefit of having a majority is that you can expect or at least dream of dictating things like policy, rules, and even meeting times and places. Much more heavily, on the world stage, a majority group can control economic and military actions across the board. Especially in these matters, the interests of a minority group or groups might very well take a back seat to the ambitions of the majority.

In this strict setup, those in the minority might find themselves uncomfortably at the drive and whims of the majority. If society allows the majority to rule, then the minority has to become the majority in order to rule; otherwise, all of their political sound and fury will signify nothing when it comes to pass laws and proposals. In a society such as the United States, in which political participation is decided by voting, the minority has no choice but to attempt to become the majority through the balloting process.

Exceptions to this abound, of course. Especially on the contentious issues of the day, lawmakers perform so-called "switches" all the time. Someone in one political party might vote with members of another political party on certain issues but support his or her own party on others. Sometimes, it is very difficult to determine who will vote which way; other times, the answers are crystal clear.

All of this conjecture and theory assumes that the majority is a solid one and that all of its members think—and, more importantly, vote—the same way. This is not always the case. A majority is not guaranteed to hold sway on every issue unless its members think the same on all of those issues. Especially in the modern political era, this kind of homogeneity is rare, if nonexistent; more likely is the majority that can count on a solid voting bloc on the major issues but which has to sweat it out on minor issues.

Especially in cases in which the majority has a very slim margin of "victory," one or two or a handful of votes here or there can make for nervous moments when vote tallies are announced. If you are in the majority and your majority is just one vote, then the absence of even two of your members can spell defeat at the hands of a determined, united minority. That concept is not always a reality, either. The common perception that those out of power will naturally band together in order to stand together in power has been proven false many times over.

The majority has to be careful not to be too autocratic in its use of power because the majority might someday be the minority. In such a case, the very benefits that the majority so recently enjoyed will suddenly be out of their reach. Especially in groups that have a slim margin of majority, this danger is very real.

A majority-rules is the system we have in America, for better or for worse. Those in the minority are often ignored, passed over, or disenfranchised in favor of the majority. This has been seen to happen in all areas of society, most notably in economic circles but also in terms of voting, property ownership, school attendance, and even social club membership. One of the ways that a majority can keep hold of its grip on society is to ensure that it doesn't get unseated, and some majorities have taken full advantage of this idea. Inventions like poll taxes and literacy tests come to mind. If you can't read or afford to read the rules of the game, then you can't possibly play in it. In this case, being in the minority really hurts. The cards are stacked against members of the minority.

One danger of keeping the minority down for too long is that the members of that minority might decide to gain the majority by violent means. This has happened countless times throughout history and will certainly happen again many more times. In some cases, the new majority set about eliminating the old one. This might seem impossible in the modern day, but desperate times can drive people to desperate measures. The majority would do well to look after at least the basic rights of the minority, if only to protect their own fundamental security.

Bearing all this in mind, one benefit of the majority-rules system is that it produces results. If two groups have the same number of members, they can theoretically deadlock on every important debate, resulting in no progress whatever. This is unlikely but possible, and that possibility is scary enough to convince most people that the majority-rules system is the way to go, even if they're in the minority.

DOMAIN 5:   PRINCIPLES OF ECONOMICS

COMPETENCY 5.1   ECONOMIC TERMS AND CONCEPTS AND ECONOMIC REASONING

Skill 5.1a   Describe the causal relationship between scarcity and choices, and explain opportunity cost and marginal benefit and marginal cost.

The fact that resources are scarce is the basis for the existence of economics. Economics is defined as a study of how scarce resources are allocated to satisfy unlimited wants. Resources refer to the four factors of production: **labor, capital, land and entrepreneurship**. The fact that the supply of these resources is finite means that society cannot have as much of everything that it wants. There is a constraint on production and consumption and on the kinds of goods and services that can be produced and consumed.

Scarcity means that choices have to be made. If society decides to produce more of one good, this means that there are fewer resources available for the production of other goods. Assume a society can produce two goods, good A and good B. The society uses resources in the production of each good. If producing one unit of good A results in an amount of resources used to produce three units of good B then producing one more unit of good A results in a decrease in three units of good B. In effect, one unit of good A "costs" three units of good B. This cost is referred to as opportunity cost.

Opportunity cost is the value of the sacrificed alternative, the value of what had to be given up in order to have the output of good A. Opportunity cost does not just refer to production. Your opportunity cost of studying with this guide is the value of what you are not doing because you are studying, whether it is watching TV, spending time with family, working, or whatever. Every choice has an opportunity cost.

Marginal analysis is used greatly in the study of economics. The term marginal always means "the change in". There are benefits and costs associated with every decision. The benefits are the gains or the advantages of a decision or action. If we are talking about production, the gains are the increases in output. If we are talking about an additional hour of study with this guide, the gains are the amount of material covered. There are also costs associated with each. The **production costs** involve the cost of the resources involved and the cost of their alternative uses. The costs of studying are the **opportunity costs** of what you have to give up, whether it is sleep, socializing, working, etc.

In terms of marginal analysis, what are the marginal benefits and marginal costs of an additional unit of output or amount of a change is there in benefits and costs from producing the additional unit? The marginal benefits of the additional unit is the change in total benefits from a one unit change in output, or mathematically, the change in total benefits divided by the change in the quantity of output. The same is true for marginal cost.

Marginal cost is the increase in costs from producing one more unit of output, or the change in total cost divided by the change in quantity of output. Looking at costs and benefits in this way is referred to as making decisions at the margin and this is the methodology used in the study of economics.

Skill 5.1b   Identify the difference between monetary and non-monetary incentives and how changes in incentives cause changes in behavior.

Economics differs from other disciplines in that it considers both monetary and non-monetary factors in decision making. Monetary factors are those that have a dollar value attached, like the cost of a unit of input. The dollar cost of something is a monetary cost and is expressed in dollars. These are referred to as explicit costs or accounting costs. Non-monetary factors are referred to as implicit costs. These include opportunity costs or the value of the sacrificed alternative.

If we are talking about entrepreneurial activities, then we have to include the value of what that factor could be earning in its next best activity, because this is the minimum amount of return that is required to keep that factor performing its present function. If a factory can earn X dollars in its next best alternative activity, then X dollars is the minimum amount required to keep that factor performing its present activity. If it doesn't earn those X dollars, it will shift into its next best alternative activity. In calculating the total cost of a decision, both monetary and non-monetary factors have to be considered.

The economic costs of a decision will always be greater than the accounting costs of the same decision, because economics includes the non-monetary aspects of that decision. For example, using this study guide has monetary and non-monetary costs associated with it. The **monetary costs** are the cost of the book and the supplies and other outlay costs, and the increase in income you will have after receiving your teacher certification. The **non-monetary costs** are the value of what you are not doing because you are studying. If there is a change in the cost of any of these monetary or non-monetary factors or incentives, there will be a change in behavior.

For example, if teacher salaries double, obtaining that teaching certificate becomes more important because it represents higher future income. Therefore, the student will work harder to obtain it. On the other hand, if your present salary doubles, then you are not willing to sacrifice hours of work to study and the teaching certificate is not as valuable as it was before.

The same thing is true for other factors of production. If the rate of return in widget production is higher than the rate of return in other industries in the economy, you will see an expansion of the widget industry as factors of production shift into widget production. This shift is caused by a change in monetary incentives in the widget and other industries. This change in a monetary incentive causes a realignment of resources throughout the economy as resources shift out of the relatively lower return industries into the relatively higher return industry. We have considered, for the most part, monetary incentives here.

How do we explain the decision of the spouse to stay home with the children? The spouse that quits working to stay at home with the children makes a large monetary sacrifice in terms of the foregone income, or the salary that he/she is not earning. In this situation, the non-monetary incentives of staying home and caring for the children outweigh the monetary incentives of working and paying for child-care. In each of these examples, each decision involves a comparison of monetary and non-monetary incentives in determining the total cost of the decision. A change in either monetary or non-monetary incentives brings about a change in behavior and the total costs of decisions and actions change accordingly.

Skill 5.1c   Debate the role of private property as an incentive in conserving and improving scarce resources, including renewable and nonrenewable natural resources.

Private property rights play an important role in the conservation of resources and the improvement in the allocation of scarce resources. We have problems in our society that result from the lack of ownership of resources, whether they are renewable or non-renewable. An example of this is pollution. Why does air and water pollution occur? Why do firms emit obnoxious emissions into the air, if they are not restrained from doing so? Nobody owns the air; therefore the air is treated as a free input into the production process. It doesn't cost the firm anything to use the air, in terms of monetary costs. The firm, for the most part, just opens the doors and windows and expels the obnoxious emission.

If the firm couldn't do this, it would have to devise and pay for a technology that would eliminate the obnoxious emissions. This represents a change in the production process because of the increased equipment and labor activities required to deal with the emissions that the firm no longer can just emit into the air. The firm is treating the air as a free input. If the firm had to pay for the air, it would have higher costs of production. It wouldn't "waste" the air because it would have to pay for it, as it pays for any other input. It is the lack of ownership of the air that leads to its use as a free good and its waste. Since nobody owns the air and property rights can't be assigned, there is inefficiency and a misallocation of resources associated with the pollution.

What can government do in this situation to try to correct for the misallocation of resources? Since they can't assign property rights for the ownership of air, they can do things to put a price on the air that the polluting firm is using. This is the theory behind fines for pollution and the sale of pollution permits. They can also require the installation of new technology to prevent the pollution. Each of these remedies is a method of putting a price on the air. Air no longer is a free input into the production process and the misallocation of resources is somewhat corrected for.

Private property rights play an important role in **resource allocation** in our economy. If the pond next door to you is owned by your neighbor, you will not be using it as a garbage dump without compensating your neighbor in some way, whether it is fines or whatever. Since the owner of a resource must be compensated in some way for that resources' use, private ownership results in prices being assigned to resources. These prices, based on scarcity, result in an efficient allocation of resources, whether the resources are renewable or non-renewable. Without these prices, there is inefficiency and waste of scarce resources whether they are widgets or water. Without private ownership of resources there is no incentive to be efficient and to conserve scarce resources, as shown in the pollution examples. This is where a role is defined for government to somehow correct for the misallocation and inefficiency caused by the lack of ownership rights.

Skill 5.1d   Describe and analyze the debate concerning the role of a market economy versus a planned economy in establishing and preserving political and personal liberty.

The roles of political and personal liberty differ greatly depending on the economic regime. The cause of the difference is the role of incentives. A **market economy** functions on the basis of the financial incentive. Firms use society's scarce resources to produce the goods that consumers want. Firms know they have a good that society wants when they earn profit. Firms have a good that consumers don't want when they consistently incur losses. Firms with consistent losses eventually go out of business and those resources shift into other industries, producing goods that consumers do want.

Consumers are, in effect, voting for the goods and services they want and don't want, with their dollars. Technological progress is advanced because of the financial incentives, whether they are personal or corporate. Firms invest in research and development activities to find newer and more efficient technologies that result in greater output at lower prices. Individuals risk their own time and money on inventions because of the potential financial rewards. They live in the structure of a market economy that allows them the liberty of choosing what to do with their own resources within the confines of the law. Students study whatever it is that they want to major in. There are more scholarships available for certain needed occupations, but the student can still obtain an education if he doesn't want to be in one of those needed areas.

In a **planned economy**, particularly one based on public ownership of the means of production, a planning entity substitutes for the market, to varying degrees from partial to total. Instead of consumers voting with their dollars, they have a bureaucratic entity trying to substitute for the functions of supply and demand in making production decisions. This is why planned economies are often plagued by a misallocation of resources that result in shortages and surpluses. In most cases, the incentive for technological progress and innovation is absent because of the lack of financial rewards. There is no financial incentive for the inventor. There is no financial incentive for the firm to engage in research and development activities, even if they have the authorization to do so. What's in it for them?

Many planned economies have less personal and political freedom than do market economies. The economy needs resources for a particular area. The labor force is directed into that area by assignment, for the most part, not by financial incentives. They attract more engineers not by offering a higher salary and more perks for engineers, but by assigning people to be engineers. Their schooling isn't financed if they don't study the required disciplines.

It is obvious why there is a differing degree of political freedom in each of the above paradigms. The lack of freedom of choice in a planned economy carries over to the political area. Most planned economies are usually headed by dictators whereas market economies have elected officials. A populace does not vote for and elect those officials who suppress them. So, for the most part, a market economy allows for more political and personal freedoms than a planned economy does.

COMPETENCY 5.2   **ELEMENTS OF AMERICA'S MARKET ECONOMY IN A GLOBAL SETTING**

Skill 5.2a   **Describe and analyze the relationship of the concepts of incentives and substitutes to the law of supply and demand.**

Supply and demand perform important functions in a market economy. Supply and demand are what make markets function efficiently. **Supply** is defined as the quantity of a good or service that a producer is willing to make available at different prices during a specified period of time. The producers' decisions are based on costs of production. **Demand** is defined as the quantity of goods and services that a buyer is willing and able to buy at different prices during a specified period of time.

The consumers' decisions are based on both income and preferences. I may want a Ferrari, but I cannot afford one, therefore, I am not a part of the relevant market demand. I have to make do by substituting a Toyota for the Ferrari I can't afford. On the other hand, I may be able to afford a Ferrari, but I don't want one. Again, I am not a part of the relevant market demand.

A **market equilibrium** occurs where the selling decisions of producers are equal to the buying decisions of consumers, or where the supply and demand curves intersect. This gives us the market equilibrium price and quantity and results in an efficient allocation of resources in accordance with consumer preferences. In other words, producers are using society's resources to produce the goods and services that society wants. Producers know this because they have a profitable business.

Incentives and **substitutes** affect the market situation. Incentives for consumers are things like sales, coupons, rebates, etc. The incentives results in increased sales for the firm, even though there is a cost to the incentives. There is a change in the market equilibrium situation and possibly market shares. The increased demand coupled with brand loyalty means the firm will be able to raise prices at some point and not lose their customers. On the production side, incentives to innovate result in increased output at lower costs, or more profit and greater market share for the innovating firm. The individual inventor also experiences financial rewards. Many firms reward employees who propose good time or money saving suggestions.

Many of these effects are absent without the use of markets. Supply and demand serve the function of registering the wishes and decisions of producers and consumers with the market tabulating these results. This leads to efficiency. Using a bureaucrat to substitute for the role of supply and demand, leads to inefficiency in both production and consumption. Consumers are no longer directing the allocation of resources with their dollar voting. They may not be getting the goods and services that they want their society's resources used for.

Prices are not efficient because they don't have their allocation function. Incentives don't function in the same way. Consumers don't buy what they don't want even if it's on sale.

The result in trying to substitute in some way for the supply and demand functions of the market is inefficiency in both production and consumption. Society's resources are not being used efficiently and they are not being used to produce what society wants produced. This means higher production costs and more waste.

Skill 5.2b   Describe the effects of changes in supply and/or demand on the relative scarcity, price, and quantity of particular products.

The **supply curve** represents the selling and production decisions of the seller and is based on the costs of production. The costs of production of a product are based on the costs of the resources used in its production. The costs of resources are based on the scarcity of the resource. The scarcer a resource is, relatively speaking, the higher its price. A diamond costs more than paper because diamonds are scarcer than paper is. All of these concepts are embodied in the seller's supply curve. The same thing is true on the buying side of the market. The buyer's preferences, tastes, income, etc. – all of his buying decisions – are embodied in the demand curve. Where the demand and supply curves intersect is where the buying decisions of buyers are equal to the selling decisions of sellers. The quantity that buyers want to buy at a particular price is equal to the quantity that sellers want to sell at that particular price. The market is in **equilibrium**.

What happens when there is a change? Suppose a new big oil field is found. Also suppose there is a technology that allows its recovery and refining at a fraction of the present costs. The result is a big increase in the supply of oil at lower costs, as reflected by a rightward shifting oil supply curve. Oil is used as an input into almost all production. Firms now have lower costs. This means that the firm can produce the same amount of output at a lower cost or can produce a larger amount of output at the same cost. The result is a rightward shift of the firm's, and therefore, the industry supply curve. This means that sellers are willing and able to offer for sale larger quantities of output at each price. Assuming buyers' buying decisions stay the same, there is a new market equilibrium, or new point of intersection of the shifted supply curve with the buyers' demand curve. The result is a lower price with a larger quantity of output. The market has achieved a new equilibrium based on the increase in the quantity of a resource.

Let's look at another situation. Suppose consumer preferences change in favor of widgets. There is an increase or rightward shift of the demand curve for widgets. The immediate effects of this change in preference is a shortage of widgets at the given price level. Consumers want to buy more widgets at the original price than sellers want to sell at that price. Consumers who want the widgets will pay a higher price for them, or they will bid up the price of widgets. As a result, there is now a higher price for widgets. The higher price calls forth increased production of widgets to meet the increased demand.

Producing more widgets requires the use of more resources, so there is an increase in the demand for the factors used in widget production and a higher price commanded by these resources. The end result of the consumer change in preferences in favor of widgets is increased widget production and a higher cost and price. The price of the output will be affected whenever there is a change in demand or a change in the supply of the resources used to produce the product. Those changes will result in higher or lower costs to the consumer as the markets adjust to reflect the changes.

Skill 5.2c   Explain and analyze the roles of property rights, competition, and profit in a market economy.

Property rights, competition and profit are all factors involved in the efficient allocation of resources in a market economy. The assignment of property rights prevents waste and inefficient use of resources. An example of this is an industrial firm dumping waste into a river, causing water pollution. The river is a free input to the firm because there is no assignment of property rights with an owner demanding compensation for the use of his property. If the firm had to pay for the use of the river, its production costs would be higher and the firm would produce less output for the given level of costs and charge a higher price for its good. The lack of property rights' assignment results in overproduction of the good – too many resources are being used in the production of that good. This may give the firm an undue edge in the market because the firm can charge a lower price than competitors who have to pay for a way to deal with their wastes. The misallocation of resources must be corrected for in some way with fines, requiring pollution abatement technologies, the sale of pollution permits, or whatever. The result is higher costs for the firm who now lowers its production levels. This somewhat corrects for the over allocation of resources and forces the firm to be more competitive.

Competition guarantees a more efficient use of society's resources. Firms have to compete with other firms for the available supply of resources to use in production. They have to compete with other firms to win the consumer's dollar. Competition means that they have to be efficient in order to survive. If they aren't using an efficient production process, they will have higher costs than their competitors. This means they will have to charge a higher price for their product than their competitors do. Consumer's who shop around will buy the product at the lowest possible price. Eventually the higher cost, more inefficient firm will be forced out of business. Consumers, who are voting with their dollars, are buying the same product at a lower price from the competitors of the higher priced firm. The lower priced, more efficient firms will have higher sales and profits while the inefficient, higher cost firms will experience losses. Lack of profits result in the inefficient firms leaving the industry as the owner's resources are shifted into industries where they earn a better rate of return. Consumers are basically telling the inefficient firms that they don't want their inefficient waste of resources.

Markets function on the basis of competition and competition leads to efficiency in the use of resources. Resource owners want to get the best price for their resource. Producers want to get the best price for their output. Buyers want to get the best deal for the product they are purchasing. All of these factors combine to result in an efficient allocation of resources or resources that are being used in accordance with the preferences of society. Inefficiency is eliminated by competition in the market place and the inefficient firm goes out of business due to lack of profit.

Skill 5.2d   **Explain and analyze how prices reflect the relative scarcity of goods and services and perform the function of allocation in a market economy.**

Prices serve an important function in a market economy. Prices are determined by the interaction of demand and supply in the market place. Resource prices are determined by the demand and supply for that resource. Relatively speaking, the scarcer the supply is, the higher the price of the resource is: the more abundant the supply is, the lower the price of the resource. Diamonds cost more than water. Water is more abundant than diamonds are and is easier to obtain.

Prices function to allocate the supply of a resource or good to those who are willing and able to pay for it. The supply curve is based on the production costs of sellers and embodies the sellers selling decisions, i.e., the quantities of a good he is willing and able to sell at different prices during a given period of time. If his production costs increase, he will be willing to sell fewer units of the good at each price. This is reflected by a leftward shift in his supply curve. If his production costs decrease, he will be willing to sell more units of the good at each price. This is represented by a rightward shift of his supply curve. This is the supply or **selling side** of the market.

On the **buying side** of the market, the consumers buying decisions are given by the demand curve. This curve represents the quantities of the good the consumer is willing and able to purchase at different prices during a given period of time. If a consumer is willing and able to buy more at each price, there is a rightward shift of his demand curve. A leftward shift of the demand curve represents a decrease in demand, a situation where the buyer is willing and able to buy fewer units of the good at each price. Putting the demand and supply side together, we have the market equilibrium at the intersection of demand and supply. The equilibrium price equates the buying and selling decisions of each side, respectively.

Those buyers and sellers who are willing and able to transact at the equilibrium price are included in the market. Those who can't or won't transact at the market price are excluded from the market. This is true whether the good is a resource or an output. Both input and output markets function on the basis of supply and demand. Both markets arrive at equilibrium prices that allocate the resource or good to those who are willing to transact at that price. If the resource market is labor, the wage rate is the equilibrium price for occupations like clerks.

The firm can hire all of the clerks it wants at the market rate. If he isn't willing to pay the market wage, the clerk will find employment someplace else. He has little incentive to pay higher than the market rate, because of the supply of clerks available at the market rate. If the employer wants to hire a professional, like an engineer, he has to pay a higher rate, because of the greater amount of education and skills involved in the job. If he isn't willing to pay the higher rate, he won't find an engineer who will work for him. Again, price is performing its allocation function that results in an efficient allocation of resources. If prices weren't based on scarcity, they couldn't perform this allocation function and there wouldn't be an efficient allocation of resources.

Skill 5.2e   Explain the process by which competition among buyers and sellers determines a market price.

Market prices are the result of the competition between buyers and sellers in the market place. Prices are determined by supply and demand. The supply side of the market represents the scarcity of resources that determines the price the producer pays for his inputs. The firm has to compete with other firms for the available supply of inputs. He has to be able to pay the market price or better in order to attract the inputs that he needs. The supply curve is calculated from the firm's cost curves. A change in the firm's costs results in a change in the supply curve. The lower the firm's costs are at any given price level, the greater the amount of output the firm can produce. Firms want to be cost efficient in order to be competitive because the firm also has to compete for the consumer's dollar in the output market. If the firm's production costs are higher than his competitors, then his competitors will be able to charge a lower price for their product and still be profitable. The cost inefficient firm will experience losses at that price and eventually be forced out of business.

On the buying side of the market, the consumers demand curve is based on his preferences, tastes, income and the price of other goods. The consumer has numerous goods that he wants to buy but is constrained by his income. The demand curve indicates what consumers are willing and able to do subject to their income **constraint**. An increase in the consumer's income, results in an increase in demand for most goods. These goods are referred to as normal goods. A decrease in income means that consumer demands smaller quantities of goods. The consumer's income comes from the input market where he sells whatever skills he has at the best rate. He has to compete with other laborers for the available income he receives that he can spend on goods and services.

Putting the demand side together with the supply side, we arrive at a market price. The intersection of demand and supply represents the market equilibrium price and quantity at which buyers and sellers and willing to transact. Buyers who want the product bid up the price for the available supply. A higher price will result in a larger quantity supplied because it is more profitable for the firm.

Sellers are willing and able to supply larger quantities at higher prices than they are at lower prices. All of these markets are functioning on the basis of competition and it is this competition that results in market prices that reflect an efficient allocation of resources. If prices do not accurately reflect the scarcity of an input, then there is a distortion in production costs, as in the case of pollution, that carries through to the output market and the price of the product. In this case the output price does not accurately reflect the production costs or the scarcity of the factors of production used in its production. The result is an under allocation or over allocation of resources, depending on the situation. This means that society is not getting exactly what it wants for its dollar.

Skill 5.2f   **Describe the effect of price controls on buyers and sellers.**

Price controls interfere with the market's ability to arrive at an equilibrium price that equates supply and demand. Price controls rob the market of what is called the rationing function of prices, the ability to adjust to equate demand and supply. Price controls are administratively imposed prices above or below the market equilibrium.

A price imposed above the market equilibrium price is called a **price floor**. It represents the highest price that can be charged for the good. The price of the good cannot rise above the price floor. At the imposed floor price, the market cannot equate supply and demand. The higher legally mandated price results in a larger quantity supplied as sellers are willing to supply larger quantities at higher prices than they are at lower prices. The higher price also means that buyers don't want as many units of output. Buyers are willing and able to buy larger quantities at lower prices than at higher prices. So the legally imposed floor price results in a situation where quantity supplied is greater than quantity demanded, or there is a surplus of the good and there is no way that the market can function to eliminate the surplus because it can't lower prices to attract more buyers. This has been the situation in agriculture for years. Price supports needed for the farmer's survival result in overproduction and surpluses in agricultural goods.

A **price ceiling** is a legally imposed price below the market equilibrium. Its purpose is to keep prices from rising, as in periods of severe inflation. With a price ceiling, the lower price results in a smaller quantity supplied by sellers. The lower price means an increase in quantity demanded by buyers, who want to buy larger quantities at lower prices than at higher prices. The result is a situation where quantity demanded exceeds quantity supplied, or a shortage. There is no way for the market to eliminate the shortage with buyers bidding up the price for the available quantity.

The legally imposed price means that the price can't rise to eliminate the shortage and the shortage will remain as long as the price controls are in effect. When the price ceilings are lifted, prices usually shoot upwards as buyers and sellers try to make up for lost time.

Price controls, whether they are ceilings or floors, are never a good way to deal with economic problems. The market cannot function to remove the distortion in it. They result in misallocations of resources. Price floors, as in agriculture, result in an over allocation of resources to that industry and an overproduction of output that the market cannot eliminate by lowering prices. The resources used in agriculture are not being used elsewhere where they might be more productive. The price ceiling causes the opposite – an underallocation of resources and underproduction of output. Society is not getting enough of the output that it wants and is not having its resources used in the manner it wants them used in. Any interference with the market results in a misallocation.

Skill 5.2g   Analyze how domestic and international competition in a market economy affects the quality, quantity, and price of goods and services produced.

The introduction of international competition results in greater efficiency in the allocation of resources. International trade that takes place on the basis of comparative advantage results in lower output prices and higher resource prices. According to trade theory, nations or regions should specialize in the production of the good which they can produce at a relatively lower cost than the other country can.

In other words, if in country A one unit of X costs one unit of Y, and in country B one unit of X costs three units of Y, good X is cheaper in country A and good Y is cheaper in country B. It takes only one third of a unit of X to produce one unit of Y in country B, whereas it takes one unit of Y in country A. Therefore, country B has the **comparative advantage** in the production of Y and country A has the comparative advantage in the production of good X.

Theory says that each country should specialize in the production of the good in which it has the comparative advantage and trade for the other good. This means country B should use all of its resources to produce good Y and trade for good X. Country A should do the opposite and specialize in the production of good X and trade for good Y. Specialization and trade on this basis results in lower prices in both countries, or regions, and greater efficiency in the use of resources. Each country will also experience increased consumption since it is getting the maximum amount of output from its given inputs by specializing according to comparative advantage. Each country, or region, can consume its own goods and the goods it has traded for.

The introduction of national or international competition into a market can result in greater efficiency if the trade is without restrictions, like tariffs or quotas. Consumers in both countries have more output at lower prices. The introduction of competition forces existing firms to be more efficient as they strive to be more efficient in order to be competitive. If they can't compete with the new competition and they don't have any form of protection, they will eventually go out of business. If they go out of business, there will be unemployment until the workers find new jobs.

Adjustments take place in both economies, as with NAFTA, as input and output markets adjust to the new conditions. But the end results, whether free trade is introduced into a new region or trade barriers are being removed between existing trading partners, is that consumers have a wider variety of products, usually of better quality at a lower prices than they had before. There is greater efficiency in the allocation of resources because each resource is being employed in its most productive capacity. The long run result is increased benefits for both of the trading partners. Even if the short run effect of trade is unemployment as resources shift into more productive uses, both countries will benefit in the end.

Skill 5.2h   Explain the role of profit as the incentive to entrepreneurs in a market economy.

Financial incentives are the key to the functioning of a market economy. All market participants are willing to take a risk for the opportunity of being a financial success. **Entrepreneurs** are willing to undertake the risk of new business ventures for the purpose of monetary gain. Resources move into higher than normal rate of return industries because they are attracted by the profit potential. Inventors are willing to take the **risk** of spending time and money trying to come up with new products in the hope of monetary gain. All of these represent the ways financial incentives operate in a market economy.

The existence of economic profits in an industry functions as a market signal to firms to enter the industry. **Economic profits** means there is an above normal rate of return in this industry. As the number of firms increases, the market supply curve shifts to right. Assuming cost curves stay the same, the expansion continues until the economic profits are eliminated and the industry is earning a normal rate of return. Depending on the level of capital intensity, this process might take a few years or it might take many years. The easier it is to shift resources from one industry to another, the faster the process will be. But the expansion will continue as long as there are economic profits to attract firms. Resources will go where they earn the highest rate of return especially if they were in a situation earning a lower than normal rate of return.

Without a profit incentive there would be no reason for firms to spend millions and billions on research and development and technological progress would be almost nonexistent. This was a problem in the planned economies in the Soviet era. There were little or no financial incentives to innovate. Firms met their quotas and targets, workers received their paychecks and that was that. Since the means of production were owned by the state, there was no incentive to improve technology or to develop new production processes. The individual had no reason to take the risks involved in entrepreneurial activities because there was nothing in it for him but a letter of commendation. The results were slow inefficient production processes.

The entrepreneur is willing to take the risks. He knows there is a good probability that his business will fail, but there is also a chance that it will succeed and there is a remote chance that it will be another Microsoft. Given this, entrepreneurs are willing to take the chance and risk their own money and investors are also willing to risk money on the chance that the business venture will be successful or very successful. If the venture isn't successful, meaning it isn't receiving those dollar votes that make it profitable, the consumers are telling that business that they don't want their scarce resources used in that way. Profits are the market signal that indicates the proper allocation of resources in accordance with consumer preferences. Excess profits, or an above normal rate of return, signal an expansion as resources are attracted into the industry.

Skill 5.2i   Describe the functions of the financial markets.

All markets function to effect an efficient allocation of resources, even financial markets. These markets also function on the basis of supply and demand and serve to allocate loanable funds to those who are willing to transact at the market price. The market price of loanable funds is the interest rate. The supply of loanable funds come from savings. Since savings represent dollars of postponed spending, households have to have some form of inducement to save. They have to be compensated in some way to postpone their spending and holding dollars in the form of savings. This inducement or payment for savings dollars is the interest rate. The higher the interest rate is the more dollars households will be willing to save. The interest rate is an opportunity cost. At higher interest rates, the opportunity cost of not saving dollars is higher than at lower interest rates. Thus, the supply of loanable funds curve is upward sloping.

Loanable funds are needed for investment purposes by businesses and by individuals. Borrowers are willing to pay a price for the funds they borrow.

This price is the **interest rate.** Borrowers want more funds at lower interest rates than they do at higher interest rates. This means that the demand for loanable funds curve is downward sloping. We now have the downward sloping demand for loanable funds curve and the upward sloping supply of loanable funds curve. If we put the two curves together then we have the market equilibrium at the point of intersection of demand and supply. This gives the equilibrium rate of interest that equates the quantity demanded and quantity supplied of loanable funds. Lenders and borrowers willing and able to transact at that interest rate are included in the market. Lenders and borrowers who can't or won't transact at that interest rate are excluded from the market. The market interest rate performs an allocative function just as a market price does. The interest rate will adjust to guarantee the equality of quantity demanded and quantity supplied, keeping the market in equilibrium.

Since investment is a component of **Gross Domestic Product** or GDP, the financial markets and their stability is an important part of the economy. Economies need investment funds in order to grow. Economies with higher rates of savings have higher rates of investment and therefore higher growth rates. This is what leads to economic growth. Economies with low rates of savings are economies that don't domestically supply enough funds for investment purposes. These are economies that have lower growth rates. The banking sector with its financial markets is very important for economies. Without a well developed banking center there is no mechanism for savings and therefore investment funds that are required for economic growth. This was the position the former Soviet countries were in after the dissolution of the Soviet Union. The banking system went with the country of Russia and the remainder of the countries had to form their own banking system before they could supply the savings funds needed for investment.

COMPETENCY 5.3   **THE RELATIONSHIP BETWEEN POLITICS AND ECONOMICS**

Skill 5.3a   **Analyze the effects of federal, state, and local policies on the distribution of resources and economic decision-making.**

Government policies, whether they are federal, state or local, affect economic decision-making and in many cases, the distribution of resources. This is the purpose of most economic policies imposed at the federal level. Governments don't implement monetary and fiscal policy at the state or local level, only at the national level. Most state and local laws that affect economic decision-making and the distribution of resources have to do with taxation. If taxes are imposed or raised at the state or local level, the effect is less spending. The purpose of these taxes is to raise revenues for the state and local government, not to affect the level of aggregate demand and inflation. At the federal level, the major purpose of these policies is to affect the level of **aggregate demand** and the **inflation rate** or the **unemployment rate**.

Governments at all three levels affect the distribution of resources and economic decision-making through **transfer payments**. This brings about a **redistribution of income** and to correct the problem of income inequality. Programs like Food Stamps, AFDC (welfare), unemployment compensation, and Medicaid all fall into this category. Technically, these government transfer programs result in a rearrangement of private consumption, not a real reallocation of resources. Price support programs in agriculture also result in a redistribution of income and a misallocation of resources. The imposition of artificially high prices results in too many resources going into agriculture and leads to product surpluses.

Laws can be enacted at all three levels to correct for the problem of **externalities**. An externality occurs when uninvolved third parties are affected by some market activity, like pollution. Dumping obnoxious or poisonous wastes into the air and water means that the air and water are being treated as a free input by the firm. The market does not register all of the costs of production because the firm does not have to pay to use the air or water. The result of free inputs is lower production costs for the firm and an overallocation of resources into the production of the good the firm is producing.

The role for government here is to cause a **redistribution of resources** by somehow shifting all or part of the cost onto the offending firm. They can impose fines, taxes, require pollution abatement equipment, sell pollution permits, etc. Whatever method chosen, this raises the costs of production for the firms and forces them to bear some of the cost. Policies can be enacted in order to encourage labor to migrate from one sector of the economy to another. This is primarily done at the national level. The United States economy is so large that it is possible to have unemployment in different areas while the economy is at full employment. The purpose here is to cause unemployed labor in one area to migrate to another area where there are jobs. State unemployment and labor agencies provide the information for these people.

Skill 5.3b   Describe the economic and social effects of government fiscal policies.

Fiscal policy refers to changes in the levels of government spending and taxation. All three levels of government engage in fiscal policy that has economic and social effects. At the state and local levels, the purpose of government spending and taxes is to run the state and local governments. When taxes are raised at the state or local level, the purpose is to provide revenues for the government to function, not to affect the level of aggregate spending in the economy. Even though, these taxes still have economic and social effects on the local population who has less money to spend. Local merchants may see a decrease in their revenues from less spending, in addition to having to pay taxes themselves. When state and local governments spend money through local programs, like repairing or building roads, the effect is to inject money into the local economy even though the purpose is to promote transportation. The purpose isn't to stimulate spending in the area.

Fiscal policy at the national level differs from that at the state and local levels because the purpose of the fiscal policy is to affect the level of aggregate spending in the economy. One of the functions of the federal government is to promote economic stabilization. This means to correct for inflation and unemployment. The way they do this is through changing the level of government spending and/or the level of taxation.

Inflation occurs when there is too high a level of aggregate spending. There is too much spending in the economy. Producers can't keep up with the demand and the result in rising prices. In this situation the government implements contractionary fiscal policy which consists of a decrease in government spending and/ or an increase in taxes. The purpose is to slow down an economy that is expanding too quickly by enacting policies that result in people having less money to spend. These policies, depending on how they are implemented, will affect the components of aggregate demand – consumption, investment and government spending. Spending on imports will also decrease. The result of the contractionary fiscal policy will be, hopefully, to end the inflation.

Unemployment is another macro economic problem that requires expansionary fiscal policy. Unemployment occurs due to a lack of spending in the economy. There is not enough aggregate demand in the economy to fully employ the labor force. Here the role for government is to stimulate spending. If they can increase spending, producers will increase their output and hire more resources, including labor, thus eliminating the problem of unemployment. Expansionary fiscal policy consists of increasing government spending and/or lowering taxes. The increase in government spending injects money into the economy.

Government programs to build roads mean more jobs. More jobs mean more spending and a higher level of aggregate demand. As producers see an increase in the demand for their product, they increase their output levels. As they expand, they require more resources, including labor. As more of the labor force works, the level of spending increases still further, and so on. Lowering taxes affects the consumption and possibly the investment components of aggregate demand leaving consumers and businesses with more money to spend, thus leading to a higher level of spending and eliminating unemployment.

Skill 5.3c   Describe the aims and tools of monetary policy and its economic and social effects.

Nations need a smoothly functioning banking system in order to experience economic growth. **The Federal Reserve** implements monetary policy through the banking system and it is a tool used to promote economic stability at the macro level of the economy. There are three components of monetary policy: the **reserve ratio**, the **discount rate** and **open market operations**. Changes in any of these three components affect the amount of money in the banking system and thus, the level of spending in the economy.

The **reserve ratio** refers to the portion of deposits that banks are required to hold as vault cash or on deposit with the Fed. The purpose of this reserve ratio is to give the Fed a way to control the money supply. These funds can't be used for any other purpose. When the Fed changes the reserve ratio, it changes the money creation and lending ability of the banking system. When the Fed wants to expand the money supply it lowers the reserve ratio, leaving banks with more money to loan. This is one aspect of expansionary monetary policy. When the reserve ratio is increased, this results in banks having less money to make loans with, which is a form of contractionary monetary policy, which leads to a lower level of spending in the economy.

Another way in which monetary policy is implemented is by changing the **discount rate**. When banks have temporary cash shortages, they can borrow from the Fed. The interest rate on the funds they borrow is called the discount rate. Raising and lowering the discount rate is a way of controlling the money supply. Lowering the discount rate encourages banks to borrow from the Fed, instead of restricting their lending to deal with the temporary cash shortage.

By encouraging banks to borrow, their lending ability is increased and this results in a higher level of spending in the economy. Lowering the discount rate is a form of **expansionary monetary policy**. Discouraging bank lending by raising the discount rate, then is a form of **contractionary monetary policy**.

The final tool of monetary policy is called **open market operations**. This consists of the Fed buying or selling government securities with the public or with the banking system. When the Fed sells bonds, it is taking money out of the banking system. The public and the banks pay for the bonds, thus resulting in fewer dollars in the economy and a lower level of spending. The Fed selling bonds is a form of contractionary monetary policy that leads to a lower level of spending in the economy. The Fed is expanding the money supply when it buys bonds from the public or the banking system because it is paying for those bonds with dollars that enter the income-expenditures stream. The result of the Fed buying bonds is to increase the level of spending in the economy.

Skill 5.3d Assess the tradeoff between efficiency and equality in modern mixed economies, using social policies as examples.

Modern mixed economies do not result in an equal distribution of income for all of their members. Some people are very rich and some people are very poor. The remainder of the population is somewhere in-between. The reason is that not everyone has the same resource skills to supply in the input market from which they derive their income. The fact that they don't supply the same skills means that they don't all receive the same factor income. Resource owners supplying highly demanded rare skills receive more compensation than those supplying little or no skills: the more abundant the factor skill or lack of skills, the lower the factor compensation.

An efficient economy does not result in an equal or equitable distribution of income. This is a fact of capitalism. A role for government then is to implement certain kinds of social policies to try to correct for the income inequality resulting from a market economy. These policies basically effect a redistribution of income from those in the higher income brackets to those in the lower income brackets. There are different ways of accomplishing this income redistribution.

One way of redistributing income is through the federal income tax system. Taxes can be progressive, regressive or proportional. A **progressive tax** is when the tax rate increases as income increases. Those in higher income brackets pay a larger percentage of their income in taxes than those in lower income brackets do. The federal income tax is a progressive tax. A **regressive tax** is the opposite, where the tax rate decreases as the level of income increases. Here, the tax rate is higher on lower income brackets than on higher income brackets. The social security tax is in this category. A **proportional tax** is where the tax rate is the same for all income levels. The progressive tax is based on the idea of equity, that the tax burden should be heavier on people with higher income than on people with lower incomes.

There are many social programs that distribute transfer payments. This is another way of bringing about a redistribution of income and trying to correct for the inequities of a mixed economy. Transfers payment programs are programs like food stamps, Aid to Families with Dependent Children (AFDC) which people refer to as welfare, Medicaid, etc. All of these programs are redistributing tax dollars from the upper income levels to the lower income levels. Most of these programs provide aid to the lower income levels for a specific purpose, whether its food, medical care, support of children or whatever. With the exception of AFDC, they are known as in-kind programs because the aid is geared to a specific area and supplies the good or service instead of just supplying dollars for them to spend in whatever way they want.

Agricultural price support programs also bring about a redistribution of income from the population to the agricultural sector by legally mandating prices higher than the market. The farmers could not survive without this program and they produce the food for the nation. All of these programs are implemented to try to correct for some of the inequities that result from a market economy.

Skill 5.3e   Apply the principles of economic decision-making to a current or historical social problem in America.

America, like other countries, has experienced the social problem of discrimination. **Discrimination** occurs when one group does not have the same opportunities in spite of having the same qualifications as other members of society. **Opportunities** refer to things like salary, job access, promotion and occupations. **Qualifications** mean things like education, training, abilities and experiences. Equals are not treated equally.

The existence and practice of discrimination are contrary to economic theory. Economics assumes that all economic agents act rationally. The practice of discrimination, especially in labor markets, is not consistent with economic theory because it is not rational because it prevents people from working in their most productive capacity. This results in lower output levels and higher costs.

There are several economic theories that try to explain discrimination. Theorists tried explaining discrimination in terms of market power: a discriminating agent has enough market power to exploit the discriminated against entity. In the output market this would mean charging a higher price to the discriminated against entity and in the input market this means paying a lower wage to the discriminated against entity. Discrimination would have to be industry wide for the practice of wage discrimination to exist or the discriminated against worker would just find employment elsewhere. However, if there is industry wide wage discrimination, the result is a lower wage bill for the employer. If this is true, then the conclusion is that the market promotes discrimination and it won't be eliminated without some kind of legal action to eliminate the practice. The market power model is not based on prejudice.

What if discrimination is based on prejudice of some kind? Then you have a situation where the employer is willing to pay to distance themselves from the discriminated against group. Employer prejudice results in the employer paying the discriminated against employee a lower wage than he pays to other workers: the greater the amount of prejudice, the lower the wage, even if the employee is a better worker. In other words, the employer is willing to pay a premium wage to employees that are not a member of the discriminated against group. This explains the existence of wage differentials. Discrimination has to be in some way profitable for the employer or it couldn't last. Discrimination with prejudice can involve non-monetary factors that enter into the situation.

There are other kinds of labor market discrimination. Human capital discrimination refers to individuals not having the same training or educational opportunities. Wage, employment and job discrimination occur in the labor market when individuals don't have the same opportunities in these areas. Employment discrimination refers to the working group that bears the burden of unemployment, wage and job discrimination mean that a group does not have the same opportunity in terms of salary and occupation.

COMPETENCY 5.4   ELEMENTS OF THE U.S. LABOR MARKET IN A GLOBAL SETTING

Skill 5.4a   Describe the circumstances surrounding the establishment of principal American labor unions, procedures that unions use to gain benefits for their members, and the effects of unionization, the minimum wage, and unemployment insurance.

Labor unions in America arose in response to deplorable working conditions. Employees had no say in their working conditions and began to join forces to try to obtain some input. Viewed in this perspective, the history of the labor movement can be traced back to the colonial period as workers banded together and with other organizations in support of different goals. The workers that engaged in these activities were subject to actions from dismissal to blacklisting. It wasn't until 1881 that the first permanent union structure was founded on the principles of **Samuel Gompers**. This became known as the **American Federation of Labor** and was based on three principles.

The first principle is **practical business unionism**, which is the belief that unions should only concern themselves with the problems of their members: working conditions, hours, wages, job security, etc. The second principle is **political neutrality**. Unions should stay out of politics, and the government should stay out of the union movement and the collective bargaining process. The third principle is **trade autonomy**, the belief that unions should be organized on the basis of trade. There should be one union for each craft or trade; there should not be unions consisting of members from all trades. The AFL organized only craft or trade workers, and not industrial workers. The large pool of industrial workers was eventually organized by the Congress of Industrial Organization, and in 1955 the two merged to become the AFL-CIO.

The unions have various methods they can use to obtain benefits for their members. They have supported the enactment of various kinds of labor law legislation that eventually regulated both sides of the labor market, union and employer from various unfair labor and union practices, like **yellow-dog contracts, boycotts, featherbedding,** and **hot cargo clauses**. They have also supported legislation that resulted in minimum wage and unemployment insurance.

Supporting and opposing legislation isn't the only way of obtaining benefits for members. The most direct way of obtaining benefits is through the collective bargaining process. **Collective bargaining** refers to the negotiating of a labor agreement or the settling of a grievance under an existing contract. When the union and the employee can't come to terms, there is always the weapon of the strike. During a **strike** the union members withhold their labor services. The purpose is to put financial pressure on the employer. The employer can respond with a lock-out, which puts pressure on the union and the workers. Eventually an agreement is reached, with or without a strike or lock-out.

Unions have benefited their members tremendously over the years in terms of gaining wage and benefit concessions from employers. **Minimum wage** legislation is a legally mandated price support that doesn't really affect union members since their wages are usually well above the minimum. **Unemployment Insurance** is a program that provides income for unemployed workers. The unemployed individual does not have to be a union member to collect unemployment.

Skill 5.4b   Analyze the current U.S. economy and the global labor market.

The United States is a well endowed economy with a diversified resource base, yet it is still dependent on the global economy to supply goods and labor that it cannot supply itself or to perform tasks that it cannot perform at the same level of costs. The United States can best be characterized as a **capital-technology intensive economy**. This means that its strength is in the production of goods requiring capital and technology, which is why we import so many labor intensive goods that other countries can produce relatively cheaper than we can. This is why there is so much foreign outsourcing with call centers moving to India, Pakistan and other countries. But the United States also needs foreign labor for its agricultural sector. Without this low-cost foreign labor, farmers would have to pay much higher wages to attract domestic workers to the agricultural sector. This would result in higher food costs.

Despite its well diversified resource base, the United States cannot and does not produce all of the goods it consumes, even in agriculture. Coffee and tea are imported, as well as other foods, because we do not have sufficient resources conducive to the production of coffee and tea. We import a great deal of labor intensive clothing products because they can be produced at a relatively lower cost in other parts of the world, which is also a way of providing employment to workers in other parts of the world. There is not too much of a demand for labor intensive workers in the United States. There is more of a demand for capital intensive workers or technology workers or technologically oriented providers of services.

Rapid technological change causes effects throughout the economy as firms, industries and workers try to keep up. Rapidly changing technology costs money to implement. Firms have to determine whether or not they should innovate and when by looking at what they gain and if it is profitable. Do they have the labor capability? If not, how do they attract the labor they need? Today's labor force is highly mobile and moves around the country for employment purposes. A new plant opening in a particular region will possibly attract labor from other areas as workers go where the jobs are. So inter- and intra-regional shifts in employment are not uncommon as workers train for new jobs and move around to take employment. Some of this is also in response to international competition that makes certain job skills obsolete as plants move out of the country to benefit from lower wages or outsource for the same reason.

International competition brings about a restructuring of the labor market as firms leave the high-wage countries like the United States and locate their operations in low-wage countries to keep their costs low. The displaced workers must acquire new skills to make them employable in areas where there is a demand for labor. This may mean more than just retraining – it may mean acquiring the skills for an entirely different occupation.

The current United States economy is undergoing these changes and will continue to adjust as NAFTA continues and as practices like outsourcing and locating overseas continue.

Skill 5.4c   Analyze wage differences between jobs and professions.

When we talk about **wage differentials**, we are not always referring to skill level. If all workers and all jobs were homogeneous, there would be no wage differences. All workers and all jobs would be identical. Where the supply of labor curve intersects the demand for labor curve would result in one equilibrium wage rate. But this isn't the case. Workers and jobs are not all alike. There are differences, or workers are heterogeneous and jobs are heterogeneous.

Heterogeneity gives rise to wage differences. Wage differences can exist for a variety of reasons. There can be heterogeneity in jobs or differences in jobs which result in a compensating factor to wage differentials. There is some undesirable aspect to a certain employment. It might be location, danger, benefits, etc., whatever it is the employee has to be compensated for it or he won't accept the employment. These non-wage characteristics affect the placement of the supply of labor curve, i.e., the number of workers willing and able to work at different wage rates. The greater the differences between the jobs, the larger the wage differentials will be. Compare the danger involved in high-rise window washing and a groundskeeper. The window washer is exposed to greater danger and must therefore have a higher wage than the groundskeeper in order to compensate him for the risk and danger.

Heterogeneity among workers also results in wage differences. All workers are not alike. They differ in terms of education, training, skills, abilities, etc. Workers belong to different groups based on these characteristics. There is competition between workers within the same group but not with workers of other groups. For example, waitresses compete with other waitresses for the available jobs. Waitresses do not compete with bank presidents for the same jobs. They are basically in different labor markets with different demand and supply curves.

The way people move to different groups is to acquire education, training and skills that qualify them for the characteristics of a different group. This is technically called **investing in human capital**. The amount of investment in human capital then is a source of wage differences. Workers should be paid based on their skills, education and productivity. More highly skilled workers are paid more than those without skills.

There may be higher paying jobs in a different region that the laborer doesn't know about, or if he knows about them, there is something that prevents migration to the high wage area. The end result of migration is equalization of wages as the supply of labor curves shift in both areas reflecting the changes in quantity of workers.

Skill 5.4d   Analyze the effects of international mobility of capital, labor, and trade on the U.S. economy.

Markets, today, are international in almost all respects. In this age of computers and technology, doing business across international borders is almost as easy as doing business with the firm down the block. The **international mobility** of capital, labor and trade affects all markets and sectors of the economy, except defense. International mobility of factors means that the factors will go where they earn the highest rate of return, whether the factor is capital or labor.

These events are happening today with foreign **outsourcing** and relocating plants overseas in response to lower costs. Call centers are being relocated or established in foreign countries like Pakistan, India and other countries because of lower labor and other costs and a technology that is permissive. These lower costs make the company more profitable. Foreign outsourcing accomplishes the same goal. It represents a lower cost that allows a firm to be more profitable. Relocating a plant in another country means the differential is great enough to cover shipping costs.

Financial capital also belongs to international markets. Investment funds are truly international, going wherever the highest rate of return is. If interest rates are higher in country A than in country B, funds will flow from country B to country A in response to the higher rate of return. This interest rate differential results in an appreciation in country A's currency relative to country B's currency, as units of currency from country B are converted into country A's currency. The flow will continue as long as the interest rate differential exists. Borrowers needing loans will also engage in an international search for the best interest rate instead of confining themselves to domestic markets with higher rates. None of these activities is difficult in the era of computers.

All of these factors tie in tightly with international trade. Markets are international. Firms locate plants where labor costs are low in order to increase their profitability. Workers migrate across international borders in response to better employment terms and conditions. Countries specialize in the production of the goods which they can produce at a lower cost than their trading partners. All these factors combine to cause structural changes in the economy as the various sectors adjust to the changes brought about by membership in the international economy. These displaced workers have to find employment and may require retraining. Businesses must diversify and innovate enough to make them competitive in the international economy. This may mean developing new products and services that are demanded in international markets.

COMPETENCY 5.5   AGGREGATE ECONOMIC BEHAVIOR OF THE AMERICAN ECONOMY

Skill 5.5a   Describe how measures of economic output are adjusted using indexes.

Most measures of economic output are expressed in terms of dollars. The purchasing power of the dollar can change due to inflation and economic growth. Therefore, the price level and the purchasing power of the dollar are very important. Comparing output figures, like **Gross Domestic Product**, over the years, shows fluctuations from year to year. Are these fluctuations due to actual differences in the level of output or are they due to inflation and changes in the price level? There is no way to know unless the figures are expressed in terms of constant dollars. This is a way of adjusting for inflation or controlling for the changes in the value of the dollar. **Real GDP** or **constant dollar GDP** is GDP adjusted for inflation. **Nominal, current dollar** or **unadjusted GDP** refers to GDP figures in dollars that have not been adjusted for inflation.

The construction and use of the GDP deflator is rather simple. The first step is to select one year to be the base year and then use that year to construct the price index. It doesn't matter what year is selected as long as the information is stated. The formula is very simple.

$$\text{Price Index} = \frac{\text{Price in any year}}{\text{Price in base year}} \times 100$$

This index number then is used to compute the real GDP figure. The formula is given below:

$$\text{Real GDP} = \frac{\text{Nominal GDP}}{\text{Index Number}}$$

The above formula takes the GDP figure for any year and expresses it in base year dollars. Now perusing a column of GDP figures over any period of time has all of them expressed in dollars that have the same value as the dollar has in the base year. That's why it doesn't matter which year is used as the base year. Any differences in GDP are the result of real changes in the level of output and not due to changes in the dollar's value. Now meaningful comparisons can be made between the years. Economists never want to work with raw unadjusted data. You can look at the figures over the years but they are literally meaningless because you don't know if the changes are from actual output levels or changes in the dollar.

You will rarely have to construct your own price index and GDP deflator. Data figures are usually reported both ways and will say so in a footnote or somewhere around the table. The year used as the base year will also be reported somewhere near the figures. When you use these output figures for anything, you always state whether they are adjusted or unadjusted, and if the figures are adjusted, what year is used as the base year. If you are working with unadjusted figures, you must state that fact and be very careful of any inferences and conclusion that you draw.

Skill 5.5b **Define, calculate, and analyze the significance of the changes in rates of unemployment, inflation, and real Gross Domestic Product.**

Real GDP, the unemployment rate and the inflation rate are economic indicators. They are revealing what is happening in the economy, how poorly or how well it is doing. Inflation refers to a rise in the general level of prices which causes a decrease in the purchasing power of the dollar. This basically means that one dollar does not buy as much as it did before. Policy makers need information on inflation because it calls for contractionary policies in an economy that is expanding too rapidly. The inflation rate is computed from index numbers. The formula is very simple.

$$\text{Price Index} = \frac{\text{Price in any year}}{\text{Price in base year}} \times 100$$

Any year in the series can be selected as the base year and it is then used to compute the index number for the rest of the years, as given in the above formula.

The index numbers are then used to compute the inflation rate using the formula below:

$$\text{Inflation Rate} = \frac{\text{this year's index \# - last years index \#}}{\text{Last year's index \#}}$$

The unemployment rate refers to the percentage of the labor force that is unemployed, or:

$$\text{Unemployment Rate} = \frac{\text{Number of People Unemployed}}{\text{Number of People in Labor Force}} \times 100$$

The labor force is not one hundred percent of the population. It includes people who are capable of working and are willing to work and are either working or actively seeking employment. Excluded are people who can't work (under age sixteen, institutionalized) or who could work but chose not to work, like stay at home moms, full-time students, and retirees. The labor force is roughly one-half of the population.

The Gross Domestic Product is a measure of the economy's current output. It is calculated as the sum of its components: consumption, investment, government spending and net exports.

$$GDP = C + I + G + (X-M)$$

Since GDP is a measure of current output and expressed in current dollars, it must be converted to real terms by using the GDP deflator

This index number then is used to compute the real GDP figure. The formula is given below:

$$\text{Real GDP} = \frac{\text{Nominal GDP}}{\text{Index Number}}$$

Real GDP figures, along with the unemployment figures tell us the state of the economy. An economy in a recession needs to be stimulated with expansionary monetary and fiscal policy; just as an economy that is expanding too rapidly and with inflation needs to be slowed down with contractionary monetary and fiscal policy. Economists and government policy makers can work with the figures and determine the strength of the policy that is needed. They also watch the unemployment, inflation and GDP figures to ascertain whether the policy is working, and, if not, what else needs to be done.

Skill 5.5c   Distinguish between short- and long-term interest rates and explain their relative significance.

The **interest rate** is the price the borrower pays to the lender for the privilege of borrowing funds. Since loans are for different periods of time, there are different money market instruments that have different time durations that have different rates of interest. This is where the terms short-term and long-term interest rates comes from. What we are talking about here are the debt obligations of the United States government, or **U.S. Treasury securities**. These are T-bills, T-notes and T-bonds and they differ from one another in time to maturity.

A **T-bill** is a short-term instrument that matures in one year or less. A **T-note** is an intermediate term instrument with a maturity time from one to ten years. The **T-bond** is the long term instrument that matures in over ten years. These fixed income securities are a way of lending money to the U.S. government and carry a specified rate of interest called the coupon. There is an inverse relationship between bond prices and interest rates. This means that when interest rates rise, bond prices fall and vice-versa.

All interest rates are related. Different kinds of bonds of the same time duration that have different coupons differ in terms of risk. This is called the **risk structure of interest rates** and it is affected by risk, liquidity and income tax rules. An example of this would be the difference between a T-note and a municipal bond. Risk refers to the chance of default. U.S. government debt obligations are considered to be free of risk. This is not true of other bonds, especially private bonds. Some bonds have a risk premium, an additional amount of interest to compensate the holder for the risk of default.

Another factor affecting the risk structure is **liquidity**. Bonds do not have to be held to maturity – they can be sold. Liquidity refers to the ease with which the bond can be sold. The more difficult it is to sell the bond, the greater the amount of interest required to compensate the holder of the bond. The income tax rules treat different kinds of bonds in different ways. This also enters into the interest rate.

The **term structure of interest rates** refers to bonds that differ only in their terms of maturity. These bonds have the same risk, liquidity and tax treatment so the only difference between them is the amount of time to maturity. The bonds are all identical with the maturities linked through the term structure of interest rates. Each maturing time period has its own sequence of interest rate bond yields and is referred to as the term structure. The difference between any two securities that mature at different times is the expected interest rate. A plot of the yields on these different maturities results in what is called the yield curve. This plot describes the term structure of interest rates or the relationship between interest rates during different times to maturity. Longer term interest rates are based on short term interest rate factors and corporate expectations about future interest rates is probably the simplest way of explaining this.

COMPETENCY 5.6   INTERNATIONAL TRADE AND THE AMERICAN ECONOMY

Skill 5.6a   Use the concept of comparative advantage to identify the costs of and gains from international trade.

The theory of **comparative advantage** says that trade should be based on the comparative opportunity costs between two nations. The nation that can produce a good more cheaply should specialize in the production of that good and trade for the good in which it has the comparative disadvantage. In this way both nations will experience gains from trade. A basis for trade exists if there are differing comparative costs in each country. Suppose country A can produce ten units of good X or ten units of good Y with its resources. Country B can produce 30 units of X or 10 units of Y with its resources. What are the relative costs in each country? In country A, one X costs one unit of Y and in country B one X costs three units of Y. Good Y is cheaper in country B than it is in country A, 1/3X = 1 Y in country B versus 1Y = 1X in country A. Country B has the comparative advantage in the production of Y and country A has the comparative advantage in the production of good X. According to trade theory each country should specialize in the production of the good in which it has the comparative advantage. Country B will devote all of its resources to the production of good Y and country A will devote all of its resources to the production of good X. Each country will trade for the good in which it has the comparative disadvantage.

To determine the gains from trade, we must first consider the pre-trade production and consumption positions of both countries. In A, the pre-trade position was where they could have either 10 units of X or 10 units of Y or any combination in between. Let's assume country A chose a combination of 7Y and 3X. In country B, their resources allowed either 30 units of Y or 10 units of X or any combination in between. Let's assume country B chose the combination of 18Y and 4 X. Now let's consider the production and consumption situation before and after trade. Before trade, the total production of good Y was 18 from country B and 7 from country A for a total of 25Y. After trade, total world production is 30Y, with country B specializing in the production of Y. For good X, the pre-trade situation was 3 units of X from country A and 4 units of X from country B, for a total of 7 units of X. After trade, with country A specializing in the production of X, total world production of X is 10 units. Specialization and trade according to comparative advantage results in the world having 30Y rather than 25Y and 10X instead of 7X. This increase is referred to as the gains from trade. Both countries have higher consumption levels of both good due to specialization. This example refers to free unrestricted trade. Trade barriers introduce distortions.

Skill 5.6b   Compare and contrast the arguments for and against trade restrictions during the Great Depression with those among labor, business, and political leaders today.

Trade theory tells us that free unrestricted trade, without any barriers is best. Free trade leads to the most efficient use of world resources. Any kind of protective measure reduces the volume of world trade and causes higher levels of unemployment and lower levels of income and consumption. Yet nations of the world resort to protective measures when they experience economic difficulties.

During the Great Depression in the 1930s, the U.S. enacted the **Smoot-Hawley Tariff Act** which raised tariffs to their highest level in U.S. history. The result was retaliation from other countries. These actions contributed to the severity and duration of the Depression. These were basically what are called **Beggar Thy Neighbor** policies because the purpose was to protect domestic jobs at the expense of the trading partners.

The arguments heard for protection today are pretty much the same as they were in the 1930s. The job protection argument is still being heard. The way to protect American jobs is to restrict imports. Americans will buy more domestically produced goods thus leading to an increase in demand for domestic workers. This is the usual argument heard during periods of recession. Beggar Thy Neighbor policies export unemployment to the trading partners.

Another commonly used argument is based on **national security**. This argument says that industries vital to national defense should be protected from foreign competition – that a nation should be self-sufficient in goods it needs for national defense. There is some truth to this argument but how do you decide which industries are vital and necessary. Fighters and bombers are essential but what about the inputs used to make them like computers and paper clips? Where do you draw the line?

New industries usually ask for protection from the more developed foreign competitors. This is called the Infant Industry argument which says give the new industries protection until they can grow and compete in the world market. It makes some economic sense, except the industry will adjust to operating with protection because its removes the pressure for them to be competitive.

Another common argument is that the high wage domestic labor should be protected from the low wage country imports. People will buy the lower priced foreign imports thus lowering demand for the domestically produced product and leading to unemployment in those high wage industries. The problem is that these high wage industries should not be trying to compete with the comparative advantage of the low wage countries. This kind of behavior isn't consistent with trade theory.

And finally, there is the call for an **anti-dumping tariff** when a nation catches another selling a good at a lower price in the foreign market than in its own domestic market. Dumping is very difficult to prove. So even though we are seventy years past the Great Depression, we still have the same arguments being used for protective trade measures.

Skill 5.6c Analyze the significance of the changing role of international political borders and territorial sovereignty in a global economy.

GATT, NAFTA, WTO and EU are all forms of **trade liberalization**. The **GATT** or **General Agreements on Tariffs and Trade** was founded in 1947 and today, as the **World Trade Organization** or **WTO**, has 147 member nations. It was based on three principles. The first was Most Favored National status for all members. This means trade based on comparative advantage without tariffs or trade barriers. The second principle was elimination of quotas and third, reduction of trade barriers through multi-lateral trade negotiations. The WTO is the successor to the GATT and came into being in 1995. Its objective is to promote free trade. As such it administers trade agreements, settles disputes, and provides a forum for trade discussions and negotiations.

The **North American Free Trade Agreement** or **NAFTA** and the **EU** are both forms of regional economic integration. Economic integration is a method of trade liberalization on a regional basis. NAFTA represents the lowest form or first step in the regional trade integration process. A **free trade area** consists for two or more countries that abolish tariffs and other trade barriers among themselves but maintain their own trade barriers against the rest of the world. A free trade area allows for specialization and trade on the basis of comparative advantage within the area. The next stage in the integration process is a customs union, which is a free trade area that has common external tariffs against non-members. The third stage is a common market which is a customs union with free factor mobility within the area. Factors migrate where they find the best payment within the area. The fourth state is economic union where the common market members have common or coordinated economic and social policies. The final stage is monetary union where the area has a common currency. This is what Europe is working toward. They have a common market with elements of the fourth and fifth stages of integration.

The WTO does not change or blur the significance of political borders and territorial sovereignty in the same way that economic integration does, although the WTO is a way of settling trade disputes that arise from the different integration agreements. In the advanced stages of economic integration the political borders remain, but economic and social policies are common or coordinated and in monetary union, there is one common currency. Each nation is its own independent entity but they give up some sovereignty in the interest of having a successful union.

Trade agreements proliferate in the world today. The Smoot Hawley Tariffs and the rounds of retaliation in the 1930s are what laid the basis for what today are the WTO and the European Union (EU). The GATT and the beginnings of what is now the EU came into being as organizations trying to undo the effects of the Great Depression and the world war. Free trade without trade barriers results in the most efficient use of resources, with higher consumption, employment and income levels for all participants. This is why there are so many free trade agreements being negotiated in today's world.

Skill 5.6d   Describe how international currency exchange rates are determined and their significance.

Nations are free to choose their own form of exchange rate regime. Most major world currencies **float**, with their exchange rate value being determined by supply and demand. This has been the situation since the early 1970s when the regime of fixed exchange rates collapsed. Currency values are relative prices: one currency is expressed in terms of another currency, i.e., U.S. dollars per Deutsche mark, Italian lira per French franc, etc. The term one U.S. dollar has no meaning in world markets without being expressed in terms of another currency. Currency values can be expressed as U.S. dollars per British pound, which is another way of saying how much one British pound cost. They can also be expressed as British pounds per U.S. dollar, or how many British pounds do you get for one U.S. dollar. One is just the reciprocal of the other.

In a **clean float**, supply and demand factors for each currency in terms of another are what determine the equilibrium price or the **exchange rate**. A clean float is a market functioning without any government interference, purely on the basis of demand and supply. Sometimes nations will intervene in the market to affect the value of their currency vis-à-vis the other currency. This situation is referred to as a **managed or dirty float**. A government is not required to intervene to maintain a currency value, as they were under a regime of fixed exchange rates. A government that intervenes in the currency market now does so because it wants to, not because it is required to intervene to maintain a certain exchange rate value.

For example, if the U.S. government thinks the dollar is depreciating too much against the Canadian dollar, the U.S. government will buy U.S. dollars in the open market and pay for them with Canadian dollars. This increases the demand for U.S. dollars and increases the supply of Canadian dollars. The U.S. dollar appreciates, or increases in value, and the Canadian dollar depreciates, or decreases in value, in response to the government intervention. A stronger U.S. dollar means Canadian goods are cheaper for Americans, and American goods are more expensive for Canadians.

Not all nations have floating exchange rate regimes. Some nations base the value of their currency on another nation's currency, or they **tie** or peg their currency value to another currency, usually a trading partner's currency. Then the tied currency moves up or down in the market as the currency it is tied to does. The exchange rate is basically fixed against the currency it is tied to but floats versus the rest of the world. This practice used to be very common.

Fixed exchange rates can lead to various economic problems through the **Balance of Payments**. The only way that nations could correct for Balance of Payment problems was through the imposition of trade restrictions and they tried to bring their exports and imports under control. Since the movement today is towards free trade and specialization according to comparative advantage, floating exchange rates are much more suitable for the goals of the world.

COMPETENCY 6.1   **TOOLS AND PERSPECTIVES OF GEOGRAPHIC STUDY**

Skill 6.1a   **Describe the criteria for defining regions and identify why places and regions are important.**

The earth's surface is made up of 70% water and 30% land. Physical features of the land surface include mountains, hills, plateaus, valleys, and plains. Other minor landforms include deserts, deltas, canyons, mesas, basins, foothills, marshes and swamps. Earth's water features include oceans, seas, lakes, rivers, and canals.

Mountains are landforms with rather steep slopes at least 2,000 feet or more above sea level. Mountains are found in groups called mountain chains or mountain ranges. At least one range can be found on six of the earth's seven continents. North America has the Appalachian and Rocky Mountains; South America the Andes; Asia the Himalayas; Australia the Great Dividing Range; Europe the Alps; and Africa the Atlas, Ahaggar, and Drakensburg Mountains.

Hills are elevated landforms rising to an elevation of about 500 to 2000 feet. They are found everywhere on earth including Antarctica where they are covered by ice.

Plateaus are elevated landforms usually level on top. Depending on location, they range from being an area that is very cold to one that is cool and healthful. Some plateaus are dry because they are surrounded by mountains that keep out any moisture. Some examples include the Kenya Plateau in East Africa, which is very cool. The plateau extending north from the Himalayas is extremely dry while those in Antarctica and Greenland are covered with ice and snow.

Plains are described as areas of flat or slightly rolling land, usually lower than the landforms next to them. Sometimes called **lowlands** (and sometimes located along **seacoasts)** they support the majority of the world's people. Some are found inland and many have been formed by large rivers. This resulted in extremely fertile soil for successful cultivation of crops and numerous large settlements of people. In North America, the vast plains areas extend from the Gulf of Mexico north to the Arctic Ocean and between the Appalachian and Rocky Mountains. In Europe, rich plains extend east from Great Britain into central Europe on into the Siberian region of Russia. Plains in river valleys are found in China (the Yangtze River valley), India (the Ganges River valley), and Southeast Asia (the Mekong River valley).

Valleys are land areas found between hills and mountains. Some have gentle slopes containing trees and plants; others have steep walls and are referred to as canyons. One example is Arizona's Grand Canyon of the Colorado River.

Deserts are large dry areas of land receiving ten inches or less of rainfall each year. Among the better known deserts are Africa's large Sahara Desert, the Arabian Desert on the Arabian Peninsula, and the desert Outback covering roughly one third of Australia.

Deltas are areas of lowlands formed by soil and sediment deposited at the mouths of rivers. The soil is generally very fertile and most fertile river deltas are important crop-growing areas. One well-known example is the delta of Egypt's Nile River, known for its production of cotton.

Mesas are the flat tops of hills or mountains usually with steep sides. Sometimes plateaus are also called mesas. Basins are considered to be low areas drained by rivers or low spots in mountains. Foothills are generally considered a low series of hills found between a plain and a mountain range. Marshes and swamps are wet lowlands providing growth of such plants as rushes and reeds.

Oceans are the largest bodies of water on the planet. The four oceans of the earth are the **Atlantic Ocean**, one-half the size of the Pacific and separating North and South America from Africa and Europe; the **Pacific Ocean**, covering almost one-third of the entire surface of the earth and separating North and South America from Asia and Australia; the **Indian Ocean**, touching Africa, Asia, and Australia; and the ice-filled **Arctic Ocean**, extending from North America and Europe to the North Pole. The waters of the Atlantic, Pacific, and Indian Oceans also touch the shores of Antarctica.

Seas are smaller than oceans and are surrounded by land. Some examples include the Mediterranean Sea found between Europe, Asia, and Africa; and the Caribbean Sea, touching the West Indies, South and Central America. A lake is a body of water surrounded by land. The Great Lakes in North America are a good example.

Rivers, considered a nation's lifeblood, usually begin as very small streams, formed by melting snow and rainfall, flowing from higher to lower land, emptying into a larger body of water, usually a sea or an ocean. Examples of important rivers for the people and countries affected by and/or dependent on them include the Nile, Niger, and Zaire Rivers of Africa; the Rhine, Danube, and Thames Rivers of Europe; the Yangtze, Ganges, Mekong, Hwang He, and Irrawaddy Rivers of Asia; the Murray-Darling in Australia; and the Orinoco in South America. River systems are made up of large rivers and numerous smaller rivers or tributaries flowing into them. Examples include the vast Amazon Rivers system in South America and the Mississippi River system in the United States.

Canals are man-made water passages constructed to connect two larger bodies of water. Famous examples include the **Panama Canal** across Panama's isthmus connecting the Atlantic and Pacific Oceans and the **Suez Canal** in the Middle East between Africa and the Arabian peninsula connecting the Red and Mediterranean Seas.

Weather is the condition of the air which surrounds the day-to-day atmospheric conditions including temperature, air pressure, wind and moisture or precipitation which includes rain, snow, hail, or sleet.

Climate is average weather or daily weather conditions for a specific region or location over a long or extended period of time. Studying the climate of an area includes information gathered on the area's monthly and yearly temperatures and its monthly and yearly amounts of precipitation. In addition, a characteristic of an area's climate is the length of its growing season. Four reasons for the different climate regions on the earth are differences in:

- Latitude,
- The amount of moisture,
- Temperatures in land and water, and
- The earth's land surface.

There are many different climates throughout the earth. It is most unusual if a country contains just one kind of climate. Regions of climates are divided according to latitudes:

- 0 - 23 1 /2 degrees are the "low latitudes"
- 23 1/2 - 66 1/2 degrees are the "middle latitudes"
- 66 1/2 degrees to the Poles are the "high latitudes"

The **low latitudes** are comprised of the rainforest, savanna, and desert climates. The tropical rainforest climate is found in equatorial lowlands and is hot and wet. There is sun, extreme heat and rain--everyday. Although daily temperatures rarely rise above 90 degrees F, the daily humidity is always high, leaving everything sticky and damp. North and south of the tropical rainforests are the tropical grasslands called "savannas," the "lands of two seasons"--a winter dry season and a summer wet season. Further north and south of the tropical grasslands or savannas are the deserts. These areas are the hottest and driest parts of the earth receiving less than 10 inches of rain a year. These areas have extreme temperatures between night and day. After the sun sets, the land cools quickly dropping the temperature as much as 50 degrees F.

The **middle latitudes** contain the Mediterranean, humid-subtropical, humid-continental, marine, steppe, and desert climates. Lands containing the Mediterranean climate are considered "sunny" lands found in six areas of the world: lands bordering the Mediterranean Sea, a small portion of southwestern Africa, areas in southern and southwestern Australia, a small part of the Ukraine near the Black Sea, central Chile, and Southern California. Summers are hot and dry with mild winters. The growing season usually lasts all year and what little rain falls are during the winter months. What is rather unusual is that the Mediterranean climate is located between 30 and 40 degrees north and south latitude on the western coasts of countries.

The humid **subtropical climate** is found north and south of the tropics and is moist indeed. The areas having this type of climate are found on the eastern side of their continents and include Japan, mainland China, Australia, Africa, South America, and the United States--the southeastern coasts of these areas. An interesting feature of their locations is that warm ocean currents are found there. The winds that blow across these currents bring in warm moist air all year round. Long, warm summers; short, mild winters; a long growing season allow for different crops to be grown several times a year. All contribute to the productivity of this climate type which supports more people than any of the other climates.

The **marine climate** is found in Western Europe, the British Isles, the U.S. Pacific Northwest, the western coast of Canada and southern Chile, along with southern New Zealand and southeastern Australia. A common characteristic of these lands is that they are either near water or surrounded by it. The ocean winds are wet and warm bringing a mild, rainy climate to these areas. In the summer, the daily temperatures average at or below 70 degrees F. During the winter, because of the warming effect of the ocean waters, the temperatures rarely fall below freezing.

In northern and central United States, northern China, south central and southeastern Canada, and the western and southeastern parts of the former Soviet Union is found the **"climate of four seasons,"** the **humid continental climate--spring,** summer, fall, and winter. Cold winters, hot summers, and enough rainfall to grow a variety of crops are the major characteristics of this climate. In areas where the humid continental climate is found are some of the world's best farmlands as well as important activities such as trading and mining. Differences in temperatures throughout the year are determined by the distance a place is inland, away from the coasts.

The **steppe or prairie climate** is located in the interiors of large continents like Asia and North America. These dry flatlands are far from ocean breezes and are called prairies or the Great Plains in Canada and the United States and steppes in Asia. Although the summers are hot and the winters are cold as in the humid continental climate, the big difference is rainfall. In the steppe climate, rainfall is light and uncertain, 10 to 20 inches a year mainly in spring and summer and is considered normal. Where rain is more plentiful, grass grows; in areas of less, the steppes or prairies gradually become deserts.

These are found in the Gobi Desert of Asia, central and western Australia, southwestern United States, and in the smaller deserts found in Pakistan, Argentina, and Africa south of the Equator.

The two major climates found in the high latitudes are **"tundra" and "taiga."** The word "tundra" meaning "marshy plain" is a Russian word and aptly describes the climatic conditions in the northern areas of Russia, Europe, and Canada. Winters are extremely cold and very long. Most of the year the ground is frozen but becomes rather mushy during the very short summer months. Surprisingly less snow falls in the area of the tundra than in the eastern part of the United States. However, due to the harshness of the extreme cold, very few people live there and no crops can be raised. Despite having a small human population, many plants and animals are found there.

The **"taiga"** is the northern forest region and is located south of the tundra. In fact, the Russian word "taiga" means 'forest." The world's largest forestlands are found here along with vast mineral wealth and furbearing animals. The climate is extreme that very few people live here, not being able to raise crops due to the extremely short growing season. The winter temperatures are colder and the summer temperatures are hotter than those in the tundra are because the taiga climate region is farther from the waters of the Arctic Ocean. The taiga is found in the northern parts of Russia, Sweden, Norway, Finland, Canada, and Alaska with most of their lands covered with marshes and swamps.

In certain areas of the earth there exists a type of climate unique to areas with high mountains, usually different from their surroundings. This type of climate is called a **"vertical climate"** because the temperatures, crops, vegetation, and human activities change and become different as one ascends the different levels of elevation. At the foot of the mountain, a hot and rainy climate is found with the cultivation of many lowland crops. As one climbs higher, the air becomes **cooler,** the climate changes sharply and different economic activities change, such as grazing sheep and growing corn. At the top of many mountains, snow is found year round.

Skill 6.1b   Explain the nature of map projections and use maps, as well as other geographic representations and technologies to acquire, process, and report information from a spatial perspective.

We use **illustrations** of various sorts because it is often easier to demonstrate a given idea visually instead of orally. Sometimes it is even easier to do so with an illustration than a description. This is especially true in the areas of education and research because humans are visually stimulated. It is a fact that any idea presented visually in some manner is always easier to understand and to comprehend than simply getting an idea across verbally, by hearing it or reading it. Among the more common illustrations used are various types of **maps, graphs and charts**.

Photographs and **globes** are useful as well, but as they are limited in what kind of information that they can show, they are rarely used. Unless, as in the case of a photograph, it is of a particular political figure or a time that one wishes to visualize.

Although maps have advantages over globes and photographs, they do have a major disadvantage. This problem must be considered as well. The major problem of all maps comes about because most maps are flat and the Earth is a sphere. It is impossible to reproduce exactly on a flat surface an object shaped like a sphere. In order to put the earth's features onto a map they must be stretched in some way. This stretching is called **distortion.**

Distortion does not mean that maps are wrong, it simply means that they are not perfect representations of the Earth or its parts. **Cartographers,** or mapmakers, understand the problems of distortion. They try to design them so that there is as little distortion as possible in the maps.

The process of putting the features of the Earth onto a flat surface is called **projection**. All maps are really map projections. There are many different types. Each one deals in a different way with the problem of distortion. Map projections are made in a number of ways. Some are done using complicated mathematics. However, the basic ideas behind map projections can be understood by looking at the three most common types:

(1) **Cylindrical Projections** - These are done by taking a cylinder of paper and wrapping it around a globe. A light is used to project the globe's features onto the paper. Distortion is least where the paper touches the globe. For example, suppose that the paper was wrapped so that it touched the globe at the equator, the map from this projection would have just a little distortion near the equator. However, in moving north or south of the equator, the distortion would increase as you moved further away from the equator. The best known and most widely used cylindrical projection is the **Mercator Projection.** It was first developed in 1569 by Gerardus Mercator, a Flemish mapmaker.

(2) **Conical Projections** - The name for these maps come from the fact that the projection is made onto a cone of paper. The cone is made so that it touches a globe at the base of the cone only. It can also be made so that it cuts through part of the globe in two different places. Again, there is the least distortion where the paper touches the globe. If the cone touches at two different points, there is some distortion at both of them. Conical projections are most often used to map areas in the **middle latitudes**. Maps of the United States are most often conical projections. This is because most of the country lies within these latitudes.

(3) **Flat-Plane Projections** - These are made with a flat piece of paper. It touches the globe at one point only. Areas near this point show little distortion. Flat-plane projections are often used to show the areas of the north and south poles. One such flat projection is called a **Gnomonic Projection**. On this kind of map all meridians appear as straight lines, Gnomonic projections are useful because any straight line drawn between points on it forms a **Great-Circle Route**.

Great-Circle Routes can best be described by thinking of a globe and when using the globe the shortest route between two points on it can be found by simply stretching a string from one point to the other. However, if the string was extended in reality, so that it took into effect the globe's curvature, it would then make a great-circle. A great-circle is any circle that cuts a sphere, such as the globe, into two equal parts. Because of distortion, most maps do not show great-circle routes as straight lines, Gnomonic projections, however, do show the shortest distance between the two places as a straight line, because of this they are valuable for navigation. They are called Great-Circle Sailing Maps.

To properly analyze a given map one must be familiar with the various parts and symbols that most modern maps use. For the most part, this is standardized, with different maps using similar parts and symbols, these can include:

The Title - All maps should have a title, just like all books should. The title tells you what information is to be found on the map.

The Legend - Most maps have a legend. A legend tells the reader about the various symbols that are used on that particular map and what the symbols represent, (also called a **map key**).

The Grid - A grid is a series of lines that are used to find exact places and locations on the map. There are several different kinds of grid systems in use, however, most maps do use the longitude and latitude system, known as the **Geographic Grid System**.

Directions - Most maps have some directional system to show which way the map is being presented. Often on a map, a small compass will be present, with arrows showing the four basic directions, north, south, east, and west.

The Scale - This is used to show the relationship between a unit of measurement on the map versus the real world measure on the Earth. Maps are drawn to many different scales. Some maps show a lot of detail for a small area. Others show a greater span of distance, whichever is being used one should always be aware of just what scale is being used. For instance the scale might be something like 1 inch = 10 miles for a small area or for a map showing the whole world it might have a scale in which 1 inch = 1,000 miles. The point is that one must look at the map key in order to see what units of measurements the map is using.

Maps have four main properties. They are (1) the size of the areas shown on the map. (2) The shapes of the areas, (3) Consistent scales, and (4) Straight line directions. A map can be drawn so that it is correct in one or more of these properties. No map can be correct in all of them.

Equal areas - One property which maps can have is that of equal areas, In an equal area map, the meridians and parallels are drawn so that the areas shown have the same proportions as they do on the Earth. For example, Greenland is about 118th the size of South America, thus it will be show as 118th the size on an equal area map. The **Mercator projection** is an example of a map that does not have equal areas. In it, Greenland appears to be about the same size of South America. This is because the distortion is very bad at the poles and Greenland lies near the North Pole.

Conformality - A second map property is conformality, or correct shapes. There are no maps which can show very large areas of the earth in their exact shapes. Only globes can really do that, however Conformal Maps are as close as possible to true shapes. The United States is often shown by a Lambert Conformal Conic Projection Map.

Consistent Scales - Many maps attempt to use the same scale on all parts of the map. Generally, this is easier when maps show a relatively small part of the earth's surface. For example, a map of Florida might be a Consistent Scale Map. Generally maps showing large areas are not consistent-scale maps. This is so because of distortion. Often such maps will have two scales noted in the key. One scale, for example, might be accurate to measure distances between points along the Equator. Another might be then used to measure distances between the North Pole and the South Pole.

Maps showing physical features often try to show information about the elevation or **relief** of the land. **Elevation** is the distance above or below the sea level. The elevation is usually shown with colors, for instance, all areas on a map which are at a certain level will be shown in the same color.

Relief Maps - Show the shape of the land surface, flat, rugged, or steep. Relief maps usually give more detail than simply showing the overall elevation of the land's surface. Relief is also sometimes shown with colors, but another way to show relief is by using **contour lines**. These lines connect all points of a land surface which are the same height surrounding the particular area of land.

Thematic Maps - These are used to show more specific information, often on a single **theme**, or topic. Thematic maps show the distribution or amount of something over a certain given area. Things such as population density, climate, economic information, cultural, political information, etc ...

Information can be gained looking at a map that might take hundreds of words to explain otherwise. Maps reflect the great variety of knowledge covered by political science. To show such a variety of information maps are made in many different ways. Because of this variety, maps must be understood in order to make the best sense of them.

COMPETENCY 6.2   GEOGRAPHIC DIVERSITY OF NATURAL LANDSCAPES AND HUMAN SOCIETIES

Skill 6.2a   Analyze how unique ecologic settings are encouraged by various combinations of natural and social phenomena, including bio-geographic relationships with climate, soil, and terrain.

Ecology is the study of how living organisms interact with the physical aspects of their surroundings (their environment), including soil, water, air, and other living things. **Biogeography** is the study of how the surface features of the earth – form, movement, and climate – affect living things.

Three levels of environmental understanding are critical:

1. An **ecosystem** is a community (of any size) consisting of a physical environment and the organisms that live within it.

2. A **biome** is a large area of land with characteristic climate, soil, and mixture of plants and animals. Biomes are made up of groups of ecosystems. Major biomes are: desert, chaparral, savanna, tropical rain forest, temperate grassland, temperate deciduous forest, taiga, and tundra.

3. A **habitat** is the set of surroundings within which members of a species normally live. Elements of the habitat include soil, water, predators, and competitors.

Within habitats interactions between members of the species occur. These interactions occur between members of the same species and between members of different species. Interaction tends to be of three types: competition, predation, and symbiosis.

Competition occurs between members of the same species or between members of different species for resources required to continue life, to grow, or to reproduce. For example, competition for acorns can occur between squirrels or it can occur between squirrels and woodpeckers. One species can either push out or cause the demise of another species if it is better adapted to obtain the resource. When a new species is introduced into a habitat, the result can be a loss of the native species and/or significant change to the habitat. For example, the introduction of the Asian plant Kudzu into the American South, has resulted in the destruction of several species because Kudzu grows and spreads very quickly and smothers everything in its path.

Predation occurs when one animal feeds upon another. Predators are organisms that live by hunting and eating other organisms. The species best suited for hunting other species in the habitat will be the species that survives. Larger species that have better hunting skills reduce the amount of prey available for smaller and/or weaker species. This affects both the amount of available prey and the diversity of species that are able to survive in the habitat.

Symbiosis is a condition in which two organisms of different species are able to live in the same environment over an extended period of time without harming one another. In some cases one species may benefit without harming the other. In other cases both species benefit.

Different organisms are by nature best suited for existence in particular environments. When an organism is displaced to a different environment or when the environment changes for some reason, its ability to survive is determined by its ability to adapt to the new environment. **Adaptation** can take the form of structural change, physiological change, or behavioral modification.

Biodiversity refers to the variety of species and organisms, as well as the variety of habitats available on the earth. Biodiversity provides the life-support system for the various habitats and species. The greater the degree of biodiversity, the more species and habitats will continue to survive.

When human and other population and migration changes, climate changes, or natural disasters disrupt the delicate balance of a habitat or an ecosystem, species either adapt or become extinct.

Natural changes can occur that alter habitats – floods, volcanoes, storms, earthquakes. These changes can affect the species that exist within the habitat, either by causing extinction or by changing the environment in a way that will no longer support the life systems. Climate changes can have similar effects. Inhabiting species, however, can also alter habitats, particularly through migration. Human civilization, population growth, and efforts to control the environment can have many negative effects on various habitats. Humans change their environments to suit their particular needs and interests. This can result in changes that result in the extinction of species or changes to the habitat itself. For example, deforestation damages the stability of mountain surfaces. One particularly devastating example is in the removal of the grasses of the Great Plains for agriculture. Tilling the ground and planting crops left the soil unprotected. Sustained drought dried out the soil into dust. When wind storms occurred, the topsoil was stripped away and blown all the way to the Atlantic Ocean.

Skill 6.2b   Analyze the patterns and networks of economic interdependence across the earth's surface during the agricultural, industrial, and post-industrial revolutions, including the production and processing of raw materials, marketing, consumption, transportation, and other measures of economic development.

The **Agricultural Revolution**, initiated by the invention of the plow, led to a thoroughgoing transformation of human society by making large-scale agricultural production possible and facilitating the development of agrarian societies. During the period during which the plow was invented, the wheel, numbers, and writing were also invented. Coinciding with the shift from hunting wild game to the domestication of animals, this period was one of dramatic social and economic change.

Numerous changes in lifestyle and thinking accompanied the development of stable agricultural communities. Rather than gathering a wide variety of plants as hunter-gatherers, agricultural communities become dependent on a limited number of plants or crops that are harvested. Subsistence becomes vulnerable to the weather and dependent upon planting and harvesting times.

Agriculture also required a great deal of physical labor and the development of a sense of discipline. Agricultural communities become sedentary or stable in terms of location. This makes the construction of dwellings appropriate. These tend to be built relatively close together, creating villages or towns.

Stable communities also free people from the need to carry everything with them and the move from hunting ground to hunting ground. This facilitates the invention of larger, more complex tools. As new tools are envisioned and developed it begins to make sense to have some specialization within the society. Skills begin to have greater value, and people begin to do work on behalf of the community that utilizes their particular skills and abilities. Settled community life also gives rise to the notion of wealth. It is now possible to keep possessions.

In the beginning of the transition to agriculture, the tools that were used for hunting and gathering were adequate to the tasks of agriculture. The initial challenge was in adapting to a new way of life. Once that challenge was met, attention turned to the development of more advanced tools and sources of energy. Six thousand years ago the first plow was invented in Mesopotamia. This plow was pulled by animals. Agriculture was now possible on a much larger scale. Soon tools were developed that make such basic tasks as gathering seeds, planting, and cutting grain faster and easier.

It also becomes necessary to maintain social and political stability to ensure that planting and harvesting times are not interrupted by internal discord or a war with a neighboring community. It also becomes necessary to develop ways to store the crop and prevent its destruction by the elements and animals. And then it must be protected from thieves.

Settled communities that produce the necessities of life are self-supporting. Advances in agricultural technology and the ability to produce a surplus of produce create two opportunities: first, the opportunity to trade the surplus goods for other desired goods, and second, the vulnerability to others who steal to take those goods. Protecting domesticated livestock and surplus, as well as stored, crops become an issue for the community. This, in turn, leads to the construction of walls and other fortifications around the community.

The ability to produce surplus crops creates the opportunity to trade or barter with other communities in exchange for desired goods. Traders and trade routes begin to develop between villages and cities. The domestication of animals expands the range of trade and facilitates an exchange of ideas and knowledge.

The **Industrial Revolution** of the eighteenth and nineteenth centuries resulted in even greater changes in human civilization and even greater opportunities for trade, increased production, and the exchange of ideas and knowledge.

The first phase of the Industrial Revolution (1750-1830) saw the mechanization of the textile industry, vast improvements in mining, with the invention of the steam engine, and numerous improvements in transportation, with the development and improvement of turnpikes, canals, and the invention of the railroad.

The second phase (1830-1910) resulted in vast improvements in a number of industries that had already been mechanized through such inventions as the Bessemer steel process and the invention of steam ships. New industries arose as a result of the new technological advances, such as photography, electricity, and chemical processes. New sources of power were harnessed and applied, including petroleum and hydroelectric power. Precision instruments were developed and engineering was launched. It was during this second phase that the Industrial Revolution spread to other European countries, to Japan, and to the United States.

The direct results of the industrial revolution, particularly as they affected industry, commerce, and agriculture, included:

- Enormous increases in productivity
- Huge increases in world trade
- Specialization and division of labor
- Standardization of parts and mass production

- Growth of giant business conglomerates and monopolies
- A new revolution in agriculture facilitated by the steam engine, machinery, chemical fertilizers, processing, canning, and refrigeration

The political results included:

- Growth of complex government by technical experts
- Centralization of government, including regulatory administrative agencies
- Advantages to democratic development, including extension of franchise to the middle class, and later to all elements of the population, mass education to meet the needs of an industrial society, the development of media of public communication, including radio, television, and cheap newspapers
- Dangers to democracy included the risk of manipulation of the media of mass communication, facilitation of dictatorial centralization and totalitarian control, subordination of the legislative function to administrative directives, efforts to achieve uniformity and conformity, and social impersonalization.

The economic results were numerous:

- The conflict between free trade and low tariffs and protectionism
- The issue of free enterprise against government regulation
- Struggles between labor and capital, including the trade-union movement
- The rise of socialism
- The rise of the utopian socialists
- The rise of Marxian or scientific socialism

The social results of the Industrial Revolution include:

- Increase of population, especially in industrial centers
- Advances in science applied to agriculture, sanitation and medicine
- Growth of great cities
- Disappearance of the difference between city dwellers and farmers
- Faster tempo of life and increased stress from the monotony of the work routine
- The emancipation of women
- The decline of religion
- Rise of scientific materialism
- Darwin's theory of evolution

Increased mobility produced a rapid diffusion of knowledge and ideas. Increased mobility also resulted in wide-scale immigration to industrialized countries. Cultures clashed and cultures melded.

Skill 6.2c   Describe the processes, patterns, and functions of human settlements from subsistence agriculture to industrial metropolis.

Human communities subsisted initially as **gatherers** – gathering berries, leaves, etc. With the invention of tools it became possible to dig for roots, hunt small animals, and catch fish from rivers and oceans. Humans observed their environments and soon learned to plant seeds and harvest crops. As people migrated to areas in which game and fertile soil were abundant, communities began to develop. When people had the knowledge to grow crops and the skills to hunt game, they began to understand division of labor. Some of the people in the community tended to agricultural needs while others hunted game.

As habitats attracted larger numbers of people, environments became crowded and there was competition. The concept of division of labor and sharing of food soon came, in more heavily populated areas, to be managed. Groups of people focused on growing crops while others concentrated on hunting. Experience led to the development of skills and of knowledge that make the work easier. Farmers began to develop new plant species and hunters began to protect animal species from other predators for their own use. This ability to manage the environment led people to settle down, to guard their resources, and to manage them.

Camps soon became villages. Villages became year-round settlements. Animals were domesticated and gathered into herds that met the needs of the village. With the settled life it was no longer necessary to "travel light." **Pottery** was developed for storing and cooking food.

By 8000 BCE, culture was beginning to evolve in these villages. Agriculture was developed for the production of grain crops, which led to a decreased reliance on wild plants. Domesticating animals for various purposes decreased the need to hunt wild game. Life became more settled. It was then possible to turn attention to such matters as managing water supplies, producing tools, making cloth, etc. There was both the social interaction and the opportunity to reflect upon existence. Mythologies arose and various kinds of belief systems. Rituals arose that re-enacted the mythologies that gave meaning to life.

As farming and animal husbandry skills increased, the dependence upon wild game and food gathering declined. With this change came the realization that a larger number of people could be supported on the produce of farming and animal husbandry.

Two things seem to have come together to produce cultures and civilizations: a society and culture based on agriculture and the development of centers of the community with literate social and religious structures. The members of these hierarchies then managed water supply and irrigation, ritual and religious life, and exerted their own right to use a portion of the goods produced by the community for their own subsistence in return for their management.

Sharpened skills, development of more sophisticated tools, commerce with other communities, and increasing knowledge of their environment, the resources available to them, and responses to the needs to share goods, order community life, and protect their possessions from outsiders led to further division of labor and community development.

As trade routes developed and travel between cities became easier, trade led to specialization. Trade enables a people to obtain the goods they desire in exchange for the goods they are able to produce. This, in turn, leads to increased attention to refinements of technique and the sharing of ideas. The knowledge of a new discovery or invention provides knowledge and technology that increases the ability to produce goods for trade.

As each community learns the value of the goods it produces and improves its ability to produce the goods in greater quantity, industry is born.

Skill 6.2d   Analyze the forces of cooperation and conflict among peoples and societies that influence the division and control of the earth's surface.

Competition for control of areas of the earth's surface is a common trait of human interaction throughout history. This competition has resulted in both destructive conflict and peaceful and productive cooperation. Societies and groups have sought control of regions of the earth's surface for a wide variety of reasons including religion, economics, politics and administration. Numerous wars have been fought through the centuries for the control of territory for each of these reasons.

At the same time, groups of people, even societies, have peacefully worked together to establish boundaries around regions or territories that served specific purposes in order to sustain the activities that support life and social organization.

Individuals and societies have divided the earth's surface through conflict for a number of reasons:

- The domination of peoples or societies, e.g., colonialism
- The control of valuable resources, e.g., oil
- The control of strategic routes, e.g., the Panama Canal

Conflicts can be spurred by religion, political ideology, national origin, language, and race. Conflicts can result from disagreement over how land, ocean or natural resources will be developed, shared, and used. Conflicts have resulted from trade, migration, and settlement rights. Conflicts can occur between small groups of people, between cities, between nations, between religious groups, and between multi-national alliances.

Today, the world is primarily divided by political/administrative interests into state sovereignties. A particular region is recognized to be controlled by a particular government, including its territory, population and natural resources. The only area of the earth's surface that today is not defined by state or national sovereignty is Antarctica.

Alliances are developed among nations on the basis of political philosophy, economic concerns, cultural similarities, religious interests, or for military defense. Some of the most notable alliances today are:
- The United Nations
- The North Atlantic Treaty Organization
- The Caribbean Community
- The Common Market
- The Council of Arab Economic Unity
- The European Union

Large companies and multi-national corporations also compete for control of natural resources for manufacturing, development, and distribution.

Throughout human history there have been conflicts on virtually every scale over the right to divide the Earth according to differing perceptions, needs and values. These conflicts have ranged from tribal conflicts to urban riots, to civil wars, to regional wars, to world wars. While these conflicts have traditionally centered on control of land surfaces, new disputes are beginning to arise over the resources of the oceans and space.

On smaller scales, conflicts have created divisions between rival gangs, use zones in cities, water supply, school districts; economic divisions include franchise areas and trade zones.

COMPETENCY 6.3   CULTURE AND THE PHYSICAL ENVIRONMENT

Skill 6.3a   Describe and analyze ways in which human societies and settlement patterns develop in response to the physical environment, and explain the social, political, economic, and physical processes that have resulted in today's urban and rural landscapes.

By nature, people are essentially social creatures. They generally live in communities or settlements of some kind and of some size. Settlements are the cradles of culture, political structure, education, and the management of resources. The relative placement of these settlements or communities are shaped by the proximity to natural resources, the movement of raw materials, the production of finished products, the availability of a work force, and the delivery of finished products. The composition of communities will, at least to some extent, be determined by shared values, language, culture, religion, and subsistence.

Settlements begin in areas that offer the natural resources to support life – food and water. With the ability to manage the environment one finds a concentration of populations. With the ability to transport raw materials and finished products, comes mobility. With increasing technology and the rise of industrial centers, comes a migration of the workforce.

Cities are the major hubs of human settlement. Almost half of the population of the world now lives in cities. These percentages are much higher in developed regions. Established cities continue to grow. The fastest growth, however, is occurring in developing areas. In some regions there are "**metropolitan areas**" made up of urban and sub-urban areas. In some places cities and urban areas have become interconnected into "**megalopoli**" (e.g., Tokyo-Kawasaki-Yokohama).

The concentrations of populations and the divisions of these areas among various groups that constitute the cities can differ significantly. North American cities are different from European cities in terms of shape, size, population density, and modes of transportation. While in North America, the wealthiest economic groups tend to live outside the cities, the opposite is true in Latin American cities.

There are significant differences among the cities of the world in terms of connectedness to other cities. While European and North American cities tend to be well linked both by transportation and communication connections, there are other places in the world in which communication between the cities of the country may be inferior to communication with the rest of the world.

Rural areas tend to be less densely populated due to the needs of agriculture. More land is needed to produce crops or for animal husbandry than for manufacturing, especially in a city in which the buildings tend to be taller. Rural areas, however, must be connected via communication and transportation in order to provide food and raw materials to urban areas.

Skill 6.3b   Recognize the interrelationship of environmental and social policy.

The purpose and aim of social policy is to **improve human welfare** and to **meet basic human** needs within the society. **Social policy** addresses basic human needs for the sustainability of the individual and the society. The concerns of social policy, then, include food, clean water, shelter, clothing, education, health, and social security. Social policy is part of **public policy**, determined by the city, the state, the nation, or the multi-national organization responsible for human welfare in a particular region.

Environmental policy is concerned with the sustainability of the earth, the region under the administration of the governing group or individual or a local habitat. The concern of environmental policy is the preservation of the region, habitat or ecosystem.

Because humans, both individually and in community, rely upon the environment to sustain human life, social and environmental policy must be mutually supportable. Because humans, both individually and in community, live upon the earth, draw upon the natural resources of the earth, and affect the environment in many ways, environmental and social policy must be mutually supportive.

If modern societies have no understanding of the limitations upon natural resources or how their actions affect the environment, and they act without regard for the sustainability of the earth, it will become impossible for the earth to sustain human existence. At the same time, the resources of the earth are necessary to support the human welfare. Environmental policies must recognize that the planet is the home of humans and other species.

For centuries, social policies, economic policies, and political policies have ignored the impact of human existence and human civilization upon the environment. Human civilization has disrupted the ecological balance, contributed to the extinction of animal and plant species, and destroyed ecosystems through uncontrolled harvesting.

In an age of global warming, unprecedented demand upon natural resources, and a shrinking planet, social and environmental policies must become increasingly interdependent if the planet is to continue to support life and human civilization.

Bibliography

Adams, James Truslow. (2006). "The March of Democracy," Vol 1. "The Rise of the Union". New York: Charles Scribner's Sons, Publisher.

Barbini, John & Warshaw, Steven. (2006). "The World Past and Present." New York: Harcourt, Brace, Jovanovich, Publishers.

Berthon, Simon & Robinson, Andrew. (2006. "The Shape of the World." Chicago: Rand McNally, Publisher.

Bice, David A. (2006). "A Panorama of Florida II". (Second Edition). Marceline, Missouri: Walsworth Publishing Co., Inc.

Bram, Leon (Vice-President and Editorial Director). (2006). "Funk and Wagnalls New Encyclopedia." United States of America.

Burns, Edward McNall & Ralph, Philip Lee. (2006. "World Civilizations Their History and Culture" (5th ed.). New York: W.W. Norton & Company, Inc., Publishers.

Dauben, Joseph W. (2006). "The World Book Encyclopedia." Chicago: World Book Inc. A Scott Fetzer Company, Publisher.

De Blij, H.J. & Muller, Peter O. (2006). "Geography Regions and Concepts" (Sixth Edition). New York: John Wiley & Sons, Inc., Publisher.

Encyclopedia Americana. (2006). Danbury, Connecticut: Grolier Inc, Publisher.

Heigh, Christopher (Editor). (2006). "The Cambridge Historical Encyclopedia of Great Britain and Ireland." Cambridge: Cambridge University Press, Publisher.

Hunkins, Francis P. & Armstrong, David G. (2006). "World Geography People and Places." Columbus, Ohio: Charles E. Merrill Publishing Co. A Bell & Howell Company, Publishers.

Jarolimek, John; Anderson, J. Hubert & Durand, Loyal, Jr. (2006). "World Neighbors." New York: Macmillan Publishing Company. London: Collier Macmillan Publishers.

McConnell, Campbell R. (2006). "Economics-Principles, Problems, and Policies" (Tenth Edition). New York: McGraw-Hill Book Company, Publisher.

Millard, Dr. Anne & Vanags, Patricia. (2006). "The Usborne Book of World History." London: Usborne Publishing Ltd., Publisher.

Novosad, Charles (Executive Editor). (2006). "The Nystrom Desk Atlas." Chicago: Nystrom Division of Herff Jones, Inc., Publisher.

Patton, Clyde P.; Rengert, Arlene C.; Saveland, Robert N.; Cooper, Kenneth S. & Cam, Patricia T. (2006). "A World View." Morristown, N.J.: Silver Burdette Companion, Publisher.

Schwartz, Melvin & O'Connor, John R. (2006). "Exploring A Changing World." New York: Globe Book Company, Publisher.

"The Annals of America: Selected Readings on Great Issues in American History 1620-1968." (2006). United States of America: William Benton, Publisher.

Tindall, George Brown & Shi, David E. (2006). "America-A Narrative History" (Fourth Edition). New York: W.W. Norton & Company, Publisher.

Todd, Lewis Paul & Curti, Merle. (2006). "Rise of the American Nation" (Third Edition). New York: Harcourt, Brace, Jovanovich, Inc., Publishers.

Tyler, Jenny; Watts, Lisa; Bowyer, Carol; Trundle, Roma & Warrender, Annabelle (2006) 'The Usbome Book of World Geography." London: Usbome Publishing Ltd., Publisher.

Willson, David H. (2006). "A History of England." Hinsdale, Illinois: The Dryder Press, inc., Publisher

Sample Test

1. The Fertile Crescent was bounded by:
(Rigorous)(Skill 1.1b)

A. Mediterranean Sea

B. Arabian Desert

C. Taurus Mountains

D. Ural Mountains

2. Which ancient civilization is credited with being the first to develop irrigation techniques through the use of canals, dikes, and devices for raising water?
(Rigorous) (Skill 1.1c)

A. The Sumerians

B. The Egyptians

C. The Babylonians

D. The Akkadians

3. The study of past human cultures based on physical artifacts is:
(Easy) (Skill 1.1a)

A. History

B. Anthropology

C. Cultural Geography

D. Archaeology

4. Development of a solar calendar, invention of the decimal system, and contributions to the development of geometry and astronomy are all the legacy of:
(Rigorous) (Skill 1.1c)

A. The Babylonians

B. The Persians

C. The Sumerians

D. The Egyptians

5. The world religion which includes a caste system is:
(Average) (Skill 1.1e)

A. Buddhism

B. Hinduism

C. Sikhism

D. Jainism

6. An early cultural group was so skillful in navigating on the seas that they were able to sail at night guided by stars. They were the:
(Rigorous) (Skill 1.1c)

A. Greeks

B. Persians

C. Minoans

D. Phoenicians

7. **Which of the following is an example of a direct democracy?**
(Averagel 1.1c)

A. Elected representatives

B. Greek city-states

C. The United States Senate

D. The United States House of Representative

8. **The Roman Empire gave so much to the world, especially the Western world. Of the legacies below, the most influential, effective and lasting is:**
(Rigorous) (Skill 1.1c)

A. The language of Latin

B. Roman law, justice, and political system

C. Engineering and building

D. The writings of its poets an historians

9. **Charlemagne's most important influence on Western civilization is seen today in:**
(Rigorous) (Skill 1.1f)

A. Respect for and encouragement of learning

B. Strong military for defense

C. The criminal justice system

D. Cruel dictatorship

10. **The study of a people's culture would be part of all of the following except:**
(Average) (Skill 1.1a)

A. Science

B. Archaeology

C. History

D. Anthropology

11. **"Participant observation" is a method of study most closely associated with and used in:**
(Average) (Skill 1.1a)

A. Anthropology

B. Archaeology

C. Sociology

D. Political Science

12. The principle of zero in mathematics is the discovery of the ancient civilization found in:
(Rigorous) (Skill 1.1c)

A. Egypt

B. Persia

C. India

D. Babylon

13. The early ancient civilizations developed systems of government:
(Average) (Skill 1.1c)

A. To provide for defense against attack

B. To regulate trade

C. To regulate and direct the economic activities of the people as they worked together in groups

D. To decide on the boundaries of the different fields during planting seasons

14. The end to hunting, gathering, and fishing of prehistoric people was due to:
(Easy) (Skill 1.1b)

A. Domestication of animals

B. Building crude huts and houses

C. Development of agriculture

D. Organized government in villages

15. Bathtubs, hot and cold running water, and sewage systems with flush toilets were developed by the:
(Rigorous) (Skill 1.1c)

A. Minoans

B. Mycenaeans

C. Phoenicians

D. Greeks

16. The chemical process of radiocarbon dating would be most useful and beneficial in the field of:
(Easy) (Skill 1.1a)

A. Archaeology

B. Geography

C. Sociology

D. Anthropology

17. The first ancient civilization to introduce and practice monotheism was the:
(Average) (Skill 1.1d)

A. Sumerians

B. Minoans

C. Phoenicians

D. Hebrews

18. Native South American tribes included all of the following except:
(Easy) (Skill 1.1c)

A. Aztec

B. Inca

C. Minoans

D. Maya

19. An ancient Indian civilization known for its worshipping of the dead was the:
(Rigorous) (Skill 1.2g)

A. The Mayans

B. The Atacamas

C. The Incas

D. The Tarapacas

20. The belief that man was rationale and capable of creative thought was a philosophy of:
(Rigorous) (Skill 1.2k)

A. Rousseau

B. Immanuel Kant

C. Montesquieu

D. John Locke

21. Which one of the following did not contribute to the early medieval European civilization?
(Rigorous) (Skill 1.2b)

A. The heritage from the classical cultures

B. The Christian religion

C. The influence of the German Barbarians

D. The spread of ideas through trade and commerce

22. In Western Europe, the achievements of the Renaissance were unsurpassed and made these countries outstanding cultural centers on the continent. All of the following were accomplishments except: (Average) (Skill 1.2i)

A. Investment of the printing press

B. A rekindling of interest in the learning of classical Greece and Rome

C. Growth in literature, philosophy and art

D. Better military tactics

23. Who is considered to be the most important figure in the spread of Protestantism across Switzerland? (Average) (Skill 1.2j)

A. Calvin

B. Zwingli

C. Munzer

D. Leyden

24. China's last imperial ruling dynasty was one of its most stable and successful and, under its rule, Chinese culture made an outstanding impression on Western nations. This dynasty was: (Rigorous) (Skill 1.2h)

A. Min

B. Manchu

C. Han

D. Chou

25. The ideas and innovations of the period of the Renaissance were spread throughout Europe mainly because of: (Average) (Skill 1.2i)

A. Extensive exploration

B. Craft workers and their guilds

C The invention of the printing press

D. Increased travel and trade

26. India's greatest ruler is considered to be:
(Rigorous) (Skill 1.2h)

A. Akbar

B. Asoka

C. Babur

D. Jahan

27. The "father of anatomy" is considered to be:
(Rigorous) (Skill 1.2i)

A. Vesalius

B. Servetus

C. Galen

D. Harvey

28. The changing focus during the Renaissance when artists and scholars were less concerned with religion but centered their efforts on a better understanding of people and the world was called:
(Average) (Skill 1.2i)

A. Realism

B. Humanism

C. Individualism

D. Intellectualism

29. Which one of the following is not an important legacy of the Byzantine Empire?
(Rigorous) (Skill 1.2b)

A. It protected Western Europe from various attacks from the East by such groups as the Persians, Ottoman Turks, and Barbarians

B. It played a part in preserving the literature, philosophy, and language of ancient Greece

C. Its military organization was the foundation for modern armies

D. It kept the legal traditions of Roman government, collecting and organizing many ancient Roman laws

30. Studies in astronomy, skills in mapping, and other contributions to geographic knowledge came from:
(Rigorous) (Skill 1.2i)

A. Galileo

B. Columbus

C. Eratosthenes

D. Ptolemy

31. **The major force in eighteenth and nineteenth century politics was:**
    (Average) (Skill 1.3e)

    A. Nationalism

    B. Revolution

    C. War

    D. Diplomacy

32. **The Age of Exploration begun in the 1400s was led by:**
    (Average) (Skill 1.3a)

    A. The Portuguese

    B. The Spanish

    C. The English

    D. The Dutch

33. **The English explorer who gave England its claim to North American was:**
    (Average) (Skill 1.3a)

    A. Raleigh

    B. Hawkins

    C. Drake

    D. Cabot

34. **Marxism believes which two groups are in continual conflict?**
    (Rigorous) (Skill 1.3i)

    A. Farmers and landowners

    B. Kings and the nobility

    C. Workers and owners

    D. Structure and superstructure

35. **Which one of the following would not be considered a result of World War II?**
    (Average) (Skill 1.3j)

    A. Economic depressions and slow resumption of trade and financial aid

    B. Western Europe was no longer the center of world power

    C. The beginnings of new power struggles not only in Europe but in Asia as well

    D. Territorial and boundary changes for many nations, especially in Europe

36. The first European to see Florida and sail along its coast was:
(Rigorous) (Skill 1.3a)

A. Cabot

B. Columbus

C. Ponce de Leon

D. Narvaez

37. A political philosophy favoring or supporting rapid social changes in order to correct social and economic inequalities is called:
(Average) (Skill 1.3e)

A. Nationalism

B. Liberalism

C. Conservatism

D. Federalism

38. The results of the Renaissance, Enlightenment, Commercial and Industrial Revolutions were more unfortunate for the people of:
(Average)(Skill 1.3c)

A. Asia

B. Latin America

C. Africa

D. Middle East

39. Colonial expansion by Western European powers in the 18th and 19th centuries was due primarily to:
(Average) (Skill 1.3d)

A. Building and opening the Suez Canal

B. The Industrial Revolution

C. Marked improvements in transportation

D. Complete independence of all the Americas and loss of European domination and influence

40. Which one of the following is not a reason why Europeans came to the New World?
(Average 1.3)

A. To find resources in order to increase wealth

B. To establish trade

C. To increase a ruler's power and importance

D. To spread Christianity

41. **The only colony not founded and settled for religious, political or business reasons was:**
(Average) (Skill 2.1c)

    A. Delaware

    B. Virginia

    C. Georgia

    D. New York

42. **What country did not have a colonial stake in America?**
(Easy) (Skills 2.1b & 3.1b)

    A. France

    B. Spain

    C. Mexico

    D. China

43. **The year 1619 was a memorable for the colony of Virginia. Three important events occurred resulting in lasting effects on US history. Which one of the following is not one of the events?**
(Rigorous) (Skill 2.1c)

    A. Twenty African slaves arrived.

    B. The London Company granted the colony a charter making it independent.

    C. The colonists were given the right by the London Company to govern themselves through representative government in the Virginia House of Burgesses

    D. The London Company sent to the colony 60 women who were quickly married, establishing families and stability in the colony.

44. **The foundation of modern democracy is embodied in the ideas of:**
(Rigorous) (Skill 2.2a)

    A. St. Thomas Aquinas

    B. Rousseau

    C. John Locke

    D. Montesquieu

45. **France decided in 1777 to help the American colonies in their war against Britain. This decision was based on: (Rigorous) (Skill 2.2a)**

A. The naval victory of John Paul Jones over the British ship Serapis"

B. The survival of the terrible winter at Valley Forge

C. The success of colonial guerilla fighters in the South

D. The defeat of the British at Saratoga

46. **The source of authority for national, state, and local governments in the US is: (Average) (Skill 2.2a)**

A. The will of the people

B. The US Constitution

C. Written laws

D. The Bill of Rights

47. **Under the brand new Constitution, the most urgent of the many problems facing the new federal government was that of: (Easy) (Skills 2.2 a & b)**

A. Maintaining a strong army and navy

B. Establishing a strong foreign policy

C. Raising money to pay salaries and war debts

D. Setting up courts, passing federal laws, and providing for law enforcement officers

48. **The principle of "popular sovereignty" allowing people in any territory to make their own decision concerning slavery was stated by; (Rigorous) (Skill 2.3h)**

A. Henry Clay

B. Daniel Webster

C. John C. Calhoun

D. Stephen A. Douglas

49. **As a result of the Missouri Compromise: (Rigorous) (Skill 2.3h)**

    A. Slavery was not allowed in the Louisiana Purchase

    B. The Louisiana Purchase was nullified

    C. Louisiana separated from the Union

    D. The Embargo Act was repealed

50. **Pre Civil War American policy did not include: (Easy) (Skill 2.3c)**

    A. Isolationism

    B. Imperialism

    C. Nationalism

    D. No entangling alliances

51. **Leaders in the movement for woman's rights have included all but: (Rigorous) (Skill 2.3i)**

    A. Elizabeth Cady Stanton

    B. Lucretia Borgia

    C. Susan B. Anthony

    D. Lucretia Mott

52. **The Federalists: (Rigorous) (Skill 2.3a)**

    A. Favored state's rights

    B. Favored a weak central government

    C. Favored a strong federal government

    D. Supported the British

53. **The belief that the United States should control all of North America was called: (Easy) (Skill 2.3c)**

    A. Westward Expansion

    B. Pan Americanism

    C. Manifest Destiny

    D. Nationalism

54. **The three day Battle of Gettysburg was the turning point of the Civil War for the North leading to ultimate victory. The winning commander was: (Average) (Skill 2.4c)**

    A. McDowellle

    B. Lee

    C. Jackson

    D. McClellan

55. **The Radical Republicans who pushed the harsh Reconstruction measures through Congress after Lincoln's death lost public and moderate Republican support when they went too far:**
(Rigorous) (Skill 2.4d)

A. In their efforts to impeach the President

B. By dividing ten southern states into military-controlled districts

C. By making the ten southern states give freed African Americans the right to vote

D. Sending carpetbaggers into the South to build up support for Congressional legislation

56. **Jim Crow refers to:**
(Average) (Skill 2.4f)

A. Equality

B. Labor Movement

C. Racism

D. Free trade

57. **The Union had many strengths over the Confederacy. Which was not a strength?**
(Easy)(Skill 2.4b)

A. Railroads

B. Industry

C. Slaves

D. Manpower

58. **It can be reasonably stated that the change in the United States from primarily an agricultural country into an industrial power was due to all of the following except:**
(Rigorous) (Skill 2.4d)

A. Tariffs on foreign imports

B. Millions of hardworking immigrants

C. An increase in technological developments

D. The change from steam to electricity for powering industrial machinery

59. The post-Civil War years were a time of low public morality, a time of greed, graft, and dishonesty. Which one of the reasons listed would not be accurate?
(Rigorous) (Skill 2.5a)

A. The war itself because of the money and materials needed to carry on the War

B. The very rapid growth of industry and big business after the War

C. The personal example set by President Grant

D. Unscrupulous heads of large impersonal corporations

60. What was the impact of industrialization on the United States?
(Easy)(Skill 2.5e)

A. Decrease in population

B. Fewer jobs

C. Better transportation system

D. Decline in Infrastructure

61. In the United States, federal investigations into business activities are handled by the:
(Average) (Skill 2.5c)

A. Department of Treasury

B. Security & Exchange Commission

C. Government Accounting Office

D. Federal Trade Commission

62. After the Civil War, the US adapted an attitude of isolation from foreign affairs. But the turning point marking the beginning of the US becoming a world power was:
(Rigorous) (Skill 2.6a)

A. World War I

B. Expansion of business and trade overseas

C. The Spanish-American War

D. The building and financial of the Panama Canal

63. **During the 1920s, the United States almost completely stopped all immigration. One of the reasons was:**
(Rigorous) (Skill 2.7c)

A. Plentiful cheap unskilled labor was no longer needed by industrialists

B. War debts from World War I made it difficult to render financial assistance

C. European nations were reluctant to allow people to leave since there was a need to rebuild populations and economic stability

D. The United States did not become a member of the League of Nations

64. **The term Red Scare refers to:**
(Average) (Skill 2.7a)

A. The Halloween holiday

B. The fear of communists

C. Sun Spots

D. Labor strikes

65. **Drought is a problem in Africa and other places because:**
(Average) (Skill 2.8b)

A. There is flooding

B. The rivers change course

C. People flock to see the drought

D. The dried out soil turns to dust and cannot grow food

66. **Which of the following contributed to the severity of the Great Depression in California?**
(Rigorous) (Skill 2.8b)

A. An influx of Chinese immigrants   .

B. The dust bowl drove People out of the cities.

C. An influx of Mexican immigrants.

D. An influx of Oakies.

67. **The international organization established to work for world peace at the end of the Second World War is the:**
(Average) (Skill 2.9d)

    A. League of Nations

    B. United Federation of Nations

    C. United Nations

    D. United World League

68. **Which country was not a part of the Axis in World War II?**
(Easy) (Skill 2.9b)

    A. Germany

    B. Italy

    C. Japan

    D. United States

69. **Of all the major causes of both World Wars I and II, the most significant one is considered to be:**
(Average) (Skill 2.9a)

    A. Extreme nationalism

    B. Military buildup and aggression

    C. Political unrest

    D. Agreements and alliances

70. **After World War II, the United States:**
(Average) (Skill 2.10b)

    A. Limited its involvement in European affairs

    B. Shifted foreign policy emphasis from Europe to Asia

    C. Passed significant legislation pertaining to aid to farmers and tariffs on imports

    D. Entered the greatest period of economic growth in its history

71. **A significant change in immigration policy occurred after World War II when the United States:**
(Average) (Skill 2.10a)

    A. Eliminated restrictions

    B. Prevented Japanese immigration

    C. Imposed policies based on ethnicity and country of origin

    D. Banned immigration

72. Which country was a Cold War foe?
(Easy) (Skill 2.11a)

A. Russia

B. Brazil

C. Canada

D. Argentina

73. Which one of the following was not a post World War II organization?
(Easy) (Skill 2.11b)

A. Monroe Doctrine

B. Marshall Plan

C. Warsaw Pact

D. North Atlantic Treaty Organization

74. Which of the following is not a name associated with the Civil Rights movement?
(Rigorous) (Skill 2.12a)

A. Rosa Parks

B. Emmett Till

C. Tom Dewey

D. Martin Luther King, Jr.

75. During the period of Spanish colonialism, which of the following was not a key to the goal of exploiting, transforming and including the native people?
(Rigorous) (Skill 3.1b)

A. Missions

B. Ranchos

C. Presidios

D. Pueblos

76. Native communities in early California are commonly divided into several cultural areas. How many cultural areas?
(Rigorous) (Skill 3.1a)

A. 4

B. 5

C. 6

D. 7

77. From about 1870 to 1900 the settlement of America's "last frontier", the West, was completed. One attraction for settlers was free land but it would have been to no avail without:
(Easy) (Skill 3.2b)

A. Better farming methods and technology

B. Surveying to set boundaries

C. Immigrants and others to seek new land

D. The railroad to get them there

78. Historians state that the West helped to speed up the Industrial Revolution. Which one of the following statements was not a reason for this?
(Rigorous) (Skill 3.2a)

A. Food supplies for the ever increasing urban populations came from farms in the West

B. A tremendous supply of gold and silver from western mines provided the capital needed to built industries

C. Descendants of western settlers, educated as engineers, geologists, and metallurgists in the East, returned to the West to mine the mineral resources needed for industry

D. Iron, copper, and other minerals from western mines were important resources in manufacturing products

79. What event sparked a great migration of people from all over the world to California? (Rigorous) (Skill 3.2a)

A. The birth of Labor Unions

B. California statehood

C. The invention of the automobile

D. The gold rush

80. Which of the following does not differentiate provisions of the California constitution from the U.S. Constitution? (Rigorous) (Skill 3.2c)

A. The governor of California has the pocket veto

B. In California representation in both houses of the legislature is based on population

C. The Governor and Lt. Governor are elected separately

D. The equivalent of cabinet positions are elected rather than appointed.

81. The United States legislature is bi-cameral, this means: (Average) (Skill 3.2c)

A. It consists of several houses

B. It consists of two houses

C. The Vice-President is in charge of the legislature when in session

D. It has an upper and lower house

82. Who applied Locke's principles to the American situation? (Rigorous) (Skill 4.1a)

A. Thomas Paine

B. Samuel Adams

C. Benjamin Franklin

D. Thomas Jefferson

83. **There is no doubt of the vast improvement of the US Constitution over the weak Articles of Confederation. Which one of the four accurate statements below is a unique yet eloquent description of the document?**
(Rigorous) (Skill 4.1c)

A. The establishment of a strong central government in no way lessened or weakened the individual states.

B. Individual rights were protected and secured.

C. The Constitution is the best representation of the results of the American genius for compromise.

D. Its flexibility and adaptation to change gives it a sense of timelessness.

84. **Of the thirteen English colonies, the greatest degree of religious toleration was found in:**
(Easy) (Skill 4.2a)

A. Maryland

B. Rhode Island

C. Pennsylvania

D. Delaware

85. **The Pilgrims came to America to:**
(Average) (Skill 4.2a)

A. To drill for oil

B. To be the official representatives of the king

C. To take over the East India Company

D. To flee religious persecution

86. **The Constitution can:**
(Easy) (Skill 4.3d)

A. Never be changed

B. Be rewritten

C. Be discarded

D. Be amended

87. **In the United States government, power or control over public education, marriage, and divorce is:**
(Average) (Skill 4.3e)

A. Implied or suggested

B. Concurrent or shared

C. Delegated or expressed

D. Reserved

88. **In the US government, the power of coining money is: (Rigorous) (Skill 4.3a)**

    A. Implied or suggested

    B. Concurrent or shared

    C. Delegated or expressed

    D. Reserved

89. **Which is not a branch of the federal government? (Easy) (Skill 4.3a)**

    A. Popular

    B. Legislative

    C. Executive

    D. Judicial

90. **In the United States government, the power of taxation and borrowing is: (Average) (Skill 4.3a)**

    A. Implied or suggested

    B. Concurrent or shared

    C. Delegated or expressed

    D. Reserved

91. **The term that best describes how the Supreme Court can block laws that may be unconstitutional from being enacted is: (Average) (Skill 4.4b)**

    A. Jurisprudence

    B. Judicial Review

    C. Exclusionary Rule

    D. Right of Petition

92. **What Supreme Court ruling dealt with the issue of civil rights? (Rigorous) (Skill 4.4c)**

    A. Jefferson vs Madison

    B. Lincoln vs Douglas

    C. Dred Scott v. Sanford

    D. Marbury vs Madison

93. **"Marbury vs Madison (1803)" was an important Supreme Court case which set the precedent for: (Average) (Skill 4.4b)**

    A. The elastic clause

    B. Judicial review

    C. The supreme law of the land

    D. Popular sovereignty in the territories

94. **The Electoral College:**
(Average) (Skill 4.5c)

    A. Elects the Senate but not the House

    B. Elects the House but not the Senate

    C. Elects both the House and Senate

    D. Elects the President

95. **Which one of the following is not a function or responsibility of the US political parties?**
(Easy) (Skill 4.5a)

    A. Conducting elections or the voting process

    B. Obtaining funds needed for election campaigns

    C. Choosing candidates to run for public office

    D. Making voters aware of issues and other public affairs information

96. **On the spectrum of American politics, the label that most accurately describes voters to the "right of center" is:**
(Average) (Skill 4.5d)

    A. Moderates

    B. Liberals

    C. Conservatives

    D. Socialists

97. **The study of the exercise of power and political behavior in human society today would be conducted by experts in:**
(Easy) (Skill 4.6b)

    A. History

    B. Sociology

    C. Political Science

    D. Anthropology

98. **When referring to government, who said: "the good of the many outweighs the good of the few and also of the one"?**
(Rigorous) (Skill 4.6b)

    A. Plato

    B. Aristotle

    C. Cicero

    D. Gaius

99. The function of government is to provide for the welfare of the people is the philosophy of:
(Rigorous) (Skill 4.6B)

A. Aristotle

B. John Locke

C. Plato

D. Thomas Hobbes

100. The significance of a free press does not include which of the following:
(Average) (Skill 4.7a)

A. Providing information

B. Reporting illegal actions

C. Libel

D. Reporting in a responsible and civic-minded manner

101. A political system in which there is a one party state, centralized control, and a repressive police system with private ownership is called:
(Average) (Skill 4.8a)

A. Communism

B. Fascism

C. Socialism

D. Constitutional Monarchy

102. The "wall of separation between church and state' came from:
(Rigorous) (Skill 4.9a)

A. Aristotle

B. Alexander Hamilton

C. Thomas Jefferson

D. Thomas Paine

103. The study of the ways in which different societies around the world deal with the problems of limited resources and unlimited needs and wants is in the area of:
(Easy) (Skill 5.1a)

A. Economics

B. Sociology

C. Anthropology

D. Political Science

104. A planned economy functions on the basis of:
(Rigorous) (Skill 5.1d)

A. Public ownership

B. Private ownership

C. Stockholder control

D. An elected management board

105. Potential customers for any product or service are not only called consumers but can also be called a: (Easy) (Skill 5.2a)

   A. Resource

   B. Base

   C. Commodity

   D. Market

106. In a market economy, markets function on the basis of: (Rigorous) (Skill 5.2a)

   A. Government control

   B. Manipulation

   C. Demand and Supply

   D. Planning

107. Competition leads to: (Rigorous) (Skill 5.2c)

   A. Fights

   B. Waste

   C. Overproduction

   D. Efficient use of resources

108. The economic system promoting individual ownership of land, capital, and businesses with minimal governmental regulations is called: (Average) (Skill 5.2h)

   A. Macro-economy

   B. Micro-economy

   C. Laissez-faire

   D. Free enterprise & market economy

109. Which of the following is not a tool of monetary policy? (Average) (Skill 5.3c)

   A. Open market operations

   B. Changing the discount rate

   C. Changing the exchange rate

   D. Changing the reserve ratio

110. The idea that increasing government spending would end depressions was: (Average) (Skill 5.3a)

   A. The basis of modern economics

   B. Called Classical economics

   C. Known as federalism

   D. Called isolationism

111. The programs such as Medicaid and Food Stamps are the responsibility of: (Easy) (Skill 5.3a)

   A. Federal government

   B. Local government

   C. State government

   D. Communal government

112. Unions were founded on the basis of the beliefs of: (Average) (Skill 5.4a)

   A. Thomas Robert Malthus

   B. John Stuart Mill

   C. Samuel Gompers

   D. John Maynard Keynes

113. The American labor union movement started gaining new momentum: (Average) (Skill 5.4a)

   A. During the building of the railroads

   B. After 1865 with the growth of cities

   C. With the rise of industrial giants such as Carnegie and Vanderbilt

   D. During the war years of 1861-1865

114. Gross Domestic Product is: (Average) (Skill 5.5a)

   A. A measure of well being

   B. A well known social indicator

   C. A measure of a nation's output

   D. A measure of a nation's trade

115. One method of trade restriction used by some nations is: (Average) (Skill 5.6b)

   A. Limited treaties

   B. Floating exchange rate

   C. Bill of exchange

   D. Import quotas

116. The doctrine of comparative advantage explains: (Average) (Skill 5.6a)

   A. Why nations trade

   B. How to fight a war

   C. Time zones

   D. Political divisions

117. **Which one of the following does not affect climate? (Rigorous) (Skill 6.1a)**

A. Elevation or altitude

B. Ocean currents

C. Latitude

D. Longitude

118. **Geography was first studied in an organized manner by: (Rigorous) (Skill 6.1)**

A. The Egyptians

B. The Greeks

C. The Romans

D. The Arabs

119. **Meridians, or lines of longitude, not only help in pinpointing locations but are also used for: (Average) (Skill 6.1b)**

A. Measuring distance from the Poles

B. Determining direction of ocean currents

C. Determining the time around the world

D. Measuring distance on the equator

120. **A famous canal is the: (Easy) (Skill 6.1a)**

A. Pacific Canal

B. Arctic Canal

C. Panama Canal

D. Atlantic Canal

121. **In which of the following disciplines would the study of physical mapping, modern or ancient, and the plotting of points and boundaries be least useful? (Easy) (Skill 6.1a)**

A. Sociology

B. Geography

C. Archaeology

D. History

122. **The study of "spatial relationships and interaction" would be done by people in the field of: (Easy) (Skill 6.1)**

A. Political Science

B. Anthropology

C. Geography

D. Sociology

123. **The study of how living organisms interact is called: (Average) (Skill 6.2a)**

    A. Ecology

    B. Sociology

    C. Anthropology

    D. Political Science

124. **Which of the following is an organization or alliance for defense purposes? (Average) (Skill 6.2d)**

    A. North Atlantic Treaty Organization

    B. The Common Market

    C. The European Union

    D. North American Free Trade Association

125. **What term does not describe a settlement in the physical and cultural sense? (Average) (Skill 6.3A)**

    A. Climate

    B. Religion

    C. Shared values

    D. Shared language

Answer Key

1. D	41. C	81. B	121. A
2. A	42. D	82. D	122. C
3. D	43. B	83. C	123. A
4. D	44. C	84. B	124. A
5. B	45. D	85. D	125. A
6. D	46. A	86. D	
7. B	47. C	87. D	
8. B	48. D	88. C	
9. A	49. A	89. A	
10. A	50. B	90. B	
11. A	51. B	91. B	
12. C	52. C	92. C	
13. C	53. C	93. B	
14. C	54. B	94. D	
15. A	55. A	95. A	
16. A	56. C	96. C	
17. D	57. C	97. C	
18. C	58. A	98. B	
19. C	59. C	99. A	
20. B	60. C	100. C	
21. D	61. D	101. B	
22. D	62. C	102. C	
23. A	63. A	103. A	
24. B	64. B	104. A	
25. C	65. D	105. D	
26. A	66. D	106. C	
27. A	67. C	107. D	
28. B	68. D	108. D	
29. C	69. A	109. C	
30. D	70. D	110. A	
31. A	71. C	111. C	
32. A	72. A	112. C	
33. D	73. A	113. B	
34. C	74. C	114. A	
35. A	75. B	115. D	
36. A	76. C	116. A	
37. B	77. D	117. D	
38. C	78. C	118. B	
39. B	79. D	119. C	
40. B	80. A	120. C	

Rigor Table

	Easy %20	Average Rigor %40	Rigorous %40
Question #	3, 14, 16, 18, 42, 47, 50, 53, 57, 60, 68, 72, 73, 77, 84, 86, 89, 95, 97, 103, 105, 111, 120, 121, 122	5, 7, 11, 13, 17, 22, 23, 25, 28, 31, 32, 33, 35, 37, 38, 39, 40, 54, 56, 61, 64, 65, 67, 59, 70, 71, 81, 85, 87, 90, 91, 93, 94, 96, 100, 101, 108, 109, 110, 112, 113, 114, 115, 116, 119, 123, 124, 125	1, 2, 4, 6, 8, 9, 12, 15, 19, 20, 21, 24, 26, 27, 29, 30, 34, 36, 43, 44, 45, 46,48, 49, 51, 52, 55, 58, 59, 62, 63, 66, 74, 75, 76, 78, 79, 80, 82, 83, 88, 92, 98, 99, 102, 104, 106, 107, 117, 118

Rationales with Sample Questions

1. **The Fertile Crescent was bounded by:**
   (Rigorous) (Skill 1.1b)

   A. Mediterranean Sea

   B. Arabian Desert

   C. Taurus Mountains

   D. Ural Mountains

Answer:

D. Ural Mountains

(A) Mediterranean Sea forms the Western border of the Fertile Crescent (B) the Arabian Desert is the Southern boundary and (C) the Taurus Mountains form the Northern boundary. (D) The Ural Mountains are further North in Russia and form the border between Russia and Europe.

2. **Which ancient civilization is credited with being the first to develop irrigation techniques through the use of canals, dikes, and devices for raising water?**
   (Rigorous) (Skill 1.1c)

   A. The Sumerians

   B. The Egyptians

   C. The Babylonians

   D. The Akkadians

Answer:

A. The Sumerians

The ancient (A) Sumerians of the Fertile Crescent of Mesopotamia are credited with being the first to develop irrigation techniques through the use of canals, dikes, and devices for raising water. The (B) Egyptians also practiced controlled irrigation but that was primarily through the use of the Nile's predictable flooding schedule. The (C) Babylonians were more noted for their revolutionary systems of law than their irrigation systems.

3.   The study of past human cultures based on physical artifacts is:
      (Easy) (Skill 1.1a)

      A. History

      B. Anthropology

      C. Cultural Geography

      D. Archaeology

Answer:

D. Archaeology

Archaeology is the study of past human cultures based on physical artifacts such as fossils, carvings, paintings, and engraved writings.

4.   Development of a solar calendar, invention of the decimal system, and contributions to the development of geometry and astronomy are all the legacy of:
      (Rigorous) (Skill 1.1c)

      A. The Babylonians

      B. The Persians

      C. The Sumerians

      D. The Egyptians

Answer:

D. The Egyptians

The (A) Babylonians of ancient Mesopotamia flourished for a time under their great contribution of organized law and code, called Hammurabi's Code (1750 B.C.), after the ruler Hammurabi. The fall of the Babylonians to the Persians in 539 B.C. made way for the warrior-driver Persian Empire that expanded from Pakistan to the Mediterranean Sea until the conquest of Alexander the Great in 331 B.C. The Sumerians of ancient Mesopotamia were most noted for their early advancements as one of the first civilizations and their contributions towards written language known as cuneiform. It was the (D) Egyptians who were the first true developers of a solar calendar, the decimal system, and made significant contributions to the development of geometry and astronomy.

5. **The world religion, which includes a caste system, is:**
(Average) (Skill 1.1e)

A. Buddhism

B. Hinduism

C. Sikhism

D. Jainism

Answer:

B. Hinduism

Buddhism, Sikhism, and Jainism all rose out of protest against Hinduism and its practices of sacrifice and the caste system. The caste system, in which people were born into castes, would determine their class for life including who they could marry, what jobs they could perform, and their overall quality of life.

6. **An early cultural group was so skillful in navigating on the sea that they were able to sail at night guided by stars. They were the:**
(Rigorous) (Skill 1.1c)

A. Greeks

B. Persians

C. Minoans

D. Phoenicians

Answer:

D. Phoenicians

Although the Greeks were quite able sailors and developed a strong navy in their defeat of the Persians at sea in the Battle of Marathon, it was the Eastern Mediterranean culture of the Phoenicians that had first developed the astronomical skill of sailing at night with the stars as their guide. The Minoans were an advanced early civilization off the Greek coast on Crete more noted for their innovations in terms of sewage systems, toilets, and running water.

7. **Which of the following is an example of a direct democracy? (Average 1.1c)**

A. Elected representatives

B. Greek city-states

C. The Constitution

D. The Confederate States

Answer:

B. Greek city-states

The Greek city-states are an example of a direct democracy as their leaders were elected directly by the citizens and the citizens themselves were given voice in government. (A) Elected representatives in the United States as in the case of the presidential elections are actually elected by an electoral college that is supposed to be representative of the citizens. As we have learned from the elections of 2000, this is a flawed system. The United States Congress, the Senate, and the House of Representatives are also examples of indirect democracy as they represent the citizens in the legislature as opposed to having citizens represent themselves.

8. **The Roman Empire gave so much to the world, especially the Western world. Of the legacies below, the most influential, effective and lasting is:**
    (Rigorous) (Skill 1.1c)

    A. The language of Latin

    B. Roman law, justice, and political system

    C. Engineering and building

    D. The writings of its poets and historians

Answer:

B. Roman law, justice, and political system

Of the lasting legacies of the Roman Empire, it is their law, justice, and political system that has been the most effective and influential on our Western world today. The idea of a Senate and different houses is still maintained by our United

States government and their legal justice system is also the foundation of our own. We still use many Latin words in our justice system, terms such as *habeas corpus* and *voir dire*. English, Spanish, Italian, French, and others are all based on Latin. The Roman language, Latin itself has died out. Roman engineering and building and their writings and poetry have also been influential but not nearly to the degree that their government and justice systems have been.

9. **Charlemagne's most important influence on Western civilization is seen today in:**
   (Rigorous) (Skill 1.1f)

   A. Respect for and encouragement of learning

   B. Strong military for defense

   C. The criminal justice system

   D. Cruel dictatorship

Answer:

A. Respect for and encouragement of learning

Charlemagne was the leader of the Germanic Franks responsible for the promotion of the Holy Roman Empire across Europe. Although he unified governments and aided the Pope, he re-crowned himself in 802 A.D. to demonstrate that his power and right to rule was not a grant from the Pope, but rather a secular achievement. Therefore, although he used much of the Church's power in his rise to power, the Pope in turn used Charlemagne to ascend the Church to new heights. Thus, Charlemagne had an influence on the issues between Church and state and was well-known for his respect of learning.

10. **The study of a people's culture would be part of all of the following except:**
    (Average) (Skill 1.1a)

    A. Science

    B. Archaeology

    C. History

    D. Anthropology

Answer:

A. Science

The study of a people's culture would be a part of studies in the disciplines of archaeology, (study of ancient artifacts including written works), and history (the study of the past) and anthropology, the study of the relationship between man and his culture. Culture would be less important in science that is based on hard facts.

11. **"Participant observation" is a method of study most closely associated with and used in:**
     (Average) (Skill 1.1a)

     A. Anthropology

     B. Archaeology

     C. Sociology

     D. Political science

Answer:

A. Anthropology

"Participant observation" is a method of study most closely associated with and used in (A) anthropology or the study of current human cultures. (B) Archaeologists typically the study of the remains of people, animals or other physical things. (C) Sociology is the study of human society and usually consists of surveys, controlled experiments, and field studies. (D) Political science is the study of political life including justice, freedom, power and equality in a variety of methods.

12. **The principle of zero in mathematics is the discovery of the ancient civilization found in:**
     (Rigorous) (Skill 1.1c)

     A. Egypt

     B. Persia

     C. India

     D. Babylon

Answer:

C. India

Although the Egyptians practiced algebra and geometry, the Persians developed an alphabet, and the Babylonians developed Hammurabi's Code, which would come to be considered among the most important contributions of the Mesopotamian civilization, it was the Indians that created the idea of zero in mathematics changing drastically our ideas about numbers.

13. **The early ancient civilizations developed systems of government:**
(Average) (Skill 1.1c)

A. To provide for defense against attack

B. To regulate trade

C. To regulate and direct the economic activities of the people as they worked together in groups

D. To decide on the boundaries of the different fields during planting seasons

Answer:

C. To regulate and direct the economic activities of the people as they worked together in groups

Although ancient civilizations were concerned with defense, trade regulation and the maintenance of boundaries in their fields, they could not have done any of them without first regulating and directing the economic activities of the people as they worked in groups. This provided for a stable economic base from which they could trade and actually had something worth providing defense for.

14. **The end to hunting, gathering, and fishing of prehistoric people was due to:**
(Easy) (Skill 1.1b)

A. Domestication of animals

B. Building crude huts and houses

C. Development of agriculture

D. Organized government in villages

Answer:

C. Development of agriculture

Although the domestication of animals, the building of huts and houses and the first organized governments were all very important steps made by early civilizations, it was the development of agriculture that ended the once dominant practices of hunting, gathering, and fishing among prehistoric people. The development of agriculture provided a more efficient use of time and for the first time a surplus of food. This greatly improved the quality of life and contributed to early population growth.

15. **Bathtubs, hot and cold running water, and sewage systems with flush toilets were developed by the:**
    (Rigorous) (Skill 1.1c)

    A. Minoans

    B. Mycenaeans

    C. Phoenicians

    D. Greeks

Answer:

A. Minoans

The (A) Minoans were one of the earliest Greek cultures and existed on the island of Crete and flourished from about 1600 B.C. to about 1400 B.C. During this time, the (B) Mycenaean were flourishing on the mainland of what is now Greece. However, it was the Minoans on Crete that are best known for their advanced ancient civilization in which such advances as bathtubs, hot and cold running water, sewage systems and flush toilets were developed. The (C) Phoenicians also flourished around 1250 B.C., however, their primary development was in language and arts. The Phoenicians created an alphabet that has still considerable influence in the world today. The great developments of the (D) Greeks were primarily in the fields of philosophy, political science, and early ideas of democracy.

16. **The chemical process of radiocarbon dating would be most useful and beneficial in the field of:**
    (Easy) (Skill 1.1a)

    A. Archaeology

    B. Geography

    C. Sociology

    D. Anthropology

Answer:

A. Archaeology

Radiocarbon dating is a chemical process that helps generate a more absolute method for dating artifacts and remains by measuring the radioactive materials present in them today and calculating how long it takes for certain materials to decay. Since geographers mainly study locations and special properties of earth's living things and physical features, sociologists mostly study human society and social conditions and anthropologists generally study human culture and humanity, the answer is archaeology because archeologists study past human cultures by studying their remains.

17. **The first ancient civilization to introduce and practice monotheism was the:**
    (Average) (Skill 1.1d)

    A. Sumerians

    B. Minoans

    C. Phoenicians

    D. Hebrews

Answer:

D. Hebrews

The (A) Sumerians and (C) Phoenicians both practiced religions in which many gods and goddesses were worshipped. Often these gods/goddesses were based on a feature of nature such as a sun, moon, weather, rocks, water, etc. The (B) Minoan culture shared many religious practices with the Ancient Egyptians. It seems that the king was somewhat of a god figure and the queen, a goddess. Much of the Minoan art point to worship of multiple gods. Therefore, only the (D) Hebrews introduced and fully practiced monotheism, or the belief in one God.

18. **Native South American tribes included all of the following except:**
    (Easy) (Skill 1.1c)

    A. Aztec

    B. Inca

    C. Minoans

    D. Maya

Answer:

C. Minoans

The (A) Aztec were a tribe in Mexico and Central America. (B) The Inca and (D) the Maya were South American tribes. The Minoans were an early civilization but not from the Americas.

19. **An ancient Indian civilization known for its worshipping of the dead was the:**
(Rigorous) (Skill 1.2g)

A. The Mayans

B. The Atacamas

C. The Incas

D. The Tarapacas

Answer:

C. The Incas

The Incas of Peru were an ancient civilization that practiced the worship of the dead.

20. **The belief that man was rationale and capable of creative thought was a philosophy of:**
(Rigorous) (Skill 1.2k)

A. Rousseau

B. Immanuel Kant

C. Montesquieu

D. John Locke

Answer:

B. Immanuel Kant

Immanuel Kant (1724-1804) was the German metaphysician and philosopher, who believed in the rationality of man and believed that man was capable of creative thought.

21. **Which one of the following did not contribute to the early medieval European civilization?**
(Rigorous) (Skill 1.2b)

A. The heritage from the classical cultures

B. The Christian religion

C. The influence of the German Barbarians

D. The spread of ideas through trade and commerce

Answer:

D. The spread of ideas through trade and commerce

The heritage of the classical cultures such as Greece, the Christian religion which became dominant, and the influence of the Germanic Barbarians (Visigoths, Saxons, Ostrogoths, Vandals and Franks) were all contributions to early medieval Europe and its plunge into feudalism. During this period, lives were often difficult and lived out on one single manor, with very little travel or spread of ideas through trade or commerce. Civilization seems to have halted progress during these years.

22.   **In Western Europe, the achievements of the Renaissance were unsurpassed and made these countries outstanding cultural centers on the continent. All of the following were accomplishments except:**
(Average) (Skill 1.2i)

A. Invention of the printing press

B. A rekindling of interest in the learning of classical Greece & Rome

C. Growth in literature, philosophy, and art

D. Better military tactics

Answer:

D. Better military tactics

The Renaissance in Western Europe produced many important achievements that helped push immense progress among European civilization. Some of the most important developments during the Renaissance were Gutenberg's invention of the printing press in Germany and a reexamination of the ideas and philosophies of classical Greece and Rome that eventually helped Renaissance thinkers to approach more modern ideas. Also important during the Renaissance was the growth in literature (Petrarch, Boccaccio, Erasmus), philosophy (Machiavelli, More, Bacon) and art (Van Eyck, Giotto, da Vinci). Therefore, improved military tactics is the only possible answer as it was clearly not a characteristic of the Renaissance in Western Europe.

23. **Who is considered to be the most important figure in the spread of Protestantism across Switzerland?**
(Average) (Skill 1.2j)

A. Calvin

B. Zwingli

C. Munzer

D. Leyden

Answer:

A. Calvin

While Huldreich Zwingli (1484-1531) was the first to spread the Protestant Reformation in Switzerland around 1519, it was John Calvin (1509-1564), whose less radical approach to Protestantism who really made the most impact in Switzerland. Calvin's ideas separated from the Lutherans over the "Lord's Supper" debate over the sacrament, and his branch of Protestants became known as Calvinism. Calvin certainly built on Zwingli's early influence but really made the religion widespread throughout Switzerland. Thomas Munzer (1489-1525) was a German Protestant reformer whose radical and revolutionary ideas about God's will to overthrow the ruling classes and his siding with the peasantry got him beheaded. Munzer has since been studied and admired by Marxists for his views on class. Leyden (or Leiden) was a founder of the University of Leyden, a Protestant place for study in the Netherlands.

24. **China's last imperial ruling dynasty was one of its most stable and successful and under its rule, Chinese culture made an outstanding impression on Western nations. This dynasty was: (Rigorous) (Skill 1.2h)**

A. Ming

B. Manchu

C. Han

D. Chou

Answer:

B. Manchu

The (A) Ming Dynasty lasted from 1368-1644 and was among the more successful dynasties but focused attention towards foreign trade and encouraged growth in the arts. Therefore, it was the (B) Manchu Dynasty, the last imperial ruling dynasty, which came to power in the 1600s and expanded China's power in Asia greatly that was and still is considered to be among the most important, most stable, and most successful of the Chinese dynasties. The (C) Han and (D) Chou Dynasties were part of the "ancient" dynasties of China and while important in Chinese History, their influence did not hold impression on Western nations as the Manchu.

25. **The ideas and innovations of the period of the Renaissance were spread throughout Europe mainly because of:**
(Average) (Skill 1.2i)

    A. Extensive exploration

    B. Craft workers and their guilds

    C. The invention of the printing press

    D. Increased travel and trade

Answer:

C. The invention of the printing press

The ideas and innovations of the Renaissance were spread throughout Europe for a number of reasons. While exploration, increased travel, and spread of craft may have aided the spread of the Renaissance to small degrees, nothing was as important to the spread of ideas as Gutenberg's invention of the printing press in Germany.

26. **India's greatest ruler is considered to be:**
(Rigorous) (Skill 1.2h)

    A. Akbar

    B. Asoka

    C. Babur

    D. Jahan

Answer:

A. Akbar

Akbar (1556-1605) is considered to be India's greatest ruler. He combined a drive for conquest with a magnetic personality and went so far as to invent his own religion, Dinillahi, a combination of Islam, Christianity, Zoroastrianism, and Hinduism. Asoka (273 B.C.-232 B.C.) was also an important ruler as he was the first to bring together a fully united India. Babur (1483-1540) was both considered to be a failure as he struggled to maintain any power early in his reign, but later to be somewhat successful in his quest to reunite Northern India. Jahan's (1592-1666) rule of India is considered to be the golden age of art and literature in the region.

27. The "father of anatomy" is considered to be:
     (Rigorous) (Skill 1.2i)

     A. Vesalius

     B. Servetus

     C. Galen

     D. Harvey

Answer:

A. Vesalius

Andreas Vesalius (1514-1564) is considered to be the "father of anatomy" as a result of his revolutionary work on the human anatomy based on dissections of human cadavers. Prior to Vesalius, men such as Galen, (130-200) had done work in the field of anatomy, but they had based the majority of their work on animal studies.

28. The changing focus during the Renaissance when artists and scholars were less concerned with religion but centered their efforts on a better understanding of people and the world was called:
     (Average) (Skill 1.2i)

     A. Realism

     B. Humanism

     C. Individualism

     D. Intellectualism

Answer:

B. Humanism

Realism is a medieval philosophy that contemplated independence of existence of the body, the mind, and God. The idea of individualism is usually either a reference to an economic or political theory. Intellectualism is the placing of great importance and devotion to the exploring of the intellect. Therefore, the changing focus during the Renaissance when artists and scholars were less concerned with religion but centered their efforts on a better understanding of people and the world was called humanism.

29. **Which one of the following is not an important legacy of the Byzantine Empire?**
(Rigorous) (Skill 1.2b)

A. It protected Western Europe from various attacks from the East by such groups as the Persians, Ottoman Turks, and Barbarians

B. It played a part in preserving the literature, philosophy, and language of ancient Greece

C. Its military organization was the foundation for modern armies

D. It kept the legal traditions of Roman government, collecting and organizing many ancient Roman laws.

Answer:

C. Its military organization was the foundation for modern armies

The Byzantine Empire (1353-1453) was the successor to the Roman Empire in the East and protected Western Europe from invaders such as the Persians and Ottomans. The Byzantine Empire was a Christian incorporation of Greek philosophy, language, and literature along with Roman government and law. Therefore, although regarded as having a strong infantry, cavalry, and engineering corps along with excellent morale amongst its soldiers, the Byzantine Empire is not particularly considered a foundation for modern armies.

30. **Studies in astronomy, skills in mapping, and other contributions to geographic knowledge came from:**
    (Rigorous) (Skill 1.2i)

    A. Galileo

    B. Columbus

    C. Eratosthenes

    D. Ptolemy

Answer:

D. Ptolemy

Ptolemy (2nd century AD) was important in the fields of astronomy and geography. His theory stated that the earth was the center of the universe and all the other planets rotated around it, a theory that was later proven false. Ptolemy, however, was important for his contributions to the fields of mapping, mathematics, and geography. Galileo (1564-1642) was also important in the field of astronomy but did not make the mapping and geographic contributions of Ptolemy. He invented and used the world's first telescope and advanced Copernicus' theory that the earth revolved around the sun, much to the dismay of the Church.

31. **The major force in eighteenth and nineteenth century politics was:**
    (Average) (Skill 1.3e)

    A. Nationalism

    B. Revolution

    C. War

    D. Diplomacy

Answer:

A. Nationalism

Nationalism was the driving force in politics in the eighteenth and nineteenth century. Groups of people that shared common traits and characteristics wanted their own government and countries. This led to some revolution, war and the failure of diplomacy.

32. **The Age of Exploration begun in the 1400s was led by:**
(Average) (Skill 1.3a)

A. The Portuguese

B. The Spanish

C. The English

D. The Dutch

Answer:

A. The Portuguese

Although the Age of Exploration had many important players among them, the Dutch, Spanish and English, it was the Portuguese who sent the first explorers to the New World.

33. **The English explorer who gave England its claim to North America was:**
(Average) (Skill 1.3a)

A. Raleigh

B. Hawkins

C. Drake

D. Cabot

Answer:

D. Cabot

Sir Walter Raleigh (1554-1618) was an English explorer and navigator, who was sent to the New World in search of riches. He founded the lost colony at Roanoke, Virginia, and was later imprisoned for a supposed plot to kill the King for which he was later released. Sir John Hawkins (1532-1595) and Sir Francis Drake (1540-1596) were both navigators who worked in the slave trade, made some voyages to the New World, and commanded ships against and defeated the Spanish Armada in 1588. John Cabot (1450-1498) was the English explorer who gave England claim to North America.

34. **Marxism believes which two groups are in continual conflict:
     (Rigorous) (Skill 1.3i)**

     A. Farmers and landowners

     B. Kings and the nobility

     C. Workers and owners

     D. Structure and superstructure

Answer:

C. Workers and owners

Marxism believes that the workers and owners are in continual conflict. Marxists refer to these two groups as the proletariat and the bourgeoisie. The proletariat is exploited by the bourgeoisie and will, according to Marxism, rise up over the bourgeoisie in class warfare in an effort to end private control over the means of production.

35. **Which one of the following would not be considered a result of
     World War II?
     (Average) (Skill 1.3j)**

     A. Economic depressions and slow resumption of trade and financial aid

     B. Western Europe was no longer the center of world power

     C. The beginnings of new power struggles not only in Europe but in Asia as well

     D. Territorial and boundary changes for many nations, especially in Europe

Answer:

A. Economic depressions and slow resumption of trade and financial aid

Following World War II, the economy was vibrant and flourished from the stimulant of war and an increased dependence of the world on United States industries. Therefore, World War II didn't result in economic depressions and slow resumption of trade and financial aid. Western Europe was no longer the center of world power. New power struggles arose in Europe and Asia and many European nations underwent changing territories and boundaries.

36. **The first European to see Florida and sail along its coast was: (Rigorous) (Skill 1.3a)**

    A. Cabot

    B. Columbus

    C. Ponce de Leon

    D. Narvaez

Answer:

A. Cabot

(A) John Cabot (1450-1498) was the English explorer who gave England claim to North America and the first European to see Florida and sail along its coast. (B) Columbus (1451-1506) was sent by the Spanish to the New World and has received false credit for "discovering America" in 1492, although he did open up

the New World to European expansion, exploitation, and Christianity. (C) Ponce de Leon (1460-1521), the Spanish explorer, was the first European to actually land on Florida. (D) Panfilo de Narvaez (1470-1528) was also a Spanish conquistador, but he was sent to Mexico to force Cortes into submission. He failed and was captured.

37. **A political philosophy favoring or supporting rapid social changes in order to correct social and economic inequalities is called:**
    (Average) (Skill 1.3e)

    A. Nationalism

    B. Liberalism

    C. Conservatism

    D. Federalism

Answer:

B. Liberalism

A political philosophy favoring rapid social changes in order to correct social and economic inequalities are called Liberalism. Liberalism was a theory that could be said to have started with the great French philosophers Montesquieu (1689-1755) and Rousseau (1712-1778). It is important to understand the difference between political, economic, and social liberalism, as they are different and how they sometimes contrast one another in the modern world.

38. **The results of the Renaissance, Enlightenment, Commercial and the Industrial Revolutions were more unfortunate for the people of:**
(Average) (Skill 1.3c)

A. Asia

B. Latin America

C. Africa

D. Middle East

Answer:

C. Africa

The results of the Renaissance, Enlightenment, Commercial and Industrial Revolutions were quite beneficial for many people in much of the world. New ideas of humanism, religious tolerance, and secularism were spreading. Increased trade and manufacturing were surging economies in much of the world. The people of Africa, however, suffered during these times as they became largely left out of the developments. Also, the people of Africa were stolen, traded, and sold into slavery to provide a cheap labor force for the growing industries of Europe and the New World.

39. **Colonial expansion by Western European powers in the 18ᵗʰ and 19ᵗʰ centuries was due primarily to:**
(Average) (Skill 1.3d)

A. Building and opening the Suez Canal

B. The Industrial Revolution

C. Marked improvements in transportation

D. Complete independence of all the Americas and loss of   European domination and influence

Answer:

B. The Industrial Revolution

Colonial expansion by Western European powers in the late eighteenth and nineteenth centuries was due primarily to the Industrial Revolution in Great Britain that spread across Europe and needed new natural resources and therefore, new locations from which to extract the raw materials needed to feed the new industries.

40. **Which one of the following is not a reason why Europeans came to the New World?**
(Average 1.3)

A. To find resources in order to increase wealth

B. To establish trade

C. To increase a ruler's power and importance

D. To spread Christianity

Answer:

B. To establish trade

The Europeans came to the New World for a number of reasons; often they came to find new natural resources to extract for manufacturing. The Portuguese, Spanish and English were sent over to increase the monarch's power and spread influences such as religion (Christianity) and culture. Therefore, the only reason given that Europeans didn't come to the New World was to establish trade.

41. **The only colony not founded and settled for religious, political, or business reasons was:**
     (Average) (Skill 2.1c)

     A. Delaware

     B. Virginia

     C. Georgia

     D. New York

Answer:

C. Georgia

The Swedish and the Dutch established Delaware and New York as Middle Colonies. They were established with the intention of growth by economic prosperity from farming across the countryside. The English, with the intention of generating a strong farming economy settled Virginia, a Southern Colony. Georgia was the only one of these colonies not settled for religious, political or business reasons as it was started as a place for debtors from English prisons.

42. **What country did not have a colonial stake in America?**
     (Easy) (Skills 2.1b & 3.1b)

     A. France

     B. Spain

     C. Mexico

     D. China

Answer:

D. China

(A) France, (B) Spain and (C) Mexico all had colonies in America. The country that didn't was (D) China. There were Chinese immigrants but no Chinese colonies.

43. **The year 1619 was a memorable year for the colony of Virginia. Three important events occurred resulting in lasting effects on US history. Which one of the following was not one of the events? (Rigorous) (Skill 2.1c)**

   A. Twenty African slaves arrived.

   B. The London Company granted the colony a charter making it independent.

   C. The colonists were given the right by the London Company to govern themselves through representative government in the Virginia House of Burgesses.

   D. The London Company sent to the colony 60 women who were quickly married, establishing families and stability in the colony.

Answer:

B. The London Company granted the colony a charter making it independent.

In the year 1619, the Southern colony of Virginia had an eventful year including the first arrival of twenty African slaves, the right to self-governance through representative government in the Virginia House of Burgesses (their own legislative body), and the arrival of sixty women sent to marry and establish

families in the colony. The London Company did not, however, grant the colony a charter in 1619.

44. **The foundation of modern democracy is embodied in the ideas of: (Rigorous) (Skill 2.2a)**

A. St. Thomas Aquinas

B. Rousseau

C. John Locke

D. Montesquieu

Answer:

C. John Locke

(A) It was St. Thomas Aquinas (1225-1274) who merged Aristotelian ideas with Christianity, who helped lay the ideas of modern constitutionalism and the limiting of government by law. (B) Rousseau (1712-1778) and (D) Montesquieu (1689-1755) were political philosophers who explored the idea of what has come to be known as liberalism. They pushed the idea that through understanding the interconnectedness of economics, geography, climate and psychology, that changes could be made to improve life. (C) John Locke (1632-1704), whose book *Two Treatises of Government* has long been considered a founding document on the rights of people to rebel against an unjust government, was an important figure in the founding of the US Constitution and on general politics of the American Colonies. Locke is the one who laid the basis for modern democracy.

45. **France decided in 1777 to help the American colonies in their war against Britain. This decision was based on:**
    (Rigorous) (Skill 2.2a)

    A. The naval victory of John Paul Jones over the British ship "Serapis"

    B. The survival of the terrible winter at Valley Forge

    C. The success of colonial guerilla fighters in the South

    D. The defeat of the British at Saratoga

Answer:

D. The defeat of the British at Saratoga

The defeat of the British at Saratoga was the overwhelming factor in the Franco-American alliance of 1777 that helped the American colonies defeat the British. Some historians believe that without the Franco-American alliance, the American Colonies would not have been able to defeat the British and American would have remained a British colony.

46. **The source of authority for national, state, and local governments in the United States is:**
    (Average) (Skill 2.2a)

    A. The will of the people

    B. The United States Constitution

    C. Written laws

    D. The Bill of Rights

Answer:

A. The will of the people

The source of authority for national, state, and local governments in the United States is the will of the people. Although the United States Constitution, the Bill of Rights, and the other written laws of the land are important guidelines for authority, they may ultimately be altered or changed by the will of the people.

47. **Under the brand new Constitution, the most urgent of the many problems facing the new federal government was that of:**
(Easy) (Skills 2.2 a & b)

A. Maintaining a strong army and navy

B. Establishing a strong foreign policy

C. Raising money to pay salaries and war debts

D. Setting up courts, passing federal laws, and providing for law enforcement officers

Answer:

C. Raising money to pay salaries and war debts

Maintaining strong military forces, establishment of a strong foreign policy, and setting up a justice system were important problems facing the United States under the newly ratified Constitution. However, the most important and pressing issue was how to raise money to pay salaries and war debts from the Revolutionary War. Alexander Hamilton (1755-1804) then Secretary of the Treasury proposed increased tariffs and taxes on products such as liquor. This

money would be used to pay off war debts and to pay for internal programs. Hamilton also proposed the idea of a National Bank.

48. **The principle of "popular sovereignty", allowing people in any Territory to make their own decision concerning slavery was stated by:**
(Rigorous) (Skill 2.3h)

A. Henry Clay

B. Daniel Webster

C. John C. Calhoun

D. Stephen A. Douglas

Answer:

D. Stephen A. Douglas

(A) Henry Clay (1777-1852) and (B) Daniel Webster (1782-1852) were prominent Whigs whose main concern was keeping the United States one nation. They opposed Andrew Jackson and his Democratic party around the 1830s in favor of promoting what Clay called "the American System". (C) John C. Calhoun (1782-1850) served as Vice-President under John Quincy Adams and Andrew Jackson, and then as a state senator from South Carolina. He was very pro-slavery and a champion of states' rights. The principle of "popular sovereignty", in which people in each territory could make their own decisions concerning slavery, was the doctrine of (D) Stephen A. Douglas (1813-1861). Douglas was looking for a middle ground between the abolitionists of the North and the pro-slavery Democrats of the South. However, as the polarization of pro- and anti-slavery sentiments grew, he lost the presidential election to Republican Abraham Lincoln, who later abolished slavery.

49.   **As a result of the Missouri Compromise:**
       (Rigorous) (Skill 2.3h)

       A. Slavery was not allowed in the Louisiana Purchase

       B. The Louisiana Purchase was nullified

       C. Louisiana separated from the Union

       D. The Embargo Act was repealed

Answer:

A. Slavery was not allowed in the Louisiana Purchase

The Missouri Compromise was the agreement that eventually allowed Missouri to enter the Union. It did not nullify (B) the Louisiana Purchase and (D) the Embargo Act and did not (C) separate Louisiana from the Union. (A) As a result of the Missouri Compromise slavery was specifically banned north of the boundary 36° 30'.

50.   **Pre Civil War American policy did not include:**
       (Easy) (Skill 2.3c)

       A. Isolationism

       B. Imperialism

       C. Nationalism

       D. No entangling alliances

Answer:

B. Imperialism

(A) Isolationism, (C) nationalism and (D) a practice of no entangling alliances characterized pre-Civil War practices. (B) Imperialism, or the establishment of colonies was not a policy of the United States.

51. **Leaders in the movement for woman's rights have included all but:**
    (Rigorous) (Skill 2.3i)

    A. Elizabeth Cady Stanton

    B. Lucretia Borgia

    C. Susan B. Anthony

    D. Lucretia Mott

Answer:

B. Lucretia Borgia

The only name not associated with the woman's rights movement is Lucretia Borgia. The others were all pioneers in the movement with Susan B. Anthony and Elizabeth Cady Stanton being the founders of the National Woman Suffrage Association in 1869.

52. **The Federalists:**
    (Rigorous) (Skill 2.3a)

    A. Favored state's rights

    B. Favored a weak central government

    C. Favored a strong federal government

    D. Supported the British

Answer:

C. Favored a strong federal government

The Federalists were opposed to (A) state's rights and a (B) weak federal government. (D) Most of them opposed the British. (C) The Federalists favored a strong federal government.

53.   The belief that the United States should control all of North
       America was called:
       (Easy) (Skill 2.3c)

       A. Westward Expansion

       B. Pan Americanism

       C. Manifest Destiny

       D. Nationalism

Answer:

C. Manifest Destiny

The belief that the United States should control all of North America was called (B)
Manifest Destiny. This idea fueled much of the violence and aggression towards
those already occupying the lands such as the Native Americans. Manifest Destiny
was certainly driven by sentiments of (D) nationalism and gave rise to (A)
westward expansion.

54.   The three-day Battle of Gettysburg was the turning point of the
       Civil War for the North leading to ultimate victory. The battle in
       the West reinforcing the North's victory and sealing the South's
       defeat was the day after Gettysburg at:
       (Average) (Skill 2.4c)

       A. Perryville

       B. Vicksburg

       C. Stones River

       D. Shiloh

Answer:

B. Vicksburg

The Battle of Vicksburg was crucial in reinforcing the North's victory and sealing
the South's defeat for a couple of reasons. First, the Battle of Vicksburg potentially
gave the Union full control of the Mississippi River. More importantly, the battle
split the Confederate Army and allowed General Grant to reach his goal of
restoring commerce to the important northwest area.

55. **The Radical Republicans who pushed the harsh Reconstruction measures through Congress after Lincoln's death lost public and moderate Republican support when they went too far: (Rigorous) (Skill 2.4d)**

A. In their efforts to impeach the President

B. By dividing ten southern states into military-controlled districts

C. By making the ten southern states give freed African-Americans the right to vote

D. Sending carpetbaggers into the South to build up support for Congressional legislation

Answer:

A. In their efforts to impeach the President

The public support and the moderate Republicans were actually being drawn towards the more radical end of the Republican spectrum following Lincoln's death during Reconstruction. Because many felt as though Andrew Johnson's policies towards the South were too soft and were running the risk of rebuilding the old system of white power and slavery. Even moderate Republicans in the North felt as though it was essential to rebuild the South but with the understanding that they must be abide by the Fourteenth and Fifteenth Amendment assuring Blacks freedom and the right to vote. The radical Republicans were so frustrated that the President would make concessions to the old Southerners that they attempted to impeach him. This turned back the support that they had received from the public and from moderates.

56.   **Jim Crow refers to:**
        (Average) (Skill 2.4f)

  A. Equality

  B. Labor Movement

  C. Racism

  D. Free trade

Answer:

C. Racism

(C) Jim Crow is a term used to describe the policies of racism and discrimination. It has nothing to do with the (B) labor movement or (D) free trade and is the opposite of (A) the concept of equality.

57.   **The Union had many strengths over the Confederacy. Which was not a strength?**
        (Easy) (Skill 2.4b)

  A. Railroads

  B. Industry

  C. Slaves

  D. Manpower

Answer:

C. Slaves

At the time of the Civil War, the South was mostly a plantation economy based on using slaves. The industry, railroads and manpower was located in the North, which made transportation and weapons easy for the North to obtain and use than the South.

58. **It can be reasonably stated that the change in the United States from primarily an agricultural country into an industrial power was due to all of the following except:**
     (Rigorous) (Skill 2.4d)

    A. Tariffs on foreign imports

    B. Millions of hardworking immigrants

    C. An increase in technological developments

    D. The change from steam to electricity for powering industrial machinery

Answer:

A. Tariffs on foreign imports

It can be reasonably stated that the change in the United States from primarily an agricultural country into an industrial power was due to a great degree of three of the reasons listed above. It was a combination of millions of hard-working immigrants, an increase in technological developments, and the change from steam to electricity for powering industrial machinery. The only reason given that really had little effect was the tariffs on foreign imports.

59. **The post-Civil War years were a time of low public morality, a time of greed, graft, and dishonesty. Which one of the reasons listed would not be accurate?**
(Rigorous) (Skill 2.5a)

  A. The war itself because of the money and materials needed to carry on war

  B. The very rapid growth of industry and big business after the war

  C. The personal example set by President Grant

  D. Unscrupulous heads of large impersonal corporations

Answer:

C. The personal example set by President Grant

The post-Civil War years were a particularly difficult time for the nation and public morale was especially low. The war had plunged the country into debt and ultimately into a recession by the 1890s. Racism was rampant throughout the South and the North where freed Blacks were taking jobs for low wages. The rapid growth of industry and big business caused a polarization of rich and poor, workers and owners. Many people moved into the urban centers to find work in the new industrial sector, jobs were typically low-wage, long hours, and poor working conditions. The heads of large impersonal corporations were arrogant in treating their workers inhumanely and letting morale drop to a record low. The heads of corporations showed their greed and malice towards the workingman by trying to prevent and disband labor unions.

60. **What was the impact of industrialization on the United States? (Easy) (Skill 2.5e)**

   A. Decrease in population

   B. Fewer jobs

   C. Better transportation system

   D. Decline in Infrastructure

Answer:

C. Better transportation system

(A) Industrial resulted in more jobs which actually resulted in an increase in the population and people moved to where the jobs were. (B) Industrialization created jobs and more output. The income earned from the jobs gave people the money to purchase the increased output which in turn created more jobs. (D) Industrialization represented an increase in the infrastructure as new factories were built. (C) One of the aspects of industrialization was a better transportation system as railroads came into being.

61. **In the United States, federal investigations into business activities are handled by the: (Average) (Skill 2.5c)**

   A. Department of Treasury

   B. Security and Exchange Commission

   C. Government Accounting Office

   D. Federal Trade Commission

Answer:

D. Federal Trade Commission

The Department of Treasury (A), established in 1789, is an executive government agency that is responsible for advising the president on fiscal policy. There is no such thing as a Government Accounting Office. In the United States, Federal Trade Commission or FTC handles federal investigations into business activities. The establishment of the FTC in 1915 as an independent government agency was done so as to assure fair and free competition among businesses.

62. **After the Civil War, the United States adapted an attitude of isolation from foreign affairs. But the turning point marking the beginning of the US becoming a world power was: (Rigorous) (Skill 2.6a)**

A. World War I

B. Expansion of business and trade overseas

C. The Spanish-American War

D. The building and financing of the Panama Canal

Answer:

C. The Spanish-American War

The turning point marking the beginning of the United States becoming a super power was the Spanish-American War. This was seen as an extension of the Monroe doctrine, calling for United States dominance in the Western Hemisphere and removal of European powers in the region. The United States' relatively easy defeat of Spain in the Spanish-American War marked the beginning of a continuing era of dominance for the United States. In addition, in the post-Civil War era, Spain was the largest land owner in the Americas. Their easy defeat at the hands of the United States in Cuba, the Philippines, and elsewhere showed the strength of the United States across the globe.

63. **During the 1920s, the United States almost completely stopped all immigration. One of the reasons was:**
   (Rigorous) (Skill 2.7c)

   A. Plentiful cheap, unskilled labor was no longer needed by industrialists

   B. War debts from World War I made it difficult to render financial assistance

   C. European nations were reluctant to allow people to leave since there was a need to rebuild populations and economic stability

   D. The United States did not become a member of the League of Nations

Answer:

A. Plentiful cheap, unskilled labor was no longer needed by industrialists

The primary reason that the United States almost completely stopped all immigration during the 1920s was because their once, much needed, cheap, unskilled labor jobs, made available by the once booming industrial economy, were no longer needed. This has much to do with the increased use of machines to do the work once done by cheap, unskilled laborers.

64. **The term Red Scare refers to:**
   (Average) (Skill 2.7a)

   A. The Halloween holiday

   B. The fear of communists

   C. Sun Spots

   D. Labor strikes

Answer:

B. The fear of communists

(B) Communists were known as Reds so the term Red Scare referred to a fear of Communists in the government.

65. **Drought is a problem in Africa and other places because: (Average) (Skill 2.8b)**

A. There is flooding

B. The rivers change course

C. People flock to see the drought

D. The dried out soil turns to dust and cannot grow food

Answer:

D. The dried out soil turns to dust and cannot grow food

Since a drought is a period of dryness and a lack of rain, there (A) is no flooding and (B) the rivers do not change course especially since most of them are dry.

People may go to see the area but for the most part, (D) drought is accompanied by famine since the soil cannot grow food.

66. **Which of the following contributed to the severity of the Great Depression in California? (Rigorous) (Skill 2.8b)**

A. An influx of Chinese immigrants.

B. The dust bowl drove people out of the cities.

C. An influx of Mexican immigrants.

D. An influx of Oakies.

Answer:

D. An influx of Oakies

The answer is "An influx of Oakies" (D). The Dust Bowl of the Great Plains destroyed agriculture in the area. People living in the plains areas lost their livelihood and many lost their homes and possessions in the great dust storms that resulted from a period of extended drought. People from all of the states affected by the Dust Bowl made their way to California in search of a better life. Because the majority of the people were from Oklahoma, they were all referred to as "Oakies." These migrants brought with them their distinctive plains culture. The great influx of people seeking jobs exacerbated the effects of the Great Depression in California.

67. **The international organization established to work for world peace at the end of the Second World War is the :
(Average) (Skill 2.9d)**

    A. League of Nations

    B. United Federation of Nations

    C. United Nations

    D. United World League

    Answer:

C. United Nations

The international organization established to work for world peace at the end of the Second World War was the United Nations. From the ashes of the failed League of Nations, established following World War I, the United Nations continues to be a major player in world affairs today.

68. **Which country was not a part of the Axis in World War II?
(Easy) (Skill 2.9b)**

    A. Germany

    B. Italy

    C. Japan

    D. United States

Answer:

D. United States

(A) Germany, (B) Italy and (C) Japan were the member of the Axis in World War II. (D) The United States was a member of the Allies which opposed the Axis.

69. **Of all the major causes of both World Wars I and II, the most significant one is considered to be:**
    (Average) (Skill 2.9a)

    A. Extreme nationalism

    B. Military buildup and aggression

    C. Political unrest

    D. Agreements and alliances

Answer:

A. Extreme nationalism

Although military buildup and aggression, political unrest, and agreements and alliances were all characteristic of the world climate before and during World War I

and World War II, the most significant cause of both wars was extreme nationalism. Nationalism is the idea that the interests and needs of a particular nation are of the utmost and primary importance above all else. Some nationalist movements could be liberation movements while others were oppressive regimes, much depends on their degree of nationalism. The nationalism that sparked WWI included a rejection of German, Austro-Hungarian, and Ottoman imperialism by Serbs, Slavs and others culminating in the assassination of Archduke Ferdinand by a Serb nationalist in 1914. Following WWI and the Treaty of Versailles, many Germans and others in the Central Alliance Nations, malcontent at the concessions and reparations of the treaty started a new form of nationalism. Adolf Hitler and the Nazi regime led this extreme nationalism. Hitler's ideas were an example of extreme, oppressive nationalism combined with political, social and economic scapegoating and was the primary cause of WWII.

70. **After World War II, the United States:**
    (Average) (Skill 2.10b)

    A. Limited its involvement in European affairs

    B. Shifted foreign policy emphasis from Europe to Asia

    C. Passed significant legislation pertaining to aid to farmers and tariffs on imports

    D. Entered the greatest period of economic growth in its history

Answer:

D. Entered the greatest period of economic growth in its history

After World War II, the United States did not limit or shift its involvement in European affairs. In fact, it escalated the Cold War with the Soviet Union at a swift pace and attempted to contain Communism to prevent its spread across Europe. There was no significant legislation pertaining to aid to farmers and tariffs on imports. In fact, since World War II, trade has become more liberal than ever. Free trade, no matter how risky or harmful to the people of the United States or other countries, has become the economic policy of the United States called neo-liberalism. Due to this, the United States after World War II entered the greatest period of economic growth in its history and remains a world superpower.

71. **A significant change in immigration policy occurred after World War II when the United States:**
    (Average) (Skill 2.10a)

    A. Eliminated restrictions

    B. Prevented Japanese immigration

    C. Imposed policies based on ethnicity and country of origin

    D. Banned immigration

Answer:

C. Imposed policies based on ethnicity and country of origin

(A) The policies that changed after the war did not include the elimination of restrictions. (B) Japanese immigration was not prevented and (D) immigration itself was not banned. (C) Policies were aimed at allowable limits based on ethnicity and country of origin.

72. **Which country was a Cold War foe?**
(Easy) (Skill 2.11a)

A. Russia

B. Brazil

C. Canada

D. Argentina

Answer:

A. Russia

(B) Brazil and (D) Argentina are in South America and (C) Canada is in North America. (A) Russia is the country that was a Cold War superpower and foe of the United States.

73. **Which one of the following was not a post World War II organization?**
(Easy) (Skill 2.11b)

A. Monroe Doctrine

B. Marshall Plan

C. Warsaw Pact

D. North Atlantic Treaty Organization

Answer:

A. Monroe Doctrine

(B) The Marshall Plan provided funds for the reconstruction of Europe after World War II. (C) The Warsaw Pact and (D) NATO were both organizations that came into being for defense purpose. The Warsaw Pact was for the defense of Eastern Europe and NATO was for the defense of Western Europe. (A) The Monroe Doctrine was a nineteenth century agreement in which the United States was committed to defend all countries in the hemisphere.

74. **Which of the following is not a name associated with the Civil Rights movement?**
    (Rigorous) (Skill 2.12a)

    A. Rosa Parks

    B. Emmett Till

    C. Tom Dewey

    D. Martin Luther King, Jr.

Answer:

C. Tom Dewey

(A) Rosa Parks was the black lady who wouldn't move to the back of the bus. (B) Emmett Till was the civil rights worked who was killed. (C) Martin Luther King, Jr. was a Civil Rights leader. (C) Tom Dewey was never involved in the Civil Rights movement.

75. During the period of Spanish colonialism in California, which of the following was not a key to the goal of exploiting, transforming and including the native people?
(Rigorous) (Skill 3.1b)

A. Missions

B. Ranchos

C. Presidios

D. Pueblos

Answer:

B. Ranchos

The answer is "Ranchos" (b). The goal of Spanish colonialism was to exploit, transform and include the native people of California. The Spanish empire sought to do this first by gathering the native people into communities where they could both be taught Spanish culture and be converted to Roman Catholicism and its value system. The social institutions by which this was accomplished was the encouragement of the Mission System, which established a number of Catholic missions a day's journey apart. Once the native people were brought to the missions, they were incorporated into a mission society and indoctrinated in the teachings of Catholicism. The Presidios were fortresses that were constructed to protect Spanish interests and the communities from invaders. The Pueblos were small civilian communities that attracted settlers with the gift of land, seed, and farming equipment. The function of the Pueblos was to produce food for the missions and for the presidios.

76.	Native communities in early California are commonly divided into several cultural areas. How many cultural areas?
(Rigorous) (Skill 3.1a)

	A.	4

	B.	5

	C.	6

	D.	7

Answer:

C. 6

The answer is 6 (C). Due to the great diversity of the native communities, the state is generally divided into six "culture areas." The culture areas are: (1) the Southern Culture Area, (2) the Central Culture Area, (3) the Northwestern Culture Area, (4) the Northeastern Culture Area, (5) the Great Basin Culture Area, and (6) the Colorado River Culture Area. These areas are geographically distinct and supported different sorts of cultures depending upon the availability of an adequate water supply, the ability to cultivate the land, and the availability of game.

77.	From about 1870 to 1900, the last settlement of America's "last frontier", the West, was completed. One attraction for settlers was free land but it would have been to no avail without:
(Easy) (Skill 3.2b)

	A. Better farming methods and technology

	B. Surveying to set boundaries

	C. Immigrants and others to see new lands

	D. The railroad to get them there

Answer:

D. The railroad to get them there

From about 1870 to 1900, the settlement for America's "last frontier" in the West was made possible by the building of the railroad. Without the railroad, the settlers never could have traveled such distances in an efficient manner.

78. **Historians state that the West helped to speed up the Industrial Revolution. Which one of the following statements was not a reason for this?**
    (Rigorous) (Skill 3.2a)

    A. Food supplies for the ever-increasing urban populations came from farms in the West.

    B. A tremendous supply of gold and silver from western mines provided the capital needed to build industries.

    C. Descendants of western settlers, educated as engineers, geologists, and metallurgists in the East, returned to the West to mine the mineral resources needed for industry.

    D. Iron, copper, and other minerals from western mines were important resources in manufacturing products.

Answer:

C. Descendants of western settlers, educated as engineers, geologists, and metallurgists in the East, returned to the West to mine the mineral resources needed for industry.

The West helped to speed up the Industrial Revolution in a number of important and significant ways. First, the land yielded crops for the growing urban populations. Second, the gold and silver supplies coming out of the Western mines provided the capital needed to build industries. Also, resources such as iron and copper were extracted from the mines in the West and provided natural resources for manufacturing. The descendants of western settlers typically didn't become educated and then returned to the West as miners. The miners were typically working class with little or no education.

79. **What event sparked a great migration of people from all over the world to California?**
(Rigorous) (Skill 3.2a)

   A. The birth of Labor Unions

   B. California statehood

   C. The invention of the automobile

   D. The gold rush

Answer:

D. The gold rush

The discovery of gold in California created a lust for gold that quickly brought immigrants from the eastern United States and many parts of the world. To be sure, there were struggles and conflicts, as well as the rise of nativism. Yet this vast migration of people from all parts of the world began the process that has created California's uniquely diverse culture.

80. **Which of the following does not differentiate provisions of the California constitution from the U.S. Constitution?**
    (Rigorous) (Skill 3.2c)

    A. The governor of California has the pocket veto

    B. In California representation in both houses of the legislature is based on population

    C. The Governor and Lt. Governor are elected separately

    D. The equivalent of cabinet positions are elected rather than appointed.

Answer:

A. The governor of California has the pocket veto.

The answer is (A) "The governor of California has the pocket veto." One of the differences between the California constitution and the U.S. Constitution concerns the executive power to veto and nullify legislation enacted by the legislature. The pocket veto, a policy that permits the President of the United States to nullify an act of Congress by simply withholding signature on a bill, is not shared by the Governor of California. Although the Governor of California does not have this particular power, the Governor holds a power that has not been extended to the President of the United States. This is the "Line-Item Veto" which permits the Governor to veto individual items that are part of a piece of legislation without nullifying the entire piece of legislation.

81. **The United States legislature is bi-cameral, this means:**
(Average) (Skill 3.2c)

A. It consists of several houses

B. It consists of two houses

C. The Vice-President is in charge of the legislature when in session

D. It has an upper house and a lower house

Answer:

B. It consists of two houses

The bi-cameral nature of the United States legislature means that it has two houses, the Senate and the House of Representatives, that make up the Congress. The Vice-President is part of the Executive branch of government but presides over the Senate and may act as a tiebreaker. An upper and lower house would be parts of a Parliamentary system of government such as the governments of Great Britain and Israel.

82. **Who applied Locke's principles to the American situation?**
(Rigorous) (Skill 4.1a)

A. Thomas Paine

B. Samuel Adams

C. Benjamin Franklin

D. Thomas Jefferson

Answer:

D. Thomas Jefferson

Thomas Paine (1737-1809), the great American political theorist, wrote "these are the times that try men's souls" in his 16 part pamphlet *The Crisis*. Paine's authoring of *Common Sense* was an important step in spreading information to the American colonists about their need for independence from Great Britain. It was Thomas Jefferson who took the ideals and principles of John Locke and applied them to the situation in America.

83. **There is no doubt of the vast improvement of the U.S. Constitution over the weak Articles of Confederation. Which one of the four statements below is not a description of the document? (Rigorous) (Skill 4.1c)**

    A. The establishment of a strong central government in no way lessened or weakened the individual states

    B. Individual rights were protected and secured

    C. The Constitution demands unquestioned respect and subservience to the federal government by all states and citizens

    D. Its flexibility and adaptation to change gives it a sense of timelessness

Answer:

C. The Constitution demands unquestioned respect and subservience to the federal government by all states and citizens.

The U.S. Constitution was indeed a vast improvement over the Articles of Confederation and the authors of the document took great care to assure longevity. It clearly stated that the establishment of a strong central government in no way lessened or weakened the individual states. In the Bill of Rights, citizens were assured that individual rights were protected and secured. Possibly the most important feature of the new Constitution was its flexibility and adaptation to change which assured longevity.

Therefore, the only statement made that doesn't describe some facet of the Constitution is "The Constitution demands unquestioned respect and subservience to the federal government by all states and citizens". On the contrary, the Constitution made sure that citizens could critique and make changes to their government and encourages such critiques and changes as necessary for the preservation of democracy.

84. **Of the thirteen English colonies, the greatest degree of religious toleration was found in:**
     (Easy) (Skill 4.2a)

    A. Maryland

    B. Rhode Island

    C. Pennsylvania

    D. Delaware

Answer:

B. Rhode Island

Roger Williams, founder of Providence and Rhode Island, had objected to the Massachusetts colonial seizure of Indian lands and settlements and the relationship between these seizures and the Church of England. Williams was banished from Massachusetts and purposely set up Rhode Island as the first colony with a true separation of church and state.

85. **The Pilgrims came to America to:**
     (Average) (Skill 4.2a)

    A. To drill for oil

    B. To be the official representatives of the king

    C. To take over the East India Company

    D. To flee religious persecution

Answer:

D. To flee religious persecution

The Pilgrims and others suffered religious persecution and because of this came to America.

86. **The Constitution can:**
(Easy) (Skill 4.3d)

A. Never be changed

B. Be rewritten

C. Be discarded

D. Be amended

Answer:

D. Be amended

The Constitution is the law of the land. As such, it cannot be discarded. It can be changed officially through the amendment process.

87. **In the United States government, power or control over public education, marriage, and divorce is:**
(Average) (Skill 4.3e)

A. Implied or suggested

B. Concurrent or shared

C. Delegated or expressed

D. Reserved

Answer:

D. Reserved

In the United States government, power or control over public education, marriage, and divorce is reserved. This is to say that these powers are reserved for the people of the states to decide for themselves.

88.   **In the United States government, the power of coining money is:**
        (Rigorous) (Skill 4.3a)

   A. Implied or suggested

   B. Concurrent or shared

   C. Delegated or expressed

   D. Reserved

Answer:

C. Delegated or expressed

In the United States government, the power of coining money is delegated or expressed. Therefore, only the United States government may coin money, the states may not coin money for themselves.

89.   **Which is not a branch of the federal government?**
        (Easy) (Skill 4.3a)

   A. Popular

   B. Legislative

   C. Executive

   D. Judicial

Answer:

A. Popular

The three branches of government are the (B) legislative, (C) executive and (D) judicial branches. Each has its own distinct functions and duties. There is not such branch as the (A) popular.

90. **In the United States government, the power of taxation and borrowing is:**
(Average) (Skill 4.3a)

A. Implied or suggested

B. Concurrent or shared

C. Delegated or expressed

D. Reserved

Answer:

B. Concurrent or shared

In the United States government, the power of taxation is concurrent or shared with the states. An example of this is the separation of state and federal income tax and the separate filings of tax returns for each.

91. **The term that best describes how the Supreme Court can block laws that may be unconstitutional from being enacted is:**
(Average) (Skill 4.4b)

A. Jurisprudence

B. Judicial Review

C. Exclusionary Rule

D. Right of Petition

Answer:

B. Judicial Review

(A) Jurisprudence is the study of the development and origin of law. (B) Judicial review is the term that best describes how the Supreme Court can block laws that they deem as unconstitutional as set forth in Marbury vs Madison. The (C) "exclusionary rule" is a reference to the Fourth Amendment of the Constitution and says that evidence gathered in an illegal manner or search must be thrown out and excluded from evidence. There is nothing called the (D) "Right of Petition", however the Petition of Right is a reference to a statement of civil liberties sent by the English Parliament to Charles I in 1628.

92. **What Supreme Court ruling dealt with the issue of civil rights? (Rigorous) (Skill 4.4c)**

    A. Jefferson vs Madison

    B. Lincoln vs Douglas

    C. Dred Scott v. Sanford

    D. Marbury vs Madison

Answer:

C. Dred Scott v. Sanford

Marbury vs Madison established the principal of judicial review. The Supreme Court ruled that it held no authority in making the decision (regarding Marbury's commission as Justice of the Peace in District of Columbia) as the Supreme Court's jurisdiction (or lack thereof) in the case, was conflicted with Article III of the Constitution. (C) The Dred Scot case is the well-know civil rights case that had to do with the rights of the slave.

93. **"Marbury vs Madison (1803)" was an important Supreme Court case which set the precedent for: (Average) (Skill 4.4b)**

    A. The elastic clause

    B. Judicial review

    C. The supreme law of the land

    D. Popular sovereignty in the territories

Answer:

B. Judicial review

Marbury vs Madison (1803) was an important case for the Supreme Court as it established judicial review (B). In that case, the Supreme Court set precedence to declare laws passed by Congress as unconstitutional. Popular sovereignty (D) in the territories was a failed plan pushed by Stephen Davis to allow states to decide the slavery question for themselves. In his attempt to appeal to the masses in the pre-Civil War elections. The supreme law of the land (C) is just that, the law that rules. (A) The elastic clause is not a real term.

94. **The Electoral College:**
    (Average) (Skill 4.5c)

    A. Elects the Senate but not the House

    B. Elects the House but not the Senate

    C. Elects both the House and Senate

    D. Elects the President

Answer:

D. Elects the President

The Electoral College only exists to casts its votes for the President of the United States. Both Senators or Representatives are elected by majority vote.

95. **Which one of the following is not a function or responsibility of the US political parties?**
    (Easy) (Skill 4.5a)

    A. Conducting elections or the voting process

    B. Obtaining funds needed for election campaigns

    C. Choosing candidates to run for public office

    D. Making voters aware of issues and other public affairs information

Answer:

A. Conducting elections or the voting process

The US political parties have numerous functions and responsibilities. Among them are obtaining funds needed for election campaigns, choosing the candidates to run for office, and making voters aware of the issues. The political parties, however, do not conduct elections or the voting process, as that would be an obvious conflict of interest.

96.	On the spectrum of American politics the label that most accurately describes voters to the "right of center" is:
	(Average) (Skill 4.5d)

	A. Moderates

	B. Liberals

	C. Conservatives

	D. Socialists

Answer:

C. Conservatives

(A) Moderates are considered voters who teeter on the line of political centrality or drift slightly to the left or right. (B) Liberals are voters who stand on the left of center. (C) Conservative voters are those who are "right of center". (D) Socialists would land far to the left on the political spectrum of America.

97.	The study of the exercise of power and political behavior in human society today would be conducted by experts in:
	(Easy) (Skill 4.6b)

	A. History

	B. Sociology

	C. Political Science

	D. Anthropology

Answer:

C. Political Science

Experts in the field of political science today would likely conduct the study of exercise of power and political behavior in human society. However, it is also reasonable to suggest that such studies would be important to historians (study of the past, often in an effort to understand the present), sociologists (often concerned with power structure in the social and political worlds), and even some anthropologists (study of culture and their behaviors).

98. **When referring to government, who said: "the good of the many outweighs the good of the few and also of the one"?**
    (Rigorous) (Skill 4.6b)

    A. Plato

    B. Aristotle

    C. Cicero

    D. Gaius

Answer:

B. Aristotle

Aristotle is the one who wrote the quote. It showed his true insight as one of the great political and social commentators and philosophers of all time.

99. **The function of government is to provide for the welfare of the people is the philosophy of:**
(Rigorous) (Skill 4.6B)

A. Aristotle

B. John Locke

C. Plato

D. Thomas Hobbes

Answer:

A. Aristotle

(D) Thomas Hobbes (1588-1679) wrote the important work *Leviathan* in which he pointed out that people are by all means selfish, individualistic animals that will always look out for themselves and therefore, the state must combat this nature desire. (B) John Locke (1632-1704) whose book *Two Treatises of Government* has long been considered a founding document on the rights of people to rebel against an unjust government was an important figure in the founding of the US Constitution and on general politics of the American Colonies. (C) Plato (427-347 B.C.) and Aristotle (384-322 B.C.) both contributed to the field of political science.

Both believed that political order would result in the greatest stability. In fact, Aristotle studied under Plato. Both Plato and Aristotle studied the ideas of causality and the Prime Mover, but their conclusions were different. Aristotle, however, is considered to be "the father of political science" because of his development of systems of political order the true development, a scientific system to study justice and political order.

100. **The significance of a free press does not include which of the following:**
(Average) (Skill 4.7a)

A. Providing information

B. Reporting illegal actions

C. Libel

D. Reporting in a responsible and civic-minded manner

Answer:

C. Libel

(A) Providing information is definitely one of the functions of a free press as well as (B) reporting on illegal actions of others and (D) acting in a professional and responsible civic-minded manner. (C) Libel, or the provision of what is known to be false and damaging information is not part of the functions.

101. **A political system in which there is a one party state, centralized control, and a repressive police system with private ownership is called:**
(Average) (Skill 4.8a)

A. Communism

B. Fascism

C. Socialism

D. Constitutional Monarchy

Answer:

B. Fascism

(A) Communism and (C) Socialism both are based on the public ownership of the means of production. (D) A constitutional monarchy would have private ownership. (B) Fascism is the only form of government that has all of the characteristics mentioned in the statement.

102. The "wall of separation between church and state' came from:
(Rigorous) (Skill 4.9a)

A. Aristotle

B. Alexander Hamilton

C. Thomas Jefferson

D. Thomas

Answer:

C. Thomas Jefferson

Thomas Jefferson is the owner of the above quote which expresses one of the founding beliefs of America, the separation of church and state.

103. The study of ways in which different societies around the world deal with the problems of limited resources and unlimited needs and wants is in the area of:
(Easy) (Skill 5.1a)

A. Economics

B. Sociology

C. Anthropology

D. Political Science

Answer:

A. Economics

The study of the ways in which different societies around the world deal with the problems of limited resources and unlimited needs and wants is a study of Economics. Economists consider the law of supply and demand as fundamental to the study of the economy. However, Sociology and Political Science also consider the study of economics and its importance in understanding social and political systems.

104. **A planned economy functions on the basis of:**
(Rigorous) (Skill 5.1d)

A. Public ownership

B. Private ownership

C. Stockholder control

D. An elected management board

Answer:

A. Public ownership

(B) Private owner ship is a facet of capitalism and (C) stockholder control and (D) elected management board are parts of private ownership. (A) Public ownership is a part of a planned economy.

105. **Potential customers for any product or service are not only called consumers but can also be called a:**
(Easy) (Skill 5.2a)

A. Resource

B. Base

C. Commodity

D. Market

Answer:

D. Market

Potential customers for any product or service are not only customers but can also be called a market. A resource is a source of wealth; natural resources are the basis for manufacturing goods and services. A commodity is anything that is bought or sold, any product.

106. **In a market economy, markets function on the basis of:**
     (Rigorous) (Skill 5.2a)

    A. Government control

    B. Manipulation

    C. Demand and Supply

    D. Planning

Answer:

C. Demand and Supply

(A) Government control is not a manifestation of the functioning of free markets since government interferes with the operating mechanism of the market. (C) Manipulation refers to the interfering with the price-quantity adjustment mechanism that prevents markets from operating efficiently. (D) Planning is a mechanism that replaces the market. (C) Demand and supply describes the basis for the adjustment mechanism which is how free markets function.

107. **Competition leads to:**
     (Rigorous) (Skill 5.2c)

    A. Fights

    B. Waste

    C. Overproduction

    D. Efficient use of resources

Answer:

D. Efficient use of resources

Competition is the basis for the functioning of markets. It may cause a few a disagreement between market participants but it does not lead to (B) waste or (C) overproduction since competition results in (D) the efficient use of resources.

108. **The economic system promoting individual ownership of land, capital, and businesses with minimal governmental regulations is called:**
(Average) (Skill 5.2h)

A. Macro-economy

B. Micro-economy

C. Laissez-faire

D. Free enterprise or market economy

Answer:

D. Free Enterprise or market economy

(D) Free enterprise, market economy is the economic system that promotes private ownership of land, capital, and business with minimal government interference. (C) Laissez-faire is the idea that an "invisible hand" will guide the free enterprise system to the maximum potential efficiency.

109. **Which of the following is not a tool of monetary policy?**
(Average) (Skill 5.3c)

A. Open market operations

B. Changing the discount rate

C. Changing the exchange rate

D. Changing the reserve ratio

Answer:

C. Changing the exchange rate

(A) Open Market Operations is the buying and selling of government securities and is a way of increasing or decreasing bank reserves. (B) The discount rate is the rate of interest banks pay to borrow from the Federal Reserve System. (D) The reserve ration is the percentage of deposits that the bank must hold and can't make available for loans. (C) The exchange rate is determined in foreign exchange markets and is not a tool of monetary policy.

110. **The idea that increasing government spending would end depressions was:**
(Average) (Skill 5.3a)

A. The basis of modern economics

B. Called Classical economics

C. Known as federalism

D. Called isolationism

Answer:

A. The basis of modern economics

John Maynard Keynes (1883-1946) advocated an economic system in which government regulations and spending on public works would stimulate the economy and lead to full employment. This broke from the classical idea that free markets would lead to full employment and prosperity and thus became known as the basis for modern macroeconomics. He was still a firm believer in capitalism, but in a less classical sense than Adam Smith (1723-1790), whose *Wealth of Nations* advocated for little or no government interference in the economy.

Smith claimed that an individual's self-interest would bring about the public's welfare. It is important to note that Smith was firmly against the free market systems of monopoly power and warned that the private sector, particularly large manufacturers, if left unregulated could potentially stand in opposition to the public welfare.

111. **The programs such as Medicaid and Food Stamps are the responsibility of:**
     (Easy) (Skill 5.3a)

     A. Federal government

     B. Local government

     C. State government

     D. Communal government

Answer:

C. State Government

Assistance programs, such as Medicaid and Food Stamps are the responsibility of state governments.

112. **Unions were founded on the basis of the beliefs of:**
(Average) (Skill 5.4a)

A. Thomas Robert Malthus

B. John Stuart Mill

C. Samuel Gompers

D. John Maynard Keynes

Answer:

C. Samuel Gompers

(A) Thomas Malthus (1766-1834) was a British economist who introduced the study of population and early on considered famine, war, and disease to be the primary checks on world population. He later modified his views and recognized his early theoretical shortcomings and shifted his focus to the causes of unemployment. (B) John Stuart Mill (1806-1873) was a progressive British philosopher and economist, whose ideas came closer to socialism than to the classical capitalist ideas of Adam Smith. Mill constantly advocated for political and social reforms, including emancipation for women, labor organizations, and farming cooperatives. (D) John Maynard Keynes 1883-1946) was also an important economist. He advocated an economic system in which government regulations and spending on public works would stimulate the economy and lead to full employment. (C) Samuel Gompers was a labor leader whose beliefs of practical business unionism formed the basis for the modern labor union.

113. **The American labor union movement started gaining new momentum:**
     (Average) (Skill 5.4a)

     A. During the building of the railroads

     B. After 1865 with the growth of cities

     C. With the rise of industrial giants such as Carnegie and Vanderbilt

     D. During the war years of 1861-1865

Answer:

B. After 1865 with the growth of cities

The American Labor Union movement had been around since the late eighteenth and early nineteenth centuries. The Labor movement began to first experience persecution by employers in the early 1800s. The American Labor Movement remained relatively ineffective until after the Civil War. In 1866, the National Labor Union was formed, pushing such issues as the eight-hour workday and new policies of immigration. This gave rise to the Knights of Labor and eventually the American Federation of Labor (AFL) in the 1890s and the Industrial Workers of the World (1905). Therefore, it was the period following the Civil War that empowered the labor movement in terms of numbers, militancy, and effectiveness.

114. Gross Domestic Product is:
(Average) (Skill 5.5a)

A. A measure of nation's output

B. A well known social indicator

C. A measure of well being

D. A measure of a nation's trade

Answer:

A. A measure of nation's output

The Gross Domestic Product cannot be used as a (B) social indicator or a (C) measure of well being. (D) It contains information about trade but goes much further in that it is (A) a measure of a nation's output. Since it doesn't say anything about hours worked or hours of leisure, it can't be used as a measure of well-being.

115. One method of trade restriction used by some nations is:
(Average) (Skill 5.6b)

A. Limited treaties

B. Floating exchange rate

C. Bill of exchange

D. Import quotas

Answer:

D. Import quotas

One method of trade restriction used by some nations is import quotas. The amount of goods imported are regulated in an effort to protect domestic enterprise and limit foreign competition. Both the United States and Japan, two of the world's most industrialized nations have import quotas to protect domestic industries.

116. **The doctrine of comparative advantage explains:**
(Average) (Skill 5.6a)

    A. Why nations trade

    B. How to fight a war

    C. Time zones

    D. Political divisions

Answer:

A. Why nations trade

The principle of comparative advantage is the basis for the theory of international trade and says that nations engage in trade with other nations when they can produce the good at a comparatively lower price than the other nation can.

117. **Which one of the following does not affect climate?**
(Rigorous) (Skill 6.1a)

    A. Elevation and altitude

    B. Ocean currents

    C. Latitude

    D. Longitude

Answer:

D. Longitude

Latitude is the primary influence of earth's climate as it determines the climatic region in which an area lies. Elevation or altitude and ocean currents are considered to be secondary influences on climate. Longitude is considered to have no important influence over climate.

118. **Geography was first studied in an organized manner by the:**
     (Rigorous) (Skill 6.1)

     A. Egyptians

     B. Greeks

     C. Romans

     D. Arabs

Answer:

B. Greeks

The Greeks were the first to study geography, possibly because of the difficulties they faced as a result of geographic conditions. Greece had difficulty uniting early

on as their steep, treacherous, mountainous terrain made it difficult for the city-states to be united. As the Greeks studied their geography, it became possible to defeat more powerful armies on their home turf, such as the great victory over the Persians at Marathon.

119. **Meridians, or lines of longitude, not only help in pinpointing locations, but are also used for:**
     (Average) (Skill 6.1b)

     A. Measuring distance from the Poles

     B. Determining direction of ocean currents

     C. Determining the time around the world

     D. Measuring distance on the Equator

Answer:

C. Determining the time around the world

Meridians, or lines of longitude, are the determining factor in separating time zones and determining time around the world.

120. **A famous canal is the:**
     (Easy) (Skill 6.1a)

     A. Pacific Canal

     B. Arctic Canal

     C. Panama Canal

     D. Atlantic Canal

Answer:

C. Panama Canal

(C) the only canal is the selection of answers is the Panama Canal. The Pacific, Artic and Atlantic are oceans, not canals.

121. **In which of the following disciplines would the study of physical mapping, modern or ancient, and the plotting of points and boundaries be least useful?**
     (Easy) (Skill 6.1a)

     A. Sociology

     B. Geography

     C. Archaeology

     D. History

Answer:

A. Sociology

In geography, archaeology, and history, the study of maps and plotting of points and boundaries is very important as all three of these disciplines hold value in understanding the spatial relations and regional characteristics of people and places. Sociology, however, mostly focuses on the social interactions of people and while location is important, the physical location is not as important as the social location such as the differences between studying people in groups or as individuals.

122. **The Study of "spatial relationships and interaction" would be done by people in the field of:**
(Easy) (Skill 6.1)

   A. Political Science

   B. Anthropology

   C. Geography

   D. Sociology

Answer:

C. Geography

Geography is the discipline within Social Science that most concerns itself with the study of "spatial relationships and interaction".

123. **The study of how living organisms interact is called:**
(Average) (Skill 6.2a)

   A. Ecology

   B. Sociology

   C. Anthropology

   D. Political Science

Answer:

A. Ecology

(B) Sociology is the study of human society and usually consists of surveys, controlled experiments, and field studies. (C) anthropology or the study of current human cultures. (D)) Political science is the study of political life including justice, freedom, power and equality in a variety of methods. (A) Ecology is a study of the interaction of living organisms.

124. **Which of the following is an organization or alliance for defense purposes?**
(Average) (Skill 6.2d)

A. North Atlantic Treaty Organization

B. The Common Market

C. The European Union

D. North American Free Trade Association

Answer:

A. North Atlantic Treaty Organization

(B) The Common Market, (C) The European Union and (D) the North American Free Trade Organization are all forms of economic integration and are in place to promote free trade and factor mobility. (D) The North Atlantic Treaty Organization, NATO, is the organization that provides for the defense of Europe.

125. **What term does not describe a settlement in the physical and cultural sense?**
(Average) (Skill 6.3A)

A. Climate

B. Religion

C. Shared values

D. Shared language

Answer:

A. Climate

(B) religion, (C) shared values and (D) shared language are common factors of a settlement. People settle where they have something in common with the other people. (A) Climate is a part of the environment and science and not a shared trait of a settlement.

XAMonline, INC. 21 Orient Ave. Melrose, MA 02176

Toll Free number 800-509-4128

TO ORDER Fax 781-662-9268 OR www.XAMonline.com

CALIFORNIA SUBJECT EXAMINATIONS   - CSET - 2008

PO#   Store/School:

Address 1:

Address 2 (Ship to other):

City, State Zip

Credit card number_____-_____-_____-_____   expiration_____

EMAIL _____

PHONE   **FAX**

ISBN	TITLE	Qty	Retail	Total
978-1-58197-816-2	RICA Reading Instruction Competence Assessment			
978-1-58197-800-1	CBEST CA Basic Educational Skills			
978-1-58197-901-5	CSET French Sample Test 149, 150			
978-1-58197-622-9	CSET Spanish 145, 146, 147			
978-1-58197-803-2	CSET MSAT Multiple Subject 101, 102, 103			
978-1-58197-261-0	CSET English 105, 106, 107			
978-1-58197-608-3	CSET Foundational-Level Mathematics 110, 111			
978-1-58197-285-6	CSET Mathematics 110, 111, 112			
978-1-58197-340-2	CSET Social Science 114, 115			
978-1-58197-342-6	CSET General Science 118, 119			
978-1-58197-809-4	CSET Biology-Life Science 120, 124			
978-1-58197-395-2	CSET Chemistry 121, 125			
978-1-58197-571-0	CSET Earth and Planetary Science 122, 126			
978-1-58197-817-9	CSET Physics 123, 127			
978-1-58197-299-3	CSET Physical Education, 129, 130, 131			
978-1-58197-813-1	CSET Art Sample Subtest 140			
			SUBTOTAL	
			Ship	$8.70
			TOTAL	

CPSIA information can be obtained at www.ICGtesting.com
Printed in the USA
BVOW05s2001270116

434512BV00005B/43/P

9 781581 973402